P9-ARS-944

WHOLE LANGUAGE VOICES
IN TEACHER EDUCATION

WHOLE LANGUAGE VOICES IN TEACHER EDUCATION

Coordinating Editors

Kathryn F. Whitmore
THE UNIVERSITY OF IOWA

Yetta M. Goodman
UNIVERSITY OF ARIZONA

CENTER FOR EXPANSION OF LANGUAGE
AND THINKING

Stenhouse Publishers York, Maine

Stenhouse Publishers, 226 York Street, York, Maine 03909

Copyright © 1996 by the Center for Expansion of Language and Thinking

All rights reserved. With the exception of the individually copyrighted protocol pages, which may be photocopied for use within the purchaser's own institution only, no part of this publication may be reproduced or transmitted in any form or by any means, electronic or mechanical, including photocopy, or any information storage and retrieval system, without permission from the publisher.

Every effort has been made to contact copyright holders and students for permission to reproduce borrowed material. We regret any oversights that may have occurred and will be pleased to rectify them in reprints of the work.

Page 154: Reprinted with permission from *Science News,* the weekly newsmagazine of science, copyright 1990 by Science Service, Inc.

Library of Congress Cataloging-in-Publication Data

Whole language voices in teacher education
   / coordinating editors, Kathryn F. Whitmore, Yetta M. Goodman ;
Center for Expansion of Language and Thinking.
      p.   cm.
   Includes bibliographical references and index.
   ISBN 1-57110-028-8 (alk. paper)
   1. English teachers—Training of.   2. English teachers--In-service
training.   3. Language experience approach in education.
4. Language arts teachers—Training of.   I. Whitmore, Kathryn F.,
1959-   . II. Goodman, Yetta M., 1931-   . III. Center for
Expansion of Language and Thinking.
PE1066.P73   1996
420'.71'1—dc20   95-42717
                                                              CIP

Cover and interior design by Ron Kosciak, *Dragonfly Design*
Typeset by Pre-Press Company, Inc.

Manufactured in the United States of America on acid-free paper
99 98 97 96 8 7 6 5 4 3 2 1

The thought collective of the Center for Expansion of Language and Thinking fondly dedicates this work to our colleagues, members, and friends who have passed away but are remembered in these pages and in our daily lives as whole language thinkers and educators:

P. David Allen　　　　*Barry W. Sherman*

Kathy O'Brien　　　　*James Tortelli*

William D. Page　　　　*John Woodley*

CONTENTS

CONTENTS OF PROTOCOLS/ENGAGEMENTS

CONTRIBUTORS

Coordinating Editors

Kathryn F. Whitmore
N274 Lindquist Center
The University of Iowa
Iowa City, IA 52242
Whitmore@blue.weeg.uiowa.edu

Yetta M. Goodman
Room 504 College of Education
University of Arizona
Tucson, AZ 87121
Goodman@ccit.arizona.edu

The following additional CELT members conceptualized this book and nurtured it through to completion:

Shirley Crenshaw
Research and Training Associates
Overland Park, Kansas

Kathy G. Short
University of Arizona
Tucson, Arizona

Dorothy F. King
Research and Training Associates
Flagstaff, Arizona

Dorothy Watson
University of Missouri at Columbia
Columbia, Missouri

The following additional CELT members edited the major parts of the book:

Linda Crafton
Center for Learning and Literacy
Deerfield, Illinois

David Heine
St. Cloud State University
St. Cloud, Minnesota

Shirley B. Ernst
Eastern Connecticut State University
Willimantic, Connecticut

Patricia Heine
St. Cloud State University
St. Cloud, Minnesota

Karen Feathers
Wayne State University
Detroit, Michigan

Dorothy Menosky
Jersey City State College
Jersey City, New Jersey

Carol Gilles
University of Missouri at Columbia
Columbia, Missouri

David L. Tucker
Illinois State University
Normal, Illinois

The following additional authors contributed to issues or narrative chapters and/or protocol/engagements:

Sharon V. Andrews
Indiana State University
Terre Haute, Indiana

Margaret A. Atwell
California State University
Fullerton, California

Mary Bixby
University of Missouri at Columbia
Columbia, Missouri

Ellen H. Brinkley
Western Michigan University
Kalamazoo, Michigan

Genevieve Brown
Sam Houston State University
Huntsville, Texas

Beverly A. Busching
University of South Carolina
Columbia, South Carolina

Brian Cambourne
University of Wollongong
Wollongong, New South Wales,
Australia

Jean Anne Clyde
University of Louisville
Louisville, Kentucky

Mark W. F. Condon
University of Louisville
Louisville, Kentucky

M. Ruth Davenport
Eastern Oregon State College
La Grande, Oregon

Jayne DeLawter
Sonoma State University
Rohnert Park, California

Janet Files
Coastal Carolina University
Conway, South Carolina

Dana L. Fox
University of Arizona
Tucson, Arizona

Elizabeth A. Franklin
University of Nebraska–Lincoln
Lincoln, Nebraska

David E. Freeman
Fresno Pacific College
Fresno, California

Yvonne S. Freeman
Fresno Pacific College
Fresno, California

Kenneth S. Goodman
University of Arizona
Tucson, Arizona

Karen Guilfoyle
University of Idaho
Genesee, Idaho

Roxanne Henkin
National–Louis University
Wheaton, Illinois

Stephen E. Hornstein
St. Cloud University
St. Cloud, Minnesota

Gail Huffman-Joley
Indiana State University
Terre Haute, Indiana

Joan Irvine
University of Manitoba
Winnipeg, Manitoba

Patricia W. Jenkins
Columbia Public Schools
Columbia, Missouri

Virginia W. Juettner
Anchorage School District
Anchorage, Alaska

Wendy C. Kasten
Kent State University
Kent, Ohio

Janice V. Kristo
University of Maine
Orono, Maine

Stephen B. Kucer
California State University
at San Marcos
San Marcos, California

Myna L. Matlin
Tucson Unified School District
Tucson, Arizona

Richard J. Meyer
University of Nebraska–Lincoln
Lincoln, Nebraska

Heidi Mills
University of South Carolina
Columbia, South Carolina

Kay Moss
Illinois State University
Normal, Illinois

Bess Osborn
Sam Houston State University
Huntsville, Texas

Leslie Patterson
University of Houston
Houston, Texas

Margaret Yatsevitch Phinney
University of Minnesota
Minneapolis, Minnesota

Joan Livingston Prouty
Sam Houston State University
Huntsville, Texas

Lynn Rhodes
University of Colorado at Denver
Denver, Colorado

Mary Robbins
Sam Houston State University
Huntsville, Texas

Ruth Sáez-Vega
University of Arizona
Tucson, Arizona

Wayne Serebrin
University of Manitoba
Winnipeg, Manitoba

Yvonne Siu-Runyan
University of Northern Colorado
Greeley, Colorado

Helen Slaughter
University of Hawaii at Manoa
Honolulu, Hawaii

Laura A. Smith
Walter White Elementary School
River Rouge, Michigan

Phil Swicegood
Sam Houston State University
Huntsville, Texas

Carole Urzúa
Fresno, California

Rahima Wade
The University of Iowa
Iowa City, Iowa

Jane White
East Texas State University
Commerce, Texas

Sandra Wilde
Portland State University
Portland, Oregon

Katie Wood
Western Carolina University
Cullowhee, North Carolina

PRACTICING WHAT WE TEACH:
THE PRINCIPLES THAT GUIDE US

Kathryn F. Whitmore and Kenneth S. Goodman

The idea for this book began several years ago as a discussion among the members of a thought collective, the Center for Expansion of Language and Thinking (CELT)—much like many wonderful ideas for classroom practice begin in Teachers Applying Whole Language (TAWL) support groups. CELT is a nonprofit educational corporation, international in scope, whose members believe in the principles of education for democracy with a focus on natural language learning and inquiry. This is the first book to be collaboratively written by the membership of CELT. In it, we present how we practice the whole language philosophy in our teacher education classes and inservice programs, with the intent to raise questions and cause reflection in our professional community.

Several elements consistent with our whole language philosophy have been essential to CELT's progress on this book over the years. We have worked collaboratively, negotiating our differences of opinions and checking our ideas against one another's for confirmation and extension. We have advocated for holistic practice at all levels of the educational process, recognizing that classroom teachers deserve as much professional respect as university faculty. We have pushed the function and purpose of our writing to lead the form of presentation, so that the shape of this book has an integrity in keeping with its message. These goals have meant that the conceptual framework of the book, its organization, and our revision, editing, and publication processes are a transaction of our collective texts in written form.

We invite you to experience the stories we value in our educational practice. We encourage you to respond to what you read in this book by reflecting on the theoretical principles and assumptions that guide and ground your interactions with professional educators. And as you consider initiating or continuing a whole language teacher education philosophy in your practice, we encourage you to join our conversation by contacting a CELT member. The editors' addresses and e-mail addresses, as well as the locations of all authors, are found in the List of Contributors.

The whole language philosophy is significantly impacting curriculum in elementary and secondary schools around the world, thereby creating the need for a shift in the education of potential teachers and the continuing education of those already working in schools. Our shift in thinking about whole language teacher education has affected the content we explore in our university classes and inservice workshops and the methods we use to assist teachers and teacher education students to learn about whole language and its curricular implications. In our efforts, we create whole language learning environments for our learners (Short and Burke 1989).

This chapter serves as an introduction to the book by way of exploring the dynamic principles that inform, guide, explain, and justify our teaching. We explain how these principles center our journey around the theme cycle of whole language teacher education that organizes the parts of the book. Then the writing of one student, whom we call Beth, will bring the principles on which our teaching is grounded to life through her intense graduate school learning experience.

BASING WHAT WE DO ON WHAT WE KNOW

Although learning experiences and teaching issues for adult learners are different from those for school-aged learners, the principles embodied in a whole language philosophy inform instructional decision making for learners of all ages and experiences. These principles are supported by beliefs in learners and learning, teachers and teaching, language curriculum, culture, and community. They enable us to improve education through a greater understanding of the relationships among language, thought, and learning.

The whole language philosophy has emerged as a grass-roots movement of educators who develop practice from their shared beliefs about how learning occurs (K. Goodman 1986). Our philosophy is based on the rich history of sociopsycholinguistic theory (Y. Goodman 1989), and influenced by the work of Lev Vygotsky, Jean Piaget, John Dewey, Louise Rosenblatt, Frank Smith, and others, as well as by our own research. This theoretical foundation tells us that knowledge is constructed by individual learners within the social context of interactions with people and objects in their cultural experiences. Whole language teacher educators, like whole language teachers, base what they do on what they know. We develop experiences for learners that are theoretically consistent with this foundation and enable students to reach their potentials as learners and thinkers in school and out (Whitmore and Y. Goodman 1995).

One unwarranted criticism of whole language has been that it looks very different from teacher to teacher. That's as it should be. Each teacher is an independent professional, a decision maker who builds his or her own teaching on a common knowledge base, a common belief system, and a common set of principles. So each whole language classroom will reflect the unique voice of the teacher, but it will also reflect this common set of principles.

In this book we begin with the premise that the same principles that underlie whole language also apply to teacher education. Our teaching of teachers must be consistent with the principles we advocate. Following are some of those key principles, which we develop throughout this book:

Language Principles

- Language is the medium of communication, thought, and learning. It's central to whole language programs.

- Language is authentic when it serves real language purposes in real speech acts and literacy events.
- Language must be whole and functional to be comprehended and learned.
- Written language is language: a parallel semiotic system to oral language.
- Reading and writing are processes of making sense through written language.
- Making sense of print involves three language cue systems: graphophonic, syntactic, and semantic.

Learning Principles

- Language learning is universal. All people can think symbolically and share a social need to communicate.
- Invention and convention are two forces that shape language development and concept development.
- Each learner invents language within the convention of the social language.
- Learning language, learning through language, and learning about language take place simultaneously (Halliday, undated).
- Written language is learned like oral language: in the context of its use.
- Learning is an ongoing process. It occurs over time, in a supportive, collaborative context, and is unique for each learner.
- Reflection is a central part of the learning process, and self-evaluation is a major part of the reflection process.
- What you know affects what you learn.
- There is a zone of proximal development (Vygotsky 1978) that develops in learners: the range of what they are capable of learning at any point in time.

Teaching Principles

- Learners must be trusted to assume responsibility for their own learning.
- Whole language teachers are curriculum makers; they initiate appropriate learning opportunities for their pupils and invite them to participate.
- Whole language teachers mediate learning; they do not intervene and take control of it.
- Whole language teachers are kidwatchers (Y. Goodman 1985); they know their students. Whole language teacher educators are teacher watchers. They also know their students.
- Teachers are sensitive, as kidwatchers, to learners' zones of proximal development and provide enough (but not too much) support and mediation.
- Teachers support learners' ownership over their own learning.
- Teachers must enable students to empower and liberate themselves.
- Teachers need to accept diversity and teach for it.
- Whole language teachers are advocates for their students.

Curriculum Principles

- The whole language curriculum is whole in two senses: it is complete, and it is integrated.
- The whole language curriculum integrates all aspects of the curriculum and the whole student around themes and inquiries.

- The whole language curriculum is a dual curriculum: it builds thought and language at the same time that it builds knowledge and concepts.
- The curriculum involves learners in using and practicing new concepts and ideas.
- The curriculum starts with learners, building on who they are, what they know and believe, and where they are going.
- The curriculum reflects the culture and realities of the community.
- The whole language curriculum is broad enough to include the interests and needs of all learners and deep enough to support substantive learning at all levels.
- There are no artificial floors and ceilings in whole language. Learners may start where they are and go as far as their interests and needs take them.

Social Principles

- Whole language brings the outside world into the classroom by valuing and then relating learners' life experiences to classroom learning experiences.
- Each whole language classroom invents itself as a learning community (Whitmore and Crowell 1994).
- A major aspect of education is being socialized into a community: joining the literacy club (Smith 1988).
- Whole language teachers value collaborative learning communities and consciously work to create a sense of shared involvement.
- Only in democratic classrooms can children learn to be citizens in a democracy. College classrooms and staff development programs need to be democratic, too.

PRACTICING WHAT WE TEACH

In a study group at the 1994 Winter Workshop on Miscue Analysis and Language Processes in Tucson, Arizona, about twenty teachers and teacher educators spent ten days considering the ways in which whole language teacher educators can practice what they teach. The group began with a brainstorming of objectives, questions, and goals for the learning we were about to engage in together. When the goals were summarized and synthesized, a central issue became clear: As whole language teacher educators, we want to encourage others to believe what we believe about teaching and learning, language, thinking, culture, and school. But in this goal there is an explicit contradiction because we know that each learner has to construct his or her own meaning and knowledge. Thus, the problem is how to encourage teachers and colleagues to believe and practice a whole language philosophy without directly telling them what they should believe and how they should act. As Mem Fox, an award-winning Australian author of books for children and also a teacher educator, phrases the issue, it's "the problem of teaching what can't be taught" (1993, p. 105).

Our response to this question became conceptualized in terms of Altwerger and Flores' (1992) theme cycle model for inquiry-centered curriculum (Figure 1). It is a "cycle in which learning issues, problems, and questions lead to learning experiences and literacy uses. Initial questions are answered and problems

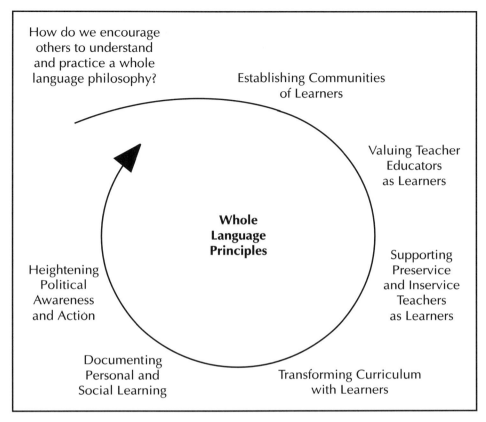

How do we encourage others to understand and practice a whole language philosophy?

Establishing Communities of Learners

Valuing Teacher Educators as Learners

Whole Language Principles

Supporting Preservice and Inservice Teachers as Learners

Heightening Political Awareness and Action

Documenting Personal and Social Learning

Transforming Curriculum with Learners

FIGURE 1   The theme cycle for whole language teacher education

solved, and new learning issues, problems, and questions are posed, leading to further learning" (p. 295).

Each of the points of reference on the cycle of inquiry in Figure 1 represents a component of whole language teacher education that we explore in this book. Each part in this book is introduced by the CELT members who edited the part, followed by narratives from teacher educators and protocols/engagements about the topic. The cycle begins and continues in each revolution with questions about the experiences of teacher education students and practicing educators. It is centered in the principles of whole language that guide all of the experiences around the path of the cycle.

ESTABLISHING COMMUNITIES OF LEARNERS

The role of community discussed in Chapter 2 is pivotal in whole language teacher education. Valuing the creation of communities of learners affects how classrooms look, how classroom interactions occur and are shaped, and what types of experiences and evaluation are planned. Building a community of learners reminds us to value the affective component of learning in our teaching. From relieving the anxiety of new students, through mentoring students into initiating and taking control of their own learning and evaluation, and on to supporting teachers in whole language support groups and professional development, the social conditions that we set up for building relationships between educators and learners and learners with each other are essential. Just like very young learners, adult learners need to be valued, have a valid sense of control in their lives as students, and find pleasure in learning to make the most of it. Fox in her essays *Radical Reflections* (1993) passionately describes the role of affect in education, literacy, and life as related to her teaching:

> Although we're deeply serious about teaching and learning, we're rarely serious in the act of teaching. We cavort through our classes, exposing our students to a variety of language experiences, many of them lighthearted, in order to demonstrate the vivacity and potential of reading and writing, speaking and listening. We try to use language energetically to amuse. We hope we're successfully modeling the fact that language is a vital tool that can be employed with power and enjoyment for many different purposes. (pp. 27–28)

VALUING TEACHER EDUCATORS AS LEARNERS

Whole language teacher educators recognize themselves as learners along with the professionals they guide as described in Part A. A constant reflection on teaching and research and a commitment to dynamic, active learning for all participants are consistent parts of the practice of the whole language teacher educator. We hold a holistic view of our varied professional roles as teachers, researchers, consultants, and authors. We grapple with finding ways to share our expertise, while ensuring that our students' voices aren't silenced or minimized. We push the limits of innovation and change, often while challenged by roadblocks that are cemented in the institutions and traditions where we work. We are visible learners in our classrooms, inviting our students into our own questioning as well as our blunders and miscues, and changing our practices based on what we learn.

SUPPORTING PRESERVICE AND INSERVICE TEACHERS AS LEARNERS

Next on the cycle of teacher education and described in Part B, preservice and inservice teachers are regarded as active learners, constructing themselves as professional teachers, a clear departure from the past teacher training model. Whereas historically undergraduates in education programs have been taught to recite basal lessons, asked to write tightly controlled, narrowly scripted lesson plans, and assigned to memorize behavior management techniques, usually to be evaluated by their performance on tests, whole language teacher educators recognize the engagement necessary on the part of students to be participants in the construction of learning about teaching.

Even our terminology manifests these beliefs; students are referred to as apprentices, preservice professionals, or teacher-learners, for example. They are regarded as members of the profession, not separate from the profession they are entering. As such, their personal histories as learners and literate members of a community are valued, and their questions about educational theory and practice, their purposes for their college educations, and their goals and objectives are negotiated into both undergraduate and graduate courses and inservice sessions.

A shared strategy among CELT members is *metapedagogy*. It works well when things are going well, as in the midst of a powerful discussion, and also when things are not going well, as when an assignment hasn't had the impact that was intended or few got the point of a shared experience. The participants are asked to step outside the immediate experience and think about what the teacher educator has planned, why it is working (or not), and what it means for their own practice. The question, "What's going on here?" can lead into reflective sharing that impacts learning on everyone's part.

The Vygotskian notion of mediation is helpful in understanding our role as teachers in whole language classrooms (Moll 1990; Moll and Whitmore 1993). The decisions teacher educators make in their professional lives are often based on the dynamic principles that guided them as classroom teachers. We take into consideration each individual learner's background experience, carefully guard their risk-taking confidence, invite and demonstrate, expect highly intellectual engagement, work with determination to keep a tension alive between the forces of invention and convention in learning, and continuously act as advocates for learners and teachers. Our goal is to work within our students' zones of proximal development, nudging them toward the upper limits of those zones.

TRANSFORMING CURRICULUM WITH LEARNERS

Part C describes how we create curriculum for students that demonstrates the content related to our courses, the methods we want our students to carry into their own teaching settings, and the social objectives that are achieved through building a community of learners in college classrooms. Typical content in whole language teacher education programs includes the relationship between teaching and learning and language and thinking, the processes involved in learning and using language and literacy, and the reality of democratic teaching. Whole language teacher educators create transformative curriculum that empowers teachers as professionals and lifelong inquirers by reflecting the principles of whole language in their practice. We share power in our classrooms with students and in doing so help them to value each other. We do more than teach democracy; we practice and demonstrate it.

DOCUMENTING PERSONAL AND SHARED LEARNING

Both during and following whole language teacher education classes, it is essential to take time—lots of time—to reflect on the experiences a group of learners is sharing in order to assess our progress and document our personal and shared learning as is described in Part D. Most learners have very limited experience in self-evaluation, given our histories as learners who were evaluated by standardized comparative means in our own schooling. Yet it is in the process of self-evaluation that the most dynamic and passionate learning occurs in whole language settings.

Whole language teacher educators value the process of reflection to the extent that it occurs continuously as an integrated part of curriculum, as well as at the conclusion of a learning experience. Case studies, portfolios, discussions, journals, kidwatching, and other strategies enable us to document the learning occurring in teacher education settings and to analyze these strategies for potential use in elementary and secondary classrooms.

HEIGHTENING POLITICAL AWARENESS AND ACTION

A common result of such intense personal and social reflection is a heightened political awareness on the part of the participants and a resulting need to act more confidently professional. Chapter 24 is both an epilogue and a prologue that discusses how teachers become aware that professional decisions are also political ones. Choosing not to use a basal reader may bring the teacher into conflict with administrative policy or powerful colleagues. Advocating for learners may antagonize those who would label and pigeonhole learners. Having excellent children's books in the classroom may lead to confrontations with some members of the extreme political and religious right. And sometimes just saying, "I'm a whole language teacher; I teach my own way," is enough to cause political strife. Is it possible to be a whole language teacher or teacher educator and remain politically neutral? As teachers gain control of their own learning in whole language experiences, they often become inspired to take a more active role in decision making in their buildings and districts and are compelled to be less complacent about the decisions made for them regarding materials selection, methodology mandates, censorship, and the like. They, like other professionals, may develop minimal criteria needed to function as professional teachers. They may leave teaching jobs where they cannot teach according to their own standards. Would doctors use treatments or procedures they felt were detrimental to their patients because some authority said they must?

Teacher educators with a whole language perspective face the political constraints of university and district settings too. We are constantly challenged to work comfortably within our theoretical framework while maintaining the tasks and responsibilities of the institutions within which we work. Our struggles range from major philosophical tensions—such as those related to promotion and tenure and intellectual freedom—to specific tensions—such as assigning grades and teaching in physical environments that are not conducive to whole language. Acting on the political nature of our profession and encouraging our students to do so as well simultaneously resolves our inquiry in teacher education contexts and initiates a new revolution of the theme cycle. Our theoretical contributions to the profession and our personal learning are never-ending processes, but they have little or no value if they don't result in action.

[handwritten margin note: This doesn't have to map onto our trad'l notions of gov't politics, does it?]

BETH: A CASE IN POINT

The complexities and passions of a whole language classroom can be illustrated through the written dialogue of one graduate student, Beth, and Kathy, the teacher educator in the course and co-author of this chapter. Beth is a typical student in a whole language teacher education classroom for many reasons. She takes her learning seriously, she has valid questions about theory and practice, and she frames her new learning within the context of her past experiences as a student, just as all of us do. We present this case study because we believe that though we build communities of learners in our classrooms, we must see ourselves teaching individual learners, each with unique experiences and each responding differently to the shared experiences. They invent themselves within the conventions we create together in our classrooms.

As you get to know Beth, pay particular attention to the special skill with which she conveys her message. She was selected as a representative learner in a teacher education classroom because she brings to light all of the dynamics of whole language illustrated in Figure 1, the cycle of teacher education inquiry. She does so with finesse and the eloquence of language that is a unique part of who she is.

Beth is now a teacher in a rural community. She and Kathy became acquainted when she was enrolled in her first graduate school class, just after she received her elementary certification. Beth had received a degree in English and secondary education certification twenty years earlier. She had one adult child and another in elementary school.

When Beth enrolled in Kathy's class, she was highly confident. She possessed an exceptional and well-deserved history as a successful student, and she was energetic and interested. She was a little cautious about how other students would perceive her lack of elementary teaching experience because she had been substituting but had never taught in her own elementary classroom.

Journals are an essential part of instructional strategies in Kathy's classroom. Like other whole language teacher educators, Kathy needs to know her students well, personally and professionally, in order to be an effective mediator. She needs to know what they think about, how their learning at the university is filtered through their personal experiences with learning since they were children themselves, and what questions they have related to the issues of the class. The students' regular journal writing provides constant information to Kathy for planning developmentally appropriate experiences for the students. (Other strategies for getting to know students and encouraging professional dialogue are the choice of other teacher educators and are described in detail elsewhere in this book.) Beth's journal provided a means to hash out some of the central issues surrounding the principles of whole language, a concept Beth certainly had mixed feelings about. For this particular four-week summer school graduate class, the students shared their journal with Kathy once a week.

Following Kathy's lead, the students introduced themselves on the first day of class, and Beth became intimidated by the range and amount of experiences represented in the group. In fact, she was tempted to drop the course, feeling out of place and less credible than the others. She was convinced to stay because Kathy recognized an opportunity to influence a new teacher's early professionalism. Also, Beth's initial journal writing demonstrated that she was a thoughtful student and an excellent writer, and Kathy recognized her strong potential. Kathy's first anecdotal record about Beth's journal said: "Lengthy, eloquent, personal, responsive. She's a writer. Good goals to build lit text set to use w/writing workshop. Wants to correct." A week later, she noted, "hope she'll continue." When Beth wrote in her journal, "Something must be going right for me in this class when I can't wait to get home from class and start writing!" Kathy replied, "Yea! I'm so glad you stayed."

Early on, Beth read *What's Whole in Whole Language?* (K. Goodman 1986), and responded to it heatedly in her journal. She began by acknowledging that

> . . . no two people see the same event in precisely the same way [because of their personal school histories]. That filter of experience we use can be modified, but never entirely dispensed with. My own filter is based on my particular educational experiences. Goodman's filter is clearly quite different.

Next, Beth listed several quotations from *What's Whole* that troubled her. All dealt with the power relationships inherent in language in society, but one in particular says, "They [whole language teachers] believe all children have language and the ability to learn language, and they reject negative, elitist, racist views of linguistic purity that would limit children to arbitrary 'proper' language" (p. 25). Beth reacted strongly to this suggestion regarding correct English. Below we enter the middle of Beth's journal with Kathy's handwritten responses in the margins:

> I love the English language. For me, the PBS program, "The Story of English," was heaven-sent. I hung on every episode like some devotees hang on *The Young and the Restless*. In college, I actually *bought* the *Oxford English Dictionary,* all 4,116 pages of it. I am fascinated by the derivation of words. I *liked* to diagram sentences in elementary school. The rules of grammar which we chanted in those parallel rows of desks in sixth grade are with me still. There are, indeed, correct ways and less correct ways and, yes, even *incorrect* ways to express our thoughts and ideas. And so, Ken Goodman, does all of this make me at once "negative, elitist, and racist"? *Possibly! Let's discuss this some more. Is there a connection here? (over)*
> I wanted to attend a small, exclusive, expensive private college where I was convinced I would receive a superior education in comparative literature. No one else from my middle-class suburban high school had even *heard* of the place. The way I was able to realize this dream was to win two scholarships, one from the state of California and one from the shoe industry for which my father toiled, based on academic merit and high S.A.T. scores.

Then Beth proceeded to explain the family histories of herself and her highly successful husband. Each had grown up in a working-class family and each, as Beth wrote, "succeeded in life based on arbitrary test scores." She continued to describe her husband's struggle:

> He worked twenty hours a week at a fast food restaurant carrying an academic load of eighteen to twenty credit hours in the pre-law major for the first two years at a local community college. When I met him, he was a senior at that expensive

private college and I was a freshman. No one in his family had ever gone to college. No one had graduated from high school, either. . . . Those arbitrary and disjointed standardized tests permitted him to attend the finest law school in Texas.

Kathy's reply upon reading this scenario, which continued at length, was to write, "I would hate to give a measly test so much credit." And later, "No, the tests didn't permit him, I don't think. For many, many more folks who are equally intelligent and deserving, such tests are gatekeepers."

At this point in the course, Beth believed that tests, and learning the purest, most accurate English, as well as how to play by the rules, had enabled her family to climb out of one social class and succeed *at the top* of another. "That is why Goodman and I come to a parting of the ways when it comes to Standard English," Beth wrote. Success as measured by tests and formal English is a common assumption held by preservice and inservice teachers, whether they've beaten the system or been a victim of it in their own schooling histories. It's one of the many assumptions that whole language teacher education experiences work to change, and it often leads to dramatic rethinking on the part of our students.

In the following excerpts Beth found more troublesome spots in Ken's work. Again, you can read Kathy's handwritten responses.

1. "There is a strong whole language movement in the United States, but it is harder to see against the background of irrational demands for excellence that only translate into standardized test scores, back-to-basics movements, and pressures for narrowed curricula from moral majority and elitist groups" (p. 62). (Gee, I wonder if the author is a Democrat by any chance?) *Does that matter to you? How about his religious beliefs?*
2. "A staff that wanted to change to a positive, humanistic/scientific approach" (p. 67). (There is lots of talk about the 'humanistic/scientific' base upon which whole language is based. I never felt that the superlative language arts teachers who shared their love of literature with me were somehow less than human. *Where* is the science in whole language? What about long-term replicable studies with controls?)

Beth ended her second week's journal with these comments:

Despite my reservations regarding some of the language (i.e., Goodman's coining words such as "oralcy") and the us-against-them siege mentality (even going so far as to liken the movement to resistance knots of true believers meeting in secret to support THE CAUSE!), I think the author's intentions are clearly good, albeit somewhat blazingly fervent. Children do need to read and write in meaningful ways to meet their own needs and wants. Anything teachers can do to facilitate those ends should be welcomed and supported. Time will reveal whether or not the whole language movement is the panacea Goodman imagines it to be. In contrast to much of what has gone before it, however, it is certainly a move in the right direction.

I'd have to look back to see what you mean here.

> Would you call your comments, "fervent?

P.S. K—Yipes, it's sort of awful trying to write objectively about an author with whom your professor is personally acquainted (on a very friendly basis). I don't mean to seem picky, but sometimes the language chosen to describe a teaching method and the tendency toward politicizing it, even a movement I support as I

It isn't imagined -- it's researched, studied and documented in current practice & practice for the last 20-30 yrs.

Are you sure you support it? Seems you're not so sure and do this one, tends to raise my hackles just a bit. Where I come from, the experi-*that's ok.* ences of my husband and I, tend to naturally color my biases. Could Goodman celebrate that diversity, do you suppose?—B *Absolutely. I think he would love to talk through these issues with you.*

In Kathy's comments to Beth's journal, she had several goals. First was to value the experiences Beth brought to her learning from her history because all learners need a safety net to take risks and all learners' histories are a valid component in their current learning. Also, given the strength and confidence in Beth's writing, Kathy felt comfortable calling attention to the contradictions that she set forth. She said she supported the "movement," for example, but certainly argued hard against its most basic ideals. She clearly expected superior education for herself and her family and yet bridled at the accusation that she may hold elitist points of view about language and schooling. She refused to be political, yet most of her comments were stridently political, albeit of a more conservative persuasion. Another goal for Kathy's responses was to meet Beth on her own intellectual terms. Kathy was conscious not to water down her reaction or to placate the emotional nature of Beth's writing, because she recognized her student's highly intellectual and analytic nature. She returned Beth's journal with some of the comments you've read as well as others, not knowing what to expect for a reaction.

Meanwhile, during class time, the members of the class explored the developmental moments that occur in early literacy through the kinds of curriculum and protocols/engagements that are described throughout this book. The class listened to Kathy's daughter Monica, taped as a first grader as she painfully read from a terribly reduced basal text. They played with the reading process through transacting with "The Boat in the Basement" (see Protocol/Engagement B-10). The groups analyzed the inventions in children's early writing and began to explore their own miscues using written language. Professional literature study groups, using books like Dyson's *Multiple Worlds of Child Writers* (1989), Peterson's *Life in a Crowded Place* (1992), and Taylor's *Learning Denied* (1990), among others, met, discussed, and presented to each other. The students published a collection of their original writing that represented their personal literacy histories and completed projects that they designed and completed about early literacy. Snacks and regular sharing times in each class period enabled the participants of the class to get to know one another and build a social community. Daily, the class read children's literature that evoked emotional responses to issues of language, culture, literacy, race, and gender. Many days everyone, including Beth, was tearfully engaged in humorous and troubling issues that engulf teachers.

Beth appeared to be content and often touched during these experiences. She turned in her journal for the third time, this time with her response to Kathy's comments from the week before and Kathy's subsequent response.

> Well, I stuck my neck out on my journal response to the Goodman book and got it lopped off! When I was younger, I never would have taken such a risk. I knew precisely how to spit back what was expected, how to toe the party line. That was how you played the game and only a fool ignored the rules. Here, though, I didn't think that was necessary. It seems I was mistaken. . . .
>
> . . . There are many things which go on in every life, in each personal history. I simply meant to share a bit of mine, to offer some explication for my beliefs. From

this point, however, I believe I ought to stick to the script. Honesty, sometimes, is a costly policy.

When Kathy read these entries, she invited Beth to join her at a coffee shop. Kathy knew they needed to talk about these exchanges and wanted to demonstrate the principles of whole language face to face as well as in the shared classroom setting. Over coffee they shared details of their personal lives and deepened their respect for one another as women, readers and writers, and professionals. The following excerpts from the third week's journal entries show Beth's reaction:

I'm starting to think "volatile" is an adjective which can be aptly applied to my state of mind this summer. It seems as if my mood could be charted like some spiking temperature reading—up and down, *way* up and *way* down. . . . It was very thoughtful to meet with me at [the coffee shop] to talk things over. Was it the graduate level equivalent of McDonalds? I usually am able to get by without grappling with troublesome issues in my schoolwork. This class has certainly been a challenge to me, philosophically and emotionally. My mind seems to throb with all I am reading and thinking about. It seems, perhaps unfairly so, that many teachers do not come to terms with these issues on any fundamental level, but are instead content to learn and recite and implement the current party line as opposed to chiseling out a personal and meaningful version which is their own. Maybe they do, and I just don't see it.

. . . I'm not used to being pushed academically. It's sort of surprising, and also refreshing (and sometimes distressing!). I had a professor of English literature at college my first year who did that. He wore the Oxford don's cap and gown and had forgotten more than most of us would ever know. I came as the shining light of my high school, Mensa card in hand, to conquer letters. Dr. Owen pulled the rug out from under me, figuratively speaking of course (!), and taught me how to study, to write, and to critically examine what I read. Ever afterward, when something is rigorous yet beneficent I term it "Owenesque." This course is rapidly, for me, becoming "Owenesque."

. . . This is enough about it all for now. I have much to ponder, much to assimilate. Thank you for providing this opportunity to grow. I'd almost forgotten what it felt like.

At the end of Kathy's courses, students regularly spend time in a self-evaluation process that asks them to reflect on what they've learned and how. In Beth's class, Kathy asked students to respond to two requests for reflection. The first was "All semester we've been talking, reading, and thinking about how young children develop literacy. Write a few ideas about how you think children become literate, and how your view of reading and writing may have changed as a result of this course. How do you feel reading and writing instruction should be planned in conjunction with these ideas?" Beth responded with an eloquent summary of literacy development and the need for teachers to keep language whole in the process of using it for authentic purposes. Then she wrote:

For me, this course has been something of a revelation. It is perhaps the first time I have participated in a course where the concept of intent and reality merged.

. . . For the first time in many years, I experienced that heady excitement which comes from personal exploration and discovery. I agonized. Teeth gnashed. Tears flowed—but so did words, ideas, and pictures. I felt the stirrings of something in me I thought long gone. How strange, and how exciting, to find that it was merely dormant. It is the gem I will carry away with me. . . . For if an old and jaded perennial student like myself can be made (albeit kicking and screaming) to reexamine and reinvent herself as a learner, how very much more hope exists for children not victims of years of educational atrophy. This illumination, along with a resolve to help instead of hinder each child's voyage toward personal literacy, will surely serve to guide my own path as a teacher.

Next, students were asked, "Suggest for me the grade you feel best records your learning during the course. Explain why you feel you should receive this grade according to the expectations of the course, including completing the journal, your professional literature study group, the personal literacy reflection, the final project, and your participation in class." Beth wrote:

In my own estimation, the grade I earned for this course is an A. From my own perspective, the most unique part of my summer experience is that I took risks. Not knowing me very well, this sentence may not strike you as particularly earth-shattering. Again, you'll have to take my word for it. Risk taking is something I do not do.

. . . For someone who has played it very safely for many years, this summer was a phoenix of rebirth from an educational standpoint. Almost never do I care to argue with a professor, nor to share my thoughts. Many seem to have minds cast in stone. What would be the point? [In] this [class], though, every day I went home with thoughts teeming. I pondered and read and wrote and drew and talked in ways almost forgotten over the years in school, both as teacher and student.

I can say that I honestly learned things I wanted to know for my own sake. I can say, too, that for the first time in recent memory I came to respect a teacher for daring to confront and challenge me, thus enabling my intellectual and emotional growth to flourish when it might just as easily have withered and died. Strictly apart from attempting to quantify this experience, I just want to say that I am glad I came and glad I stayed.

WHAT DOES BETH TEACH US ABOUT WHOLE LANGUAGE TEACHING AND LEARNING?

Beth's honest writing captures the essence of a real learning experience in a whole language teacher education classroom. When we read Beth's ideas and listen to her, we see the power that slowly and carefully blooms in learners when they are challenged but simultaneously nurtured. Beth's experience is like many other students' experiences in whole language classes. She came to know, up close and personal, what it feels like to confront the disequilibrium necessary for real learning as she worked through the relationship between what she knows and what others know. Another student once came to Kathy's office to tell her, with all seriousness, that he thought he was going crazy. In his comments, we can hear the familiar strains: "My head hurts from thinking so much about what I read. Everything that I thought I believed in and practiced for years [like remediating the low group in his first-grade classroom] is under question. I feel like I'm going to explode with so many new ideas that I'm not sure about." When this student was assured that he was experiencing the phenomenon of disequilibrium, or cognitive dissonance, his face visibly relaxed and his eyes widened with understanding about the learning process from the inside out.

Sometimes learning isn't easy, and change, when traditions are so deeply and historically rooted, can be slow and painful. The rewards, as Beth experienced, can be life changing and certainly can empower learners in teacher education settings in their professional and personal lives.

David Doake (1994) writes of similar experiences in his classes. As his students become aware of the lack of expected conventions from their transmission paradigm-laden histories in school, they are very uncomfortable and near panic, especially concerning evaluation. But as Doake describes, "At the end of the course, however, they are almost always deeply appreciative of finally being given control over their own learning and the opportunity to develop an understanding of what it means to be an independent learner" (p. 135).

Trusting students and inviting them to assume ownership for their own learning creates tension in our roles as faculty. This shift requires a redefinition of teacher as mediator rather than information dispenser and an effective method of demonstrating to students that the rules and roles have changed. This book illustrates how CELT members are redefining themselves as they practice what they teach.

The following CELT members were also key contributors to this chapter: Patty Anders, Carole Edelsky, Karen Feathers, David E. Freeman, Yvonne S. Freeman, Yetta M. Goodman, Dorothy Menosky, Kathryn Mitchell Pierce, Lynn Rhodes, and Diane Stephens.

REFERENCES

Altwerger, B., and B. Flores. 1992. "The Theme Cycle: An Overview." In *The Whole Language Catalog* (p. 295). K. S. Goodman, L. B. Bird, and Y. M. Goodman, eds. Santa Rosa, CA: American School Publishers.

Doake, D. 1994. "The Myths and Realities of Whole Language: An Educational Movement at Risk." In *Under the Whole Language Umbrella* (pp. 125–157). A. D. Flurkey and R. J. Meyer, eds. Urbana, IL: National Council of Teachers of English and Bloomington, IN: Whole Language Umbrella.

Dyson, A. H. 1989. *Multiple Worlds of Child Writers: Friends Learning to Write*. New York: Teachers College Press.

Fox, M. 1993. *Radical Reflections: Passionate Opinions on Teaching, Learning, and Living*. San Diego, CA: Harcourt Brace.

Goodman, K. S. 1986. *What's Whole in Whole Language?* Portsmouth, NH: Heinemann.

Goodman, Y. M. 1985. "Kidwatching: Observing Children in the Classroom." In *Observing the Language Learner* (pp. 9–18). A. Jaggar and M. T. Smith-Burke, eds. Newark, DE and Urbana, IL: Co-published by International Reading Association and National Council of Teachers of English.

————. 1989. "Roots of the Whole-Language Movement." In *The Elementary School Journal*, 90, 2: 113–127.

Halliday, M. A. K. undated. "Three Aspects of Children's Language Development: Learning Language, Learning Through Language, Learning About Language." In *Language Research: Impact on Educational Settings*. G. S. Pinnell and M. Matlin Haussler, eds. Unpublished manuscript.

Moll, L. C. 1990. Introduction. In *Vygotsky and Education: Instructional Implications and Applications of Sociohistorical Psychology* (pp. 1–27). L. C. Moll, ed. Cambridge, UK: Cambridge University Press.

Moll, L. C., and K. F. Whitmore. 1993. "Vygotsky in Classroom Practice: Moving from Individual Transmission to Social Transaction." In *Contexts for Learning: Sociocultural Dynamics in Children's Development* (pp. 19–42). E. A. Forman, N. Minick, and C. A. Stone, eds. New York: Oxford University Press.

Peterson, R. 1992. *Life in a Crowded Place: Making a Learning Community*. Portsmouth, NH: Heinemann.

Short, K. G., and C. Burke. 1989. "New Potentials for Teacher Education: Teaching and Learning as Inquiry." In *The Elementary School Journal*, 90, 2: 193–206.

Smith, F. 1988. *Joining the Literacy Club*. Portsmouth, NH: Heinemann.

Taylor, D. 1990. *Learning Denied*. Portsmouth, NH: Heinemann.

Vygotsky, L. S. 1978. *Mind in Society*. Cambridge, MA: Harvard University Press.

Whitmore, K. F., and C. G. Crowell. 1994. *Inventing a Classroom: Life in a Bilingual, Whole Language Learning Community*. York, ME: Stenhouse.

Whitmore, K. F., and Y. M. Goodman. 1995. "Transforming Curriculum in Language and Literacy" In *Reaching Potentials: Transforming Early Childhood Curriculum and Assessment*, Vol. 2. (pp. 145–166). S. Bredekamp, ed. Washington, DC: NAEYC.

2

CREATING COMMUNITIES OF LEARNERS

Dorothy Watson, Patricia W. Jenkins, and Dorothy F. King

The idea of creating a congenial climate in classrooms isn't news for most whole language educators. We go out of our way to learn students' names, interests, and experiences; encourage everyone to participate in discussion; provide special resources for those with diverse interests; and in general make every person feel challenged and comfortable. We use our expertise to create a warm and caring atmosphere for all learners, then set the stage for individual and group players. In our congenial classrooms, we teach students about literacy and literacy education; we do our best to help students understand learning as functional, mediated, and collaborative.

Despite all our hard work, many of us have come to realize that our classroom practices have not always been consistent with our beliefs and our teaching. We have advocated community but have fallen short by providing only congeniality. In truth, when it comes to the social order of our classrooms, we often find that we are not practicing what we teach. What we advocate and must provide is a social organization in which learning takes place in a democratic setting. Our advocacy is grounded on the work of Lev Vygotsky, Paulo Freire, David Bloome, Malcolm Knowles, and Michael Halliday, to name but a few. Vygotsky (1986) regarded education as the ultimate sociocultural activity. He maintained that thought and language begin with the social (the interpsychological) and develop into the personal (the intrapsychological). Freire (1985) provided impressive examples of small communities of adult learners working together in order to become literate and to bring about social and political reform. Bloome (1985) wrote that through social interaction, students find ways of gaining status, solving problems, and valuing and feeling. Knowles (1973) defined ways that capitalize on characteristics of adult learners. Halliday (1987) defined learning as a social semiotic in which the components of the learning situation (context) are ones that teachers can directly influence.

Acceptance of the idea that optimal potential for learning can be achieved through social experiences and that these social encounters direct our thinking led us to investigate our own teaching and profession. In searching for experiences to be introduced into our classrooms, we became aware of professional groups that could contribute to our own growth. The idea of the power of community led us to consider two major themes in our experiences with preservice and inservice teachers: (1) the existing professional communities outside our classrooms—communities that are in place and are immediately available and supportive—and (2) the one that got us thinking about this issue in the first place, how to develop a community of learners within our own classrooms.

PROFESSIONAL COMMUNITIES

The belief that teaching is work done in isolation, totally devoid of collegial relationships, is often confirmed by the social structure of teachers' undergraduate experiences. Students in teacher preparation programs may be unaware of their professors', much less their own, connections with a larger professional community of educators. They may feel that their teaching, ultimately their life's work, is accomplished as a lonely enterprise. Evidence they've gained over years of schooling supports the prospect of an isolated and solitary career; indeed undergraduates may never have witnessed teachers' discussing professional concerns with each other. If they have overheard conversations, the talk may have taken the form of complaining, often about students or administrative issues. The fact is that our students may never have observed or experienced a community of professional educators.

Our collaborative inquiry has led us to conclude that as teacher educators, we need to invite students into the larger body of professionals that is immediately available to them. We must issue the invitation to join the club now. With supportive membership within their profession, novice teacher-students can avoid falling into an isolation that works against collegiality and professional growth. By becoming connected, teachers have the opportunity to join rather than separate from decision making about curriculum, learning, teaching, and life in the classroom. Genuine involvement ensures that decisions about teachers and teaching get made by those who are most knowledgeable: teachers themselves.

Because the inclusion of learners within professional communities is crucial to professional growth, as well as to ownership and pride, we present the following invitations for encouraging both undergraduate and graduate students to join the larger professional community:

- Provide access to national and international organizations such as the Whole Language Umbrella, the National Council of Teachers of English (NCTE), and the International Reading Association (IRA). Take student membership forms and examples of the organization's publications to class, and offer to sign up students on the spot. Use articles from the journals throughout the semester and identify the groups that publish the pieces.
- Encourage and mentor education students to participate in professional organizations by serving on committees, chairing and presenting or copresenting with a more experienced colleague, and submitting a manuscript for publication. Students never forget their first conference; they often comment that the experience made them feel as if they were an accepted member of an important professional community. We share our own professional involvement in professional organizations by reporting back to students after participating in a conference or seminar.
- Encourage students to attend—as colleagues, not guests—local, state, and regional meetings of professional organizations. Many TAWL (Teachers Applying Whole Language) groups extend special invitations to students to

attend monthly meetings, as well as annual conferences. Reduced registration fees are made available to full-time students.

- Establish a student association of TAWL, NCTE, or IRA. Whole language teachers often share their experience and knowledge at such meetings. Small study groups are formed when several individuals have an interest in a topic. We can be helpful in pointing these study groups to reading materials and to individual professionals who have dealt with or are dealing with the issues studied.
- Organize students through cohort groups in which experienced teachers (perhaps TAWL) and teacher educators mentor those entering the profession. Mentoring might begin with one's advisees. Groups might be organized analogous to the "home base" idea in middle schools. A healthy balance of experience can be provided by mixing membership so that graduate and undergraduate students, as well as teachers, are in the groups. Meetings of these groups might be called professional seminars, in which students get credit; in the best of all possible worlds, faculty would get recognition and credit.
- Make continuous in-school involvement a part of every class. Exchange pen pal letters with children and classroom teachers. Make oracy and literacy experiences and evaluation come alive by organizing for college students to work with children and adolescents in schools. To discover the real issues and trends that teachers are dealing with, invite students to interview educators.
- Plan student visits to whole language classrooms for observation of specific experiences such as literature study discussions; authors' circles; learning through drama, art, and music; and researchers (students and teachers) at work. Arrange for conference calls among students and the teachers they have observed.
- Invite elementary and secondary school teachers to share their classroom artifacts with college students. Reactions of the college students are sent to the classroom teacher and children, who respond in turn.
- Investigate ways of breaking out of the turf and territory dilemma of content area separation of classes. At the University of Maine, full-time students enroll for a six-credit literacy block along with one credit of fieldwork. Sections of literacy and a content area such as science, social studies, and math are presented together so that students witness professors' team teaching, negotiating, and sharing ideas and information. The increased amount of time allows visits to classrooms and having classes and groups of children visit the college classes.

A college classroom community can become part of the larger community of professional educators through participation in the network of educational organizations, district offices, schools, classrooms, and even groups within the college and university. If teacher-learners are to believe that they can make changes in the world, they need to feel linked with communities that are in touch with the resources to bring about such changes.

COMMUNITIES WITHIN OUR CLASSROOMS

When students talk about classroom communities from their personal school histories, they are likely to describe them as a "group of students under the direction of one teacher." They report that the criteria for grouping within these so-called communities had to do with children's ages, perceived abilities, and test scores. They also assume that grouping made it easier for students to master a body of knowledge within a specific amount of time. Success or failure in achieving the identified goals (set by someone other than themselves) was determined by how well students regurgitated the prescribed knowledge identified by the teacher and the textbook, usually by way of tests. High scores were usually attributed to the amount of energy and dedication devoted individually to transferring that prescribed knowledge to each solitary student. From a whole language perspective, these are the wrong reasons for grouping learners.

It is very likely that our students will attempt to create the same atmosphere and structure in their own classrooms. In keeping with their earlier experiences, as new teachers they may emphasize the individualization and isolation of learning, to the exclusion of the socialization and integration of learning. Once again, textbooks and tests may be prioritized and valued over students. Such practices are particularly inappropriate in settings in which the potential for social communication and collaboration is so great.

Given that the social context of education classrooms has such a powerful effect on what happens in future classrooms, we offer the following to colleagues who strive to practice what they teach:

- Invite members of the college classroom community to get to know each other. Students may begin to establish community by learning each others' names, but must go beyond that rudimentary effort if they are to know and trust each other. A bulletin board on which students and teacher post something about themselves, especially something about their expertise, is one way of learning about peers. Teachers and students need to learn about their classmates' histories, present circumstances, and their hopes for the days and years ahead. Friendships that extend into their teaching careers may be forged when there is a real community spirit during students' college years.

- Help members of the classroom community to know themselves. Invite students to reflect on their own abilities by creating a publicly shared portfolio that promotes self-evaluation. This collection of beliefs and assets is reviewed and revised periodically. The portfolio must encourage socialization of learners and the never-ending process of learning rather than emphasize isolation of students and a finished product. This portfolio will help meet the need that adults have to be viewed as self-directive and to be respected for their experiences (Knowles 1973).

- Ask each class member at the beginning of the semester to fill out a four-by-six-inch information card that in addition to the usual data (address, telephone, adviser's name, etc.) includes information about previous experiences with children and a note about the ways in which they most comfortably share their ideas and resources with others.

- Facilitate intellectually important and stimulating experiences. In order to invite students to contribute to its process and content, the curriculum must be open for discussion and revision. If the curriculum is to be both important and applicable, students are expected to offer suggestions and make choices about its content and to participate in instructional procedures. This negotiation of curriculum ensures inquiry and research into themes that are meaningful and important to learners.

- Help members of the community to live in an environment that is appealing and that promotes learning and teaching. The appearance of the classroom is important to all those who share time, space, and purpose. How does the arrangement of the desks, tables, chairs, lectern facilitate social interactions? Is there a message board, an artifact table, a book browsing area? Who greets the learners, takes care of housekeeping chores and administrivia? Who presides over the learning experiences?

- Members of a genuine community of learners may find themselves in roles that are not always encouraged in conventional college classrooms. An important place to begin developing this concept may be with substituting the term *teacher-learner* for *student-teacher*. This new term helps us all understand that these young teachers are already members of the professional club; they aren't just getting ready to join it. It also moves ownership and responsibility of learning directly to the teacher-learner and provides an exciting and spirited atmosphere for all involved.

If we practice our teaching of collaborative learning within a democratic social setting, we must facilitate an environment in which all scholars function as both expert and novice, teacher and student. Not only to accommodate and value the individual, but also to establish a community that is open, fair, accepting, and democratic, the teacher educator must reconsider the role of expert and in doing so come to realize the teacher-learner has expertise that can be brought to fulfillment through the larger professional community as well as by participation and commitment within the college classroom. Establishing a community of teacher-learners is an integral part of a teacher's education, and it strengthens the possibility of similar communities coming to life in the classrooms of the future.

Contributors to this chapter include Patty Anders, Mary Bixby, Carolyn Burke, Linda Crafton, Shirley Crenshaw, Jayne DeLawter, Carole Edelsky, Karen Feathers, Yetta M. Goodman, Francis Kazemek, Janice Kristo, Myna L. Matlin, Dorothy Menosky, Heidi Mills, Lynn Rhodes, Helen Slaughter, Diane Stephens, and Carole Urzúa.

REFERENCES

Bloome, D. 1985. "Reading as Social Process." In *Language Arts,* 62, 2: pp. 134–142.

Freire, P. 1985. *Pedagogy of the Oppressed.* New York: Herder and Herder.

Halliday, M. A. K. 1987. *Language as Social Semiotic: The Social Interpretation of Language and Meaning.* Baltimore, MD: University Park Press.

Knowles, M. 1973. *The Adult Learner: A Neglected Species.* Houston, TX: Gulf Publishing.

Vygotsky, L. S. 1986. *Thought and Language.* Cambridge, MA: MIT Press.

VALUING TEACHER EDUCATORS
AS LEARNERS

Dorothy F. King and Shirley Crenshaw, editors

The chapters in Part A relate personal stories of teacher educators who have transformed their teaching to reflect an evolving understanding of language and learning. Unlike a "how-to" book, these narratives provide demonstrations from which readers are free to reflect, ask their own questions, seek their own answers, and join in on the whole language conversations.

Karen Guilfoyle, in "My Journey Through the Land of Transformation: Navigating Uncharted Territory," sets the tone for the chapters that follow as she takes us through her own changes in teaching. She compellingly describes how her own feelings and thinking were transformed to reflect more closely what she saw as whole language teaching and learning.

Next, Margaret Atwell, in "Creating Community and Support Among New Faculty," distinguishes between the concepts of orientation and mentoring of new faculty. In an open letter to deans of colleges of education, she describes how whole language beliefs can inform and support new faculty.

"Balancing Action and Reflection in Student Teaching" is Kathy Short's story. She describes how she helped her students to generate their own questions as they experienced student teaching. A cycle of inquiry began in which reflection became the force behind the action. Short gives excellent examples of important changes in the student teaching program as a result of her reflection as the teacher educator.

Carol Gilles describes the journey from doctoral student to teacher educator in "Everybody Needs a 'Grip': Support Groups for Doctoral Students." Gilles reminds us of the power of collaboration in the personal aspects of our lives as well as in fostering our thinking in academic tasks. She shows that "we get by with a little help from our friends."

Wendy Kasten's "Teaching and Learning in a Professional Development School" presents her rationale for field-based instruction and describes her dynamic experience and learning as she taught a preservice class on site in an elementary school.

The authors of these chapters are teacher educators who are changing to meet the goals of their shared philosophical stance. They are in the process of learning while teaching. They are moving away from the chalkboards and lecture podiums at the fronts of classrooms to join their students in negotiated learning experiences. They are openly taking the risks alongside their students that are necessary for real learning. Their positive changes bring new challenges as they adapt the conventions of teacher education—evaluation, syllabus writing, and programmatic organization—to their philosophies and goals.

3

My Journey Through the Land
of Transformation:
Navigating Uncharted Territory

Karen Guilfoyle

I have spent many hours thinking about my experience with whole language as a learner, teacher, and researcher. It has been a powerful learning experience and a challenging one. This is my story, told through my reflections and actions, of my journey to understand learning and teaching with whole language in teacher education.

I have constructed my story through a qualitative study I began in fall 1989 as a beginning teacher educator. Numerous artifacts serve as data sources: field notes in a teacher-researcher journal, teaching notebooks, dialogue journals with four teacher educators in another study, students' journal entries and self-assessments, student evaluations, teaching videotapes, notes from meetings and conferences, and informal and formal interviews with preservice and inservice teachers and graduate students. The analysis is ongoing and continues to guide my reflection, inquiry, and practice.

My personal interpretation of this experience is grounded in the theories, beliefs, and experience I bring to the study (Lyons 1990). My lenses are influenced by my personal history, which includes being a product of the sixties; teaching in the seventies in an open concept school using language experience, individualized reading, and Glasser's class meetings (Glasser 1969); and being involved in the eighties in an alternative school in Montana, a three-room rural school, and a Teacher Corps project on the Blackfeet Reservation. Through these experiences, I developed the foundation to understand the whole language philosophy when I was introduced to it in the mid-1980s. I studied the philosophy with K. and Y. Goodman and observed it in practice over a three-year period, conducting my dissertation study (Guilfoyle 1988). Now I am using whole language in teacher education as a means to transform my practice and to support others in transforming their practice with this philosophy.

EXPLORING THE HILLS AND VALLEYS

In the following sections, I present my challenges, struggles, and celebrations to illustrate the process of changing and shifting, making visible the problems as well as possibilities in restructuring. I use them to demonstrate that teaching is learning (Boomer 1987).

Year One: The Uphill Climb

My initial attempt at implementing whole language at the college level was in an introduction to education course. It was a traumatic experience, for both the students and me. To teach the course, I was handed a notebook, developed over the past thirteen years, that contained the prescribed syllabus and told me "what to do on which day." In a letter to a friend, I wrote, "I realized that this is what you faced in your classroom all the time with basals and mandated curriculum. . . . I thought about what you had done. I wonder if I am brave enough to do that at the college level?" (personal correspondence, September 7, 1989).

I tried negotiating a revision of the curriculum with the faculty member who had developed the guide but was unsuccessful. I made some cosmetic revisions (Short and Burke 1991) and handed out a revised syllabus. These revisions were still too restrictive, so five weeks into the semester, I revised for the third time. I introduced the use of journals and group projects, opened the class to small and large group discussions, and tried to restructure the predetermined point system for evaluation. A student suggested later in the semester that I should have started "with the outline of the class we have now. It worked better because it was what you believe in more than the first couple of outlines we revised."

In that first semester, I struggled to help the students understand my use of the whole language philosophy as I attempted to implement it. During the last class meeting, I formally described the philosophy and shared my reflections on how I had used it to influence our experience. Although most of the students seemed to accept the organization of instruction, my explanation of the assessment process created an uproar:

1. For all of you who made the effort to complete assignments, attended class, and worked at a level that was appropriate for you, you have earned a grade of B.
2. Those of you who made the effort to really get involved, completed the assignments in a quality manner, attempted to introduce to the class something they had learned during the semester, really took the time to reflect and analyze in your journals, made the effort to explore a variety of materials for the papers, you will earn an A.
3. Those of you who put only minimal effort into the course, attended class on an irregular basis, turned in assignments in an inappropriate time frame and didn't make the effort to make other arrangements, minimal entries in journals, minimal effort on research cards, etc. In other words, met requirements at a minimal level, you will earn a C.

I graded on effort, commitment, and competency.

Some students were upset with the qualitative aspects I had added to the point system of evaluation. They voiced resentment at being in a "game where they felt the instructor had changed the rules."[1] Because of my limited experience at the college level and in using the philosophy, their actions caught me off-guard. I had not recognized that I was encountering one of the major problems in restructuring: fitting a new structure into an existing context that does not support the shift.

My first semester ended in discord, but it did not change my beliefs about whole language. I used the philosophy, the students' journal entries and evaluations, and my analysis of that experience to reorganize the course. Since whole language is a way of viewing learning and teaching, you can go back to it to rethink your practice. By focusing on the why (theories) rather than the how (methods), you can continually review and reorganize your practice. I could not address all their issues, but the students' comments and concerns helped me learn more about preservice teachers' views of learning and teaching and how strongly they are impacted by the transmission approach. Following are some of their suggestions:

At some point, though, those why's have to be transformed into how's.

A little more structure to lectures. Studying for tests and papers is where I learn the most—not to say tests are a learning aid, but something to think about.

Possibly less talk and more work in class. I don't have any ideas on what type that could be. However, there was too much discussion.

I would give specific due dates and stick with them because students will take advantage of handing in late work. Myself included.

During second semester, I continued to learn about the content of the course, as well as what it meant to teach it. In addition to providing more choices, I helped students explore the process and content of participation in small and large groups and implemented contracting for grades. I learned that some students have more difficulty interacting in a whole language classroom than others. My challenges were to read and respond to the many journals, support forty learners in a classroom during a fifty-minute period, and deal with students who resisted the paradigm shift and taking responsibility for their own learning. I wondered how I would ever be able to meet the other demands of academia when teaching consumed so much of my time.

Year Two: More Mountains and Cliffs

In my second year (1990–1991), my assignment changed and I began teaching an upper-division, literacy methods course, Alternatives to Basals. I treated this as an opportunity to practice whole language and teach about its implications for literacy development. In this context, new challenges arose. Not only did my organization of the course create disequilibrium for the students, but I also asked them to reconsider their notions about literacy, learning, and teaching. It posed a dilemma for the students because the psycholinguistic view of reading and critical exploration of literacy (e.g., Freire 1970; Freire and Macedo 1987) did not fit with their current beliefs or past experiences. Two students wrote:

It is not fair for you to do this at the end of our program. We need to know how to teach students, not worry about how we are learning. I need to know what you expect so I can do the work.

How will we be able to use whole language out in the schools when most places are using basals? I want to know how to get a job.

During that second year, I searched for ways to facilitate the learning of students caught in this paradigm shift. I openly discussed my purposes for the organization of the course and learning events. I attempted to help students connect their experience in my classroom to the theories we were studying. I used the journals to address individual needs, and I held conferences with students. I addressed evaluation by inviting students to develop their own criteria for grading. Students continued to struggle with my use of the philosophy, and so did I;[2] but I was learning more about the issues that make transitions so difficult for both learners and teachers (e.g., personal beliefs, past experiences, inconsistent policies, schedules, grades).

Year Three: Some Valleys Among the Hills

Student voices and my developing understanding of whole language and how knowledge is constructed socially guided me to make further changes. I immersed the students more gently into the structure of my classroom by organizing activities to create a learning community as a means to support the transition and learning. I held conferences with all the students early in the semester and asked them to assess their own progress. Support was provided to those who were inexperienced in directing their own learning as they moved to taking more responsibility (Vygotsky 1978). During this third year, using an article by Short and Burke (1989) as support, I extended the length of time the class was scheduled to accommodate a transactional framework and added a field experience in classrooms where teachers were using whole language.

These shifts helped the social context, but the learning environment continued to be problematic. My expecting students to be actively involved in reflective journal writing, a collaborative learning community (Short 1991), and personal assessment of learning after many years of participating in the transmission model created tension. Pushing students to examine their beliefs, critically rethink them, and shift to whole language added stress. In their journals, students wrote the following comments:

I have been thrown into a state of disequilibrium from the beginning of this class. I have had many conflicts with what I thought education was all about and now the new shift in education.

This class is definitely giving me a challenge. I have never been exposed to this type of teaching in college and it is challenging to write in a learning log and to get used to not having a syllabus.

I'm having a very difficult time with this new paradigm of teaching and learning. My time in this class is spent being frustrated and often angry no matter how hard I try to remain calm. I think the biggest reason for this is the huge change in my whole way of thinking that this paradigm is asking me to make. I'm not sure if I believe enough in the theories to make that change.

I was becoming aware of how difficult it is to move learners to shift their paradigms. Deconstructing beliefs and experience takes time and requires commitment to change. Learners who had been successful in the transmission model and had limited experience with failure in school or society found it difficult to see the need to transform their beliefs or views of learning and teaching.

Year Four: Rugged Terrain

During the fall semester 1992, I took a break from the Alternatives to Basals course to develop and teach two graduate classes. My learning in these courses, my interaction with graduate students and classroom teachers, and time to reflect clarified my theories and beliefs. Spring semester 1993, I returned to teach Alternatives to Basals with new hopes. An entry in my teaching journal read as follows:

> I began the semester excited about teaching undergraduates again. I felt that I had learned about organizing my course to better support them as they made the transition from traditional instruction AND was ready to put my extended understanding into practice.

I thought I now knew how to organize the course to create a student-centered, process-oriented, inquiry-based classroom and reduce the amount of resistance. My goals—to support students in being critical, reflective thinkers; actively involve them in the learning process; respect each learner through celebrating diversity; and help students assume more responsibility for their own learning by providing further ownership and choice in what they learned—seemed attainable. I thought adding walking journals in which students exchange journals with each other in small groups (see Protocol/Engagement C-8) would ease the tension. The journals are designed to "provide an opportunity for students to share thoughts, concerns, and resources" (Hornstein, Heine, and Heine 1992, p. 3) and give self-assessment a more central role in the curriculum (Short and Kauffman 1992).

The journals didn't help. I had a large class of thirty-eight students, and by the third week we were still struggling with becoming a community. The social context was strained by apprehensive, defensive, and resistant feelings. In a journal entry I shared with colleagues in another study, I wrote the following reflection on February 9:

> [The Alternatives to Basals course] has been the focus of much of my research as it is where I often introduce undergraduates not only to a constructivist/whole language view of teaching/learning but to being in a transformational classroom. I have a commitment to making that class work because I see this framework needed in the schools to support the learning of all students to participate in our changing society. All elementary education students are required to take this class so it is a cross-section of views, beliefs, and experiences similar to teachers in the field.
> . . . The course has always been a struggle for me but I have remained determined to continue using a constructivist view of teaching/learning and treat the challenge

as a learning experience. Well, this semester I'm not sure the learning is worth the pain. It raises so many issues that I am not sure what meaning it really holds.

The process of self-assessment seemed to be the straw that broke the camel's back. After the students had written their first assessments and I had responded with a narrative based on my qualitative interpretation of their learning journey, their discontent with the course became open. One student wrote,

> I don't think that it is fair. I know that when I do work for a class I put my best effort that I can into it. . . . I think it is only fair that the teacher comment on it and return it so I know how they have evaluated it. . . . Without them, I don't know how I am doing, what I need to improve, exactly the place in my work that needs improvement, or that the teacher has understood what I have done.

Others indicated that they were being asked to reflect too much, to read too much, and to write too often. Another student added that if it were an English class so much reading, writing, and reflecting might be acceptable.

I understood that the students' past experience influenced this reaction, but I was nevertheless disheartened; I had thought I could create a learning environment that would transform their beliefs about learning and teaching. As I questioned my use of the philosophy and struggled with my beliefs about learning, teaching, and assessment, I wrote in a journal entry on February 9:

> The thing that is bothering me most is that I can't understand why this is happening. My teaching is the strongest it has ever been. I am clear about my beliefs and expectations. I support their transition and have spent time discussing it. I conferenced sooner. I reduced the amount of work to allow time for in depth reading, writing, and reflection. I am putting into practice my expanded understanding of whole language and the constructivist view of teaching/learning. I am better able to assess both the students' progress and the organization of the course. But the classroom environment is not better.
>
> I thought about the words of my colleague, E. Michel. I spent all last semester restructuring the content area reading course to match what is currently known about reading/writing/teaching/learning. I know it is effective but the students are so resistant to being involved at the level needed to effectively implement this organization of instruction that they end up hating the course. Have I gained anything?

Throughout the remainder of the semester, I repeatedly reflected on my practice, held conferences with resistant and uninvolved students, and tried to connect with the students' experiences to understand the meaning of their actions and interactions. Still, the classroom never moved to being a collaborative community. Three students chose not to join the learning community, and others seemed only to learn how to "play a new game" to get through the course.

I ended my fourth year of teaching feeling much the same as I did after my first semester and uncertain as to whether I wanted to return to the college classroom. During the summer, I tried putting my experience into perspective. I analyzed data from the Alternatives to Basals class, read several texts (Mayher 1990; Simon 1991; Weiler 1988), reflected in my journal, attended the Center for Expansion of Language and Thinking (CELT) Rejuvenation Conference—Making Curriculum More Explicitly Political, and talked to colleagues.

I have learned that in whole language the terrain can be difficult and rough for all participants. The following analysis, by a graduate student studying my classroom (Edson 1993), depicts the experience:

> Through the semester, the class found that the journey could not be represented by a straight line. The path was not smooth and errorless. Instead it was winding, with hairpin turns and detours. Rocks appeared as the students and professor took risks, and sometimes the rocks became boulders as the students mucked through their approximations at thinking critically. (p. 22)

UNDERSTANDING THE JOURNEY

I have put a great amount of time and effort into implementing and studying the meaning of whole language in teacher education, for both the students and me. I have done this in a system that wants higher education to be restructured yet without changing any of its existing structures and policies. It has influenced my participation in academia where research is valued over teaching and publishing is valued over scholarship.

In my ongoing process of constructing the meaning of learning and teaching with whole language, I have developed knowledge about learning, teaching, and the social construction of knowledge. Although I still have many questions, I have generated new ways of viewing the terrain that may help me and others as we travel over the rocky and treacherous road of transformation.

Exploring the Rocks and Boulders as a Teacher

Initially it seemed that the struggles in transformation were created by the students' lack of experience in a transactional context and my limited experience in implementing whole language in teacher education. I thought that once I learned how to use the whole language philosophy, the other issue would be minimized. This is one of the reasons I was so unprepared for my experiences during my fourth year of using whole language.

When I added the lenses of critical and feminist pedagogies (Laird 1988; Leck 1987; Luke and Gore 1992) to deconstruct the experience, I began to understand the complexities involved in attempting to shift to transactional and transformational classrooms.[3] I also recognized the tension created by practicing a social constructivist view of learning and whole language, while attempting to transform others' beliefs and views of learning and teaching. My goals—to have students adopt a whole language philosophy and to view schooling through social and political lenses—*and* my beliefs and theories of learning created conflict.

The Shifting Role of Tour Guide

From the very beginning, I worked hard to change students' views (Weiler 1988). I took seriously the role of teacher as a transformative intellectual (Giroux 1988). One of my early journal entries reflects this perspective:

I want to help change teaching/learning so all kids are respected/valued and get their needs accommodated. I want to change how students are interacted with in the teaching/learning environment. I want to change the teacher education program.

I did not understand that seeing myself as a change agent, capable of changing others, was a holdover from a transmission view of learning and is also problematic with some critical pedagogies (Gore 1992; Lather 1990). My attempts to change others through an authoritative voice was responsible, in part, for the resistance I encountered. I now understand the difference between supporting and changing. I cannot change or transform anyone; that is a personal choice. As a social constructivist using whole language, my role is to use demonstration and dialogue to support others' transitions.

I have learned that I must also be able to accept some resistance since I use whole language as a form of critical pedagogy (Edelsky 1991) and "treat students as critical agents; make knowledge problematic; utilize critical and affirming dialogue; and make the case for struggling for a qualitatively better world for all people" (Giroux 1988, p. 127). Although their words may have new meaning, I hope students will continue to write about me as the following ones did:

I see her as a change agent and an inspirational leader—someone who believes in what she is doing so strongly that when others attack her ideas, she can bounce back within a short period of time, smile again, and give it another go at being a change agent.

I will remember your appreciation for celebration of the difference between students. You are a one person crusade for the moral and ethical values of the individual—especially minorities.

Because of this experience, I am reflecting on my "talk" as well as my "walk," and I am transforming my voice. I am learning the difference between "tell" versus "share," "should" versus "could," and "talk to" versus "talk with." I cannot take away the authority I have in the classroom as the teacher, but I can take the authority out of my voice to be a part of the conversation, discussion, or dialogue. In "helping students uncover words that interpret what it is that they are experiencing," I need to be careful "because it is so easy for teachers to push their own ideas off on students, thereby distancing them from their experience" (Peterson 1992, p. 99).

This, too, will not alleviate all tension. As I continue to push students in their thinking and guide them "in reconstructing their experience as they actively reorganize and reconfigure incoming information through reflective thought" (Farber and Armaline 1992, p. 102), the disequilibrium and discomfort they feel will create stress.

The Students' Roadblocks

Students came to my classes expecting me to be able to teach them everything they needed to know about the classroom. They thought they would be told how to teach. They did not see the value of exploring personal beliefs and theories. They wanted methods to organize their practice, not new ways of viewing learning and teaching.

The students struggled with the new ways of knowing they encountered in my classroom. Long years in the transmission model and their limited experience in learning by connecting, reflecting, and self-assessing placed a strain on their participation. They had not often taken risks in learning and lacked trust that they could succeed in this new framework.

When students discovered that they were expected to be actively involved, make choices, have responsibility for personal learning, and think critically about literacy and schooling, some became resistant. They had learned to play the game of school and didn't want the rules changed. A few were overwhelmed; the difference between their experience and the course was too great. Others celebrated the challenge, as shown in their responses to the question, "What will you remember most about this class?":

> The excitement of seeing a new paradigm and theory of learning that addresses my personal needs for growth as a learner and helps me redefine my theory, philosophy, and practice as a teacher.

> Karen G and her depth of knowing about whole language, students, adults, teachers, and life.

> I will definitely remember this class as a place where I found out about my own teaching philosophy and how my opinions will affect the students I teach. I have clarified my beliefs!

There continue to be passive, resistant, or defensive students in my classroom. There are also those who have taken the risk to rethink critically their beliefs and assumptions about learning and teaching and have begun their personal transformation through participating in Alternatives to Basals. I am learning more about how to guide each group on their journey.

WINDING AND TURNING AS A COMMUNITY

Neither the students nor I understood that transformation was such an intense experience. We did not fully understand the impact the traditional transmission mode of schooling had made on us. We all had to learn new roles and ways of interacting to participate in a whole language classroom. Our histories have not given us practice in this kind of context. We needed to understand the meaning of learning as a process and to celebrate approximations. We had to become a community of learners. There was a lot at stake in transforming our theories and beliefs.

DANGER IN THE LAND OF ACADEMIA

As an untenured professor in a system that values publishing over teaching, my use of whole language holds serious consequences. As a teacher educator, I am expected to teach nine credits a semester, research, write, and publish. It is a struggle to fulfill all these roles when teaching involves so much of my time and energy.

I can't dig out old lecture notes from the previous semester so I can spend time researching. My writing time is used to respond to students' journals and other writing. Office hours are filled with student conferences. Library time is spent in better understanding the events in my classroom. My research is "published" in my practice rather than educational journals. My understanding of whole language grows, but my list of publications does not. Not receiving tenure could be the consequence of exploring uncharted territory with whole language.

ONE LAST LOOK BEFORE LEAVING THE TERRAIN

This land of transformation that I chose to explore proved to be quite an adventure. As I trekked through the bogs and swamps, tripped over the rocks and boulders, soared to the tops of mountains, and tumbled down the other side, I encountered sights I had never seen before. Some were breathtaking and exhilarating; others filled me with despair. Although I wanted it to be an easier journey, I recognize that struggling with the challenges pushed me forward. (Learning is like that!)

I have used this writing to provide a sketchy map of some of the regions I discovered and hope it can serve as a guide for others, or at least as a starting point for their exploration. The following note, left on my door from a former student in Alternatives to Basals, demonstrates why, as teachers of teachers, it is important that we begin the journey into the land of transformation:

> Just a little thank-you. . . . Because of your suggestion that we write on how children learn I was able to write on that very question on a job application! I want you to know (to thank you) for making us think! (You're the only one who ever asked that question!) I'm still job hunting but wanted you to know how much I still appreciate you and all you did! Keep it up!

NOTES

[1] The issue of grades continues to be problematic although I have made several shifts in assessment. I hold conferences, write in-depth comments on assignments, and provide narratives describing progress several times during the semester. My lowest rankings on the Student Evaluation Forms are on the question, "The instructor provided adequate opportunity throughout the course for you to be informed of your progress in meeting course goals." To the students, this means a number or letter, not words.

[2] At the same time as I was struggling with the undergraduates in Alternatives to Basals, students in my graduate courses nominated me for the Outstanding Faculty Award. I was naive enough to believe that receiving this award could mean that the journey was going to get easier.

[3] The distinction I make between *transactional* and *transformational* is that in a transformational classroom, the political is added to the personal and social aspect of learning. "Making the pedagogical more political means inserting schooling

directly into the political sphere by arguing that schooling represents both a struggle to define meaning and a struggle over power relations" (Giroux 1988, p. 127).

REFERENCES

Boomer, G. 1987. "Addressing the Problem of Elsewhereness." In *Reclaiming the Classroom: Teacher Research as an Agency for Change.* D. Goswami and P. Stillman, eds. Portsmouth, NH: Heinemann.

Edelsky, C. 1991. *With Literacy and Justice for All: Rethinking the Social in Language and Education.* London, UK: Falmer Press.

Edson, F. 1993. *One Teacher's Whole Language Classroom: The Students' Perspectives.* Paper presented at the annual Northern Rocky Mountain Educational Research Association, Jackson Hole, WY.

Farber, K., and W. Armaline. 1992. "Unlearning How to Teach: Restructuring the Teaching of Pedagogy." In *Teaching Education, 5,* 1: 99–111.

Freire, P. 1970. *Pedagogy of the Oppressed.* New York: Seabury Press.

Freire, P., and D. Macedo. 1987. *Literacy: Reading the Word and the World.* Amherst, MA: Bergin & Garvey.

Giroux, H. 1988. *Teachers as Intellectuals.* Amherst, MA: Bergin & Garvey.

Glasser, W. 1969. *Schools Without Failure.* New York: Harper.

Gore, J. 1992. "What We Can Do for You! What *Can* "We" Do for "You"?: Struggling over Empowerment in Critical and Feminist Pedagogy." In *Feminisms and Critical Pedagogy.* C. Luke and J. Gore, eds. New York: Routledge.

Guilfoyle, K. 1988. *Teaching Indian Children: An Ethnography of a First-Grade Classroom.* Unpublished doctoral dissertation, University of Arizona, Tucson, AZ.

Hornstein, S., D. Heine, and P. Heine. 1992. "Whole Language Goes to College." In *Insights,* 24, 6.

Laird, S. 1988. "Reforming 'Woman's True Profession': A Case for 'Feminist Pedagogy' in Teacher Education." In *Harvard Education Review,* 58, 4: 449–463.

Lather, P. 1990. *Staying Dumb? Student Resistance to Liberatory Curriculum.* Paper presented at American Educational Research Association, Boston, MA.

Leck, G. 1987. "Review Article—Feminist Pedagogy, Liberation Theory, and the Traditional Schooling Paradigm." In *Educational Theory,* 37, 3: 343–354.

Luke, C., and P. Gore, eds. 1992. *Feminisms and Critical Pedagogy.* New York: Routledge.

Lyons, N. 1990. "Dilemmas of Knowing: Ethical and Epistemological Dimensions of Teachers' Work and Development." In *Harvard Education Review,* 60, 2: 159–180.

Mayher, J. 1990. *Uncommon Sense: Theoretical Practice in Language Education.* Portsmouth, NH: Heinemann.

Peterson, R. 1992. *Life in a Crowded Place: Making a Learning Community.* Portsmouth, NH: Heinemann.

Shor, I. 1987. "Educating the Educators: A Freirean Approach to the Crisis in Teacher Education." In *Freire for the Classroom: A Sourcebook for Liberatory Teaching.* I. Shor, ed. Portsmouth, NH: Heinemann.

Short, K. G. 1990. "Creating a Community of Learners." In *Talking About Books.* K. G. Short and K. Pierce, eds. Portsmouth, NH: Heinemann.

Short, K. G., and C. Burke. 1989. "New Potentials for Teacher Education: Teaching and Learning as Inquiry." In *Elementary School Journal,* 90, 2: 193–206.

———. 1991. *Creating Curriculum: Teachers and Students as a Community of Learners.* Portsmouth, NH: Heinemann.

Short, K. G., and G. Kauffman. 1992. "Hearing Students' Voices: The Role of Reflection in Learning." In *Teachers Networking,* 11, 3: 1–6.

Simon, R. 1991. *Teaching Against the Grain: Texts for a Pedagogy of Possibility.* Amherst, MA: Bergin & Garvey.

Vygotsky, L. S. 1978. *Mind in Society.* Cambridge, MA: Harvard University Press.

Weiler, K. 1988. *Women Teaching for Change: Gender, Class and Power.* Amherst, MA: Bergin & Garvey.

4

CREATING COMMUNITY AND SUPPORT AMONG NEW FACULTY: AN OPEN LETTER TO DEANS OF EDUCATION

Margaret A. Atwell

This is written to other university administrators who, like me, have responsibility for faculty retention and development and who may, like me, occasionally wonder why we so seldom practice what we preach. As administrators of schools of education, we too rarely apply what we know about teacher support to our own faculty. In this letter, I will share what we learned from a faculty support program that was developed over a five-year span at California State University, San Bernardino. Interestingly, our program exists on a campus where several Center for Expansion of Language and Thinking (CELT) members work, and although this was not a CELT project, it is highly compatible with the way whole language teachers—and other professors who hold constructivist points of view—teach. The success of the program was immediately evident; two years later, the university centralized the model. It remains an active program.

In discussing faculty professional development programs, it is helpful to distinguish between orientation and mentoring, two complementary yet distinct forms of support. The goal of an orientation program is to help faculty make initial adjustments to their new academic setting. If successful, it will introduce faculty members to the culture and expectations of their new campus and help them acclimate quickly. Orientation programs are short term, focused, and intense. Successful programs create a group of peers who supply social support for each other in addition to providing data and information the institution feels is important.

The goal of mentoring is to introduce a colleague to a discipline or a discipline-specific network that reaches beyond an individual campus. Mentoring is most successful when it is the result of natural selection and pairing. Most often, mentoring implies a difference in experience and status between the mentor and mentee; mentors are more established in their field and have access to professional networks they are willing to share with a promising colleague. Most successful mentoring is done on campuses that have active senior faculty.

Both orientation and monitoring activities are important aspects of a complete program of faculty professional development, and both are consistent with and support whole language teacher education.

A DEVELOPMENTAL PATTERN

Our work with new university faculty (Cooper and Atwell 1990) parallels much of what has happened with new teacher induction in the K–12 sector (Roth 1990; Sandlin 1990) and its benefits. Faculty, including those at a university, typically move through phases of adjustment (Boice 1992) and find only certain kinds of information useful at certain stages of their incorporation into and development within the new system. By borrowing from research and analyzing our own program, we pose a three-stage model of development that all faculty experience.

Stage One: Transition Needs

The initial stage begins as soon as the faculty accept their positions at a new university, although it may be months before they arrive on campus. A successful support program establishes early and frequent contact by phone and mail and continues intensely through the first term following the faculty member's arrival.

We have found that at this early stage, faculty focus on logistical matters that range from insignificant to profound. Decisions relating to moving to a new town are foremost in their minds. Choosing where to live, selecting schools for their children, transferring bank accounts and financial concerns as well as learning the basic how-to's of a new school are of great interest.

Sometimes a well-meaning chair, anxious to get to the heart of teaching, research, and service expectations for the newcomer, may seek to dispense with these mostly nonacademic matters quickly or not address them at all. We learned, however, that it is critical that time be taken to deal with each of these needs fully. Even the most experienced or dedicated newcomer will not be able to consider the subtleties of curriculum or begin a research agenda until these matters are settled. Investing time to find out what each faculty member needs and then helping him or her make the transition is imperative.

Stage Two: Personal Professional Needs

Once the newcomer has settled in and the transition needs are met, he or she is free to think about more professional matters. This stage can begin as early as the second term (if a good orientation has been provided) and typically lasts two to three years. During this time, faculty members come to identify themselves as part of a specific discipline or program group within their school, with some idea of where they fit and what specific contributions they can make. Typically, the initial focus will be on matters that directly affect the faculty member as a discipline expert—for example, refining course syllabi, seeking support for research projects or grants, and clarifying the expectations around and building a record for promotion and tenure.

Stage Three: Collaboration Professional Needs

It is not uncommon for it to take several years for faculty members to begin to feel as if they are contributors to the campus' academic program. After teaching for several terms, faculty develop a breadth of experience that helps them see the bigger picture, and they are able to become more sophisticated members of the team. At this stage, their focus becomes more social. They move outward, often beyond the program or campus, to find and incorporate current professional information into teaching and scholarly work. Ideally, this stage continues and expands throughout a career. It is at this point that the faculty can begin to help redesign and revise curriculum beyond their own specific courses. Contributions to program reviews and governance issues become of more interest. It is at this time, too, that faculty have increased concern for establishing their reputations as scholars by publishing or presenting papers and becoming known in their area of specialization. By this time, the faculty needs for orientation are well past, so their needs are better served by a mentor or mentoring network.

MENTORING AND WHOLE LANGUAGE

Liebermann and McLaughlin (1992) described specialized professional networks as an effective means for education faculty to find support and growth. Although CELT was not specifically mentioned, it easily could have been since CELT has always served as a collegial support system for its members. Put into the large framework of developmental support that I am suggesting and using the definitions I already introduced, CELT can and often does serve as an important mentoring system. CELT has always brought together experienced and well-connected professionals with younger, promising protégés. Like traditional forms of mentoring that occur in university settings, CELT uses a selection process, albeit somewhat impersonal, to enlist new members. Once accepted, new members find that CELT members actively support each other by creating opportunities to publish, present at conferences, learn together, and "rejuvenate." The level of collaboration is extremely high. For many of its members who feel isolated on individual campuses, CELT serves an important mentoring role. If paired with campus success, it can be a powerful means of continued professional development and enrichment.

WHOLE LANGUAGE BELIEFS

Establishing a program of professional development for faculty helps create a sense of community consistent with a whole language philosophy. A support program like the one described here puts into practice beliefs held by whole language teacher educators about learning and learners:

- All learners, including faculty, follow consistent developmental patterns. These patterns make it possible to plan educational experiences that will encourage continued growth.
- All learners, including faculty, are meaning makers, constructing new knowledge from past experiences. What is learned in one setting can be used in others.

- Information is only learned in context. Learners will remember what is significant to them and what makes sense at the time. Presenting information out of context or at a time it is not needed is ineffective.
- Learning, like faculty development, is social. Settings and programs that build on learners' natural drive to collaborate will enrich development while creating a supportive sense of community.

OUR PROGRAM

California State University, San Bernardino, is a relatively young campus. It is a vital and dynamic place, with a staggering rate of growth. In the five years spanning 1985 to 1990, the School of Education tripled in the size of the faculty, and it found itself in the precarious position of having far more untenured faculty than those with tenure. Because of this situation and out of a belief that faculty need support throughout their careers, and certainly at this important time, an orientation program was implemented in 1985 in the School of Education. The program was designed and revised on the basis of early and constant feedback from its participants. The results have been quite successful. Although the California economy has slowed considerably since 1990, the university has continued this program, following the basic sequence described below. Over time, the developmental patterns discussed above emerged and helped us understand the complex pattern involved in moving into a new academic setting. Two aspects of the program are critical: the topics and the sequence of those topics' presentation. Newcomers need certain information *at certain times*. Presenting topics too soon is as useless as not presenting them at all.

The First Days

During the summer before the newcomers arrive, a series of letters (one every two or three weeks) is sent containing information about what is going on in the school. A copy of the local newspaper is sent along for information about the community and classified ads for housing searches, as well as special information about banks and banking in the area. Most important, a booklet listing and describing the largest and closest school districts is sent to those needing to decide on schools for their children.

Opening Day

On the San Bernardino campus, the first official workday for faculty always begins with an all-university convocation and school, department, and program faculty meetings. For most newcomers, the schedule is confusing, and the prospect of reporting to a new place alone can be an intimidating experience. To help faculty feel comfortable and part of the group, they are invited to an all-morning meeting the day before the year officially begins. The meeting gives them a chance to meet in a small, informal, and relaxed setting and to begin to make friends. A quick tour of the campus ensures that all the newcomers will know where to report the next morning. Basics, like how to get office keys and photocopier cards, are covered, and each faculty member is given a handbook of how-to's, pertinent telephone numbers, and names to use as a reference throughout the year. The meeting is kept light and social. Most newcomers leave after arranging to meet together the next morning. Every year of the program's existence, faculty report that making a few friends so early in the year helped reduce feelings of isolation and made them feel welcome.

The First Term: Initial Transition

The first term is the most intensive phase of the orientation program and includes regularly scheduled seminars. With the help of faculty who have recently come to the university, topics have been identified and sequenced to respond best to the newcomer's situation. In order of presentation, the topics include:

Health Benefits.   California offers state employees several options for health care, and new faculty are required to select their plan by the end of their first week on campus. Established faculty who are enrolled in different plans informally discuss their experiences at this meeting.

Developing Syllabi.   Every campus has expectations, usually implicit, about what ought to be included in a course outline. Often student perceptions and evaluations of teaching competence are affected by the syllabus, and time and effort invested in making expectations overt is well spent. As part of San Bernardino's orientation program, each newcomer is given copies of syllabi that have been developed by others to use, if desired, as models for their own.

Student Advisement.   California has a maze of regulations governing teacher licensure that, to some degree, all education faculty must come to understand. Advising on the San Bernardino campus is considered to be part of the teaching load, and new faculty begin advising students, with an experienced faculty member as a partner, from their first term. Since it is so complex and includes both state and university regulations, two or three separate orientation sessions are needed on these topics, conducted by credentialing staff and faculty who are particularly effective advisers.

University Resources.   Faculty need to learn what resources the university makes available to support their work. Representatives from the university library, computer or media center, and bookstore detail their collections, databases, and textbook services.

Evaluation Process.   Faculty are quite aware, from their first days on campus, that they will be evaluated for promotion and tenure. At this time in their orientation, overall guidance as to the steps of the process, including reviewing the forms they will eventually be completing, is helpful. Special attention is paid to describing the types of documentation that will be required to give faculty maximum time to attain or locate the records they will eventually need to present. It is critically important that this session be kept focused as an overview. If too much detail is provided or too much emphasis is placed on its importance, a fact already well understood, faculty experience distress and anxiety.

The first term ends at winter break, a good time to end the intensive seminar series. If the orientation has been successful, newcomers know the basics about the university or where to seek help when needed and a sense that, although far from clearly defined, they have a unique place within the school. Most important, the newcomers should have transformed themselves into a mutually supportive group of colleagues and friends.

Next Terms and Next Phases

Following the developmental pattern, the newcomers begin to focus more outwardly as they gain control of their teaching load and scholarship, and the orientation program becomes less intense. Meetings are held monthly at first, and then only when requested. Information is provided in less and less formal ways. Topics concerning grants and other monetary support for scholarship become important, as does a curiosity about the history of the curriculum and, eventually, state frameworks. The whole group sessions tend to be replaced by collaborations between pairs or in small groups. Joint projects are sometimes developed, and groups meet to discuss a colleague's completed or in-progress work. In the natural course of events, the need for orientation is replaced by a need for mentoring.

A FINAL WORD

Recruiting and retaining high-quality faculty is expensive and exhausting work. Given the projections for increased undergraduate enrollments in the next decade and the decline in the number of potential faculty in the pipeline, it will become increasingly important to hire well and find ways to keep faculty. Programs like the one I have described are effective in building a sense of community. A sense of belonging and having a place will encourage the best and brightest to stay and to flourish.

REFERENCES

Boice, R. 1992. *The New Faculty Member.* San Francisco: Jossey-Bass.

Cooper, S., and M. A. Atwell. 1990, March. "Supporting Your Faculty: A Model for New Faculty Induction at the University Level." Paper presented at the Association of Teacher Educators Convention, New Orleans, LA.

Liebermann, A., and M. McLaughlin. 1992, May. "Networks for Educational Change: Powerful and Problematic." In *Phi Delta Kappa,* 73.

Roth, R. 1990. New Faculty Induction, National Leadership Academy on Planning and Implementing Induction, Internship, Mentoring and Beginning Teacher Programs, Association of Teacher Educators, Los Angeles, CA.

Sandlin, R. 1990, March. "A New Teacher Development Model." Paper presented at Association of Teacher Education Convention, New Orleans, LA.

Balancing Action and Reflection
in Student Teaching

Kathy G. Short

One of my goals as a teacher educator is to base my courses in inquiry and the search for questions that are significant to preservice and inservice teachers. The questions asked in inquiry should not be framed ahead of time by me or a text-book but come out of the inquiry process so that all of us are both problem posers and problem solvers. Teacher education students need the opportunity to engage in experiences to find questions that they can productively pursue. As they become immersed in exploring teaching and learning, they encounter anomalies, questions, and issues that puzzle them. Dewey (1938) argues that when problems arise, a cycle of inquiry is put into motion whereby learners form ideas or hypotheses and then act on those ideas to observe what happens. Action, however, is not enough. All learners need time to reflect on what has occurred in order to make sense of those experiences and to organize ideas for future use. Reflection, says Dewey, is the "heart of intellectual organization and of the disciplined mind" (p. 87).

While action provides the content for reflection, reflection is the driving force behind action. When action and reflection work together, learners have something on which to reflect and opportunities to pull important meanings from their experiences to continue their growth and learning (Short and Kauffman 1992). Teacher education programs for preservice teachers, however, often seem to value action at the expense of reflection. Preservice teachers become immersed in new methodologies, theories, and classroom field experiences but have little time to step away from those experiences and reflect on their own understandings and beliefs about these experiences (Short and Burke 1989).

The lack of emphasis on reflection is a major issue during student teaching; preservice teachers often feel that they are too busy teaching to have any time to think. Student teaching is often cited as having the most impact on the future teaching styles of preservice teachers, yet student teachers spend little time reflecting on who they want to become as teachers. As the director of elementary student teaching at Goshen College, I became increasingly concerned by the lack of reflection during student teaching and the resulting lack of control that student teachers felt over their own decision-making processes as teachers. I began to search for ways to build reflection into the student teaching semester during student teaching and in an intensive seminar at the end of student teaching. Because of my own reflection on the various aspects of the student teaching program, several changes were made. These changes occurred because I listened closely to the voices of preservice teachers.

RETHINKING THE STUDENT TEACHING SEMINAR EXPERIENCE

Our explorations of ways to restructure the student teaching experience to balance action and reflection, as well as meet program requirements, led to a number of different formats and schedules. These attempts reflect the formats that many other institutions have also used. In their senior year, student teachers at Goshen College return to campus early so they can start when school districts and classroom teachers officially begin the school year. They meet the state requirements for twelve weeks of student teaching and still have time for a three-week intensive course on campus. One schedule we tried had the student teachers spend the first two to three weeks full time in schools, return to campus for a three-week methods course to develop science and social studies units, and then return full time to student teaching. At the end of student teaching, they had several days of seminars on applying, interviewing, and the certification process. Most student teachers found this schedule disruptive and resented leaving the classroom when they were just beginning to feel part of the school community.

The format was changed so that students were involved in one- or two-day seminars spaced out during student teaching. These seminars were successful in addressing such issues as classroom management and evaluation and gave students a chance to share with each other, yet they still resented being pulled away from their teaching experiences. The seminars did support some reflection, but the student teachers were so involved in day-to-day survival that they found it difficult to reflect on what was happening. Often they began to adopt the beliefs and practices of the classroom teachers without considering their own beliefs.

Based on these experiences, the seminar was moved to the end of the semester with occasional after-school and half-day meetings during student teaching. The seminar was a methods course on issues of classroom management and language arts. The course content was solid, but it came at the wrong time. Student teachers returned to campus with many questions and unresolved issues, and instead of exploring those questions, they became immersed in more methods. Student teachers who had experiences that were difficult or in traditionally based classrooms often resented those who had worked in innovative classroom settings. And although some sharing occurred in the seminar, student teachers were not able to learn from each other's experiences or to process their own. I was also deeply concerned about student teachers who were willing to give up their own beliefs and assumed they had to adopt those of their cooperating teachers in order to survive in public schools.

SUPPORTING REFLECTION DURING
STUDENT TEACHING

Because of these concerns, I began making changes in the student teaching experience to support more reflection and dialogue. Students kept a reflective journal about their teaching experiences, writing in the journal at least three times a week. College supervisors received these journals from student teachers every two weeks and read and responded to each journal. The journals supported initial reflection as student teachers took a small step away from their classroom teaching experiences to reflect on their experiences. The journals also created an exchange between the college supervisor and the student teacher that allowed for a greater sense of support and dialogue. As one of the supervisors, I found that the dialogue journal gave me insights about the struggles and issues the student teacher was experiencing. I was able to focus the school visits and conferences with the student teacher in ways that were more supportive for that person and to identify major problems before they reached a crisis point.

In addition, I met with all of the student teachers after school every two to three weeks throughout the teaching experience. The meetings had a particular focus, such as integrated units or classroom management, but they were used primarily for students to share what was happening in their student teaching situations. We met both as a whole group and in small groups so they could talk about their successes, problems, and issues they were facing and to think together about ways to deal with problems. These meetings were a support network for student teachers and kept them in contact with each other. Twice we met for half-day meetings on issues of classroom management to allow for a more concentrated focus on the problems they were facing and ways they might more effectively respond to the behaviors of their students.

The dialogue journals and after-school meetings helped student teachers to reflect on their experiences, yet it still remained difficult for them to step back from these experiences because they were so busy with planning, gathering materials, and teaching. The seminar at the end of student teaching obviously needed to play a major role in supporting a more distant and deeper reflection on their experiences and in allowing them to explore their many questions about teaching.

CREATING A REFLECTIVE LEARNING ENVIRONMENT
IN SENIOR SEMINAR

Our first decision was to use the title of "Senior Seminar" to signal that this was not just another course. As I thought about the Senior Seminar, I knew we needed to create an environment that would encourage reflection and inquiry on the issues and questions that are always part of the student teaching experience. I also knew that the student teachers had difficulty with the adjustment of returning to campus life and being a student. Although we had met throughout their student teaching experience, they often felt isolated from each other and had organized themselves into small cliques based on where they had student taught. They needed time to become more comfortable with each other and feel they were part of a supportive community.

To facilitate this transition back to campus, I scheduled their last day of student teaching on a Wednesday and planned several experiences to pull us back together. At our first meeting the next morning, I asked each student teacher to come prepared to share a story from student teaching—an experience that was significant for them. We spent the morning laughing and crying as they related their experience. I then gave them information on the seminar that would start the following Monday so they would be familiar with the format and projects. On Friday, we took an all-day trip to an outdoor environmental center. After spending the morning in small groups hiking and exploring with guides from the center, we had a hot dog roast and sharing time at lunch. In the afternoon, the student teachers responded to the morning hikes through art, writing, music, construction of scientific models, and reading. After several hours of working separately and in small groups, we met to share our responses with each other. By the end of these two days, we were regaining a sense of trust and community.

For the next two weeks, we met in an intensive seminar to examine broad issues related to teacher education, such as evaluation, classroom management, curriculum reform, and educational philosophy. The student teachers set up research notebooks with dividers for each of the three to four major issues we had agreed to explore. For each major area such as evaluation, student teachers listed what they already knew and what they wanted to know more about. They wrote their questions at the top of separate pages in their notebooks so that as they read or talked with others, they could make notes about possible responses to their questions, as well as add new questions.

The first hour of every morning was a whole group session. Presentations, panels, and discussions on major issues were scheduled to encourage students to explore these issues from a wide variety of perspectives. For example, we had a panel of parents share their perspectives on evaluation and parent conferences. On another day, a panel of student teachers shared their experiences of working in classrooms where the teachers had moved away from basal reader approaches. I also shared my own teaching journey and the changes I had made (and was still making) in my beliefs and practices.

The whole group session was followed by a two-hour work time where students met in groups or worked individually to research their questions. I set up the room with many relevant professional books and with listening centers containing videotapes and filmstrips. In addition, I provided five or six copies of articles that students could use for literature circles. During work time, study groups met to discuss common topics of interest, students formed literature circles to discuss readings, small groups watched and then discussed a video, and individuals read, wrote, and reflected in their research notebooks.

We ended the morning by writing reflections on the morning's experiences in learning logs, kept at the front of their research notebooks. We wrote in silence for fifteen minutes and then talked and shared insights from the morning. These discussions often went over our official ending time without anyone even noticing, a definite indication of involvement and interest. The students also used this time to offer invitations for particular literature groups or discussion groups for the following day. During the afternoon, student teachers worked individually or with a partner on a senior project. We had discussed this project in our after-school meetings so they already had chosen a focus for their projects before the seminar began. The topics for the projects grew out of questions and issues that were of concern to them from their student teaching experiences—for example, responding to children who are manipulative, building a responsible classroom, dealing with child abuse, meeting a wide variety of learning needs, teaching in inner-city settings, and moving beyond art as "cute" activities. They researched their questions by observing in classrooms, talking to teachers and children, talking with each other, and reading in professional materials. At the end of the second week, they shared their projects with each other through presentations using learning centers, pamphlets, papers, oral discussions, demonstrations, role plays, and murals.

The seminar concluded the following week with three days that focused on job applications and resumes, interviewing, and certification. These experiences included receiving information about their placement files, talking with a panel of principals about interviewing, participating in several interviews with an administrator, and beginning the process of filling out paperwork for the career office. We also spent time talking about first-year teaching and reading accounts of first-year teachers' experiences. We hired substitute teachers for several second-year teachers so they could come and talk about their first-year experiences. Based on these discussions, student teachers wrote themselves letters of advice, which they sealed and self-addressed. The Teacher Education office mailed these letters the next fall.

This Senior Seminar was a powerful experience. I left each day drained yet exhilarated by the thinking and questioning that was going on. Some students' teaching experiences had been negative and caused them to lose self-confidence or to question the possibility of change in schools. As they spoke with their peers, I saw them regain confidence and commitment. They thought about what *they* really believed and the kind of learning environment they wanted for their classrooms. They realized how much they needed the support of colleagues if they were not going to follow the status quo.

Creating collaborative learning environments in their classrooms was not going to be easy. In every way, schools as institutions seem to work against powerful teaching. The students were going to face many difficult times as they tried to put their beliefs into action in classrooms. Before the seminar, many no longer believed it was possible to make a difference in schools; the seminar gave them the chance to see that they could make a difference. Idealism and realism came together in a better balance as they considered the kinds of learning environments they wanted to create and their need for dialogue with colleagues. The one or two students who made the decision to leave teaching felt good about this decision because they had time to process their experiences with peers.

TAKING CONTROL OF LEARNING THROUGH REFLECTION

Through reflection, these student teachers took control of their learning. They distanced themselves from their teaching experiences, considered new perspectives, saw new alternatives, and developed more generalized understandings and knowledge. They reflected on what they had learned, how they had learned, and why they were learning. These reflections on the content, process, and purposes of their teaching experiences gave them a deeper sense of their own beliefs and strategies for teaching and learning. They knew their options as teachers and learners and so had the tools to reconsider their circumstances. Learning and teaching had become more predictable to them because they had greater control of their learning. Although their world would continue to shift and change, it was now under their control.

If we as teacher educators want preservice teachers to integrate their experiences into a focused whole, they need to have time and opportunities to reflect on those experiences. Through reflection, all learners can bring alive their experiences in ways that bring new meanings to the present and new potentials for the future.

REFERENCES

Dewey, J. 1938. *Experience and Education.* New York: Collier.

Short, K. G., and C. Burke. 1989. "New Potentials for Teacher Education: Teaching and Learning as Inquiry." In *Elementary School Journal,* 90, 2: 193–206.

Short, K. G., and G. Kauffman. 1992. "Hearing Students' Voices: The Role of Reflection in Learning." In *Teachers Networking: The Whole Language Newsletter,* 11, 3: 1–6.

EVERYBODY NEEDS A "GRIP": SUPPORT GROUPS FOR DOCTORAL STUDENTS

*Carol Gilles**

"Wow, your course work is over! All you need to do now is comps and write the dissertation! You're practically done. You must feel great."

I didn't feel great; nor do many other doctoral students as they realize that the comfortable routine of attending classes, reading, studying, and writing papers in collaboration with a group of colleagues will suddenly halt. At this point in my doctoral program there was a new challenge: comprehensive exams and the dissertation became the focus of attention. There were few deadlines, no schedules. I was free to decide when, where, and how to study. Although my adviser and mentor had been wonderfully helpful to me, suddenly I felt that I had to do this part on my own. Perhaps it was pride—a feeling that at this point I should be able to carry on independently. Even with the help of attentive advisers, many doctoral students come to feel without moorings and very alone.

Formal and informal support groups are necessary for the mental, emotional, and intellectual health of doctoral students. In this chapter, I compare two such groups: an experimental, year-long, one-credit graduate seminar organized by faculty advisers and an informal group organized for and by the students that met every Monday for lunch over the course of a year.

THE DOCTORAL READING SEMINAR

The doctoral reading seminar was organized by professor of education Dorothy Watson, who felt that students would benefit from a chance to meet together with reading faculty to share ideas, suggestions, and research with one another. This seminar was scheduled to meet four hours once a month for a year, for one hour of graduate credit. All reading doctoral students were encouraged to register for the seminar. At one of the first meetings, students were encouraged to brainstorm the topics that they wanted to discuss over the months, which included using the library facilities, sharing proposals or initial investigations, and discussing relevant research.

*The author acknowledges the contributions of Mary Bixby to this chapter.

Monthly meetings were often held in the homes of faculty members. Generally the sessions began by having a potluck dinner. Each student brought a dish or shared payment with those who provided food. Many times the faculty (or their thoughtful spouses) volunteered to cook. After dinner and perhaps a glass of wine, the meeting began with the presentation of one of the doctoral student's research, followed by a question and answer session. When I presented the initial findings from my dissertation, I was nervous because I was presenting "rough draft" findings to peers who were further along in the process than I was; moreover, I was sharing my attempts at scholarly work with faculty members.

Nevertheless, the warm living room setting and interest of the group made me feel quite at home, and we had a lively discussion about my data. Besides hearing about ongoing doctoral research, the group also discussed current research studies they had chosen. For example, one evening we had a spirited conversation about Lisa Delpit and her ideas about the viability of whole language instruction with students of color.

Although the seminar provided a place to discuss and try out ideas with faculty and peers in a social atmosphere, there were some disadvantages. First, a month was a long time between meetings. Some group members would find and read research articles immediately after the seminar and then have to wait a month before they could discuss them. Second, sometimes it was disconcerting to present "rough draft" findings to the same people who would eventually critique the research in a formal manner. The faculty members were very careful to be helpful and positive; nevertheless, the experience sometimes fostered nervous presenters. Third, those nitty-gritty doctoral student questions about writing a dissertation were rarely asked because members of the doctoral faculty were sitting there: How can you ask what format a particular professor prefers in Chapter 3 when he or she is a member of the group? Consequently the seminar was a pleasant activity that gave some of us a chance to present our ideas in a small group, gave us reasons to read and discuss research findings, and gave everyone opportunities to mingle in a more social atmosphere. Yet the insider lore was left untold.

THE "GET A GRIP" GROUP

When the informal lunch group was formed, I was on the other side, my degree was finished. Early in the year several doctoral students who were beginning to write the second chapter of their dissertations decided they needed a group to support their writing and thinking. Although several people who came before us had a colleague or friend to commiserate with during their processes, these students decided that a larger group, patterned somewhat after the reading seminar, might be useful. One member made a flier and invited doctoral students and friends of doctoral students to lunch on Mondays. Two of us who had completed our dissertations were invited because the doctoral students still looked upon us as peers and colleagues.

At the first lunch, we discussed the purpose of the group. This was to be a group where any question was legitimate. What do we do first to fill out forms for doctoral studies? What kind of computer and word processor would the graduate school accept? Do some professors expect different things in Chapter 2 from other professors? What is the best way to study for the comprehensive exam? We would collectively pool all of our knowledge and give one another our best advice.

We met on Mondays at 11:45 at various restaurants. There was no pressure for members to come, simply an invitation. There was no credit involved, yet the eight to ten members came to nearly every meeting.

The name for the group originated when one member began whining about comprehensive exams, "Oh, I just don't know what I'll do. This is going to be impossible. I'll never learn all this material!" One student who had just finished her own exams replied, "Oh, just get a grip!" We all laughed, and this became our motto and our name: "get a grip"—get control and don't take yourself so seriously! Although the group visited different restaurants and even changed the meeting day occasionally, one aspect of the meeting remained constant: each member took a turn and reported what she had accomplished within the previous week. Janice reported that she had figured out a strategy to attack Chapter 4, a problem area for her. Minta had applied for a job in Maine and wondered if any of us had ever been through a telephone interview. Ruthie had begun to collect her data and wanted the group to listen to her initial observations and help her organize categories. Barbara had decided that she needed to make one of her guiding questions more specific and wanted our feedback on the revised question. Sarah explained that she might be able to do research in Sweden. But what should she research? Group members suggested that Sarah make a list of all the areas that she was interested in and then those she already knew a lot about. Where the two lines intersected, she might find an intriguing possible topic.

This reporting proved very helpful to doctoral students and to those of us who had completed the degree. Occasionally a member reported that she had not written all week, and we all tried to help her move forward. The intensity of the group moved both of us who had finished our degrees too. We began new research projects and writing because we had an interested audience whose support could encourage postdoctoral efforts, as well as efforts on the dissertation.

Besides talking shop, there was lots of social talk as well. Between bites of bagels, we talked about movies that everyone should see, books that had to be read, and the perils of raising children. Some days we helped members figure out what bills were a priority when there wasn't enough money in the account to go around. We passed on news about part-time jobs or inservice workshops that some of us might want to do. Since many of our children had reached the difficult teenage period, some of our talk centered on how to make fair decisions. For example, Mary's son wanted to go on a foreign exchange trip to Germany, and she had told him that he must find a job to earn the spending money or he couldn't go. After three weeks, he hadn't looked for a job. Should she let him go anyway or stick to her initial request? The group voted that Mary should stick to her guns. Ah, therapy at affordable prices! Such social talk reaffirmed our friendships and encouraged our trust.

WHAT IS IMPORTANT ABOUT EACH GROUP?

The doctoral seminar was important because it was the first group in which doctoral students had a chance to get to know one another and faculty members. We were able to talk with the faculty about research in a comfortable social setting. As we talked, the distinction between faculty and students began to blur. Many of us had become apprentices to faculty members as teaching assistants where we watched their teaching and emulated their strategies. This group gave us a chance to begin the move from the role of apprentice to professional. Instead of just observing how faculty members discussed research among themselves, we were invited into those discussions as intellectual peers. We heard the questions they asked of one another and learned from these questions. We tried out our ideas on the group and found that we were treated not as students but as colleagues. Would we have attended if there were not credit? Probably. The food, the collegiality, and the intellectual discussions would have drawn us to the group, even without the incentive of credit.

The "Get a Grip" group was even more important for many of us. This group carried no credit, yet the benefits were enormous. This group attempted to provide the special individual support that each of us needed. No question was considered insignificant, no discussion trivial.

Sometimes group members would try out ideas on one another before they wrote them down. This process helped them to articulate their ideas and get some input as a part of the prewriting process. Some of our duties involved acting as readers for a draft of a particular chapter. As such, the group members became unofficial dissertation committee members. Asking a group member to read a chapter was a bit like taking a play on the road to Peoria before opening on Broadway—a rehearsal for the big time. Reading and reacting critically to these new ideas helped all of us to sort out what we believed and to recall research that might be pertinent. As we talked, argued, and disagreed, we saw new ideas emerging—new ideas that none of us had considered before we began our lunch. Our collaboration complemented and supplemented the previous doctoral seminar.

CONCLUSION

Writing a dissertation is a complex task, one in which doctoral students need support. Many of us are lucky to have mentors who are not only advisers but friends and, ultimately, colleagues. Good advisers are one reason that most of us decided to pursue doctorates. Yet even their consistent, powerful support and encouragement is not enough. Doctoral students need a variety of groups, from formal seminars to informal lunch groups. All three sources of support are necessary and vital: an adviser who makes you stretch, a group of faculty and students who discuss research and challenge one another, and an informal group that can solve an individual's particular problem through their shared candor, insightfulness, irreverence, humor, or any combination. The writing of the dissertation isn't a time for being alone and writing in a closed room; it should be a time to nurture, invest in, and benefit from the collegial friendships begun in course work that will continue throughout our professional careers.

TEACHING AND LEARNING IN A
PROFESSIONAL DEVELOPMENT SCHOOL

Wendy C. Kasten

Unlike the laboratory schools of an earlier era, professional development schools (PDSs) are part of a regular school district working as partners with colleges and universities. Universities do not play any major role in the hiring or managing of the professional development schools. The two institutions choose to work together in a variety of ways, which may include school-based courses, continued inservice, and field service placement. In this model, the two institutions are truly a partnership.

The style of partnership may vary as to the formality or informality of the agreement and choice to work together. Some PDSs enter into contractual arrangements, which may include purchase of a university faculty member's time, or it may simply be a mutual verbal agreement among a university, a school faculty, and the appropriate administrators.

THE VALUE OF TEACHING IN A PROFESSIONAL
DEVELOPMENT SCHOOL

At the Sarasota campus of the University of South Florida, I taught Language Arts in Childhood Education for ten years. Because of my background, I considered the content of this course right up my alley, and yet for years, it was the course with which I was the most dissatisfied. At the end of each semester, I never felt as though I had done a good job teaching it, in spite of the many innovations I had implemented.

My dissatisfaction with the course reminded me of similar feelings experienced when I was an elementary school teacher and parts of my curriculum were decontextualized from real-life language and learning. At that time, I felt many of the parts of our program prevented children from making connections and utilizing real skills for realistic purposes.

Similarly, a course that focuses on curriculum and methodology for use with children is decontextualized, no matter how innovative the teaching of that course may be, if it is taught on a university campus instead of in a school. The results of this decontextualized university teaching are disappointing and probably center around several theoretical and applied inconsistencies.

First, in a university setting where there are no children and teachers to interact and learn with, our finest teaching and demonstrations stay in the realm of the theoretical. We inform our students about what should work, ought to work, and has worked for people in other settings. In these instances, students often argue about the validity or effectiveness of strategies that are foreign to their own personal educational experience. Some students leave university classes based on a constructivist view, still thinking whole language is a passing fad or an ideal that is not for everyone. When a course occurs in a field-based setting, this is less likely to happen. Students see theory being applied; they see children growing, learning, and engaged in meaningful activities; they see the attitudes that accompany meaningful learning. In fact, it is common to have students wishing school could have "been like this" for them. As one graduating student said, reflecting on her field-based course, "I cannot begin to explain what it meant to me to see it all right there."

Second, in a decontextualized university setting, college students learn theory and strategies but do not necessarily know how to match the appropriateness of strategies to the needs of real learners. The kidwatching (Y. Goodman 1978) element is not there. The result, I have found, is the tendency to produce new teachers who have a menu of wonderful strategies at their disposal but a poor sense of when to use them to their best advantage. In a field-based setting, the presence of children provides opportunities to get to know learners' needs.

A third issue has to do with the power of demonstration and being in the presence and company of education as we are teaching about it. These demonstrations include the teachers with whom we co-teach, the artifacts around the school resulting from literacy activities and events (children's writing on display, author's study, plays in the media center, bulletin boards, etc.), and the demonstrating I do for my students when I co-teach a writing lesson with a teacher to a class of elementary students.

The most important aspect of this context is that university students who see whole language learning in practice not only learn about those practices but have the confidence to use them later. Many of my former students (previous to teaching in the professional development school setting) were excited about holistic teaching while they were in the course. But when they later joined an elementary school faculty, they were often introduced to the real world by veteran teachers at a school who considered their university education to be of the ivory tower variety and, consequently, unrealistic for their school population.

In this situation, many new teachers question their own learning and follow their colleagues' sometimes cynical ways. These new teachers lack the confidence to try what they learned in college classrooms and to confidently vow to new peers that they have seen holistic theory working successfully. Another consequence, from an educational change standpoint, is that the infusion of new teachers does not breathe new life into an old school. Instead, new teachers conform, and the status quo is maintained.

For all of these reasons, teaching certain education classes on a college campus isn't good enough. The outcomes of university-based teaching (as opposed to site-based teaching) do not support my goals of turning out the very finest teachers possible.

SCHOOL PARTNERSHIPS AND RAPPORT

The success of teaching university classes at an elementary school depends on a number of factors; most critical is good rapport with a school faculty, which includes trust and dialogue. This relationship takes time to develop. However, creating a professional development site benefits university students and also acts as a catalyst for continued teacher learning (and for my own learning as well). If we, as university faculty, are going to practice what we preach, we face the same dilemmas as the teachers we serve: developing authentic curriculum and being lifelong learners in the teaching-learning process. We need the partnership of exemplary and growing schools to help teach our courses and accomplish our goals.

My partnership with Moody Elementary School began with the initiative of its newly appointed principal, Judy Joachim, and her requests for ongoing inservice and more connection with the local university campus. I was involved with the school improvement plan, inservice, and participation in some school activities before we proposed or attempted to utilize the school as a site for the teaching of education courses. Coincidentally, that same year, the climate in Florida became one that promoted the idea of professional development schools.

An important factor in this partnership is the rapport that existed among myself, the school administrators, and the school faculty. Although the school labeled me, at times, as their school mentor, I did not play the role of expert. I played a supportive role and sometimes helped locate resources, proposed ideas, or helped to trouble-shoot classroom difficulties. In many cases, teachers approached me with a problem that was or was not related to language arts. We sat, talked, and brainstormed. Sometimes I visited the classroom to get a sense of the problem—whether it was dying enthusiasm for the writing process or one child with special needs. I offered suggestions that a teacher could choose, try, or reject, depending on her comfort with the ideas. I reminded teachers that they always know their students best, and the final choice must be up to them.

This process and the resulting rapport with teachers enabled me to co-teach with them and ask their help in teaching my language arts class. I would not feel comfortable imposing my needs on a school if I were not offering something in return. Although part of my goal in doing this course on the school campus was to strengthen our partnership, I could not have predicted the extent to which the teachers and sometimes even the children helped to reinvent the course each semester and provide authentic learning for the university students. I also could not have predicted the extent to which my own teaching would benefit.

REINVENTING THE COURSE

A field-based course is never the same from one semester to another. The children with whom we work remain there but continue to grow. The situations, contexts, and issues within the school and individual classrooms change from month to month. Because of these changes, it is also not possible to plan a course for all fifteen weeks of a semester, as I had been accustomed to doing on campus. Flexibility and fluidity become important components of our teaching, as we've long known to be true in good elementary and secondary classrooms.

Yet as I began each course, there were several elements I considered. The first was comfort and some degree of proficiency with students about the writing process and their own personal writing. I have learned, as have many colleagues, that no amount of effort toward teaching preservice teachers about the writing process will be profitable if they are privately terrified about their personal writing. I addressed this issue in a number of ways.

First, we followed the model of the National Writing Project and its affiliates. There were times when we wrote and shared, and met in conferences for our own purposes, and times when we shared and met in conferences with some children from a multiage class. The fourth and fifth graders learned that even older students struggle at times with writing. Often these youngsters were more experienced with conferencing and took the lead in asking thoughtful questions of the writer. The university students had a chance to see what writing in classrooms looks like once it has been successfully implemented, forming their expectations for their future classrooms. In addition, the university students practiced their new skills of talking to children and others about the writing process and conferencing with an eager, live audience.

Second, we each established an ongoing relationship with an emergent reader-writer. We began by being "pen pals" with first graders and expanded into other experiences with children so that students developed kidwatching abilities and recognized emergent literacy in progress. University students developed a portfolio on one child to gain insights into the role of audience; children's motivation to communicate; and children's growth in spelling and sentence structure. Portfolios were helpful if someone asked, "When will the teacher start teaching these children conventional spelling?" I suggested they examine the child's portfolio for student growth.

The child's portfolio demonstrated the constructivist nature of emergent literacy as the university students read their child's communication, followed their choices of spelling and punctuation, and saw how language became conventional over a period of time as a result of need and frequency of use. University students expressed both amazement and joy as they saw before them the signs of literacy as a developmental process and how early reading and writing are interdependent.

The third component of the course was to experience, as much as possible, writing with children of various grade levels, in a variety of genres, and for a variety of purposes. These experiences took many forms and were somewhat dependent on classroom themes, curriculum, and events. For example, one semester the university students guided a group of multiage fourth and fifth graders in selecting, designing, and writing informational books for the school library on Florida native trees. Interest was created by a schoolwide and community tree-planting initiative that added over 300 seedlings to the school grounds. Students and their families participated in the planting and subsequent care, which made learning more about trees an important and purposeful goal.

On another occasion, university students assisted this same class with their class-produced schoolwide newspaper. Assigning two university students or more to each "department" within this classroom (layout, editorials, reporters, advertising, marketing, etc.) helped direct the productions in this class of over thirty students. In the process, the teacher received support for the project, the elementary students learned new ways to work with students and their writing, and the adult learners participated in a highly authentic language arts activity.

At other times, I initiated working with a second/third grade multiage class so that the university students saw the capabilities of younger students by comparing these students to their older friends. Working in different settings allowed students to experience a variety of language arts and helped us respond to the specific needs of the classroom teacher. For example, a grade two-three teacher needed to know how to teach persuasive writing, a skill that was evaluated statewide in grades four and eight. Never having done a lesson on persuasion, the teacher and I brainstormed a lesson that we co-taught.

First, the teacher reminded students about previous times persuasion had been an issue in their class. Then I told about a time in my own childhood when I desperately wanted to persuade my parents to let me go away to camp. The children responded to my sharing and candor as I told them how badly I wanted to go to Girl Scout camp despite my parents' objections.

I asked them to think as if they were my parents and help me list on a chart the reasons my parents wouldn't want me to go. They came up with many ideas, including the cost and a possible parental concern that I might not yet be "mature enough" to go away from home. I then asked them to help me list the persuasive arguments I could propose that would speak to parental concerns in the persuasive writing. Finally, the children helped me compose a model letter to my parents that would persuade them to let me go to camp. They suggested, for example, that I find a way to help pay for going to camp and that I find baby-sitting jobs to prove my maturity for going away from home.

When we finished the letter, the classroom teacher paired the elementary students with the university students who had been observing this lesson. They were told that each person was to write a letter of persuasion on a matter of his or her own concern. Just as in the model, they were to begin by listing important points to make in their favor and counterpoints that their audience would likely offer as a rebuttal. We suggested in constructing their letter from their list that they save their most important point for last, to add impact to their presentation.

In little groups on the floor, in the hall, or at classroom tables, university students and elementary students composed a persuasive letter of their own. Later, during "author's chair," some university students and some elementary students shared their work and received response from peers. The students in the multiage second and third grade wrote on a wide variety of very personal concerns, usually to a family member. Their letters ranged from wanting a pet, or needing a new school knapsack, to needing more privacy from younger siblings. They wrote seriously on topics obviously close to their hearts.

Co-teaching experiences such as this benefited all participants. I had the opportunity to try out a new lesson. The teacher had the opportunity to explore a new area with the support of a colleague. The elementary students got a lesson in writing. The university students got a lesson in writing and in the teaching of writing. They also saw both the teacher and me demonstrating teaching behavior and management of the lesson.

"I HAVE AN IDEA"

Site-based teaching is professionally nurturing for me and others because of the continuing dialogue among university faculty, teachers, and the school administration. The dialogues with the teachers who helped me teach the course centered around the constant brainstorming of new and better ways to educate the language arts students, to teach writing to the children, and to integrate language arts in content area learning.

These discussions resulted in a constantly changing course. Often a teacher came to me, saying, "I have an idea. Why don't we . . ." The wonderful part of this was that nearly all the teachers with whom I collaborated at this site were once students in my language arts course. Consequently, they understood the objectives of the course and could project ideas based on what they wished they had been able to do when they were students.

When I initiated site-based teaching, I worried about how the course would go and wondered whether we could think of ways to work together that would be mutually beneficial; by the end of the experience we were saturated with ideas and did not have enough time to try them all. Another of my early concerns was that the presence of the university course would be burdensome to the school or be another demand on teachers who are already incredibly busy. This never became an issue. Rather, teachers told me they looked forward to our times together because they valued their continuous learning.

MEANINGFUL ASSIGNMENTS

One assignment for this course proved to be the most effective in helping university students identify children's needs. On a scheduled day, we took over four or five classrooms all at the same time, and each language arts student tried out a writing lesson with five or six children from the same class. The teachers watched the different lessons going on in their room and gleaned new ideas for the teaching of writing. We scheduled an hour so that the university students had time to complete a lesson and collect artifacts for analysis.

The objective of this one-week assignment was met after the lesson was completed. My students analyzed what they did and how it went, based on all they had read and learned about the writing process. Was the activity age appropriate? Authentic? Meaningful? Did the children's writing turn out as they expected? In doing this analysis, they revisited their course readings and found support for why aspects of their lessons went well or were problematic.

For evaluation purposes, I was most interested in students' reflections. Theoretically, their lessons might have failed, but if they explained why, cited authors to support their view, and suggested ways they would change next time, I valued their reflection.

[handwritten margin note: This may not always be true, though.]

LEARNING ON THE JOB

I'm not sure who learned the most from this partnership. Every time I taught a lesson with a teacher, I learned more about the teaching of writing. The teachers with whom I team taught learned more about the teaching of writing every time we worked together. Teachers picked up small points and examples from me just as I did from them. The children saw and learned from authentic writing as they observed university students writing the same lessons and struggling with writing as well. The children benefited from the attention they received from the language arts students.

The children learned what a university is. I heard them say to each other, "Are those real university students?" Although our campus was only nine miles away from their community, many children were not familiar with the word *university,* nor did they have any idea what it meant. Perhaps our experience planted a few seeds toward the children's postsecondary educational plans.

And the language arts students? Aside from the compelling nature of experiential learning, they realized the breadth of what they learned at H. S. Moody after the course was over. They used strategies they learned from the Moody teachers in their student teaching. A few told me they realized the scope of their learning in our site-based course later, while teaching.

I don't think I could ever teach a course such as this again on a campus. This was a partnership that was far too powerful to be dissolved or compromised for the convenience of scheduling so I insisted it no longer be offered when schools are not in session. Working in the school added to our credibility. There was no inconsistency between the material being taught in university classes and the real world of schooling because we all lived and taught and learned together in that real world. Teaching this course in an elementary school was a joyful aspect of my job. I came home tired but I always felt as though I had a truly productive and worthwhile day.

REFERENCE

Goodman, Y. M. 1978. "Kidwatching: An Alternative to Testing." In *National Elementary School Principal, 57,* 4: 41–45.

A

PROTOCOLS/ENGAGEMENTS

David L. Tucker and Dorothy Menosky, editors

Introduction by Yetta M. Goodman

How do I engage others in looking at phenomena the way I do? How do I get teachers, graduate students, or researchers to reflect on what I believe is important about learning to read? These were the questions that Ken Goodman was asking himself as a teacher educator when he realized the significance of his growing understanding of reading as a language process. How could he involve others in thinking and learning about reading with new understandings?

To accomplish his task, Ken began to fashion experiences to involve graduate and undergraduate students and audiences at conferences and workshops to reflect on and wonder about language. He created texts that reflected aspects of authentic language in order to help his audiences consider a range of language issues such as the role of syntax in language, or the reading process and how it works in adults and children.

During the early days of reading miscue research, these texts or artifacts were called protocols because they were visible texts written or selected to show language as it really is. Ken placed carefully selected excerpts from the published texts he was using in miscue analysis research on overhead transparencies or handouts. He asked the readers to read silently, write down their responses, or sketch what they remembered from their readings. Discussions about their responses, first in small groups and later with the whole group, helped the participants understand the importance of the issues they were exploring. Other protocols were audio- or videotapes of readers with accompanying transcripts so that audiences could mark miscues and work together to discuss the role of miscues in the reading process. These reflective discussions led to debate and disequilibrium that caused changes in attitudes toward and knowledge about readers and writers, speakers of a range of dialects and language, and issues related to text construction.

In one of Ken's earliest creations (see Protocol/Engagement B-11), it is obvious that he took a page from linguist–mathemetician Lewis Carroll:

A marlup was poving his kump. Parmily a narg horped some whev in his kump.
"Why did vump horp whev in my frinkle kump," the marlup jufd the narg.
"Er'm muvvily trungy," the narg grupped.

"Er heshed vump norpled whev in your kump. Do vump pove your kump frinkle."

Each protocol has a carefully thought out purpose or goal. In "A Mardsan . . ." Ken hoped to help his audiences attend to the role of syntax in the reading process. He wanted them to realize that grammar supports the construction of meaning and that examination of syntax through miscue analysis reveals what readers know about their language and how such knowledge is useful to teachers. He hoped to use such protocols to examine the orthographic and morphological system with teachers in an engaging fashion.

An early creation was Gloopy and Blit (see Protocol/Engagement B-11), which he fashioned so that teachers could examine the syntax of basal texts and develop insights into the role of various types of questions asked about a text that typically followed short basal stories.

Ken wanted to capture his students' imaginations about language and to help them realize how interesting the study of language could be and how important it is to understand reading, how students read, and the development of curriculum. Those of us involved in reading miscue research have added dramatically to the types and roles that protocols play in learning. Some of us began to use the term *engagement* instead of *protocol*. Their uses have expanded, but the overall purpose remains the same.

The objective for using protocols/engagements is to cause observers to wonder and respond and to attend to the issues being raised by considering their personal involvement in the process. Engagement with the protocols helps observers to reconsider attitudes and knowledge about language and learning processes without a professor or teacher directly telling what something means. Discussion with peers and opportunities for reflection and reconsideration is at the heart of protocols/engagements.

Protocols/engagements fit into the whole language teaching and learning framework. Brian Cambourne (1988) uses engagement as one of the conditions necessary for whole language teaching and learning. Kathy Short, Jerry Harste, and Carolyn Burke (1996) use the concept in a similar vein. Engagement, fundamental to learning, means the learner has chosen to attend to the object, the topic, or the idea at hand. Every engagement is complex because it incorporates a range of responses from the learner. Engagement involves concentrated attention, but for each member of the learning community, what is attended to will differ. Learning is unlikely if the potential learners do not decide that the protocol/engagement is important to enhance their world or to expand their knowledge base. Engagement precipitates imagining, daydreaming, wondering, and wandering (Merriam 1991) and most often leads to complex changes in the learner's views, beliefs, and concepts. It demands action and activity on the part of the learner.

Such dynamic responses can occur only if the language that accompanies and permeates the engagement is authentic and meaningful and can connect with what the learner already knows, what the learner is already wondering about, and what she or he thinks needs to be known. That's why the language of the protocol/engagement is carefully selected for authenticity by the teacher educator with the learner in mind.

As we create authentic protocols/engagements with students, we demonstrate a role of teaching that is important to whole language learning (Smith 1981). Everything teacher educators do in classes is a demonstration from which students can learn. The kinds of demonstrations we provide are the raw materials from which students construct their meanings about the role of teaching. We know that teachers most often teach as they are taught. To that end, we take the protocols/engagements that we devise seriously. We see to it that each protocol/engagement is related to a real-world event and monitor to ensure that students are actively engaged. We create settings in which the probability for deep engagement is maximized, and we create protocols/engagements that permit learners to restructure their knowledge about teaching and learning.

Each part of the book ends with a collection of relevant protocols/engagements. Within each section of protocols/engagements, you'll find detailed and specific procedures for how to create and live through the experiences within a group setting. Each suggestion is couched in an introduction that ties it to the principles of whole language that are grounded in theory. Extensions are sometimes suggested as well in the afterword section, but we encourage you to make these protocols/engagements your own, using your professional knowledge of theory, practice, and your particular students to adapt our ideas to meet your purposes.

REFERENCES

Cambourne, B. 1988. *The Whole Story: Natural Learning and the Acquisition of Literacy in the Classroom.* Aukland, Australia: Ashton Scholastic.

Merriam, E. 1991. *The Wise Woman and Her Secret.* Illus. Linda Graves. New York: Simon and Schuster.

Short, K. G., J. C. Harste, and C. Burke. 1996. *Creating Classrooms for Authors and Inquirers: The Reading-Writing Connection.* Portsmouth, NH: Heinemann.

Smith, F. 1981. "Demonstrations, Engagements, and Sensitivity: The Choice Between People and Programs." In *Language Arts, 58, 6.*

A-1 Demonstrating the Range of Evaluation Possibilities

Kathryn F. Whitmore and Rahima Wade

Introduction   The end of a course or an inservice workshop often brings a slew of evaluative procedures for all the participants. Hopefully students at universities are involved in self-evaluation in addition to faculty evaluation of their learning. Students are also frequently asked to evaluate courses, whether with a computerized bubble format that is easy for the institution to quantify, with an instructor-made form that is more qualitative and personalized to the specific experience and philosophy of the faculty member, or both. This engagement explains how a group of participants can be involved in evaluating the performance of the professor while simultaneously learning about the range of possibilities that exist in evaluation and the corresponding merits and limitations of quantitative versus increasingly qualitative techniques. The engagement provides the professor with some valuable information to inform his or her own practice.

It also meets our instructional goal for the students to understand authentic assessment better by experiencing it.

Procedure   Five evaluation forms need to be prepared (Figures A-1.1 through A-1.5). The first four are handed out randomly to the participants so that different students have different copies to complete. The instructions on each form are self-explanatory, but students usually need to be reassured that it's okay that they have a different form from the person sitting next to them, and they should do what the form asks them to. Often students are reluctant to complete the first form, which asks them to grade their professor. If they feel compelled to write an explanation for their decision, ask them to refrain from sharing it until the experience is completed.

Provide adequate time for the students to complete the forms, realizing that the forms require increasingly long periods of time with each version. While the students are responding to the directions, the professor completes the fifth form, a self-evaluation.

When the group has finished writing, ask a volunteer representative from each type of form to read his or her directions aloud and then their response. It's important to share in the order of the forms. Ask as many students to share their evaluations as are willing. Some students may be uncomfortable reading their professor evaluations of you out loud; others may have written negative comments that they prefer to keep anonymous.

After examples of all types of the student forms have been shared, discuss the increasing depth of information that is available to you from each type of evaluation. The grades are nice to hear, but they provide virtually no information that is helpful to extend our thinking and practice. As each technique becomes more qualitative and more writer controlled, the information shared becomes more valuable because it is useful and specific. The narratives written during this engagement can provide wonderful feedback for future planning and teaching.

Following the students' sharing of their evaluation of you, read your self-evaluation narrative. It will no doubt convey information about your professional development, your thinking about teaching, and your personal conditions for successful practice. It will invite your students into your personal assessment of how the course or event has progressed and what you'll do differently next time. The students are usually fascinated by the information that is shared, and they have no way of knowing it without an experience like this.

A discussion can continue about the relative merits of the range of evaluation techniques we have available to us in educational settings. At the close of the engagement, ask students to turn in their forms if they will.

[handwritten margin note: I wonder if this puts this student in a bad position b/c grades are yet to be assigned]

Please think about my performance in this course. Then, please give me a grade of A, B, C, D, or F. We will share your evaluation as a group.

FIGURE A-1.1   **Student evaluation form**

Copyright © 1996 Kathryn F. Whitmore and Rahima Wade. Stenhouse Publishers, York, Maine.

Please think about my performance in this course. Then, rank my abilities in the following categories with a 1–5, with 1 meaning the worst and 5 meaning the best. We will share your evaluation as a group.

Criteria	Rank 1–5	Reason
Style of presentation	_____	_____
Personal rapport with students	_____	_____
Quality of examples	_____	_____
Applicability of ideas for your practice	_____	_____
Responses to written work	_____	_____

FIGURE A-1.2   Student evaluation form

Please think about my performance in this course. Develop a short list of criteria that are important to you when you take an education course. Then rate me on each of your criteria with a rank of 1–5, with 1 meaning the worst and 5 meaning the best. We will share your evaluation as a group.

Criteria	Rank 1–5	Reason
1.	_____	_____
2.	_____	_____
3.	_____	_____

FIGURE A-1.3   Student evaluation form

Copyright © 1996 Kathryn F. Whitmore and Rahima Wade. Stenhouse Publishers, York, Maine.

Please think about my performance in this course. Write me a brief narrative describing my performance in terms of strengths and weaknesses. We will share your evaluation as a group.

FIGURE A-1.4   Student evaluation form

Instructor's self-evaluation. The instructor writes a reflective narrative about his or her performance and growth during the course.

FIGURE A-1.5   Teacher self-evaluation form

A-2 Understanding Student Understanding

STEPHEN B. KUCER

Introduction   I use this activity to understand how adult learners are interpreting the intentions behind my classroom demonstrations so as to view the classroom from their vantage point.

Procedures   After students have engaged in a particular demonstration in which an aspect of literacy, literacy teaching, or literacy learning has been highlighted, I give each student a Reflection Interview (Figure A-2). Under the heading "Description of Activity," I describe the particular demonstration on which I want students to focus. I then ask students to reflect on the activity identified and to describe why they think I engaged them in the activity and what specifically they learned. I also complete the interview.

In analyzing the students' responses as compared to my own, I come to a fuller understanding of how the activity impacted their thinking and the relation between my intentions and their learnings. The students' responses allow me to make modifications in my demonstrations as needed and to consider the development of other demonstrations that will promote student learning.

Copyright © 1996 Kathryn F. Whitmore and Rahima Wade. Stenhouse Publishers, York, Maine.

Name _____ **Date** _____

Description of Activity:

1. Why did I have you engage in this activity? What was I trying to teach you?

2. What specific things did you learn from engaging in this activity?

FIGURE A-2   Reflection interview

Copyright © 1996 Stephen B. Kucer. Stenhouse Publishers, York, Maine.

A-3 Changing Teaching Through Reflective Practice

SHIRLEY CRENSHAW

Introduction   As a college instructor, I realized that my whole language class-room practices were limited to the foundational components of whole language that were easiest to incorporate in a college classroom. I was uncomfortable because I had ignored many of the other components that seemed inappropriate for experienced teachers. As a guide for examining what I saw as a hypocritical stance in my application of whole language beliefs, I considered John Smyth's (1992) challenge to engage in the politics of reflection. His framework asks the following questions (p. 298):

1. What do my practices say about my assumptions, values, and beliefs about teaching?
2. What social practices are expressed?
3. What views of power are embodied?
4. Whose interests seem to be served?
5. What constrains me?

As a result of my own reflection, I worked to develop a college-level learning environment that shifts responsibility for learning to the students. The following engagement contains an outline of the foundation of whole language that is important to me to practice in my own teaching. It sets out the basic plan I now use for graduate classes and summarizes the evaluation component of a course.

Procedures   Suggested Outline for Reflecting on the Implementation of the Foundations of Whole Language

1. Read, think, and talk.
    a. Read professional articles and books.
    b. Think about what you believe about teaching and learning.
    c. Talk to others about your ideas and questions. Establish a reading circle, enlist a sharing partner, or initiate and participate in a support-study group.
2. Consider curriculum planning questions.
    a. What do we know about our students?
    b. What do we want them to know as a result of our instruction?
    c. What do they already know?
    d. What do they want to know?
    e. How can we learn along with them?
    f. How can we provide a comfortable learning community?
3. Focus on student-centered involvement.
    a. Invite students to share questions and insights about content material.
    b. Ask students what they would like to study from a list of self-generated and teacher-suggested topics.
    c. Invite students to teach the class, serving as resident experts on a topic of interest.
    d. Share classroom problems and involve students in providing solutions.
    e. Give students responsibility for learning progress and evaluation.

4. Provide choices in learning activities.
   a. Encourage student-selected topics for reading, writing, and research.
   b. Provide a variety of reading materials.
   c. Invite alternative ways of responding to text and to instruction.
5. Implement authentic reading and writing activities.
   a. Read aloud to the class each day (newspaper items, poetry, chapter books, magazine features, article excerpts, student- or teacher-authored materials).
   b. Provide time for uninterrupted, individual reading.
   c. Give students the opportunity every day to write journals, learning logs, reading response logs, written conversation, pen pal letters, personal messages, writing process pieces, research projects, science, and math processes.
   d. Encourage individual and group projects as alternatives to tests.

Sample Implementation Plan (How to Survive in a Roomful of Tired Adults)

Getting Started

- General conversation among participants.
- Shared literacy: Teacher or student shares a book, story, news item, poem, cartoon, or topic-related material by reading aloud or using an overhead projector.
- Status of the class roll call: Students respond with one comment, idea, or question from their reading or writing assignment. Nancie Atwell (1987) introduced the idea of checking on class members' progress in developing pieces of writing at the beginning of each writing workshop. Her "status of the class" checklist included students' names and columns for noting topics, drafts, revisions, or conferences, so that she could quickly determine each student's progress. I decided to extend roll call to include student reactions and questions about the topics we were sharing. I used it like a "status of the class" checklist to assess students' connections.
- Teacher presentation of focused topic (15-minute limit).
- Small group discussion (three to five persons) for making connections or generating questions about the topic. Teacher circulates and joins various groups to note topics discussed and involvement by individuals. Each group has a recorder to keep notes and a reporter to share with the larger group.
- Small groups report to whole class. Teacher listens, takes notes, and facilitates discussion, if needed.

Extending Learning Opportunities

- Presentation by students or teacher. Individuals present books they have read, conferences attended, classroom research, observations, or strategies they have experienced. Study groups may present ideas or projects that they have been working on. If students are not scheduled, teacher presents further extension of topics assigned for that class period.
- Small groups reconvene to discuss ideas presented.
- Learning log (reflective journal) entries. Students and teacher think about connections they have made, new insights gained, or questions for further study, and record these in individual learning logs or journals.

Making Connections

- Teacher or student presentation of connections made between topics, questions, insights, and background for next week's study. This section may include video viewing, case studies, strategies to try, problems to solve, or an article to read and discuss.
- Small group discussion with a different mix of group members.
- Reports to the larger group.
- Learning log entry.
- Summary (questions, clarification, assignments for next class meeting).
- Exit slips for students to record a connection, a request, or a major question. They are half-sheets of paper with the words: "I learned, I need, I wonder." Exit slips are used to give information to the teacher so that next week's preparation may include comments about the learning connections and responses to the requests and questions. Students are invited to complete at least one of the three statements. Most students choose to complete all three.

Determination of Final Grades

Evaluation is easier with reflection as a regular part of my practice because it is continuous and I have the opportunity to observe student interest and involvement as the class progresses. Also, the students evaluate their own work. For final grades, I consider student responses to the following:

- Status of the class roll call.
- Learning logs. Students review their learning logs and determine the most important things they learned. Then they write a learning summary that they turn in every two weeks.
- Individual and group presentations.
- Exit slips turned in every class.
- Collaborative quizzes or exams.
- Final projects, with self-evaluations (application of learning).

Afterword   I find Smyth's five reflective questions continuing to be appropriate as I research, write, consult, present, and teach in a variety of situations and locations. I remind myself to ask what my practices say about my beliefs about teaching, what social practices and views of power are operative, whose interests are served, and what constrains me to make a difference. We generate change and attempt to influence others because we have experienced living through our own describing, informing, confronting, and reconstructing through careful reflection.

References

Atwell, N. 1987. *In the Middle: Writing, Reading, and Learning with Adolescents.* Portsmouth, NH: Heinemann Boynton/Cook.

Smyth, J. 1992. "Teachers' Work and the Politics of Reflection." In *American Educational Research Journal,* 29: 267–300.

A-4 What's in a Name? Reflecting on Syllabus Writing

CAROLE URZÚA

Introduction During my eleventh year of teaching college students, I discovered that a rose is not necessarily a rose is not necessarily a rose, especially when that rose is a course syllabus. For me, syllabus construction has been a process of deciding what texts, projects, and examinations my students had to do and then writing it down in clear prose. With classes I repeatedly taught, the prose benefited from students' misunderstandings; I revised frequently, making each successive draft more specific, and, for students, more detailed in how their work should be done. I didn't want the syllabus to create inequity, with some students possibly performing less admirably because they didn't understand my directions.

While my syllabus was reflecting more and more control over how the students would conduct themselves, I was, at the same time, creating engagements, activities, readings, and discussions telling the students they should share responsibility with their students; they should help their students become independent and empowered. The paradox finally became obvious when I typed "Requirements." Such an objective word, *requirements*. We, teacher and students, have a pact: You will do all of the following because I have been appointed to determine what is best for you. In PE (preenlightened) times, I would have—consciously, I hope—had good reasons for including each requirement, but it never occurred to me that I might tell the students about my thought processes. It certainly had not occurred to me that requirements were actually the most teacher-centered part of my teaching, implying that there was a set of criteria (and concomitant standards?) that students must meet in order to be successful in the course.

What I wanted students—all students, but especially those in preservice education—to know was that the activities I set out for them would be frames in which they could explore, risk, experiment, and create their own piece of art, representing their own construction of knowledge. Each picture would be different, each work of art informed and influenced by a number of factors, most of them under control of the students. How could I say that in the first document the students read in my class: the syllabus?

Procedures The first change was a simple one. The word *requirements* was changed to the phrase, "How to learn the most this semester." The focus now was on how the semester could be the most help to the student in his or her individual construction of knowledge. The genre of the text also changed. Whereas "attend all classes" previously meant, "Because I say so and your grade will suffer," it now implicitly meant, "I assume you are taking this class because it means something to you, and you will make more meaning by coming to all of the sessions." The move was from persuasion to information. Then, verbs, especially modals, were changed, so that "You will . . ." became "You could . . . ," and "You should . . ." became "You might . . ."

Now that my heading stated, "How to learn the most this semester," I could move on to creating more global generalizations. For example, I had always included, "Ask questions while you read," but now I realized that the more general concept was, "Be curious, questioning, and active in class and out."

Moving to set out frames for students encouraged me to become more overt in my purposes for including certain ideas. Whenever possible, therefore, I have been including my rationale. After suggesting, for instance, that "keeping a good accounting system of all your writings and ideas" is a good way of learning through writing, I then noted that one way to do that was through a regular sharing of writing through dialogue journals. After providing some particulars, I then wrote:

> Research data are clear that dialogue journals help us to become better writers through the act of composing and through the written conversation. You may, therefore, continue on one topic as long as you want, drop topics, pick up old or new topics, etc. There is not always time in class for you to reflect on subjects as long and as deeply as we would like; writing about ideas will help you rethink, expand, change, manipulate, and review your ideas, and those of others. If you are diligent in responding to your readings and your emerging thoughts, you should be able to read through your journals at the end of the semester, and see your growth, movement, and learning.

Changing focus from the instructor's requirements to the students' responsibilities inevitably brings up the question of evaluation. Students need to know what criteria are being used. Evaluating and grading in ways that will be acceptable to our institutions while still demonstrating a belief that students know what they've constructed and learned continues to be a dilemma. In an attempt to solve it, I've connected the frame "how to learn the most this semester" to each engagement. For example, after providing several activities from which students might choose to provide data they can analyze over time, I included the following in regard to their reports:

> To be most effective, make your report well organized. I anticipate there will be a sense of development of your own learning which could be reflected in your paper. For example, "I first thought . . . about my [case study, adoptee], but further data showed . . ." Each time you observe and analyze, think of yourself as a scientist, a researcher putting forth a hypothesis about, in your case, the language and literacy development of a child. Find and provide all the data you can which will support your hypotheses; suggest, when appropriate, how the child's development and/or your own development is evident in the data you are finding. Your paper might, therefore, reflect the hypotheses and the data.

Afterword   When, in the past, I had set out the requirements for a course, those requirements were always confined to that course. As I reflected on how my students' semester could be most effective, I realized it would be most helpful to them if they could connect all their learnings from all of their teacher education classes. I told them that they needed to become global and make connections, and my postscript reminded them that the whole of their experiences in their program of study is greater than the sum of the discrete parts/courses.

Unlike Shakespeare or Stein, I found that a rose/syllabus is not a rose/syllabus when that syllabus takes on a different focus. I'm not yet positive that I am impacting my students as I would like, but at least the language of my syllabus represents a more consistent underlying philosophy of education and learning.

SUPPORTING INSERVICE AND PRESERVICE TEACHERS AS LEARNERS

Karen Feathers and Linda Crafton, editors

Whole language is not simply an instructional method that applies to elementary and secondary education, nor is it restricted to a particular age group. Rather, whole language is a complex theory of language and learning that informs teachers' work with students of all ages and abilities. Thus, as whole language teacher educators, we use our understanding of language and learning to inform our college teaching, as well as our work with children.

Effective learning occurs when teachers live the model they espouse. Nothing else will influence professional development in quite the same way. Teachers do teach the way they are taught. When we talk to teachers about community, we must become a community; if we require reading about writing and reading workshops, we must provide ongoing experiences with those curricular components; if we believe in authentic assessment, we must give opportunities for kidwatching and reflection. The activities that constitute the curriculum for each course may vary, but they share common elements. They are learner centered, involve choice, allow the learner to grow in his or her own way, are low in risk, and are embedded within the context of a community of learners.

The chapters in this part show what is possible when teacher educators seek to empower adult learners in the same way as younger, less experienced students. Jean Anne Clyde and Mark Condon share their use of kidwatching to help students understand how children learn in "'School Talk': Exploring the Uses of Language in Middle School Teacher Education." The use of a study group as a catalyst for continuing professional development is discussed by Myna Matlin and Kathy Short in "Study Groups: Inviting Teachers to Learn Together." The role of talk in promoting understanding and growth within a study group is the focus of Chapter 10, "Conversation as Exploration: Teachers Collaborating to Know What They Know," by Katie Wood and Beverly Busching.

Writing is important in whole language college classrooms, as evidenced by Sharon Andrews and Gail Huffman-Joley in Chapter 11, "Doing Theory in the

Methods Class: Focused Reflection." Finally, in "Miscue Analysis: A Mediator in the Development of a Philosophy of Literacy," Virginia Juettner provides a detailed description about how she uses miscue analysis to help undergraduate students understand and change their views of reading.

These chapters show the commitment of whole language teacher educators to demonstrate the breadth and depth of their beliefs through their actions in their own college classrooms. They show us whole language theory as practice.

"School Talk": Exploring the Uses of Language in Middle School Teacher Education

Jean Anne Clyde and Mark W. F. Condon

As whole language teachers, each of us in our own way has come to value conversation as a vehicle through which learners construct meaning about their worlds. Whether we have students studying the role of humans in the disappearance of the world's rain forests, appreciating mathematics in daily living, or understanding and celebrating cultural differences, we have learned that talk is a vital tool in assisting learners in making the personal connections that characterize real learning—that which endures as usable long after students leave the school context.

Given the teacher preparation that most of us experienced, these conclusions were drawn despite many of the things we were taught in university classes about schools and children, learning and teaching, and curriculum. Our learning to value conversation came from first-hand experiences in seeing children make and share their observations, analyses, and connections; from reflection about how our training and these observations differ; and, of course, through our own conversations with fellow teachers.

Convincing a group of preservice middle school teachers that oral and written language are important tools for learning about mathematics, science, or social studies is a substantial undertaking. This is particularly challenging when many of these preservice teachers have only romanticized memories of their own experiences as middle schoolers, or have felt successful in middle school and attached their feelings of success to traditional quiet classrooms where discussions and agendas were generally controlled by teachers.

Our undergraduate course, Oral and Written Communication in the Middle Grades, was designed to help first-semester teacher education students develop an understanding of the uses of oral and written language. Here we describe one assignment that we found to be particularly effective in helping students come to value language as a vital tool in learning about all curricular areas in the middle grades. The assignment also served, through observing the experience of our own students, to verify for us as teacher educators the universality of that dynamic.

TALKING TO LEARN

We structured our teacher education classroom so that students had frequent opportunities to work in small groups and to "talk their way into understanding" (Barnes 1992) new concepts of teaching and learning so essential to effective instruction. Throughout the course, we tried to create the kind of context that mirrored that which we were advocating. We also participated in each of the in-class activities with the students.

We began the course with an investigation of language learning, using the "Cloning an Author" (Short, Harste, and Burke 1996) strategy as a vehicle for exploring concepts presented in Judith Lindfors' (1980) work. In this strategy, learners are asked to identify key concepts or ideas as they read a passage, recording them on index cards. Eventually they select the seven they believe are most important. After selecting the concept card they believe is most central to the others, they "web" their other cards around it, such that their placement reflects relationships between the concepts. This strategy promoted a lively conversation about language learning, while demonstrating our commitment to discussion as a medium for learning.

Part of the class was devoted to a biweekly exchange of letters with middle school pen pals at a local school. Like our students, we each wrote to a pen pal, so we experienced the same challenges they did in determining how to communicate sensitively and effectively with young teenagers. We reserved class time to read and share letters and to talk about the myriad problems students revealed through their letters. Conversations about how to respond to letters helped all of us better understand the kinds of pressures and problems young adults face and highlighted the important role that language plays in establishing strong relationships with adolescents.

We chose as the text for the course Douglas Barnes' *From Communication to Curriculum* (1992), which provides an in-depth examination of how language can be used as a tool for learning across disciplines. Because the text is conceptually dense, we read one chapter per week, using "Save the Last Word for Me" (Short, Harste, and Burke 1996), to facilitate discussions. In this strategy, each reader identifies several direct quotations from the passage that she or he feels are provocative. Each of the quotations is written on one side of a three-by-five file card, with the reader's response to it written on the back of the card. By sharing their quotations, students' contributions become the focus of discussion. Members of the group respond to these quotations, exploring the content of the material, including its emotional power. When the discussion comes to an end, the student who volunteered the quotation has the last word.

As students interacted, we remained silent, avoiding even eye contact while taking anecdotal notes of important issues and questions that were raised. In this way, students were free to talk their way to deeper understandings of the material without our interference or interruption. Later in the class, our notes allowed us to revisit important or unresolved issues that emerged through the discussion. This entire engagement was supportive for the students on many levels. They experienced directly the benefits of conversation in sorting through issues from the course; at the same time they observed the roles that teachers can play in supporting and extending learners' understandings.

These weekly discussions were extremely productive. However, it seemed necessary to create a "lived-through experience" for our students to allow them to examine for themselves how the nature of talk in a classroom affects the context and, consequently, the potentials for student learning.

Our strategy for addressing the impact of context on learners was created in two parts: (1) a nonschool learning environment and (2) a school environment. For the first assignment, which we called our "kidwatching" assignment (Y. Goodman 1978), we sent our students to nonschool settings—museums and zoos—to observe how children learn when exploring independently. Because we wanted students to recognize both the commonalities and differences among learners of different ages, we asked each of them to observe one elementary school and one middle school learner. We provided a set of guide questions to help establish a focus as students investigated learners' uses of language to explore, analyze, challenge, and communicate concepts that were present in the museum and zoo exhibits.

Through this assignment, students came to appreciate the ease with which children learn within natural learning contexts and how important language is to that learning. They discovered how efficient, idiosyncratic, constant, and language-rich children's learning strategies tend to be in inviting contexts. They observed how high the level of learner engagement in the exhibits can be, even in the absence of a supervising adult, and how intrusive adult direction may be when it runs counter to children's learning agendas. They identified the supportive (and sometimes not so supportive) aspects of the exhibits and the personnel who staff them, and shared their conclusions in letters written to educational directors of the various institutions.

Having seen our students grow in the experience of kidwatching at the museums and zoos, our next assignment involved kidwatching in schools. Our initial inclination was to have our students watch teachers. We had talked in class about children's language as "kid talk" and it seemed natural to move on to teacher talk. However, we felt wary about placing teachers in a critical professional spotlight without their permission. In many ways, such a focus also seemed to abandon the centrality of children that we had sought for our course. Therefore, we shaped the assignment to focus on classroom discussion and oral language use—"school talk." Naturally, teachers play a critical role in defining the parameters of language use; however, by again placing learners at center stage as full actors in the conversation that occurs in classrooms, we succeeded in keeping the focus on children, with adults playing supportive roles in the drama. The resulting assignment (see Appendix on page 82), which required our students to observe children in middle school classrooms, is described in the remainder of this chapter.

THE ASSIGNMENT

We provided a set of guide questions to help students frame their observations around issues central to Barnes' book: agenda setting, control of talk, and the impact of context on the learners' sense of empowerment, self-concepts, and what school learning is all about.

Our students formed groups of two to three based on their discipline specialties (each of them has two). Each group then made arrangements to visit one of several local middle schools together. They asked to observe teachers who shared a group of middle schoolers and taught the subjects our students were learning to teach. During their visits each team shadowed a class of children, traveling with them for three consecutive periods. The assignment called for each set of students to compose what is known by ethnographers as a thick description (Geertz 1973) of one representative instructional episode in each class. They took comprehensive field notes on the nature of classroom interactions, instruction, and the roles they perceived teachers and students to be assuming in each class. Each member gathered independent data of the same event. They were to include careful observations of specific children and to document their behavior across the three classroom contexts.

In addition to visiting schools in teams, students were required to shape their findings into a single coauthored paper that addressed the questions posed on their assignment handout. We believed that observing middle schoolers would provide one avenue for learning about language and context, but we were hopeful that the conversation required to coauthor papers would provide a firsthand experience, and thus a deeper understanding, of the potential for learning through language.

THE PRODUCTS OF THEIR EFFORTS

The results of the "school talk" experience far exceeded our expectations. Included in students' coauthored reports and their individual self-evaluations were their attempts to recognize and characterize the divergence of conversational patterns between teachers and children and among groups of middle school learners, and the impact of each of these on the shaping of thinking and learning behavior (Barnes 1992). Excerpts from their work indicate that our students seemed to have developed a complex set of understandings about language and learning. The generalizations were among those we had identified as important goals of the course:

- Learners behave differently in different contexts.
- Conversation shapes a critical part of the context of learning.
- Oral and written language are tools for learning about the world and for clarifying one's own thinking.
- Teaching involves helping learners connect new information to old in personally meaningful ways.

In the following sections, these understandings are shared by the students themselves through excerpts of their formal papers, as well as the self-evaluations they wrote regarding what they felt they learned from the experience.

The Impact of Context on Learners

One of the most often-mentioned observations shared by students was the way in which student behavior varied by context. Teresa not only noted the impact of context, but through her observations, began to develop an understanding of the complexity of classroom society.

> Everything about a classroom affects the learning or lack of learning that will take place there. The students I watched actually took on a different role or personality in each classroom setting. They responded to the teacher's way of talking and questioning, the seating arrangements, the amount of interaction between students and teacher and/or students and students. Even the temperature of the room or the time of day affected them.

Tonya observed the difference that the teacher can make: "It really made me realize the effect that the teacher's attitude can make on students' performance. The teachers who went into the class with a bad attitude had the most discipline problems out of their students."

The Role of Conversation in Shaping the Context

Students drew many conclusions regarding the impact of conversation on context, and consequently, on learning—for example:

> I . . . discovered that the classroom where the teacher wanted silence and structure seemed to be the least effective. . . . From my observation, the more the teacher invites class discussion, the more successful it can be. (Jenny)

Observations by Jenny, Susan, and Ian corroborated this conclusion and added these reflections:

> It is interesting to note that where interaction is encouraged, the communication between students was positive and constructive in nature. Where it was prohibited, interaction was seen to be negative and inhibitive to the learning process. Students were loud, inconsiderate, and insulting to each other.

In their analysis of the classrooms they visited, Patty, Bridget, and Mary concluded that "student interaction enables students to explore themselves in search of their identity and this is the real quest for knowledge."

Dorothy noted great differences in the role of oral language across contexts and viewed many missed opportunities for student learning in contexts that restricted language use:

> I learned how important language can be in a classroom and how little it is used in a constructive manner. This stems from the fact that teachers have a limited vision of language. Many teachers use language to give away, to bestow their knowledge on their students; but they forget that communication goes two ways; it should be given and received. They restrict language for instructions, questions and answers—what a limited scope! Some [teachers] . . . do not realize how much potential and "action knowledge" that a child may contribute to the class . . . I now know, as a teacher, I can encourage students to use language hypothetically and in an exploratory manner to achieve more confidence and a greater understanding of themselves and their learning.

Oral and Written Language: Tools for Learning About the World and Clarifying One's Thinking

Mary discovered the power of language in learning:

> Realize the significance of students putting what they have learned into words. My observations would have had little meaning had I not transformed those events to fit concepts from the text and then into paper form. I really came to have a more complete understanding of creating opportunities for students to make connections, as well as the shaping which goes on in classes, often unconsciously. I now realize that teachers must constantly scrutinize their teaching styles to be sure they meet their students' needs.

Helping Learners Connect New Information to Old in Personally Meaningful Ways

Cathy and Karen discussed the teachers' sensitivity to the connections learners could make:

> It was in the science class that a student appeared to connect a discussion of venereal disease to his own world. Maybe because he had heard of it or had experienced it, this student was concerned with "jock itch." Although "jock itch" was not a correct answer to the question asked, the science teacher changed the direction of the discussion to include this topic. She validated the importance of making connections by allowing this student to try to connect something of concern to himself with the current discussion. . . . By accepting this student's answer and letting the discussion follow his lead, she was also encouraging other students to make connections to their daily lives. She was saying that what was important to her students was important to her and important enough to spend class time on. The potential for learning is high in the science classroom because the teacher's treatment of the students' answers was indicative of a classroom dialogue in which sharing predominates over presenting. This type of dialogue, Barnes [1992] suggests, "encourages pupils when they talk and write to bring out existing knowledge to be reshaped by new points of view." (p. 111)

Tonya's observations led her to conclude that students must have a central role in their own learning:

> It became clear to me that real learning can only take place when the students are directing the lessons. Especially at this age, students must be allowed to communicate their ideas with one another.

Jenny, Susan, and Ian reflected on the need to find ways to help learners labeled behaviorally disordered make knowledge and learning their own:

> Even in a class which is supposedly designed to deal with behavior problems there should be a way to make knowledge available without making a straitjacket out of it. Students need to assume responsibility for their world in order to make changes in it.

These concepts became more powerful for our students as they shared their findings when they handed in their assignments. Perhaps even more exciting than the insights they had gleaned about language learning, and middle schoolers, were their sophisticated reflections about the benefits of collaboration and conversation discovered through coauthoring.

THE RICHES OF COAUTHORSHIP

The decision to include a coauthorship component in this assignment was a deliberate one. Our work over the past few years in studying coauthoring in children (Condon and Clyde 1991, 1992) and mature learners (Condon and Clyde 1993) had convinced us that working in concert with others enables learners to handle much more challenging assignments than when working independently. Essentially, coauthoring seems to allow each contributor to operate within her or his zone of proximal development (Vygotsky 1978), benefiting from each other's capabilities as they develop their own. The process provided opportunities for conversations we believe were essential for students to make complex concepts their own.

In our class debriefing on school talk and in their self-evaluations, our students talked about their experiences in sharing data with their partner(s), the unique contributions each made in creating their reports, and how their own learning experience seemed to mirror the children they had read about in their textbook and in the classrooms they had seen. Cathy wrote:

> Karen [her co-author] often helped me to see things more clearly. By trying to explain my ideas to her I had to clarify my own thoughts. . . . At other times, Karen thought of things I had not even thought of.

Angela also found the negotiation that occurs between coauthors to be the essence of professional collaboration:

> I believe conversation was the key role in my partner and I understanding school talk. We both sat in on the same classes but we saw some different things. It wasn't until we got together to compare observations that we realized how good it was to work together on this.

Finally, Ian seemed to capture the sense of community and professionalism that resulted from coauthorship with his two partners:

> Getting the chance to discuss observations and ideas with two intelligent people who have the same desires as I do was the best learning experience of this assignment. Looking through six eyes provides more than triple the insight. Seeing things through their views offers the chance to develop a fourth view that is a combination of all or parts of each individual. This also brought about a closeness that will go beyond this assignment, semester and year.

Our students' conversations have served them well. Through those discussions, they were able to bring "to sharp awareness parts of [their] world which were upon the periphery of [their] consciousness, and to construct for [themselves] understandings which did not previously exist" (Barnes 1992, p. 106).

This experience has strengthened our belief that in the education of children or teachers, conversation and the sense of community that can grow from it are essential. They create the kinds of contexts within which individuals can feel secure in constructing their own personal connections with the curriculum.

APPENDIX:
"SCHOOL TALK" ASSIGNMENT RATIONALE

In kidwatching you have studied the roles that children can play in their own learning of language and the concepts in their world. The complement of that is to understand the role that talk in instructional settings, like school, can play in helping them to learn the language and concepts of school and academics. In middle schools, much of what is taught is new language representing the increasingly sophisticated concepts in various academic disciplines. Our interest in making this assignment is to get you tuned in to what kinds of provisions teachers make to support learning language, learning about language, and using language to learn.

General Assignment Description

Working with one classmate (or maybe two) who shares at least one of the same specialty areas as you, shadow a group of middle schoolers for three periods of their school day. Everyone will keep field notes for all of the time you are with the kids, documenting what goes on in each of the three classes you observe. Following your observations, you two (or three) will coauthor a thick description that highlights the nature of language use that is allowed, encouraged, valued, and rejected in each of the various classrooms. Then, using the following questions, you will analyze those experiences to develop an understanding of the diverse nature of classroom interaction and how it affects the kids' potentials for learning. It is our hope that this will serve as a "laboratory" experience, which will assist you in exploring some of the ideas presented in your textbook.

Specific Assignment Tasks

Part I: Thick Description (Maximum: Total of eight double-spaced pages)

Select a representative "event" from each of the classrooms you visit. Coauthor a thick description of each of those events, providing the same level of detail as found in the sample descriptions from the special education research distributed in class. Conclude each section with a summary of what you decide each teacher believes about the roles of the teacher and the students in her or his room. Support your views with evidence from your thick description.

Part II: Data Analysis (Maximum: Total of ten double-spaced pages)

Refer back to your descriptions from Part I to determine answers to questions about the two classrooms that seemed furthest apart in terms of the ways in which language was used. You will address each of the following issues:

A. Learners making "connections" with their personal lives.
B. Opportunities to interact with each other.
C. Content learning potential in the classroom.
D. How thinking and behavior are shaped.

Here are the questions under each of the four areas:

A. In your "kidwatching" adventure at the museum/zoo, you looked for ways in which kids tried to connect the new information they encountered with their prior knowledge. How do kids "make connections" in middle school? Identify the classroom context that you observed that seemed to best promote "making connections" and the one that seemed to promote that least. How did you make this decision?
B. Generally, how diverse were the opportunities for the middle schoolers to interact with one another? To what extent did the kids capitalize on these opportunities or create them if they were not provided?
C. Which classroom has the most potential for learning and which the least potential for learning? How often are the kids shaping the inquiry? How often is the teacher shaping the inquiry? What impact do these have on learning? For instance, what kinds of questions are asked during each of the classes? Who does the asking? Are they "authentic" questions (ones asked by a person who is in search of an answer she or he really does not know), or ones designed to "test" others?
D. Barnes writes, "Most teacher-class discussions that go on day after day in school are shaping not only pupils' thinking but their behaviour as learners too." What "shaping" was going on in your favorite and your least favorite classrooms?

In each of these four sections, be sure to support your explanations with concepts and issues from Barnes.

Part III: Self-Evaluation

As usual, each author must submit a separate self-evaluation for the assignment. Consider the following questions in your reflection: (1) what did you learn in the process of completing the assignment, (2) what do you view as the strengths of your efforts, (3) what "wishes" do you have for the piece, (4) what role did conversation with your coauthor play in assisting you to develop understandings about "school talk"?

REFERENCES

Barnes, D. 1992. *From Communication to Curriculum.* 2d ed. Portsmouth, NH: Heinemann Boynton/Cook.

Condon, M. W. F., and J. A. Clyde. 1991, December. "Coauthoring in the Content Areas." Paper presented at the National Reading Conference, Palm Springs, CA.

————. 1992, August. "Coauthorship: Young Authors Collaborating Beyond Individual Capabilities." Paper presented at the Whole Language Umbrella Conference, Niagara Falls, NY.

————. 1993, December. "Collaborative Authorship by Mature Learners: Preservice Teachers Learn About Literacy Through Literacy." Paper presented at the National Reading Conference, Charleston, SC.

Geertz, C. 1973. "Thick Description: Toward an Interpretive Theory of Culture." In *The Interpretation of Cultures.* C. Geertz, ed. New York: Basic Books.

Goodman, Y. M. 1978. "Kidwatching: An Alternative to Testing." *National Elementary School Principal,* 57: 41–45.

Lindfors, J. W. 1980. *Children's Language and Learning.* Englewood Cliffs, NJ: Prentice-Hall, Inc.

Short, K. G., J. C. Harste, and C. Burke. 1996. *Creating Classrooms for Authors and Inquirers.* Portsmouth, NH: Heinemann.

Vygotsky, L. S. 1978. *Mind in Society.* Cambridge, MA: Harvard University Press.

STUDY GROUPS: INVITING TEACHERS TO LEARN TOGETHER

Myna L. Matlin and Kathy G. Short

Although it is accepted that students must be active participants and problem solvers who are at the center of their learning, teachers often are not allowed to control their own inquiry. If a transmission model of learning is not deemed appropriate for children, then that model also is not appropriate for teachers. In fact, the research on change in schools indicates that no innovation has a realistic chance of succeeding unless teachers are thoroughly involved in the change process, can identify and address problems as they see them, and can make the innovation or change their own (Fullan and Pomfret 1977; Hall and Loucks 1977; Lester and Onore 1990). Instead of prescriptive mandates or packaged programs, educators need time to work with each other to think, analyze, and create conditions for change within their specific circumstances and in ways that fit their own needs (Cochran-Smith and Lytle 1990). This process takes a great deal of effort and time, yet until teachers are given the support to examine their assumptions and reflect on teaching and learning, major obstacles will impede the long-term development and implementation of instructional innovations.

A mandate for change impacted every school when the district in our community adopted a new literature program based on a different set of beliefs about teaching and learning from the previous basal reader series. The district provided a one-day workshop focused on "how-to" information about the new program and its approach to literacy learning, but then schools were left on their own to implement the mandated innovation. From experience, we knew that this type of introduction to new programs often leads to changing the materials used for instruction or adding a few new activities to what has always been done. When innovations are mandated by any district, most teachers have no real ownership in the process, so the changes are short term and superficial.

Many professional development programs focus on teacher change, a term that some say reflects a deficit model: find out what is wrong with teachers and offer a program to "fix" them (Miller 1990). If change is viewed as a natural part of learning and professional growth, then teachers are transforming themselves (Lester and Onore 1990).

Universities traditionally have not supported long-term teacher development either. The university focus on short-term inservice workshops, courses, and professional readings provides teachers with new information and theories but not long-term support for their own agendas. Teachers need professional experiences in which they actively construct knowledge instead of passively receive knowledge. They rarely have the opportunity to generate their own agendas, pose their own problems, or search out their own solutions.

As an alternative to short-term information-"passing" models of professional development, we proposed establishing a study group approach to support long-term, innovative changes in the teaching of reading. According to Luis Moll et al. (1990), study groups are settings where educators "meet to analyze literacy instruction, exchange information, and provide support for introducing practical innovations. . . . It is a place where teachers have voice and control, where they can assist each other with their work" (p. 2). The authors state that changing theory and practice is both personal and social, and study groups provide the ideal setting for prolonged supported change.

Study groups do not begin with a specific agenda or plan of staff development but with a focus on negotiating a shared agenda and encouraging professional growth. Teachers, administrators, and facilitators can take a step back from their practice and beliefs and, in a supportive environment, critique those practices and beliefs by using knowledge gained through the study group process (Short et al. 1992).

ESTABLISHING THE STUDY GROUP

Our study group, which began in August 1990, is voluntary and meets biweekly after school. To get the group started, the concept of a study group was introduced at a faculty meeting. All teachers were invited to attend and were told where and when it would meet for the first time. The fact that it was voluntary was clearly noted.

Although no added duty pay was available, during the first year the study group was joined by two-thirds of the teachers from the school. Throughout the second year, all teachers participated. In the third and fourth years, most of the teachers continued with the group.

From the beginning, the teachers set the agenda for every session. We both played support roles. Myna, a principal, participated in the study group with the teachers. Seen as a colleague, she validated problem solving and change by being a visible, integral part of the group. She learned from and with the teachers. In this informal setting, she was seen as part of the study group and shared her knowledge of teaching and learning in open exchanges.

Kathy, a university professor, served as a facilitator for the first two years. She kept the conversation flowing and helped teachers reflect by asking questions and summarizing comments. During this time, Kathy was also available to work in classrooms, doing whatever was asked of her. She demonstrated lessons for teachers, team taught, met and planned with teachers, and observed and critiqued classroom teaching and learning. Teachers were always the initiators of these experiences. Although she could provide information and advice when asked, Kathy was seen not as an outside expert who told teachers how to make the desired changes but as a colleague supporting change every step of the way.

During the third year, teachers began to facilitate the study group, and Kathy became a participant. In the fourth year, the teachers took complete leadership of the group.

STUDY GROUP FORMAT

The first session each year is devoted to brainstorming possible topics to consider in the study group. Teachers list their concerns and questions on the chalkboard, and we discuss the issues that might be the most productive to pursue. Then we decide which topic will begin the discussions and set the first semester's meeting dates. We also ask ourselves what each of us is doing differently this year than in the past.

Each group meeting begins with sharing, which gives everyone a chance to hear what is going on in other classes. The time allocated for sharing varies from very brief to much longer, depending on what is happening in classrooms, the school, or the district. Sharing is an important aspect of the study group because it builds a sense of community, removes teachers' and the principal's feelings of isolation, provides the opportunity to celebrate together, and develops mutual support through sharing concerns.

Topics and questions for each group session are initiated by teachers and may come out of the original list generated at the beginning of the year or directly from the present needs of the group. This was especially true at one point in the first year when it became clear to the teachers that the new literature-based reading program and current district forms of student assessment did not align.

When the topic calls for it, we bring in material to share and discuss. This has included portfolios and field notes, which were tried out in the classrooms first. We have read children's literature and professional articles to discuss in literature circles. Support is provided occasionally for reading professional journal articles to extend our knowledge. At first, Kathy brought articles to the meetings that seemed to relate to where discussions were going. This tended to direct the topic for the next meeting, so we switched to letting the focus develop from the group. Either Kathy or another group member could then suggest a related article, which was sent to group members to read before the next meeting.

At the end of the study group, the agenda for the next meeting is discussed and set. The topic for study is reconfirmed at the beginning of the next meeting. The topic may be changed at any time, such as when there has been a new district mandate, a crisis at school, or teachers are no longer interested in the topic.

ISSUES RELATED TO THE STUDY GROUP

Each study group must consider a number of issues in order to be successful. At every school, these considerations vary to some extent yet are similar in many ways.

Perhaps the largest issue for any new endeavor at a school is time. Every staff member must figure out where in the week to fit one more time to meet. We looked at a calendar filled with faculty meetings, after-school classes for at-risk students, child study, grade-level meetings, and informal conversations for planning and collaborating. Still, we found one and one-half hours every other week, because the faculty felt that the study group was imperative for personal and collective growth.

Although it has not been possible because of bus scheduling at our school, some study groups have been able to build meeting time into the school day by adjusting the arrival and departure times for students. By adding fifteen minutes onto the school day for four days each week, these school staffs are able to dismiss students early on the fifth day. Some groups stay later and have dinner together. For most, the time together sharing and learning is valued for itself.

Another issue is whether the study group is part of the school day or held after school on teachers' own time. The study group is voluntary. On the one hand, it is extremely important for this to be a voluntary process. People who choose to participate learn and support the learning of others rather than feeling resentful when there is no choice. On the other hand, the value of the time and energy that educators put into everything they do, including the study group, makes it regrettable that a stipend cannot be offered. The personal value and benefit for the teachers can be seen when attending our study group. It has become the school norm; it is important to each of us to be part of the group.

Within the group, confidentiality is an issue. We agreed that all topics discussed must be confidential and privileged information that is used only inside the study group. All of us needed assurance that conversations were for our own purposes of exploration and learning and would neither be shared with others outside of the group without permission nor used in any evaluation.

The principal's role as evaluator and the safety of having her as a coparticipant of the study group is an additional issue, as it was for our group at the beginning. Some discomfort was voiced at her participation, yet discussions resulted in an acceptance of her as a group member. For our school, it has been a positive experience, and further research (Short et al. 1992) has demonstrated that in general study groups are more successful when principal support and participation is present.

Principals who become interested in teacher study groups must fully come to face the idea that "you're not a prophet in your own land." Classroom changes Myna had been encouraging and supporting for several years have come to reality as teachers have learned together and with the facilitative support of a knowledgeable university teacher. Kathy acknowledges that her greatest power comes from being a member of the group and part of the changes that occur because of it.

Still another issue is the resolution of conflict. Our study group gave us time to talk as a staff but did not necessarily resolve conflict. At first, existing discord among teachers seemed to intensify as issues came out into the open. However, in the longer term, there has been improvement. The ongoing nature of our conversations has led to greater tolerance of different points of view and actions, acceptance of each others' views, and, in some cases, the establishment of respect. It has taken an extended time for us to become a cohesive group and work through relationships and norms. Establishing study groups that are long-term and ongoing provides the support needed for building trust and respect;

short-term groups may provide information but may not build collegiality or provide an environment for inquiry.

The amount of time and patience it takes to discover our own voices within a study group is another issue. In our group, it initially seemed difficult for the teachers to view both the principal and professor as part of the group, rather than as experts or dictators. At first teachers seemed impatient for Kathy to "tell them the right way to teach." Now they would not allow her to tell them, even if she tried. Myna's opinions eventually came to be seen as coming from an equal, not from "the boss," but this also took time.

INITIATING CHANGE IN A SUPPORTIVE CONTEXT

Attendance has remained consistently high at the after-school meetings, and, as time passes, teachers are addressing a wide variety of issues and concerns within the study group. Because the idea for this group emerged to support a change in the reading program mandated at the district level, we both initially believed that the topics would focus on how to use the new literature-based materials and make the change positive for students and teachers. In fact, it was not until the middle of the second year that organizing for literature groups and response to literature emerged as topics. During the first year, we briefly touched on numerous topics chosen by the teachers, including fear of change and making mistakes, whole language (fad or reality?), integration of writing into the literature program, the true meaning of curriculum, collaboration in the classroom, the role of the teacher in a collaborative setting, and student evaluation. As a result of studying the topic of student evaluation during the first year, teachers focused in much more depth during the second year on how to take field notes and develop student portfolios for both adult evaluation of student learning and student self-evaluation.

Throughout all these discussions, teachers have come to realize that the changes they want to make go far beyond adding a new practice:

> It's [an] enormous [task] to change your philosophy and practice every day. We are just thinking through all of this and working with the kids, and we're not sure where it is going to end up. We're changing our basic ways of thinking, not just putting in a new activity. This is the scariest and most exciting thinking I have ever done.

> Yes. It's scary. You need a philosophy of how children learn and why. If you don't, it's just going to be "gimmicky" forever.

> This is the first time it ever occurred to me that my agenda for teaching and learning were valid. Before I always accepted everyone else's agenda—my administrator's or my professor's. Now I realize I have a right to my agenda and I don't want to go back.

At the beginning of the study group, only a few teachers invited Kathy into their classrooms. They each seemed to begin by asking her to work with students as they observed. Over time they planned with her and eventually braved team teaching and teaching in front of her. Her feedback was nonjudgmental, extended what teachers already were doing, and focused on student interactions as much as possible. Most of the teachers invited her to their classrooms and saw her as an integral part of the school team.

Some extended their experiences with Kathy by inviting other teachers into their rooms. Over time, observing other teachers in our school has become one of the most valued experiences for continuing professional growth and collegiality. Myna has supported this by encouraging the visitations, hiring substitutes, and taking over classes to give teachers time to interact.

Teachers have used the study group to focus on many different aspects of their teaching. Many teachers have, of course, worked on ways to use literature more effectively and powerfully in their classrooms. Some have focused on big books and shared reading experiences (Holdaway 1979). Others have worked on whole class or small group discussions, or both, about literature. Many have explored thematic teaching and ways to integrate literature into science and social studies. They have not limited their thinking to literature but also have been exploring process writing (Graves 1983), collaborative learning, multicultural issues, mathematics, computers, and evaluation of student learning.

While some teachers have made significant changes in their teaching, others have made relatively small adaptations to their classroom practice. For all, however, there are changes in how they think and talk about their teaching in the study group. The conversations at the meetings make it obvious that teachers, like their students, are willing to risk change in different ways.

The study group has allowed teachers and Myna to identify conflicts in belief systems within their own school district, especially between the new literacy curriculum and the way student reading and writing is evaluated. In the past, these conflicts were accepted as the way it is, but now teachers are thinking through the inconsistencies and developing alternative evaluation strategies that are acceptable to all involved.

The presence of the study group has given focus to professional development at the school level. Teachers grow through working and learning together. When teachers see themselves as learners and have the opportunity to experience control of their own learning, they make the same experience possible for their students.

The effects of the study group are not limited to classroom inquiry. Out of the experience, some teachers have decided to return to the university for classes and advanced degrees; some have taken on the new challenge of presenting at local, state, and national conferences; and some have become deeply involved in teacher research. All have renewed their focus on teaching and learning. Teachers look at curriculum, learning, and evaluation as powerful collaborative experiences for everyone involved and so are involving students in learning through new and meaningful ways.

Because the group is voluntary, not all teachers participate. However, even nonparticipants feel the impact and excitement and, whether they work on their own, hear faculty room discussions, or receive support from the principal or other teachers, changes are being made in every classroom in the building. The collegial support and enthusiasm of the study group has drawn the majority of the faculty into the process. Although teachers have different philosophies and approaches, they have developed shared understandings as a faculty that have built continuity across grade levels and classrooms.

LEARNING FROM THE STUDY GROUP

The study group provides a powerful context for learning. We believe that the following factors provide the basis for that power:

- Teachers trust that their voices are heard; they are in control of their own learning and have power over their work. They set the agenda for the study group in collaboration with other educators; it is not set out for them.
- Study groups mesh theory and practice; teachers plan activities based on what they know about learning and curriculum.
- Teachers see themselves as decision makers; they have the power to make changes through their own reflection and actions. They decide if, when, and how they will make changes and in what areas of their curriculum and teaching.
- Teachers' confidence in themselves and their colleagues grows because the study group supports individual professional growth and the development of a strong school community of learners. Teachers do not need to rely on outside experts to give them information.
- The study group provides the time and opportunity in teachers' action-filled schedules for reflection on teaching and learning. As Dewey (1938) indicated, reflection allows learners to organize ideas for future use.
- Study groups offer opportunities for growth to teachers at all stages of experience and levels of concern. They support those who are struggling or lack confidence in their teaching while encouraging the experienced teachers to think through new issues.
- School administrators have the opportunity to provide instructional leadership and support teacher development.
- Change is seen as a natural part of professional life, not an indication that something is wrong with teachers and their work.
- The study group provides a demonstration of a collaborative learning environment in which teachers experience as adults the processes they are trying to create in their own classrooms.

The study group has provided a true professional development experience for the teachers and principal at our school. It provides each individual the foundation from which to learn and plan together as a staff. Teachers have begun to take responsibility for their own decision making instead of simply accepting the words of "experts." After attending a one-day workshop on using literature in the classroom presented by a well-known national speaker, one of the teachers told us, "For the first time in my life I didn't accept everything the expert told me. You know, I think she wasn't totally right in what she was saying." The teacher went on to explain her own views of the topic, views she formulated herself with her colleagues in the after-school study group.

Teachers in the study group can think with others, share ideas, challenge their current instructional practices, explore the relationship between theory and practice in teaching, think through professional and personal needs, and develop literacy innovations for their classrooms. The resources used by the group include peers, research literature, analysis of classroom practices, and collaborative work with other educators. Rather than imposing a program or developing a prescriptive approach that forces teachers to adopt new approaches, the study group offers a way for educators to develop innovations and think through their own beliefs. It is a strategy for strengthening the autonomy of teachers and other educators to be active thinkers about their work and to make change a natural part of their experiences.

REFERENCES

Cochran-Smith, M., and S. Lytle. 1990. "Research on Teaching and Teacher Research: The Issues that Divide." In *Educational Researcher,* 19, 2: 2–11.

Dewey, J. 1938. *Experience and Education.* New York: Collier.

Fullan, M., and A. Pomfret. 1977. "Research on Curriculum and Instructional Implementation." In *Review of Educational Change,* 47: 335–397.

Graves, D. H. 1983. *Writing: Teachers and Children at Work.* Portsmouth, NH: Heinemann.

Hall, G., and S. Loucks. 1977. "A Developmental Model for Determining Whether the Treatment Is Actually Implemented." In *American Education Research Journal,* 14, 3: 263–276.

Holdaway, D. 1979. *The Foundations of Literacy.* Sydney, Australia: Ashton Scholastic.

Lester, N. B., and C. S. Onore. 1990. *Learning Change.* Portsmouth, NH: Heinemann.

Miller, J. 1990. *Creating Spaces and Finding Voices.* Albany, NY: SUNY Press.

Moll, L. C., K. F. Whitmore, R. Andrade, J. Tapia, E. Saavedra, J. Dworin, and D. Fry. 1990. "Community Knowledge and Classroom Practice: Combining Resources for Literacy Instruction." OBEMLA Contract No: 300-87-0131. Final report. University of Arizona, Tucson, AZ.

Short, K. G., K. Crawford, L. Kahn, S. Kaser, C. Klassen, and P. Sherman. 1992. "Teacher Study Groups: Exploring Literacy Issues Through Collaborative Dialogue." In *Forty-first Yearbook of the National Reading Conference.* Chicago: NRC.

Conversation as Exploration: Teachers Collaborating to Know What They Know

Katie Wood and Beverly A. Busching

In the morning of the eighth day of our Summer Writing Institute, a conversation occurred that was so generative that one teacher recalled it as a zenith for her. All of our journals were full of insights that emerged that morning. Laura had written a mythological narrative that evoked our deepest quandaries and dreams about transforming schools, and we talked it through together. Not everyone spoke, yet the verbal interplay of ideas as we reached for what we believed engaged the private struggles of all of us, a group of twenty teachers from elementary school through college. As two teacher educators who were a participant (Katie) and leader-participant (Beverly) of the institute, we believed that we could discover something about how collaboration operates by studying the dynamics of the inner and outer dialogues in that memorable conversation.

Katie recorded and transcribed all of our whole group discussions and many of the response group meetings from the summer institute[1], and when we read through these transcripts, we discovered that collaborative exploration was not unusual. In a myriad of contexts—other morning discussions, response group meetings, impromptu pairs, lunch gatherings—the teachers who had gathered together for a month to write and study the meaning of writing instruction frequently used each other to search for meaning in their work. We are coming to think that these exploratory conversations (Barnes 1992) are a major reason that the institute had such a strong effect on teachers' beliefs and practices and why so many of them came to see themselves and their classrooms differently. In this chapter we highlight conversation as exploration of what we know and value by letting our readers eavesdrop on this conversation, drawing from it insights about how our talk grew out of and enriched our work together.

THE CONTEXT OF OUR CONVERSATION

On this morning as we did every day, we gathered to hear the log as a way of focusing on what matters from the previous day. Each day, one teacher volunteered to write a reflection on what was important about that day. Instead of giving guidelines, we just plunged into the task with a teacher who was willing to take the risk and used reflective sessions after each reading to build insights about what the log should be. We celebrated the diversity of form and style (journal entries, heavily revised narratives, extended metaphors such as sandwiches and flower gardens). We wondered how one teacher could capture meanings for the whole group ("don't worry about it; we like individual perspectives") and how long the log should be ("not too long—you have to read it to the group"). We reflected back to the author what we liked about the log (humor, creativity, reminding us about the deeper meanings of our work, mentioning each person) and interviewed the author of the log about how he or she had made decisions.

On the morning of Laura's log, we had worked together only seven days. A major emphasis for our institute was living the process of authorship, so we had already faced our fears and satisfactions as writers in bringing multiple drafts to our response groups. Some of us had offered our expertise in workshops on specialized topics for the group, and we had shared our personal lives—children, travel, illnesses, recipes, car repair—over snacks, lunch, and response group meetings. Laura, a middle school teacher, was courageously implementing a whole language reading and writing program in a conservative rural school district. The first paragraph of her log set the tone for a mythological tale that, as one teacher said, made us feel that our work was "something momentous and magnificent":

> Once upon a Carolina summer, a community of dreamers decided to retreat to the village of Potential for a time of thinking, sharing, learning, reading, writing, listening, and talking. They were a special group of dreamers because their ultimate mission was to enhance the dreams of the apprentices in their local townships. Their desire was to bring the entire Kingdom a new way of knowing, a new way of seeing. Their work was indeed important and crucial because the evil King Standardized Test was practicing a deadly form of child abuse; he was trying to destroy the dreams of the apprentices. The dreamers came together each day for various collaborative efforts so that they could strengthen the language of their voices, written and spoken.

As the story continued, the events of the previous day in the institute were recounted in fairy tale language that highlighted the struggles between good and evil—between what we believed and what had been mandated.

OPENING UP CONVERSATION

For a moment we sat quietly, caught in that magical web created by a story that gave voice to our dreams and struggles. Beverly finally commented on our thoughtfulness and then invited Laura to expand a phrase from her log that contained a key theoretical contrast:[2]

BEVERLY: Laura, talk a little more about inquiry being generative.

LAURA: Well, I see it in my classroom, but even more so in here. It really amazes me in the short time we've been together, but when we start talking, it seems that one insight generates another and it just flows and builds. I see the power of talking as so important and the implications for that in the classroom.

BEVERLY: So you don't see this as something that is special to us, but it can happen in the classroom too?

LAURA: Right. *(The group is silent.)*

BEVERLY: Is this of interest to us to discuss, or does it seem obvious?

We think that within the silence after Laura's response, the group was grappling with the multitude of meanings invested in the log, lost in their own thoughts. A few were writing in their journals. Beverly, in her role as director, saw an opportunity to let Laura teach the group about "generativeness," an important concept that had been mentioned earlier but not examined by the group. For Laura, the word had a world of meaning and was a central concept in her current theory. But she did not want to just give a definition; she wanted to share her new insights about the spirit of collaborative inquiry that seemed to be emerging in the group and how important it was with her students. Beverly, sensing that the teachers were engaged but not sure where they wanted to go, offered an invitation to define a direction for the conversation. Katie responded to the invitation:

KATIE: It seems obvious now, but I'm not sure I would have said so two weeks ago.

BECKY: I think I feel it and I understand it, but I'm still confused about this content that I feel my students have got to learn, this factual stuff, and I have to mesh the two together. That's what bothers me.

RUTH: Hey, but remember your presentation? We learned a lot of factual stuff, and we figured it out ourselves.

BECKY: Yeah, but it's so hard to do that and I spent so much time thinking about that and planning that, I know I can't possibly spend that much time on each of my lessons. It's easier for me to plan my lessons by saying this is what we need to talk about and doing it in the traditional way as opposed to switching over and saying I want my learners engaged. Does this make sense?

PHYLLIS: Well, yes and no. *(slowly, followed by a pause)*

LYN: It doesn't make sense to me any more because when I do that, I find that I am so bored that it is now not easier. It's harder for me to teach that way because I have to battle everything I believe in.

Becky, a doctoral student and adjunct instructor, invited the group into a dilemma shared by others. The conversation then became a public grappling for meaning focused by her problem. We recognize here the push and pull of learners helping one another, fulfilling alternatively for each other the support that enables them to work in areas beyond what could be accomplished alone (Vygotsky 1978). By putting her discomfort out on the table, Becky asked the others to take on the roles of teachers and authorities, but this occurred because she had become comfortable first with them as friends and supporters. Because of the many ways they had come to know each other in this community, respect was a force underlying this entire exchange. Respect for herself as an inquirer, for example, was apparent in Katie's acknowledgment that even a week earlier she would not have understood what she asserts as a belief today. Respect for self supports and grows from respect we feel from others.

Although Ruth's comment affirmed her respect for Becky's expertise, it wasn't what Becky needed to resolve her dilemma. She was seeking new insights, not support, so she continued to push her question. There was more meaning here than the transcript alone can show. The simple statements made by Ruth and Katie are informed by the text of their past experiences with Becky—her inspiring workshop and plans for inquiry-based teacher education—and Ruth later reported that Becky etched the dilemma of "skills versus meanings" with attention-getting sharpness for her. If a skilled whole language teacher such as Becky was still anxious about how to implement a negotiated curriculum, she should sit up and take notice. Lyn, on the other hand, voiced a very personal resolution, in a way saying, "Yes, it's a dilemma, but there is only one answer for me now no matter how many problems it creates for me."

Julia, a new voice, joined Becky in the process of trying to say more clearly just where the problem lies, perhaps because she shared Becky's dilemma:

BECKY: There are just certain skills out there that you've got to have, and I'm kind of caught in the midst of that. I'm not secure enough in this, even though it is structured, though it may appear to some you are just throwing it out there.

JULIA: What content are you talking about: phonics, language arts class?

BECKY: Anything that has a certain content.

JULIA: If you are talking about language arts, what content are you talking about: literature or grammar, or both?

BECKY: If it was language arts, I would feel responsible for all of that.

JULIA: Research has shown for a hundred years that it's not doing any good to give those old-fashioned lessons. I can show you in my room a kid who can mark all those little examples and get them all right, and then put it on a piece of writing and he won't do it. I don't feel that at all about not getting out those grammar books. . . . I guess I may lose my job over it eventually, but I don't think that's [grammar books] the way to learn it. I don't feel guilty about it any more.

Only a few words were spoken, but their past experiences were part of the text of the current conversation. We knew that Julia was a teacher of inner-city twelfth-grade students who were struggling to pass the state exit exam in writing. She was her students' last chance: if they wanted to graduate, they must pass this exam. In fact, Julia gave as her reason for coming to the writing institute her need for help in teaching her students to "get their subjects and verbs to agree." We respected her teaching authority, and the difficulty of implementing a whole language approach in her situation. We knew that Julia wanted to take risks with the exit exam classes but was anxious about convincing administrators, parents, and other teachers that these new approaches are effective. So although on the surface we were working on Becky's question, in actuality it was Julia's question also. At the end of the exchange, Julia surprised many of us with a strong assertion of what she had been moving toward, a strengthening moment for all of us.

After Julia's statement about not feeling guilty anymore, smiles gave her support for her affirmation of belief. Then Laura extended the thinking with an explanatory concept that was important in her belief system.

LAURA: I think it all comes back down to whether you trust the learner.

BEVERLY: What does that really mean?

ANGELA: You have to be willing to relinquish control.

BEVERLY: Trust them to do what?

MARY BARBARA: To make an investment and have a purpose to learn, and you plant that purpose. I am very science oriented, and I was just sitting here thinking that the way science is taught now is you learn by doing and you don't just read out of a book. It does make it initially much more difficult for the planning process for the teacher. But when you begin to see the product of that and the excitement and the learning that takes place, it gives you that incentive to go on. It's a big jump in science as in writing. You give the writer an investment in learning, and then he's here because he wants to learn. You can't give that to somebody. You can only plant the atmosphere and then let them come.

MARGARET: I hate to say it, but not all of them are always going to come.

Beverly, still pursuing her agenda of not letting pat phrases go unexplored, asked the group to explore the key tenet of trust in whole language that had not yet been discussed. This time she connected with an area of current growth, and the group accepted the instructor's nudge, pulling new speakers into the dialogue.

Mary Barbara's words, "I was just sitting here thinking," show how inner dialogue emerges to support the group collaboration. Her thinking drew on a wealth of past experiences as she connected what she understood to be true about science to her understanding of the present questions. Mary Barbara was stating something she thought she knew, and the opportunity to reflect publicly let her and others manipulate this thinking and create something more powerfully meaningful. This interaction of private and public dialogue is at the heart of the collaborative process.

At this point Margaret, a high school teacher, entered the conversation with a negation: "Not all of them are always going to come." Margaret did not invite the group to think with her, or even present her doubt as a dilemma, but as a corrective to the optimism of the conversation. Julia, however, was respectful of Margaret's doubt, and, for a few minutes, they talked about junior and senior high school students who are seemingly impossible to motivate. After several exchanges, Margaret offered a personal resolution that helped another teacher see more clearly that her philosophy could no longer encompass balancing theories. She invited Margaret into dialogue with her by ending with a question:

MARGARET: I have learned that it's okay to intersperse the "Dream" [from Laura's log] of nontraditional teaching with traditional skill-based instruction to get the mechanics and to get the skills. I think it's okay to balance it.

LAUREN: But I find that I can't balance it because it's a whole philosophy. . . . It's a whole way of teaching, and to go back and forth makes me feel like a hypocrite.

. . . Maybe some can teach some of both and that's fine, but when I teach traditionally, I don't see them learning. It's safe for me, but do you see them learning from that?

Margaret responded by telling about some teacher-directed teaching experiences she felt had been successful. In one, she had engaged students' interest with a teacher-selected literature textbook and in another by using the grammar book. But participants' inner dialogues were active in the process of trying to make theoretical sense of the exchange, and several teachers jumped in and tried to construct explanatory concepts. The conversation moved away from a phase of "telling what happened" in the classroom back to trying to "interpret what is important" in the classroom.

LYN: There is a difference between strategies employed and the philosophies undergirding what you're doing and why you're doing it. Just because you do a mini-lesson or even if you drag out a grammar book and use examples, that doesn't make you automatically jump philosophies. It's how you use it and why you use it that's important.

JULIA: There are some things in that grammar book that I really work hard on, but I don't feel bad about what I don't use. Of course, they have to get grades, we have to do that.

MARY BARBARA: I am being a parent the way I was taught by my parents, and I think I am fighting being a teacher the way I was taught. I just want to say that being in this setting of the summer institute has given me some balance to be able to see how the other way can work and to have the freedom to make that decision. I just never have been taught any way but by tradition.

Beverly, still concerned with not sliding too easily over these concepts, introduced a plea for continued digging into underlying meanings, especially to be able to communicate in workshops for other teachers. One teacher responded by offering Frank Smith's *Insult to Intelligence* (1986) as a source that defined for him clearly what was wrong with traditional teaching. Finally, Beverly attempted to move the group on and bring closure to the now-lengthy conversation:

BEVERLY: I hope that we will continue to help each other articulate what are the elements that are really important. Instead of saying that we don't use the basal, ask what it is that happened in the child's mind that was wrong in your experience with the basal. And how can it be used in whatever you see as important.

Her comments show respect for teachers as authorities, even as she urged them to keep testing, to keep trying to know more deeply what they believe. The group ended the session in the usual way, reflecting back to the author of the log what they thought was valuable and interviewing the author about processes of creating the log. Finally, several comments about our meaningful conversation as the ultimate demonstration of the power of her writing led Laura to a new insight that the whole process brought home to her:

PHYLLIS: The nicest demonstration is what happened to us. We were put in a state of dreaming, and then we talked for so long afterward. Laura didn't lecture her core of beliefs; she let us reflect.

LAURA: You know, through writing the log and the subsequent conversation, I learned that there is no one-to-one correspondence between teaching and learning. You all really opened my eyes to that.

JULIA: Didn't your story do exactly what you want to do, what all of us want to do in our classrooms?

LAURA: I never really thought about that.

PHYLLIS: Yes. It was a demonstration.

FRED: The log meant different things for different people.

PHYLLIS: It was so individualized.

REVISITING OUR CONVERSATION

Later a group of teachers examined the transcript and validated our intuitive belief that the group had been intensely engaged in the collaborative building of meanings. Angela, a high school teacher who spoke only once ("You have to be willing to relinquish control"), said that the relinquishing of control implicit in trusting the learner had been the hardest aspect of her new understandings during the entire summer. Though her vocal role in the conversation was minor, her silent dialogue about control was powerful. Phyllis remarked that Laura's log bound us as a group because it made it seem like we were on a real quest together. She admitted that she still got dreamy when she reread it and felt like she was in search of the mythological Holy Grail. She commented, "Laura demonstrated so nicely how we can be invited into the cycle of inquiry." Phyllis also valued the distinction between "strategies employed" and "philosophies undergirding" that emerged in the conversation because she felt these comments served to put the entire conversation into perspective. She remembered admiring Lyn for expressing what she was feeling, but could not put so artfully into words. The contrast between just these two participants clearly demonstrates an essential dynamic of exploratory conversations: each participant brings to and takes from the conversation a personal set of meanings.

DISTINGUISHING KINDS OF CONVERSATIONS

Douglas Barnes (1992) helped us better understand how exploratory collaboration, with its intricate web of inquiry and tested theory, works. He distinguishes between exploratory speech and final draft speech, which identifies differences associated with an intimate audience as compared with a distant audience. Table 10 illustrates this relationship. Each contrast between the intimate and distant audience helps define the important distinction between exploratory and final draft speech functions. The collaborative struggle for meaning is possible only when the conditions for exploratory speech are present and learners feel comfortable with those conditions.

Barnes helped us understand better the significance of our conversation that was not preplanned or instructor directed. We all orchestrated its beats and

	Intimate Audience	*Distant Audience*
Size	Small group	Large group
Source of authority	The group	The teacher
Relationships	Intimate	Public
Ordering of thought	Inexplicit	Explicit
Speech planning	Improvised	Preplanned
Speech function	Exploratory	Final draft

TABLE 10   Relationships between intimate and distant audiences
(Barnes 1992, p. 109)

crescendos. The ups and downs in intensity could draw directly from the inner struggles for meaning communicated to an intimate audience. We began to understand how this conversation was different from other kinds of conversations that were valuable but not open to the same kinds of intense, personal meaning construction. For example, when a consultant visited during our first week, an auditorium full of teachers from several summer institutes asked questions, but the audience was no longer intimate, and each question and answer seemed to have its own undigested existence. Afterward, the consultant met with our group around a large table and asked us what meanings we had constructed from the morning lecture and discussion. The exchange that resulted was a different kind of discussion, one that we now think of as an "inventory" exchange. Each person shared personally constructed meanings but without the orchestration of support, challenge, and stretching that characterized our "log" conversation. Many valuable inventory exchanges were held during the summer, and the visible results, posted on the walls, were a reminder of the rich data pool that we had collectively brought to the institute: a list of the qualities of literature we as readers valued, a list of possible artifacts for a teacher's portfolio, and so forth. They were valuable but not so richly generative of discovered meanings as exploratory conversations. In this case, the ordering of thought and the nature of the comments had preset limits, not because it was a public audience but because this kind of talk had been defined for us in past encounters. We were following our internal preset scripts.

Another valuable conversation was the kind of discussion, somewhat preplanned and leader led, that focused on a specific topic or task, usually as part of a teacher workshop or introduced by the instructor. In these discussions, for example, we struggled to clarify Rosenblatt's (1978) notion of efferent reading; we distinguished between Calkins' (1986) notion of content conferences and other kinds of conferences; we talked out the practicalities of after-school teacher workshops. No one would discount the professional importance of these discussions, but the potential for discovery of new meanings was not supported by their structure or the purposes we had defined for them.

Collaborative Exploration

In any conversation, each individual mainta͏   ͏ogues. One
dialogue is spoken: the exchange of ideas an͏   ͏s, including as many
participants as choose to speak publicly. The͏   ͏is an active internal dialogue
that is an intricate exchange between the voice of an individual's past experiences
and tested theories and the voice of present experiences and tenuous new possibilities. In a community with a shared history and purposes that has learned to
support each person's inquiry, participants are comfortable bringing the internal
dialogue into the external script. Thus, Becky felt safe to risk her initiating question, and she respected what others' internal dialogue might contribute.

By bringing our internal dialogue to the group, we invite others into our
inquiry and make a personal grappling for meaning a public one. Each reflection
adds to the collective pool of reflections from which all learners draw. When
learners cooperate only by throwing their reflections into the collective pool, as
we did in our "inventory"-type discussions, they are left to move to resolutions
on their own. Exploratory conversations that are open to the collaborative construction of meanings make available the full potential of the pool of inner dialogues as participants collaborate to build their own and others' understandings.

Confirmation and Reflexivity

Exploratory conversations offer learners a variety of opportunities for growth.
Sometimes we feel a sense of confirmation that the tested theories of our past
hold up to the questions of the present. Lyn, who offered the distinction between
strategies and philosophy, was strengthened by the confirmation that her current
theories served her well in making sense of issues important to others. Becky and
Julia were in the process of confronting an existing anomaly about ownership
and "covering the content," and the discussion provided a way for them to work
through to a reflexive resolution and new tested theories. Margaret faced questions about her struggling secondary learners that her current theory couldn't
answer. Several teachers were constructing theories that were still very new and
uncertain; it was important for them to be involved with the more experienced
learners testing their theories against the group's questions.

We believe that learning occurred in this conversation whether teachers were
faced with confirmations or anomalies. Teachers are empowered when they realize that a tested theory serves them well in a new context, and they emerge from
the exchange with strengthened beliefs. Discomfort caused by facing anomalies,
with respectful support by the group, leads to powerful inquiry and new perspectives on theory-building processes. In a community of learners who work
together over time, many meaning-building conversations are needed if teachers
are to restructure their beliefs significantly. After all, one may be confirmed and
empowered about a certain theory today and tomorrow face a revolutionary
experience that will force movement toward a reflexive resolution all over again.
Learners must always remain open to both the confirmations and the anomalies,
never being satisfied to allow experiences to go untested. This is what makes
learning so exciting—and so tiring!

COMMUNITY

The words *community* and *communication* come from the same root, *commune,* which in its original form had the same meaning as *common.* The root implies a shared understanding, purpose, or belief that allows the hearts and minds of those involved to mingle freely, as perhaps once happened on a village common.

Those who live and learn together in a community build a shared history of interactions, feelings, and experiences. Because we spent whole days together and were writing alongside our inquiry, we came to know and care for each other. We knew when Becky slept in her new house for the first time and asked how her two small girls had reacted. We applauded when Deirdre returned from a successful job interview. We knew that Laura was fearful of losing her beloved principal, and that Phyllis was fearful of losing her mother. The shared history became a common text for the group to draw from, sometimes overtly as when Ruth used Becky's workshop from the week before to make a point. We could work with unspoken meanings and incomplete verbalizations, and, as a result, we could swiftly move to fresher, newer thinking.

The shared purposes of this group—to learn about the teaching of writing by engaging in the process of writing and to reexamine our established beliefs—did not happen by accident; they were consciously nurtured from the beginning and renewed again and again. Beverly felt that one of her main roles was to keep these purposes in front of the group while valuing the different concerns and contributions of each individual. In our conversation, we can see the group using this shared sense of purpose to keep itself on track without a preplanned structure. The conversation was purposeful even though the direction might not have been discernible or the final outcome specific.

Today most who participated don't remember much, if anything, of what was actually said, but all remember the power of the summer experience. What we remember is the quest. Laura's log, like all other good literature, sent us on a journey that morning. Details of the trip may be lost to us, but the new place where we are now and the feeling of having traveled are not. There were, indeed, multiple dialogues taking place that morning—the one we have on tape and the twenty inner dialogues intertwined with the group exchange. This kind of exploratory conversation should permeate any teacher education community so that, as we learn, the power of talking can support us to help each other understand what it is that we know and care about.

NOTES

[1] Katie's dissertation (Wood 1992) provided the basis for understanding the collaborative processes of the institute. We have revisited her systematically collected data to extend our theories of how our conversations were situated in and enriched our learning. We have triangulated our insights with the perceptions of other teachers who participated.

[2] In the interest of readability, the false starts, "uhs," and repeats that are characteristic of conversation have been edited from the transcripts.

REFERENCES

Barnes, D. 1992. *From Communication to Curriculum.* 2d ed. Portsmouth, NH: Heinemann Boynton/Cook.

Calkins, L. M. 1986. *The Art of Teaching Writing.* Portsmouth, NH: Heinemann.

Rosenblatt, L. 1978. *The Reader, the Text, the Poem: The Transactional Theory of the Literary Work.* Carbondale, IL: Southern Illinois University Press.

Smith, F. 1986. *Insult to Intelligence: The Bureaucratic Invasion of Our Classrooms.* Portsmouth, NH: Heinemann.

Vygotsky, L. S. 1978. *Mind in Society.* Cambridge, MA: Harvard University Press.

Wood, M. C. 1992. "Professional Development in a Reflective Community: An Ethnographic Study of the Midlands Writing Project Summer Invitational Writing Institute". Unpublished doctoral dissertation, University of South Carolina, SC.

Doing Theory in the Methods Class:
Focused Reflection

Sharon V. Andrews and Gail Huffman-Joley

Why don't college professors—or any other teachers, for that matter—do what they know is best for learning in the classroom? Sometimes we believe we are "doing" theory, but actually we are only thinking it. For example, Sharon "knew" what she wanted her classroom to look like, feel like, and sound like, but it was risky and unpredictable to provide opportunities for it to happen:

> I couldn't believe what I was seeing on the videotape. There I was center stage for most of a three-hour language arts seminar on whole language, spouting theory and exhortations about active engagement of learners, about empowerment, learners taking ownership of the classroom, but for this seminar (which I had wanted to be so "interactive" and "learner centered") I was in complete control.
>
> Without having seen myself on tape, it would have taken me much longer to recognize the disparity between my beliefs about the way students learn best and the way I was teaching.

In Sharon's case, the focused reflection provided by videotaping made visible that she was acting outside her own theory and let her see the gaps between her beliefs and her actions.

Gail's reflection enabled her to see discontinuity in how she dealt with reading and writing:

> One night the students began to share their pieces they had been writing. I began to reflect on the infinite variety of life experiences and interests being shared because the students chose their writing topics. Although I did not assign topics for their writing, I was still selecting articles, chapters, and texts for them to read because I thought they were important. I trusted the learners and gave them responsibility for choice in their writing and I witnessed the power in the pieces which evolved, but I hadn't made the transfer to reading.

Such reflection is risky business. We have to come face to face with our shortcomings as teachers of courses concerned with literacy curricula. When the professor plans for reflection, expects everybody in class to do it, and creates an environment in which learning means taking risks and exposing gaps in knowledge, then that risk and unpredictability become manageable, particularly within the framework of the relative safety of small groups.

These two episodes illustrate what we mean by focused reflection: moments of dissonance, a recognition that your theory doesn't match your practice. But as one of my undergraduates advised, "When you are introduced to something that is a new idea, you are going to feel this upsetting of your thoughts, but I think you should stay there a while until you have made a definite decision."

Focused reflection in the classroom may be a new idea, but it is worth the time to develop. In this chapter we provide ways to reduce the risks, record and express classroom episodes, and present strategies for focused reflection.

THE CONTEXT FOR REFLECTION

In order to develop skilled and reflective teachers for public schools, preservice teachers must experience contexts that foster reflective "public thinking" in the college classroom. Teacher educators must demonstrate reflective practice in their courses. Stefanie, a preservice teacher, demonstrated that her instructional history in teacher education had done little to involve her in actively reflecting on her own learning. In Sharon's methods course, Stefanie was required to engage in reflective learning strategies for the first time. In an interview at the end of the course, she said:

Not nec. a good thing

[Education is definitely the safest area I've ever been in.] You can go slow or keep quiet in the background. But it was much more risky in this class and it made me a bigger risk taker in my other classes. At first I was really intimidated. I didn't want to talk because I didn't know how I felt or what I believed. So much more was expected of me in this class. It made me go home and think about so many things I would have closed my eyes to. You can definitely avoid thinking about things in a regular [college] classroom setting.

Like Stefanie, most preservice teachers arrive in their course settings with twelve to sixteen years of instructional history, much of which has involved a transmission mode (Barnes 1976) of teaching and learning (lectures and testing). This behaviorist model of learning has led to passive, noncritical thinkers. Reflective practice, on the other hand, enables the learner to experience theory while actively practicing. What is the reflective act? What is its relation to teaching? Watson, Harste, and Burke (1989) wrote:

[Reflectivity] refers to the ability to use yourself and others as instruments for your learning. It means that you constantly look at what people, yourself and others, do in the act of learning X or Y. . . . The process of naming experience makes interesting things happen. By putting our experience into language we take distance from it, transform it into something that can be . . . stepped back from . . . and studied, by ourselves and others. . . . In short we can begin to interrogate and understand the very constructs which we use to make sense of the world. (p. 36)

This definition is a good place to start. When we are discussing literature in small groups or writing a personal memo in a response log, we are making our thinking public. The recording of ideas in oral or written language allows the learner the opportunity to create a dialogue with herself or himself and others and allows for changes in thinking and action (Heine 1988).

Although this is a natural learning process, learners with an instructional history consisting of a transmission mode of teaching and learning need help in stepping back and seeing themselves as active learners who are growing and changing. Focused reflection provides a sounding board and a stepping back from written or spoken thinking. The signs and symbols of thinking are developed through social interaction.

One of Sharon's recent courses, a seminar in language arts methods for a group of inservice and preservice teachers, is a case in point. The authoring cycle—a process approach to curriculum that incorporates drafting, peer response, editing, and publishing of writing; classroom research projects; and literature circles (Short, Harste, and Burke 1996)—formed the framework of the course. Sharon's personal focus was on teaching as inquiry. Course events were recorded and analyzed for the purpose of improving her teaching. Her goals were to help students take responsibility for their own learning and to create curriculum that encouraged independent and meaningful inquiry. Journals, discussion groups, and interviews were ways to document reflections on teaching and learning, allowing all participants to inquire into their practice. Figure 11 shows the integration of reflective strategies into the teaching.

Journals, kept for the twelve-week period, helped students record and analyze their mismatches between theory and practice, their questions, and their frustrations during the course of their school-based field experience connected to the language arts seminar. The journals provided information for curriculum planning and course evaluation and served as the vehicle for giving students feedback. Students' responses in interviews and journals also became the means for negotiation between the students and the instructor in planning course directions.

In her graduate-level course in language arts for teachers in elementary or middle school, Gail used strategies for reflective inquiry that were similar to Sharon's. Students wrote on topics of their choice during each session and served as an audience for peers as the pieces were developed. They brought books of personal interest to talk about with classmates in literature circles. They researched a children's author and shared findings and the author's books with classmates. Gail's goal was that these teacher-learners experience in the college classroom the same processes and strategies they were trying with younger students in their own classrooms. The strategies helped teachers to identify connections better between their learning and their students' learning.

Gail's and Sharon's strategies were not a bag of teacher tricks; rather, the strategies helped learners to become aware of their own learning strategies through reflection. They were no longer as dependent on the instructor to provide interpretations for every act of learning. They could apply previous experience because that experience had been consciously analyzed and integrated into personal theory about teaching.

Seminar Events/Engagements		
Journals	Taping	Interviews

Week 1	Getting to know you
	   Authoring cycle: Experience #1
	     "Nightmares"
	       Curriculum overheads
		Debriefing

Week 2	Sharing time
	   Author's circles
	     "Best teacher/worst teacher"
	       Curriculum overheads
		Debriefing

Week 3	Sharing time
	   Author's circles
	     Literature groups
	       Curriculum models
		Debriefing

Week 4	Sharing time
	   Author's circles
	     Literature groups
	       Curriculum models
		Debriefing

Week 5	Sharing time
	   Discuss field trips
	   Large groups discussion: whole language and phonics
	   Standarized testing discussion
		Interviews

Week 6	Sharing time
	   Whole group generation of topics/responsibilities
	   for remaining sessions
	     Strategy workshop
		Debriefing

Week 7	Sharing time
	   Authoring cycle: Experience #2. Predictable Books
	     Discuss pen pal projects
	       Basal Reader presentation
		Debriefing

Week 8	Sharing time
	   "People's Choice": One-on-one chats
	Research groups. Author's circles
	       Presentation: Denise Ogren
		Debriefing

Week 9	Sharing time
	   "People's Choice": One-on-one chats
	Research groups. Author's circles
	     Human Development Activity
		Debriefing

Week 10	Sharing time
	"People's Choice": One-on-one chats
	   Literature circles. Author's circles
	   Research groups
	     Holistic scoring of writing
		Debriefing

Week 11	Sharing time
	"People's Choice": One-on-one chats
	   Author's circles. Research groups
	   Editing groups
	     Mock job interviews
		Debriefing

Week 12	Large group presentation of research projects	Interviews

FIGURE 11   Major seminar events

STRATEGIES FOR FOCUSED REFLECTION

Although we, as teacher educators, cannot direct reflectivity, we can provide the encouragement, conditions, and time for it. The first and simplest function of reflective practice is making connections. We do this daily, moment by moment, as we constantly make sense of our experiences and sort incoming information. Focused and purposeful reflection, however, takes this natural learning strategy to a conscious level and gives students more control over their learning.

A Learner's Insight of the Teaching Process: Making Connections

Connections were often made during discussion groups. A lively interaction would spark new ideas and provide links between events that at first seemed unconnected. Students' own reflections on college classroom experiences pulled together information for them and provided a broader framework for thinking. For example, Joy's new insights were based on her own response to authors' circles in Sharon's college classroom:

> We [her fifth-grade field experience classroom] did authors' circles. The kids were just like we [in our college classroom] were—really hesitant to say anything and a little bit nervous about sharing what they had to say. It's funny. If we hadn't done it first and I hadn't seen that we were a little bit nervous about saying anything, I might have been more critical of that. I might have said, "Doesn't anybody have anything to say?" Instead, I said, "Maybe next time you'll feel more comfortable saying these things. It will just take a while." I thought that was so enlightening to see that.

Being reflective about her own firsthand learning experiences gave Joy a learner's insight on the teaching process. This insight provided information for building curriculum and a broadened perspective on the learning processes of her students.

Gail documented the kinds of student actions that show connections between her course themes, such as self-selection of topics, off-stage rehearsing of writing, impact of audience on writing, and the student's own understanding of these principles through firsthand experience.

Sharing the Power of Community: Reflective Journals

Reflective journals are notebooks for the recording of insights, questions, and personal connections with reading, writing, and class events. [Students are encouraged not to use noncommittal words like *interesting* and *enjoyable* but to take a stance and express an opinion.]

Kim began Sharon's course confident that she could read about or learn from Sharon everything she needed to know for successful completion of the course. Initially, she saw little value in sharing her ideas in writing or in classroom discussion because she felt she had little to contribute. An early entry in Kim's journal shows a change in attitude. She commented not only on the power of reflection itself but also on her connections to her future students:

> I wrote my first story about my uncle's farm. It was a descriptive story. I kept myself at arm's length from the person and the place. Now I'm writing about an episode in my life. I remember my third grade in school. Some kids started the "I Hate Kim Club." I was upset for months. I didn't want to go to school. It's scary reflecting that deeply. I'm seeing how much I myself learn from this process and I can imagine its impact on younger learners. . . . I felt funny sharing my stories at first. Under pressure, I guess. But after a few times you begin to realize there is really no threat and you still have ultimate control over your story. You're the author.

The sense of community in the classroom and the shared writing opportunities allowed Kim to leave behind a safe topic and reach out for something riskier but more meaningful. Like Joy in the earlier example, Kim began to reflect on her own learning processes, and this reflection brought insight to her future teaching.

The students also recognized Sharon's struggles with her teaching as she tried to live what she thought was the best model for teaching and learning. Students' experiences of seeing themselves on tape paralleled her own. Evidence of those comparisons was recorded in their journals. For instance, Kim wrote at midterm:

> I saw my videotape today. It was really valuable watching myself. I act on tape as though I have so much to get done that I'll never be able to manage it. Also I felt I needed to sometimes look at the children more than I was. Sometimes I seemed preoccupied with trying to write down what one child just said and listen to another child's question. Next time I'll just tape so I don't write down "in real words" what their "scribbling" says. What we demonstrate is not necessarily what we want children to learn. Sound familiar?

In-Class Reflections: Rear Windows on Our Learning

In-class reflections are ten- to fifteen-minute free-writing periods—invitations for students and the instructor to struggle with some new thoughts on a topic or to make sense of changes in their thinking on a previously discussed issue. Inspiration for these in-class reflections can come from many directions. For example, one day on the way to class, it occurred to Sharon that one of the biggest blocks to change and growth is fear: fear of looking foolish, fear of losing control in the classroom, fear of not meeting administrative guidelines, and so forth.

Sharon developed an experience she called "Nightmares in My Closet" (after Mercer Mayer's [1968] book about a child who is afraid of what might be in his closet). After reading the book, Sharon invited the pre- and inservice teachers to write down for themselves the kinds of pressures and fears that keep them from trying new things in their classrooms:

Preservice Teachers' Nightmares

Fear of not getting a job.
Fear of failure, of not living up to expectations.

Fear of negatively influencing child's attitude about school.

Fear of lack of preparation for teaching.

Fear of not getting "the big picture" for all this information about teaching.

Fear of not feeling the freedom to ask questions.

Fear of not having control in the classroom.

Fear of limits and restrictions on my teaching by the school principal.

Inservice Teachers' Nightmares

Fear of what other teachers think about my teaching.

Fear of turning children off school.

Fear of not being accepted by other teachers if I do something different.

Fear of comparison to other teachers at my grade level.

Fear of state tests dictating my curriculum.

These "nightmares" became an interesting set of orienting questions or issues on which students continued to focus, consciously or unconsciously, throughout the semester. Sharon didn't recognize this phenomenon until she looked at the journals, interviews, and reflections of individual students from the whole semester. This longitudinal view of a learner's thinking can clue the instructor to fears that may block a student's growth and becomes a kind of portfolio of reflection. The instructor and more experienced reflector can then provide individual support, discussion, and readings to help students deal with those fears.

In-class reflections also give us opportunities to critique our past ideas. For example, during a reflection period in Sharon's class, students were asked to look back at some early "Where We Are" documents they had written and reflect on them in light of their current thinking. Kim wrote:

> Boy, it's interesting to look back, isn't it? We should have to do it more often . . . to realize how much information we've taken in. . . . I hope I've come a step since this "Where We Are" document. . . . I said at the beginning of this course I wanted to know how to motivate children in the area of written and oral expression. I think first-grade field experience this semester was helpful in this in some ways. . . . I really realized that the skill itself isn't the essential matter, but the feelings and reasoning behind the act of writing.

Kim's recorded thoughts gave her a reference point. Because of the in-class reflections, she was able to focus on the evolution of her thinking. At midterm she wrote,

> I understand why you had us observe in the nursery school classroom early in the semester. It was good for me to absorb what we have been learning in class and in turn look at not only this observational experience but at others as well with a more critical eye.

Reflective Questioning: Transacting as Author and Audience

Reflective questions are developed by the instructor (or gleaned from other sources) and posed in the group with the intent of sparking critical thinking about course events and assignments. Reflective questioning gave Gail's students a chance to consider how they were becoming better writers with the support of the classroom community and how they were applying the underlying theoretical principles of the course. During the first few sessions, the whole group served as an audience "receiving the writing" (Graves 1983, p. 16) that an author volunteered to read. Later, students broke into small groups so that all of them could experience being both author and audience. Notes from Gail's class journal taken in a midsemester session demonstrate this writing community:

> The author had been reading a line or two from the piece she had just written. A member of the audience interrupts: "Oh, I can't wait to hear this!" Others in the group joined in with laughter—good collegiality tonight. Later in the session, another student apologized to the group for her disorganized piece. Others disagreed after she read it and told her why. One said, "To me, it's as if she's having a conversation with herself." There was much laughing and comfortable talk among students tonight—a sense of a writing community developing.

Each time before they began, Gail's class talked about the role and responses of the audience and the author. More important, sometime during or at the end of this activity, the group was asked questions: "Why are we doing this?" "Why is this important?" "How does your experience here influence what you do in your own classroom?"

In Sharon's class, the question, "Why is this process of sharing our writing important?" was highlighted for the whole class the day that her students were sharing their family stories as part of a theme study on family issues. Sharon had written a piece about her grandmother's house. She read aloud:

> Grandma's house was dark and quiet, curtains closed and blinds pulled to keep out the heat. I sat quietly in the dining room, dusting each little figurine in the china cabinet.

The piece touched a common chord in most of the listeners, and students began recounting descriptions of their own grandparents' homes. Sharon's eyes lit up when Bill recalled the "old clock on my grandmother's mantle." Her revised piece concluded:

> Grandma is gone now and so is the house with its calm, quiet, secret places. The china cabinet sits in my aunt's dining room now, exactly as it did at Grandma's, its dusted memories receding further into the past. The clock is there, too, but it doesn't keep time anymore.

"Now it's perfect," she said when she read the piece to the group. Not only was the value of sharing our writing brought home, but the students also recognized that every writer (including the college professor) struggles with ideas, revision, and writing to an audience. Listening to others provides ideas for improving our writing.

Other questions asked at appropriate moments enable us to become aware of how we learn about writing:

- Did you think about the writing you would do in class while you were not here?

- How did you choose the topic you wrote about? (This strategy is repeated periodically because the learners' strategies in choosing topics will change and evolve.)
- Looking at your drafts, what can you learn about how you write?
- For you as a writer, is revision a continuous process?
- Did you learn something or clarify something you did not know you knew so clearly until you discovered it through writing (Murray 1984)?
- How did audience response influence your thinking?
- Why did you decide to add or change something?
- As a participant in a community of learners, are you sensing that some of your interests and strengths are being identified and affirmed by the group?
- Is working with your peers helpful to you in this process? Why or why not?

Receiving Audience Talk: The Instructor's In-Process Journal

If you walked into our classes during group time (literature circles, authors' circles, invitations to try reading/writing strategies) you would often see us jotting notes in a journal as we walked around the class. We record comments and conversations to discuss with students and to make their learning visible. We point out demonstrated theory that helps to bridge the gaps in students' knowledge.

For example, after a few sessions of modeling "receiving the writing" (Graves 1983) with the whole class, we form small groups so that more authors have the opportunity to experience peer response. We circulate, observe, listen, and make notes. We quote students' responses.

As our community of learners was becoming established during early sessions, authors tended to be apologetic, tentative, or even apprehensive. One author said, "Mine is housewifey stuff," and another, after reading aloud, said, "Okay, tear it apart," and still another, "I poured my whole heart out tonight." In the beginning, audience responses tend to be general: "I liked the part about . . ." As the sessions continued and the trust among participants built, their skills as authors and responders increased markedly. The focus remained on the ideas and content of writing, but the developing authors became aware of their style and form as well. One author said, "I noticed I've been using the same lead for every piece. Tonight I chose a new way to begin." Another was aware she could develop her thinking through writing: "I have lots of thoughts here, and they are disorganized . . . but I know I can revise." A third wrote a note to himself at the bottom of his piece: "I need a better closing, more summary, and reflection." Still another was aware of repeating certain words and knew in revision she would find more expressive ones. This audience talk, jotted down in Gail's in-process journal, became the substance of whole group discussion as the class refined their concept of audience influence.

Reflective Papers: Summarizing Experience

Reflective papers are consolidating experiences, written at midterm, the end of semester, or other logical points. Stefanie, a preservice teacher, was rethinking her ideas about early literacy. In this excerpt, she makes the connections between early writing experience, the kindergarten curriculum in her inservice teacher's classroom, and the content of her pen pal's letters:

> I can see many benefits of this pen pal project. . . . I found myself looking for strategies that would lead my pen pal, Annie, to write more content in her letters.
>
> . . . From this project I have found myself wanting to know much more about how children progress to such different writing levels when they are roughly the same age.
>
> I do think that the amount of writing experience they have at the early grades plays a major part in these differences. When I look at the written conversations and mailbox messages that are done in the kindergarten classroom, I see how very important these activities are. I have begun to look more closely at them than I did at the beginning of the year.

Stefanie's reflections on her pen pal project led her back in her thinking to view earlier experiences during the semester with new appreciation and insight.

CONCLUSIONS

Reflection is an act of temporary closure and often a much-needed sense of documenting one's growth. Reflective practice provides a pause in the complexity of classroom interaction and rigorous thinking. Reflective strategies have made us more aware of our responsibility as college instructors to provide environments that demand thoughtful, critical reflections on learning. We are convinced that the implementation of reflective strategies in the college classroom sets in motion a process that redefines teaching and learning at all levels. Our personal classroom goals have been broadened. First, we are seeking more than an improved affective dimension of teaching and learning, more than democratic practice. We want college classrooms to become dynamic contexts for theory development. Telling your theories does little to bring students into active involvement with their own ideas. Doing your theories does much. Second, our views of research have shifted. We want teacher educators to recognize the potential for research in the study of their own pedagogy right at hand in their classrooms. Third, we want to see the impact of practical theory. As our students become more aware of how they themselves learn, we want their own practices to reflect the strategies and structures that help children understand how they learn. We want critical thinking, introspection, and theory making about good teaching.

We have followed a number of our students, both preservice and inservice teachers, back to their classrooms. We have seen literature circles, process writing, journals, and learning teams in action—processes that have grown out of our own willingness to practice reflective strategies in the college classroom. Joy's description of a "lesson" for herself and the children in her field experience classroom exemplifies the ongoing and generative nature of reflective practice:

> The [fifth-grade] kids were supposed to write on a subject suggested by the school principal for National Education Week: "Why people need education and why

education needs people." The kids were really unmotivated. They decided they wanted to do things as a group.

We split the kids into two groups. I had half the kids and the subject, "Why education needs people." The kids in my group brainstormed first. Then I asked them to write some ideas down and share them. We talked about the ideas in an authoring-cycle-type way and then put them together. I felt like I should mediate, direct, or organize the discussion at first (shades of Professor Andrews!). I guess I was playing teacher too much. Then I quickly realized that wasn't working and I gave them more freedom. In the end, they seemed to be doing well without me, so I left them to work on their own.

It was interesting to see the way their thinking went on a difficult topic. At first their ideas were weak and didn't fit together—the kids were clearly only there to get the assignment over with. But by sticking to it, they kept adding little bits and pieces together. They read it over and over. Then one more time they read it and it all seemed to fall together. They knew just the way they wanted it. That's when I left them alone to iron out the details.

I really felt good about this "lesson." I feel that it was a learning experience for both me and the kids.

In the same way that Sharon had demonstrated how to give students freedom in the college classroom, Joy was learning to let go and trust the learners in her own classroom.

We have seen movement toward reflective practice in public schools because teachers have experienced such practice in our college classrooms. We have seen connections between teacher reflectiveness and teachers' confidence in themselves as learners. We have seen children become aware of how they learn, recognize what works for them as learners, take ownership of their learning, and develop better control of the signs and symbols of language. We have seen children value social interaction and peer response, become more supportive, humane, and responsive, and establish a stake in each others' learning because their teachers have experienced this themselves and have learned how to set up classrooms that provide a context for reflective practice.

Lectures are efficient modes for dispensing information, and a good lecturer can inspire respect for the topic, entertain, enthrall, and truly provide content. But pedagogy is not the science of information retrieval, nor is it entertaining the troops. Pedagogy is teaching students how they learn so that they can apply those processes in other situations. The teacher who helps students discover their own knowledge, abilities, and learning processes creates powerful and generative environments.

REFERENCES

Barnes, D. 1976. *From Communication to Curriculum*. New York: Penguin.
Graves, D. H. 1983. *Writing: Teachers and Children at Work*. Portsmouth, NH: Heinemann.

Heine, D. 1988. "A Sociosemiotic Perspective of Learning: Teaching Learning and Curriculum Exploration Through Collaboration." Unpublished doctoral dissertation, Indiana University, Bloomington, IN.

Lortie, D. 1975. *Schoolteacher: A Sociological Study*. Chicago: University of Chicago Press.

Mayer, M. 1968. *There's a Nightmare in My Closet*. New York: Dial.

Murray, D. 1984. *Write to Learn*. New York: Holt, Rinehart, and Winston.

Schon, D. 1987. *Educating the Reflective Practitioner*. San Francisco: Jossey-Bass.

Short, K. G., J. C. Harste, and C. Burke. 1996. *Creating Classrooms for Authors and Inquirers*. Portsmouth, NH: Heinemann.

Watson, D. J., J. C. Harste, and C. Burke. 1989. *Whole Language: Inquiring Voices*. New York: Scholastic.

MISCUE ANALYSIS: A MEDIATOR IN THE DEVELOPMENT OF A PHILOSOPHY OF LITERACY

Virginia W. Juettner

All of us construct our literacy beliefs based on personal experiences, interpretations, connections, and assimilated ideas. Creating a learning environment that focuses on the decisions and beliefs of emerging teachers provides a rich context for building personal beliefs about literacy. What guides an emerging teacher's development, and how do you know if they really understand the reading process and connections to literacy learning? In this chapter, I discuss an undergraduate course I taught, and analyze and describe several class activities that promoted the construction of personal belief systems using miscue analysis as a key activity to mediate understanding and development of theory.

CONTEXT FOR DEVELOPMENT OF THEORETICAL BELIEFS ABOUT LITERACY

My course, the last the students took before student teaching, was organized so that "emerging teachers" were encouraged to think like teachers. Class assignments stressed choice, reflective thinking, intellectual commitment, and teaching responsibility. Each assignment had some purpose and function important to the role of an emerging teacher. Throughout, students decided for themselves what made sense and how to present their beliefs based on a developing literacy schema: their personal understanding of literacy and the reading process.

During the first half of the semester, students learned about literacy theory, methods, practice, and evaluation, and they explored their own beliefs. A midterm experience provided an opportunity for synthesizing and organizing ideas and experiences, and a portfolio project asked students to think about their beliefs and practices. The crucial activity, however, was miscue analysis.

Miscue analysis is a process for analyzing responses to text based on the reader's use of the semantic, syntactic, and graphophonic cue systems (K. Goodman 1994). By analyzing oral reading samples and their retellings, students learn that readers' deviations from the text are not errors but miscues that occur as students bring their linguistic knowledge and strategies to the task of reading. They develop a constructive view of the student's reading that enables them to design literacy events and assess growth continuously.

The various class activities promoted the development of a personal belief system, but I also used the assignments to identify students' current beliefs, document growth in individuals and the group, and examine whether we could develop expectations for assessing the literacy growth of emerging teachers.

BELIEFS AND CONCEPTS IN THE BEGINNING

The TORP

To begin our discussions on reading instruction, I asked students to agree or disagree with statements on the DeFord Theoretical Orientation to Reading Profile (TORP), a survey of reading attitudes and beliefs (DeFord 1985). Statements in the TORP are organized to reflect a range of beliefs about reading from subskills to whole language models (see Protocol/Engagement B-7 for additional uses of the TORP).

During the first class, students completed the profile individually, then discussed their responses in a group and came to consensus. The individual responses were compiled and a class profile developed. The forced format required students to make a commitment and then defend their choice or negotiate a new choice during the group discussions.

Our discussions about the TORP were spirited, with strong beliefs expressed in some areas and tentative, qualified opinions in others. The groups used their collective opinions to come to consensus on many items; however, the survey definitely created the need to know more. Students continually asked me for the "right" answer to various items. About a third of the class did not return the TORP because they were unsure of their responses and did not feel comfortable turning in a survey without knowing "the" answers. The general opinion was that there was one right way to respond. Students stated that they did not have knowledge of reading instruction; thus, it was unfair to ask them to complete the survey. They felt it was my job to tell them how to teach reading. This attitude was at odds with the strong views they expressed in our discussions. The dissonance was characterized by my attempts to learn what they were really thinking and their attempts to provide the expected or "correct" response.

The TORP indicated opinions at all ranges of the scale for most of the items. There were no group or individual patterns that revealed an obvious reading belief system or knowledge of miscue analysis. Opinions ranged widely among individuals. Over half of the students agreed with six items that reflect a subskills model of reading. The strongest response of the class (93 percent) was agreement with the statement, "When children do not know a word, they should be instructed to sound it out." Other responses with high agreement included:

Fluency and expression are necessary components of reading and indicate comprehension: 83 percent.

Dividing words into syllables is helpful for reading new words (instruction): 65 percent.

Dictionaries are necessary in determining the meaning/pronunciation of new words: 64 percent.

Readers need to be introduced to the root form of words before reading inflected forms: 64 percent.

It is important to teach skills in relation to other skills: 64 percent.

Over 50 percent of the students disagreed with three items:

It is a sign of an ineffective reader when words and phrases are repeated: 64 percent.

Some problems in reading are caused by readers dropping the inflectional endings from words: 55 percent.

If a child says "house" for the written word "home," the response should be left uncorrected: 58 percent.

Some took the least threatening path and responded in the middle, "neither agree nor disagree," which suggested students were unsure, didn't know, or were unwilling to risk taking a stand.

Students' TORP statements reflect common practices in the classroom, practices possibly experienced by these undergraduate students when they were in elementary school. In the group discussion, students referred to past reading experiences in school or at home to support their opinions. For some students, there was a dissonance between how they learned to read at home and their views on how reading should be taught in school. One student described learning to read at home from a parent who read to her daily but defended her survey response in terms of teaching a phonics-first approach in school. It seemed as if students were willing to suspend what they knew about learning from daily experience and accept vastly different approaches due to their perceptions about what emerging teachers are expected to believe.

The TORP served as an awareness-building exercise, one that developed a need to know more about literacy theory and practice. It reflected beginning beliefs about the reading process and helped to establish one piece of baseline information from which the students and I could observe growth.

Quick Write

After the discussion, students wrote for fifteen minutes on their personal beliefs about the reading process. The opportunity to talk about beliefs, listen to new perspectives, find some agreement among their peers, and think about the issues made this an easier task than the TORP. I summarized these belief statements and put them into categories.

Thirty-three statements stressed the importance of interest, motivation, and knowledge of the reading topic. Prior experience was listed eleven times, more than any other factor. Ten responses focused on phonics and reading strategies, although the beliefs about phonics ranged from "phonics is the basis from which you learn to read," to "can be helpful with unfamiliar words." Nine responses mentioned "immersion in books and language." Other beliefs were mentioned only a few times.

These responses indicated that students entered the class with a wide range of ideas and beliefs and that there were few common beliefs about the reading process, with the exception of a belief that motivation and interest in reading are important. Even in this area, three students did not mention motivation and interest in their quick writes.

Individual students varied widely in the number of beliefs expressed and in the conceptual connectivity of their ideas. For example, John stated that reading instruction needs to be interesting and that reading is a complex process—two conceptually unconnected statements. Several students wrote lists of beliefs without attempting to express any connections or relationships among their ideas. However, there were students who did cluster their beliefs based on personal, logical connections. Anne indicated that "meaning and context are part of reading" and that teachers should use familiar material that the child understands. The statements together indicate relational knowledge of personal understanding, prior experience, and meaning in text. Beginning concepts related to miscue analysis were found in some of the quick writes. Two students made reference to the three cueing systems, and ten students mentioned prediction, use of context clues, and prior knowledge as strategies for reading.

The quick writes, along with the TORP, provided insight into the beginning beliefs and orientations of each student. These emerging teachers had pieces but no whole about how reading works, and they were most tentative in their beliefs.

BUILDING A PERSONAL BELIEF SYSTEM: THE MISCUE PROJECT

The central strategy employed during the semester to develop awareness of existing beliefs and build upon the existing belief system was miscue analysis. It was taught as both a process and a model for thinking about what occurs during reading and as an approach for collecting and analyzing information on the reading of students. As such, miscue analysis took emerging teachers from theory to practice and then back to theory as they analyzed their miscue samples, drew conclusions about their student's literacy development, and integrated this information into their growing schemas on literacy and language.

I introduced the miscue project early in the semester with the Goodman model of the reading process (1994), using examples that demonstrated each cueing system. After discussing the theoretical model, students learned how to mark miscues on typescripts. They practiced coding miscues by listening to audiotapes of student miscue sessions. Students used the procedures from *Reading Miscue Inventory* (Goodman, Watson, and Burke 1987) to collect a student's reading and retelling. For the analysis of miscues I introduced them to Procedure I (Goodman, Watson, and Burke 1987) and *Reading Process and Practice* (Weaver 1988). They also did a reading attitude survey as part of the process.

By the time the miscue project began, students had read and discussed literacy theory. They had observed and worked in classrooms and had many questions about the differences between what they saw in schools and what was advocated in class. At the time the projects were implemented, students were ready to confirm their beliefs—ready to accept or reject their evolving ideas based on the miscue experience.

We spent a full day coding and analyzing their samples. Using their analysis, students developed a one- to two-page summary of what they had learned about the reading of their subject (Kemp 1987). After presenting their miscue projects in class, the students shared their results with the readers' classroom teachers.

All of the lectures during the semester did not equal that one experience working with a child and learning how to view reading through the eyes and mind of a learner. It was here that emerging teachers realized what was involved in the process of reading and began constructing their models of literacy. Although we had lengthy class discussions about the miscue analysis assignment, the impact of miscue analysis on literacy beliefs was revealed in the assignments that followed the miscue project.

MIDTERM BELIEFS AND CONCEPTS

The students completed a midterm assessment designed as a first-draft writing experience, one they were expected to rework by the end of the semester. They developed a semantic map of their beliefs about the reading process and how literacy develops, and then they wrote a philosophy of literacy statement.

In order to document change and learning, the midterm philosophy statements were compiled in the same manner as the quick writes using the statements of students to develop the categories. I determined frequency of similar response counts for the twenty-two students in the class that revealed several changes from the beginning of the semester. Although the numbers of statements and categories were about the same, the concepts about reading changed considerably. Students moved from talking about motivation and interest in reading in the first quick write (thirty-three statements) to concepts related to meaningful, relevant contexts for learning (nine statements), real-life reasons and purposes for reading (twelve statements), and specific characteristics of the learning environment (twenty-eight statements) including the freedom to take risks (fourteen). Students identified specific conditions related to motivation and interest and discussed how these conditions fit into their personal beliefs about literacy. The importance of prior knowledge and early language development was mentioned twenty-four times, and statements about "learning from whole to part" increased from three to twenty, as did "learning to read and write is a natural process" (four to seventeen). Nine students mentioned schema building in children and its relationship to language learning.

Twenty-five statements referring to some aspect of miscue analysis were included in the philosophies, with seventeen specific references to, "The reading process involves the use of three cueing systems: graphophonic, syntax, semantics." This was the largest number of responses for a single statement of belief on the midterm. Other statements (eighteen responses) focused on the importance of meaning, including prediction, confirming, and self-correction strategies. Only one student in the group failed to make any reference to Goodman's model or concepts demonstrated through miscue analysis.

Midterm responses revealed more specific knowledge of literacy and learning and the emergence of relationships in organizing beliefs. Not only were student responses more numerous in both the number of statements made by individuals and in response to specific statements, but the class became more cohesive, firm, and specific in their beliefs. Most students moved from list making to building relationships between literacy concepts. At the beginning of the term, there were contradictions in beliefs and widely varying beliefs about the reading process. Students were not sure of their beliefs. The midterm reflected an orientation toward a whole language philosophy, although there remained variations in the personal belief patterns of students.

The midterm clearly indicated where each student stood in terms of literacy development, miscue connections, and building a personal belief system. The differences in growth became more pronounced for some, particularly those who had not acquired many of the concepts important to understanding literacy development. Looking at a summary of the concepts discussed in the midterm gave me direction for working with individuals. This list became a benchmark that was used to evaluate both student growth and effectiveness of instruction at the end of the semester.

INDIVIDUAL PROFILE OF GROWTH IN LITERACY BELIEFS

The changes that occurred in the class as a whole are reflected in Mary, one of the more mature students. She had worked outside the field of education and had a family before enrolling in school. Like many other parents of school-aged children, she came to the class with ideas about how children should be taught to read and expressed her views openly during class discussions. On the first night of class, her quick write revealed that Mary had had a difficult time with reading in school:

> I learned to read in elem. school, early 1950's. No, I was not a good reader. Actually I did not learn to read efficiently until college. Perseverance and desire made me a good reader, and also a pair of glasses—bifocals specifically.

Mary did much of her thinking on paper, submitting many pages of learning log entries each week. She learned by examining issues raised in class, reflecting on past experiences, and coming to some conclusions in the process. She was not shy about expressing opinions and challenging ideas discussed in class. The following excerpt was written prior to the second week of class:

> It's been so long since I learned to read I had forgotten many things. For example, that small children learn to read within their environments, such as reading McDonalds signs. Of course, I thought to myself, as I remembered things like selecting my favorite cereals and stuff while shopping with mom. Why else would TV advertisers spend money to educate the wee-public on what to influence mom to buy, if they couldn't recognize a product. Thus reading is largely symbolic thinking. Pre-school vocabulary tests consist of generic pictures of houses, kitties and the like.

I have not changed my opinion via this new schema or revelation, nor the group discussion re: the questionnaire, one iota (sp?) with regards to the idea that children need to learn the alphabet in order to learn to read. I believe that it is necessary to beginning a reading schema. How can one program a computer without symbols to program it with? Then, new knowledge builds and grows out from the basic fundamentals.

I am still strong about phonics and being able to make sense of sounds.

Mary was searching for connections through her writing and used writing to sort through ideas. She was aware of her existing beliefs and was seeking to understand new knowledge in light of these beliefs. Her writing, in response to the TORP and class discussions, indicated support for a phonics approach to reading using a traditional part-to-whole model of reading development. In this entry she articulated her rationale for her belief making it clear that she wasn't accepting my beliefs about reading, even though her first paragraph was about how she started reading through environmental print. However, Mary was beginning to have thoughts that would come into conflict with her current beliefs.

Exploration of her own early learning indicated a willingness to tackle new ideas within the context of her own experience and demonstrated new learning. Here was a thinker with existing schemas who would challenge, question, probe, and explore to develop her beliefs.

The next entry occurred about five weeks into the semester and revealed, as Mary puts it, a new perspective:

First, and mostly, I've learned about how much more of a mental process reading is, rather than a simple skill. When I think about it in this new perspective it really does make sense. The research results and examples clarify and exemplify lots of things you could even say you somehow knew innately. When you consciously try to observe yourself reading you can almost catch yourself predicting. You don't read road signs, but you are conscious of the context much of the time. The colors prime your awareness categories as well. And when you read music it is within a certain context and you are predicting as you are reading as well. I don't "think" C, F, A, D, etc. And it explains why some people get more out of a reading than others, even though they can operate the grapho/phonic cues just as well. It makes sense that schema is a great part of the reading process.

It is interesting that proficient readers predict, sample, then confirm. I never realized the prediction aspect before, only the sample and confirm part. My mother always told me to read the rest of the sentence, then try to guess what the word should be, and I applied the sample, or phonics approach trying to match the sound to something I've heard in the language, then the context would make sense.

This entry was almost a complete reversal of belief as compared with the first learning log entry. At this point in the class, we had introduced miscue analysis, which can be seen in Mary's discussion of prediction, sampling, confirming, and the cueing systems. Class discussion of theory and research had changed Mary's vantage point for viewing the development of literacy. She expressed her new understanding of how skills fit into the larger perspective of language learning. Mary wrote to pull together these ideas and to relate and confirm what she was learning with her experiences.

Both learning log samples indicate Mary's ability to relate concepts and build schemas prior to the midterm. She had reorganized her beginning beliefs using the miscue theoretical framework to accommodate existing knowledge and experience and assimilate new ideas. Mary used writing as a vehicle for thinking through ideas and making connections.

At the end of the semester, Mary submitted the required philosophy of literacy. An excerpt shows how she followed her own path in developing a personal philosophy and exemplifies her inclination for using theory, schemas, and concepts to make broad connections:

> Literacy occurs in children, in my opinion, in much the same manner as they acquire other basic forms of communication such as speaking, listening, or decoding visual cues like body language. It happens out of needs, the need to understand, to obtain, and to be expressed.
>
> Anyone who knows very small children has more than likely seen how precocious and sophisticated their predicting, sampling, and confirming strategies can be when they desire to obtain, and that is to say, to obtain everything from ice cream to attention. The more successful they are, the more they learn, and the faster they learn, the more success they achieve. It is ultimately natural.
>
> It follows then, that the more literary experiences they are able to have, the broader will be their learning base. The more increased their understanding becomes, the more they will be able to relate to, to remember and retain, to identify with and communicate about, and the more they will desire to learn—if, and only if, it is made meaningful for them. This means that they must be encouraged to learn about what is relevant to them, as it pertains to their world view and experiences. We can only hope as teachers to give them positive experiences, and to open the doors to the world at large, not to select or contain what they will learn in school, but allow them to choose their own way . . . .
>
> Today there is so much more information than ever before. How can one decide which knowledge to teach, or which information is correct? We can't. But, we can focus on how we know, what processes guide our thinking, and develop resourcefulness to find out that which we seek to know, and be given the opportunity to entertain ideas, and to change our way of thinking based on new information, and to strive for improvement, not perfection. Children learn by creating, making, doing, and by trial and error. They will learn to read by reading and being read to, and to write by the act of doing so meaningfully . . . .

Mary uses concepts of cue systems and reading strategies as descriptive of a single reading process to include the child's approach to constructing meaning, meeting needs, and learning throughout life. She expands her literacy philosophy to discuss concepts of democracy and life-long learning strategies, again using her knowledge and experience to confirm and validate her beliefs. She ends her literacy philosophy by stating that a whole language environment will support the development of "liberty, and justice, appreciation and acceptability for all." Mary has gone considerably beyond literacy philosophy to discuss her personal worldview.

Mary's ability to develop and articulate a personal philosophy is related to her internal system of belief and meaning, her strategies for learning, and the experiences afforded her during the semester, particularly miscue analysis. The framework for viewing the reading process made sense to Mary, who took what she already knew, rejected the ideas that no longer made sense, and incorporated the concepts that supported her evolving belief system. Miscue analysis was used as a schema for thinking about other theories, experiences, and beliefs, all the while using her life as a reality check to ask, "Does that make sense within my experience?"

THE IMPORTANCE OF PERSONAL BELIEF SYSTEMS

In *Learning Change* (1990), Lester and Onore emphasize the importance of a philosophy of instruction. They offer as examples the "language and learning policies" developed by Australian and British schools. They believe that schools in the United States lack a unified purpose. Lack of a philosophy leads to vulnerability, inability to assess the merits of various approaches, and eclecticism, where variety in methodology is valued over all other considerations.

As teacher educators we must stress the importance of a belief system for emerging and practicing teachers to use in making decisions about instruction. Conversely, discussions of curriculum and methodology should occur in a literacy learning environment that fosters belief system development. We should no longer discuss whether to teach phonics but instead explore the importance of phonics within developing language and literacy belief systems. The potential of miscue analysis and other similar strategies to provide a framework that supports literacy belief system development is beginning to be realized as we observe the construction of personal theory in emerging teachers.

REFERENCES

DeFord, D. 1985. "Validating a Construct: A Theoretical Orientation in Reading Instruction." In *Reading Research Quarterly*, 20, 3: 351–367.

Goodman, K. S. 1994. "Reading, Writing, and Written Text: A Transactional Sociopycholinguistic View." In *Theoretical Models and Processes of Reading* (pp. 1093–1130). R. B. Ruddell, M. R. Ruddell, and H. Singer, eds. Newark, DE: International Reading Association.

Goodman, Y. M., D. J. Watson, and C. Burke. 1987. *Reading Miscue Inventory: Alternative Procedures*. New York: Richard C. Owen.

Kemp, M. 1987. *Watching Children Read and Write*. Melbourne, Victoria: Thomas Nelson Australia.

Lester, N. B., and C. S. Onore. 1990. *Learning Change*. Portsmouth, NH: Heinemann Boynton/Cook.

Weaver, C. 1988. *Reading Process and Practice: From Socio-Psycholinguistics to Whole Language*. Portsmouth, NH: Heinemann.

PROTOCOLS/ENGAGEMENTS

See the introduction to the Protocols/Engagements in Part A for a full explanation of this material (page 61).

B-1 Shoebox Autobiography

MARK W. F. CONDON AND JEAN ANNE CLYDE

Introduction   The Shoebox Autobiography developed by Carolyn Burke and Dorothy Menosky, is a strategy that can be adapted for use by learners of all ages and is especially helpful if introduced during the first few meetings with a new group of learners. After a demonstration by the teacher, learners are invited (perhaps five at a time) to bring in a shoebox, decorated in some way to indicate who they are, that contains a variety of artifacts from their homes and communities. Discussion around these artifacts allows students to indicate their "authority" in ways they feel strongly about and put their values and dreams up for all to enjoy.

This version is supportive of teacher development on three levels. First, it offers a demonstration for students to get to know the culture of the classroom in which they will be spending time. Students come to value the context as a socially supportive one that focuses on the uniquenesses and strengths of the participants. Second, through the demonstration, the teacher is established as a participant alongside the students and as a risk taker and a learner. As a result a climate of trust is created within the classroom. Third, the strategy provides students engagement with the challenges of composition inherent in generating their own autobiographies. In addition, it offers a medium through which they engage and explore their orientation to audience, the development of inferential thinking through concrete manipulatives, and the rigors of the composition process. Finally, it helps students understand how important the role of authority is for authors.

Procedures   The teacher pulls together a collection of items or artifacts that represent who he or she is. The fewer the artifacts there are, the more difficult the challenge is for both the "author" and the audience. The sharing of these items serves as a demonstration of the kinds of articles students may wish to include in their own boxes. The teacher shares stories regarding the significance of each of the items and what it reveals about who she or he is.

Students are invited to bring their boxes to the next class. Through the artifacts that are shared, natural discussions about each person are developed without putting anyone on the spot to talk about himself or herself. The containers typically hold photos, hobby items, tools, toys, favorite art or literature, symbols of religious importance or personal enthusiasms, indications of social roles, teaching relics, and other mementos. The artifacts speak loudly even without the narrative that over time accompanies each one.

Shoeboxes are shared one at a time with the class or as a class exhibit. Selected items can be discussed for their meaning and communicative value (e.g., "How did you decide on that to represent X?"). Small items might be circulated.

The teacher then leads the class in a discussion of the depth of personal meaning that is represented by the collection. The discussions lead to connections among class members and between students and the course content. This experience with concrete artifacts becomes part of the class memory and represents a vivid event in the class memory and is periodically referred to during subsequent class discussions.

Afterword   These are possible variations:

- The teacher takes notes as each student's materials are shared. These notes serve as a basis for discussions later about anecdotal record keeping and subject matter for writing.
- Each person passes his or her box to the person on the left. The receiver reviews its contents and introduces its owner.

B-2 Who's Who?

MARK W. F. CONDON AND JEAN ANNE CLYDE

Introduction   All teachers need to learn to value getting to know their students and peers. "Who's Who" is a "getting to know you" strategy that invites students to explore the use of alternative communication systems as they let teachers and colleagues know who they are.

We invite students to talk about who they are. "Who's Who" emphasizes nonlinguistic avenues of communicating identities. Those whose artistic, mathematical, musical, and other strengths are often overlooked will showcase their personal resources.

Procedures   After the teacher has demonstrated a personal who's who, the students are invited to bring in artifacts over several class sessions that represent some aspect of who they are. The artifacts may be more elaborate than pictures or written prose; students must find ways to use art, drama, math, music, and dance to introduce themselves.

These items are displayed on a bulletin board for all to inspect. Each class member is provided a space, with paper posted in the area so that members of the classroom community can record predictions about the meaning of the various artifacts. Those experiencing difficulty with topic selection in open writing assignments can be encouraged to write the stories on the back of their own artifacts or those of others.

After all of the artifacts have been brought in students engage in an official sharing time, as they explain the significance of each of the items they displayed.

The experience is accompanied by discussions about the challenge of using alternative forms of communication to share who we are. This display highlights the richness of class personalities, develops camaraderie, honors talents and strengths often undiscovered, and celebrates our best efforts to communicate who we are in ways that others will understand.

B-3 Getting to Know You, Getting to Know All About You

JANICE V. KRISTO

Introduction   I first saw this activity while observing in Betty Robinson's fifth-grade classroom, at the Leonard Middle School, Old Town, Maine. Like Betty, I use this activity so that students can learn something about me as a person. This activity has proved to be worthwhile in terms of students knowing something of my interests outside the classroom. It is a way to model the brainstorming of various topics I might write about during our writer's workshop and a good example of an actual teacher demonstration—much more effective than simply talking about or describing the activity.

Procedures   I gather all kinds of artifacts from home that speak to who I am and what my interests are—for example, photos of myself growing up, photos of the family and pets, and pictures from my travels; my shell collection; favorite outside reading; regional cookbooks; poetry that I love; Victorian memorabilia; pictures of the seacoast where I live; my Penobscot Indian baskets; and my camera and binoculars. I display all of these objects on the table and invite students to come up and examine everything. Next, I create the beginning of a web on the board. The centerpiece reads, "Things Jan Kristo Likes." I next invite students to begin building the web by writing information about me from what I have brought in to share.

After the web is completed we list possible topics I might choose to write about, such as:

- My trips to Greece and England.
- What it's like to live on a piece of remote coastline in Maine.
- What my dog means to me.
- The adventures of my crazy stray cat.
- My family.
- My most notable cooking experiences.
- My love of nature.
- Favorite authors and poets.

I ask students to "step out" of this activity and look inside. What do they make of it? What are their reactions? Students report that they thoroughly enjoyed getting a firsthand look at me as a person. I'm more of a person to them now and more human—not just the instructor of the course.

As a next step, they web out things about themselves and brainstorm various topics they can write about in their writing folders. As they share with each other, they come up with writing topics and learn about each other in the process. I suggest to students that they keep a section in their notebooks to record ideas such as this that they would like to try in their classrooms some day.

Students can use this activitiy at any grade level they might teach. It helps students consider that we all have a story to tell, and that there is much from their own lives to write about.

Afterword   When Betty does this activity with students, she asks them to sign up voluntarily to bring in things about themselves to display. Each week focuses on one student.

B-4 Curricular Time Lines

JANET FILES

Introduction   This strategy is grounded on the premise that all learning is social and personal. We know that we cannot learn anything new without connecting it to previously known and personal information. Therefore, I always begin literacy courses by using strategies that activate my graduate students' prior knowledge about their own literary histories and help them reflect on what mattered in supporting or detracting from their learning. We then apply what we learn from these literacy lessons to classroom practice in order to create literacy environments that enhance rather than impede learning.

Procedures   I begin by reading a picture book such as *My Great Aunt Arizona* (1992) by Gloria Houston or Tomie de Paola's *The Art Lesson* (1989). We discuss the literacy lessons that the authors are demonstrating in these stories and how the teacher's actions in the book supported or stifled the author's growth as a learner. We also talk about the concept that who we are today is very evident in who we were as children and how events and people shaped us.

Next I invite the teachers to make a list of three teachers or learning stories that significantly supported or detracted from their growth as a reader, writer, and learner. We share these stories orally in small groups. The groups reflect on what lessons are learned from these stories and compose a list of features that made reading either easy or hard. We share these insights in a large group.

The group constructs personal curricular time lines that show on a scale of −5 to +5 the ten worst and ten best incidents in their learning lives. I request that they not only name the incident but note why it was significant. I often focus them on reading and writing, although the focus can vary according to course content. I share my time line first, as well as those of a few former students, to help them with formatting and to create connections.

The time lines are shared in small groups. The groups help individuals tease out features that made learning hard or easy. We often come up with positive features such as: time to engage in the activity without criticism, supportive response, or risk taking. As a class, we collect these features and discuss how to relate what we have learned from our discussion to our own classroom curriculums.

I often use this as a preliminary engagement to writing a literacy story and literacy lesson or a personal literary history.

References

de Paola, T. 1989. *The Art Lesson*. New York: Trumpet Club.
Houston, G. 1992. *My Great Aunt Arizona*. New York: HarperCollins.

B-5 Literacy Autobiographies

RICHARD J. MEYER

Introduction   By studying their own literacy lives and attitudes in the early part of the semester, students gain insights into themselves as teachers. My goal is for them to focus on themselves as learners and teachers as they begin to understand that their teaching experiences will always be rooted in their learning experiences. To understand how it is we came to be literate is fundamental to understanding the literacy activity in classrooms.

Procedures   We read Graves' *Discover Your Own Literacy* (1990) first. With this book as a point of departure, classroom discussions focus on literacy pasts—both pleasant and unpleasant memories. Next, we brainstorm a list of resources about our own literacy. Someone suggests that each individual is his or her own best resource about literacy development. Others point out that teachers, parents, siblings, friends, family members, and other significant people are also good sources. We discuss the types of questions one might ask about someone's literacy development.

I provide copies of the Burke interview (Goodman, Watson, and Burke 1987) and the surveys Nancie Atwell (1987) uses with her students. I give the students some time in class to start to write their earliest recollections of their own literacy. Each piece of the past seems to generate new questions: Who did you write notes to? Why? Do you remember the first thing you wrote or read? What was your favorite book? What were your family's reading habits? Were you read to each night? If so, by whom?

Some students go home and rummage through basements, closets, garages, and attics to find artifacts as evidence of the way they came to be readers and writers. Some of the class members are genuinely disappointed to find that their parents didn't save every worksheet and painting from their first years of school (especially when they have classmates whose parents saved these precious relics).

The due date for this project turns into a powerful community builder for the class. The students read their literacy autobiographies in small groups. For many, this is a surprise because they have rarely, if ever, read their own writing out loud. I ask them to read their work verbatim in order for others in their small group to hear how their colleagues write. After an individual has read, the "rules" are less strict and I encourage them to engage in conversation about what has been read. The class members take their journals to the autobiography reading so that they can make notes about other recollections that occur to them while a colleague is reading. The autobiographies are referred to frequently throughout the semester as the students fit together their lives and their responsibilities as literacy educators.

Afterword   Literacy autobiographies can be published in an anthology of writing by the class. Students can be encouraged to challenge themselves by writing in a new genre. Plays, choral readings, poetry, and short stories can be shared in an author reading at an end-of-the-semester social gathering.

References

Atwell, N. 1987. *In the Middle: Writing, Reading, and Learning with Adolescents.* Portsmouth, NH: Heinemann.

Goodman, Y. M., D. J. Watson, and C. L. Burke. 1987. *Reading Miscue Inventory: Alternative Procedures.* New York: Richard C. Owen.

Graves, D. H. 1990. *Discover Your Own Literacy.* Portsmouth, NH: Heinemann.

B-6 Examining Your Own Writing Process

STEPHEN B. KUCER

Introduction   Based on years of instruction (or misinstruction), students have strong views about the writing process and what good writers do when they put pen to paper. Not surprisingly, the notion that they themselves might be competent writers is difficult for students to accept. This demonstration helps students understand the writing process in light of their own writing behavior.

Procedures   Students are asked to write an essay on their hopes and/or fears about student teaching. Because these students will be student teaching within five weeks of this assignment, the topic is of special relevance and interest to them. Students use the following format when they write:

My hopes and/or fears about student teaching	*My thinking processes*

As they write their essays on the left-hand side of the paper, the students are asked to monitor what they are thinking about writing and to record these thoughts on the right-hand side where and when they occur. Typical thoughts are: "I reread what I wrote and decided it didn't make sense"; "I discovered something new that I wanted to say"; "I wasn't sure what to write next"; "I realized that I needed to reorder my ideas."

Because I also use this piece of writing to introduce writing conferencing, it is important that students produce a fairly complete draft. Because of time limitations, I usually introduce the demonstration in class, give the students some time to get started and ask any questions, and then ask them to complete the essay at home.

After drafts are complete, students share their thought processes and strategies in groups and then build a model of what the writing process looks like to them. The models are drawn on transparencies and shared with the class.

B-7 The Teaching of Literacy: Belief Systems in Action

STEPHEN B. KUCER

Introduction   I use this demonstration to help students understand that all instruction is theoretically driven, to reflect on their own belief systems about the teaching and learning of literacy, to understand the belief systems that underlie the behavior of classroom teachers, and to reflect on the change in their own belief systems throughout the semester.

Procedures   On the first day of class, I ask students to complete a Literacy Beliefs Profile, my modification and extension of DeFord's TORP (1985), in which I have combined reading and writing within the questions and added some questions related to biliteracy and thematic teaching. (One could, however, use the original TORP.) In small groups, students discuss those questions about which they feel the strongest and those about which they are unsure. As a class, these questions are shared, and other students are given the opportunity to respond.

During this course, the students are observing and participating within a classroom in which they will be student teaching. On a regular basis, students are asked to share a literacy activity taught by the regular classroom teacher. These activities are then analyzed using the Literacy Beliefs Profile to help students understand the conceptual belief systems that drive the activities (Figure B-7).

At the end of the year, students again complete a Literacy Beliefs Profile. I return their first profile, and students identify and discuss their beliefs that have changed and those that remained constant. This demonstration of growth and change has a powerful effect on the students, who often have difficulty realizing the shift that has occurred in their belief systems.

Afterword   Refer to Chapter 12, by Virginia Juettner, who uses the TORP in conjunction with a miscue analysis assignment to help students understand the reading process. The Whole Language Umbrella publishes *Readers' Rummy* (Burke, Egawa, and Berghof 1993), which organizes the TORP into a card game.

References

DeFord, D. 1985. "Validating a Construct: A Theoretical Orientation in Reading Instruction." In *Reading Research Quarterly,* 20, 3: 351–367.

Burke, C., K. Egawa, and B. Berghof. 1993. *Readers' Rummy.* The Whole Language Umbrella.

Name _____ **Date** _____

Directions: Read the following statements. Circle the response that best indicates your feelings about reading and writing instruction:

SA (strongly agree) <— 1 — 2 — 3 — 4 — 5 —> (strongly disagree) SD

		SA				SD
1.	Children need to know the letters of the alphabet in order to read and write.	1	2	3	4	5
2.	It is a good practice to allow children to use their own dialect and oral language patterns when learning to read and write.	1	2	3	4	5
3.	A major difference between good and poor readers and writers is that good readers and writers make fewer mistakes.	1	2	3	4	5
4.	A child needs to be able to correctly spell or to correctly recognize a number of words before being asked to read or write sentences, paragraphs, or stories.	1	2	3	4	5
5.	Reading and writing activities, even for beginners, should focus on meaning and the functional use of written language, rather than on exact word and spelling identification.	1	2	3	4	5
6.	A child needs to be able to verbalize the rules of phonics and label words according to their grammatical functions (nouns, verbs, etc.) in order to become a proficient reader and writer.	1	2	3	4	5
7.	Activities for beginning readers and writers should focus on short, simple words, sentences, paragraphs, and stories.	1	2	3	4	5
8.	The use of a glossary or dictionary is necessary in determining the meaning, grammar, and pronunciation of new words.	1	2	3	4	5
9.	Reversals (e.g., was for saw; b for d) are significant problems in the teaching of reading and writing.	1	2	3	4	5
10.	It is a good practice to tell the child when a reading or writing mistake is made and to have the child correct the mistake.	1	2	3	4	5
11.	Writing and reading should be taught separately from one another.	1	2	3	4	5
12.	It is best to teach reading and writing in the following order: letters, sounds, spelling —> words, vocabulary, sentences —> paragraphs —> stories.	1	2	3	4	5

FIGURE B-7   **Literacy beliefs profile**

Copyright © 1996 Stephen B. Kucer. Stenhouse Publishers, York, Maine.

SA (strongly agree) <— 1 — 2 — 3 — 4 — 5 —> (strongly disagree) SD

	SA				SD
13. Reading and writing can be mastered and perfected.	1	2	3	4	5
14. When evaluating reading and writing, the teacher should focus on meaning, rather than on correct word identification, spelling, etc.	1	2	3	4	5
15. Reading and writing should be taught separately from other subjects such as science and social science.	1	2	3	4	5
16. Reading and writing are best taught through frequent drill and practice.	1	2	3	4	5
17. It is a sign of ineffective reading and writing when the child rereads and rewrites.	1	2	3	4	5
18. When a child does not know a word when reading or writing, he or she should be instructed to sound it out.	1	2	3	4	5
19. Good readers and writers first focus on the overall meaning of what they are reading and writing rather than on correct word identification, spelling, punctuation, capitalization, individual facts, and details.	1	2	3	4	5
20. Reading and writing skills should be taught in isolation to ensure adequate practice and mastery.	1	2	3	4	5
21. When children encounter an unknown word, they should be encouraged to spell it as best they can, to guess based on context and meaning, but to continue reading and writing.	1	2	3	4	5
22. It is important that children practice reading and writing new words after they are introduced to ensure that the words will be learned.	1	2	3	4	5
23. Dividing words into syllables according to rules is a helpful instructional practice for reading and writing new words.	1	2	3	4	5
24. Learning to first read and write in a non-English language causes problems when learning to read and write in English.	1	2	3	4	5

FIGURE B-7 **Literacy beliefs profile** *(continued)*

Copyright © 1996 Stephen B. Kucer. Stenhouse Publishers, York, Maine.

B-8 Lines of Print

KENNETH S. GOODMAN

Introduction   This demonstration is designed to help parents or teachers understand how the brain perceives and recognizes information in the reading process and how the brain responds to quick changes. Ken Goodman's "lines of print" activity was adapted in a research study by John Woodley (1983), which provides interesting conclusions about the reading of junior high, secondary, and college students.

Procedures   Explain to the audience that you will turn on the overhead for a split second, and they are to write down what they see.

Cover all lines of print in Figure B-8 except the first and then turn the overhead on and off as quickly as possible. Proceed through the other lines in the same manner, always keeping all lines covered except the one being focused on.

After the last line, discuss what the audience read and wrote for each line, what made some lines easier to read than others, and how the brain tries to create meaning when meaning is not there. Make these points:

- The brain chunks print information into meaningful units.
- The brain organizes and perceives known information more quickly than unknown information.
- Meaningful language units are perceived more quickly even when they include more linguistic units than less meaningful ones.
- We perceive what we know, not what we see.

Record these generalizations on the board as they emerge in the discussion.

Afterword   Teachers can make up their own lines of print. See Figure B-8 for an example.

Reference

Woodley, J. W. 1983. *Perception of Tachistoscopically Presented Lines of Print.* Unpublished doctoral dissertation. Tucson, AZ: University of Arizona.

Lines of Print

? + ? + ? + ? + ? + ? + ? + ?

= ★ = ★ = ★ = ★ = ★ = ★ = ★ = ★

azqrdgfdeomslp

TRANSLATION

149162536496481

This is un desafio.

Be can reading fun!

CALCALADTOR

CAN YOU READ THIS?

Eu posso ler isto.

FIGURE B-8

Copyright © 1996 Kenneth S. Goodman. Stenhouse Publishers, York, Maine.

B-9 Perception, Texts, and the Reading Process

STEPHEN B. KUCER

Introduction   This demonstration is designed to help students understand the selective nature of perception and the relationship between visual and nonvisual information during reading. Typically, students have little formal knowledge of language and literacy and believe reading is a letter-by-letter process. This perception results in a strong belief that reading should be taught in a strictly part-to-whole process. Attempts to change this preconception through course readings and discussion usually have little lasting impact.

Procedures   I usually do these activities after the "Lines of Print" engagement (Protocol/Engagement B-8). When the students have completed the lines of print, I ask them to read chorally a short story in which all the consonants have been removed, followed by the choral reading of a story in which all vowels have been removed. Students discuss which story was easier to read and the salience of consonants over vowels in the reading process. Additional generalizations are added to the list that began with the "lines of print."

Next, students read two texts, one with the bottoms of the letters deleted and one with the tops deleted. Students discuss which story is easier to read and the salience of the tops of the letters over the bottoms. Once again, new perception generalizations are added to the list.

Following these demonstrations, students are given two stories read by a third grader: "A Pin for Dan" (a controlled text) and "The Great Big Enormous Turnip" (an authentic predictable book). All reader miscues on both stories are marked on transcripts of the stories. Although the same child read both stories, I do not inform the students of this fact and simply refer to Reader A and Reader B. Students are broken into groups and asked to compare and contrast the two readings. As a class, we then compare and contrast the readings, noting the effective strategies used by Reader B and the ineffective strategies used by Reader A. I then inform the class that the same child read both texts, and we discuss the influence of the text on perception and reading, linking this discussion back to our list of perception generalizations.

B-10 The Boat in the Basement

KENNETH S. GOODMAN

Introduction   This engagement was developed with teachers in mind, to engage them in considering aspects of the reading process. It could be used with parents, middle school, or secondary students for similar purposes. This protocol helps people understand reading is not an exact process; explore the strategies of predicting and confirming; and explore the graphophonic, syntactic, semantic, and pragmatic cue systems.

Procedures   If used as an overhead, ask the audience to read "The Boat in the Basement" (Figure B-10) through once—and once only—and then write down everything they remember they read. Turn the overhead off after reading it through twice yourself. If using a photocopy, pass it out upside down. People

The Boat in the Basement

A woman was building a boat in her basement. When she had finished the the boot, she discovered that it was too big to go though the door. So he had to take the boat a part to get it out. She should of planned ahead.

FIGURE B-10

keep it upside down until they are given instructions. They turn it over, read it once—and once only—and turn it back over again to write everything they remember on the back. They are not to turn the page over again until it is appropriate to do so during the discussion.

Ask the audience if they understood the passage and how they know, but stress they should not share any specifics.

Ask if anyone had any problems with any part of the passage but not to share specifics.

Ask someone who reported no or few problems to read the passage aloud as if he or she were reading orally to students.

Although the language systems are all integrated, the discussion of individual language features can focus on:

- *Graphophonics,* by looking at *boot/boat, though/through, a part/apart,* and *should of/should've.*
- *Syntax,* by looking at *though/through* and how readers focus on and notice difficulties with nouns first as opposed to other parts of speech.
- *Semantics/pragmatics,* by looking at *he/she* and the familiarity of the story line.

It is interesting to explore why most readers notice the *boat/boot* distinction but very few notice the two *the*s (see end of line 2, beginning of line 3).

Afterword   This passage has been used for about 30 years. Fred Gollasch (1980) researched this passage with readers of a range of ages and abilities. Teachers might want to experiment with writing their own. Teachers can use these with kids to help them explore their own reading process.

Reference

Gollasch, Frederick V. 1980. *Reader's Perception in Detecting and Processing Embedded Errors in Meaningful Text.* Unpublished doctoral dissertation. Tucson, AZ: University of Arizona.

Copyright © 1996 Kenneth S. Goodman. Stenhouse Publishers, York, Maine.

B-11 Nonsense Texts to Illustrate the Three Cue Systems: "A Mardsan Giberter for Farfie," "Gloopy and Blit," and "The Marlup"

KENNETH S. GOODMAN

Introduction   This demonstration was developed with adult readers in mind to explore the role of syntax in reading, including how syntax allows the reader to answer questions without meaning, and to explore the role of graphophonics in oral and silent reading modes. Each of the nonsense stories provides insights into different aspects of syntax and meaning.

Procedures   Ask the audience to read one of the selected stories in Figure B-11 silently. Then read the first question following the story and ask for someone to answer it using a complete sentence. Proceed through the other questions in a similar manner. Discuss how the questions can be answered with no meaning and how the syntax of language is organized to relate to meaning. Explore the role of function words.

Identify parts of speech and other components and how readers know what these features are. Also discuss how certain words are pronounced and how people might pronounce them differently. Consider how people know how to change specific words in order to answer the questions appropriately.

Ask if anyone can construct the original text by having people work in small groups to produce a collaborative text. Point out that it is not possible to produce English nonsense without first starting with meaning-based texts.

The Marlup

A marlup was poving his kump. Parmily a narg horped some whev in his kump. "Why did vump horp whev in my frinkle kump?" the marlup jufd the narg. "Er'm muvvily trungy," the narg grupped. "Er heshed vump norpled whev in your kump. Do vump pove your kump frinkle?"

1. What did the narg horp in the marlup's kump?
2. What did the marlup juf the narg?
3. Was the narg trungy?
4. How does the marlup pove his kump?

FIGURE B-11   Nonsense text and questions

Copyright © 1996 Kenneth S. Goodman, Stenhouse Publishers, York, Maine

A Mardsan Giberter for Farfie

Glis was very fraper. She had denarpen Farfie's mardsan. She didn't talp a giberter for him. So she conlanted to plimp a mardsan binky for him. She had just sparved the binky when he jibbled in the gorger.

"Clorsty mardsan!" she boffed.

"That's a croustisch mardsan binky," boffed Farfie, "but my mardsan is on Stansan. Agsan is Kelsan."

"In that ruspen," boffed Glis, "I won't whank you your giberter until Stansan."

1. Why was Glis fraper?
2. What did Glis plimp?
3. Who jibbled in the gorger when Glis sparved the binky?
4. What did Farfie boff about the mardsan binky?
5. Why didn't Glis whank Farfie his giberter?

FIGURE B-11   Nonsense text and questions (*continued*)

Copyright © 1996 Kenneth S. Goodman. Stenhouse Publishers, York, Maine.

Gloopy and Blit

GLOOPY IS A BORP.
BLIT IS A LOF.

GLOOPY KLUMS LIKE BLIT.
GLOOPY AND BLIT ARE FLOMS.

RIL HAD POVED BLIT TO A JONFY.
BUT LO HAD NOT POVED GLOOPY.

"THE JONFY IS FOR LOFS," BLIT BOFD
TO GLOOPY. "ROM ARE A BORP."

GLOOPY WAS NOT KLORPY.
THEN BLIP WAS NOT KLORPY.

1. What are Gloopy and Blit?
2. Who does Gloopy klum like?
3. What did Blit bof to Gloopy?
4. Was Blit klorpy?
5. Why wasn't Gloopy poved to the jonfy?
6. Why was Blit not klorpy?

FIGURE B-11 Nonsense text and questions *(continued)*

Copyright © 1996 Kenneth S. Goodman. Stenhouse Publishers, York, Maine.

B-12 Real Texts to Illustrate the Three Cue Systems: Downhole Heave Compensator

KENNETH S. GOODMAN

Introduction   This demonstration was developed as a way to engage adult readers in considering aspects of the reading process. It demonstrates how readers transact with text when they do not understand it, manipulating syntax to answer questions. It helps readers realize the problems in reading text with complex syntax and dense conceptual load.

Procedures   Have the audience read the text provided below and then engage in answering the questions (Figure B-12). The questions can be answered in a whole group discussion or with participants working in small groups and then all coming together to discuss them and the process. (Questions I can be answered without understanding the text. To answer Questions II, the reader needs to understand the concepts in the text.)

Discuss how the participants were able to answer the questions without understanding the text by manipulating the syntax.

Afterword   Teachers can go through old magazines related to such topics as knitting instructions or sports articles on games such as cricket or curling. The Downhole Heave Compensator is an advertisement, not a scientific article.

A Tool Designed by Hindsight, by Kirk Shirley

You might say we started building downhole heave compensators in self defense. We were trying to keep drillships and semi-submersibles from wiping out our underreamers.

You might say, too, that we were late getting into the act. We didn't begin marketing our downhole heave compensators until early 1973.

But we're pleased with the way it all worked out. Our late arrival on the scene made it possible for us to analyze the tools already in service, study their good points, take warning from their bad points. Influenced as we were by the merits and demerits of previously built hardware, you might say that A-Z International's downhole heave compensator was designed by hindsight.

There's a lot to be said for hindsight. In our case, it resulted in a tool yielding at least 500 trouble-free rotating hours. And it stopped the destruction of our underreamers.

What was happening to our underreamers before 1973 shouldn't happen to anybody's downhole tools. Run from drillships and semisubs below the then-prevalent bumper subs, they lost their cones, broke their cutter arms, and earned black eyes for underreaming in the marine environment. We completely redesigned our underreamer; but, still, report after report told of underreamer failure because unbalanced bumper subs locked under heavy torque loading and failed to reciprocate. The underreamer, then, was picked up off bottom and slammed back when the vessel heaved down.

To protect our own interests properly, we set out to develop a downhole heave compensator that would reciprocate freely at all times, regardless of torque loading.

For over two years we studied every conceivable design. We made experimental tests with all types of packing, lubricants, tool joint threads and materials to determine those types which would best satisfy the criteria established for this tool. Our objective:

1. Good material
2. Good workmanship
3. Properly designed tool joints
4. A drive section which will reciprocate under full torque loading
5. Packing which will hold up and reciprocate under high temperature and high differential pressure
6. Lubricant which will maintain its molecular structure and low coefficient of friction at all temperatures for at least 1,000 hours continuous service.

We sought minimum downtime and maintenance, a tool that would reciprocate under full torque loading for at least 500 hours on bottom without pulling the string except to change bits. At today's high rig costs for drillships and semis ($.30, $.40, and even $.50 per second) the savings realized would offset the cost of the tool in just a few runs.

What was needed, in short, was a fully-balanced downhole heave compensator. Unbalanced bumper subs, our studies convinced us, will not get the job done. These unlubricated tools are fine for fishing jobs on land where they are used intermittently to release grappling tools by jarring, or, in some cases, with minimal right or lefthand torque, but they aren't designed for continuous reciprocation under high torque loading commensurate with offshore drilling from a floating platform. Sand and mud circulate through the torque transmission section, acting like emery cloth on the driving and driven members. At best, the unlubricated bumper sub can last only a few hours, making the cost of downtime and maintenance prohibitive.

The heart of any downhole heave compensator is the torque transmission system. In the A-Z system, the drive inserts are rectangular, and in assembly, the driving and driven faces thereof are in radial contact with the mandrel and outer sleeve. In other words, if this line of contact were extended, it would pass through the center of the tool, or nearly so. On the other hand, the torque transmitted by the tool is tangential, and the force is applied at right angles to the faces of the driving and driven members described above. Thus, under torque loading, the drive inserts are not forced up into the outer sleeve; neither are they forced down into the mandrel. In a sense, they are free-floating and are not subjected to any wedging action due to torque loading.

The tool made available in 1973 was not the lowest cost design considered during the two-plus years of investigation into downhole heave compensation. In view of the logistics involved in today's worldwide offshore drilling program, the established parameters for downhole tool selection have moved price to the bottom of the list. You can't afford not to have the best, even if it costs twice as much. First comes performance. How long will it stay on bottom? Second comes maintenance. Third, spare parts, etc. But at $30,000 and $40,000 a day, price has got to be last.

Questions I

1. What kind of compensators is this article about?
2. When did A-Z International begin building compensators?
3. What two results did the design of the A-Z International tool bring?
4. What were the two things destroying the underreamers?
5. What sort of damage was caused to the underreamers?
6. In what environment were the underreamers operating?
7. What six objectives did the tool designers have?
8. If the design were successful, how long could the tool stay on the bottom without pulling the string other than to change bits?
9. What is the cost range of rigs?
10. What was the key requirement for a successful downhole heave compensator?

Questions II

1. What is the general subject matter of this article?
2. What is the basic function of a downhole heave compensator?
3. What does the author mean about the role of hindsight in design?
4. Describe the relationships of drillships, semi-submersibles, underreamers, cones, bumper subs, cutter arms, drill bits, and downhole heave compensators.
5. What difference would it make if these processes were not going on in a marine environment?
6. What business is A-Z International tool company in?
7. Suggest a name for the magazine from which this article came.

FIGURE B-12 Questions for the Downhole Heave Compensator

Copyright © 1996 Kenneth S. Goodman. Stenhouse Publishers, York, Maine.

B-13 Real Texts to Illustrate the Three Cue Systems: Poison

KENNETH S. GOODMAN

Introduction   This demonstration of the reading process helps teachers, parents, and middle or secondary students understand that reading is not an exact process. It explores the use of syntax, dialect, and punctuation, and shows readers how they set up a scenario as they read a text.

Procedures   If using an overhead, ask the audience to read the text in Figure B-13 through once—and once only—and write down everything they can remember. Another option is to have people work in pairs, with one writing what he or she remembers and the other sketching what he or she remembers.

If using a photocopy, pass it out upside down. People keep it upside down until they are given instructions. They turn it over, read it once—and once only—and turn it over to write everything they remember on the back or work with a partner as described above. They are not to turn the page over again until the discussion is almost over.

Explore these areas:

- Background knowledge we bring to reading. For example, is *I* a male or a female? Is this a sinister incident or related to a considerate act?
- Concepts such as bungalow and gates in relation to pragmatic knowledge. What kind of place is this? Who owns it? Where is it?
- More information is needed than is given in the first paragraph. It is necessary to keep reading.

Afterword   This paragraph has been used for about 30 years. Teachers may like to find other paragraphs in other texts, maybe also trying a middle or ending paragraph.

Reference

Dahl, Roald. 1958. "Poison." In *Adventures in English Literature*. New York: Harcourt.

Poison

It must have been around midnight when I drove home, and as I approached the gates of the bungalow I switched off the head lamps of the car so the beam wouldn't swing in through the window of the side bedroom and wake Harry Pope.

FIGURE B-13   Poison

Copyright © 1996 Kenneth S. Goodman. Stenhouse Publishers, York, Maine.

B-14 Cooperative Cloze Strategy

BRIAN CAMBOURNE AND YETTA M. GOODMAN

Introduction   This strategy is a way to explore prediction and to help adult readers understand what makes a text predictable or constrained. The story came from a syllabus for an Open University course in England on language in education.

Procedures   Have the participants work in groups of two or three to fill in the blanks of the story in Figure B-14. Ask them to note where they had to read on for information and when they had to reread earlier sections of the text. Which slots were easy to fill and did they feel certain about? Which slots had possibilities for options, and which were hard? Why do they think certain grammatical slots were easier than others?

Ask one group to share their responses. Discuss where other groups differed and where not, and why. Also discuss the process involved in this activity and what it demonstrates about predicting, confirming, and the reading process. What does the process reveal about the participants' intuitive knowledge about language?

Afterword   Teachers can write their own slotted passage or create one from another story. The British/Australian spelling of *pedlar* may be changed or left for a discussion of alternative spelling patterns.

B-15 Experiencing the Cue Systems of Reading

SANDRA WILDE

Introduction   This engagement helps education students and teachers develop an understanding of the graphophonic, syntactic, and semantic cue systems for reading through experiencing what reading feels like when one or more of the cue systems is missing or damaged.

You will need to prepare five handouts to complete this engagement:

- Handout 1, a paragraph of about 100 words with all the vowels removed and every fifth word underlined. I usually use a passage from children's literature, but I have used a nonfiction passage for content area literacy classes.
- Handout 2, the twenty underlined words (also with vowels missing) arranged in a list.
- Handout 3, a cloze passage of a very simple fifty-word text with every fifth word replaced with a blank; I usually use one that sounds like a beginning basal reader.
- Handout 4, a cloze passage from a very difficult text (e.g., a statistics text).
- Handout 5, a nonsense passage (one in which all words other than function words are replaced with nonsense words, although inflectional endings are preserved) with accompanying comprehension questions. I usually use Ken Goodman's "A Marlup Was Poving His Kump" (Protocol/Engagement B-11).

The Pedlar and the Tiger

One night an old tiger was out in the rain. It was very dark and the rain was falling very fast. The _____ was wet and cold. He tried to find a _____ place so that he could get out of the rain. But he could find _____. There was nothing but rain. How it did _____. At last the tiger came upon an _____ wall and lay down against it. It was not quite so _____. So he fell _____. While he slept a pedlar came _____. The pedlar had lost his donkey and he was trying to find him. It was so dark the pedlar could hardly _____. The rain fell _____ and faster. He was freezing _____ and soaking _____. The pedlar looked for _____ dry place but could find _____. At last he came to the old _____ against which the tiger lay asleep. The pedlar saw the dim form of an _____ close to the wall. "This must be my _____," he said, so he took the tiger by the ear and began to kick and _____ him. "You old rascal," he said, "At _____ I have found you. What did you run _____ for?" The tiger was very much surprised. He got up and began to stir himself. The pedlar jumped on his _____ and said, "Get up now, I want to go _____." The tiger got up and the pedlar rode home on his back.

FIGURE B-14   The Pedlar and the Tiger

Copyright © 1996 Brian Cambourne and Yetta M. Goodman. Stenhouse Publishers, York, Maine.

Procedures

Activity A

I divide the class down the middle, and tell them that they'll be involved in a competition; they'll be given a sample of written language with the vowels missing, and their task is to try to figure out what words I had in mind. I give Handout 1 to half of the class and Handout 2 to the other half. I encourage them to work in teams and keep the tone playful.

I emphasize to Group 2 as I circulate around the room that they have to settle on a *single* guess for each word and that they have to use their ESP powers to figure out which of several possible words I had in mind. Group 1 is told that they only have to worry about the underlined words, although they're obviously using the context of the passage as a whole to figure them out.

When they're done, I read off the "right" answers for the 20 words and ask them how they did. Group 2 usually reacts with consternation as they realize how comparatively badly they did. Typically Group 1 gets about nineteen words correct and Group 2 about ten. I usually tease them briefly about being "blue-birds and buzzards" before revealing that their difference in performance was a construct of the task. (I do a little talking about each activity immediately after completing it but save the bulk of the discussions until we've done all five handouts.)

Activity B

I typically say to the students, "You did so well reading words with some of the letters missing, let's see how you can do with *all* of the letters missing." Their task, again, is to guess what words I had in mind, and they again work in teams to fill in the blanks of the easy cloze passage (Handout 3). When they're done, we score their work (for consistency, only exact matches count as correct), and we talk about how even their "wrong" answers were reasonable choices.

Activity C

I typically say to the students, "You did so well on the previous cloze, let's do another one just like it." After they have struggled through Handout 4, we explore why it was so much more difficult.

Activity D

I preface my comments to Handout 5 by saying, "You've done so well with decoding, let's move on to comprehension." After silently reading "A Marlup Was Poving His Kump," we do round-robin oral reading and answer the comprehension questions orally and discuss how the students were able to do so well with them.

Activity E

The connection to the cueing systems that follows and ties together the series of activities is an interactive lecture presentation that describes the graphophonic, syntactic, and semantic systems, with many examples taken from the five handouts. For instance, I point out that our knowledge of the graphophonic system enables us to read nonsense words like *marlup,* although we don't sound them out letter by letter, and how the syntax of the two cloze passages differs in both sentence length and sentence complexity. As each cueing system is defined and described, we fill in a table that examines whether each cueing system was present or not in the activities. (Table B-15 is filled in.) Discussion of the information contained in the table helps the students realize the relatively greater importance of syntactic and semantic information in the reading process as compared to graphophonic information, since readers get the most out of Handouts 1 and 3, where the syntactic and semantic cueing systems are most present and usable.

I also usually combine this series of activities with an exploration of the reading the students have done in the past twenty-four hours as a way of examining the psychosocial context of reading. The students usually find the activities and related discussion enjoyable, and I find these activities to be an effective way to build a vocabulary for talking about literacy.

Handout	Graphophonic	Syntactic	Semantic
1: paragraph, no vowels	partial	yes	yes
2: list, no vowels	partial	no	not really
3: easy cloze	partial (4/5)	yes	yes
4: hard cloze	partial (4/5)	yes, but not easily accessible	yes, but not easily accessible
5: nonsense passage	yes	yes	not really (although some students can eventually "translate" the passage using subtle semantic cues)

TABLE B-15   Responses According to Language Cues

B-16 Teachers Exploring Their Own Reading Process Through Fiction

SANDRA WILDE

Introduction   The goal for this engagement is to help adult readers realize the pleasure of discovering for themselves as they read and to become aware of how they handle challenges and construct meaning.

The book *Left Hand of Darkness*, by Ursula LeGuin, is an adult science-fiction story in which life on the planet Gethen (which translates as "Winter") is explored. The people are biologically identical to earthlings except for their gender; everyone is effectively neuter most of the time except for a monthly period of time called *kemmer,* when they take on either male or female form, but not always the same one: a person may be the mother of one child and the father of another. Most of the story, which involves personal and political intrigue and a thrilling journey on foot across the northern rim of the planet, is told by a narrator from Earth who gradually becomes more reliable as he learns more about Gethen. Like the narrator, the reader learns about the planet and its people gradually, as more and more is revealed through the narrator's eyes, the story itself, and more directly explanatory mini-essays scattered throughout the book.

Procedures   Assign a few chapters of *Left Hand of Darkness* each session so that the students can have discussions in ongoing small groups. The class also reads and discusses Frank Smith's *Reading Without Nonsense* (1985).

Each class meeting, I suggest that the teachers first have an open-ended exploration of their responses to the reading and then use the novel to examine a specific aspect of their own psychology of reading. For instance, how did they come up with pronunciation of the unfamiliar words like *shifgrethor* that were part of the language of the planet? Did they use phonics? If so, how? How did they come up with the meaning of those words? What role did the small group discussions play in their construction of the meaning of the novel? I circulate among the groups and both respond as another reader and plant thoughts and questions that push the discussion forward.

This novel is especially rewarding for this activity, partly because it's not easy to read. It includes the disconcerting sentence, "The king was pregnant," as well as many confusing passages until the readers learn their way around this strange planet.

The discussions move from the psychology of reading to instructional issues. I raise the comment, "Imagine if I had begun our reading of the novel as if it were a basal reader by putting all of LeGuin's coined words on the blackboard with definitions, explaining how the king could be pregnant and how the characters' biology worked." The teachers realize, of course, how they would have lost the pleasure of discovering for themselves as they went along, and that for me to have provided information up front would have been a violation of the author's intentions. If LeGuin had wanted us to know all about the planet before reading, she would have done an introduction herself.

My role as a teacher isn't just to leave the students as individuals to deal with reading such a challenging book on their own. The small group structure, coupled with my subtle scaffolding as I interact with the groups, gives them a different kind of support, growing out of a less directive, more delicate conceptualization of the teacher's role, and showing them that reading in a classroom community can provide pleasures that go beyond those of reading alone.

References

LeGuin, U. 1969. *The Left Hand of Darkness.* New York: Walker.

Smith, F. 1985. *Reading Without Nonsense.* 2d ed. New York: Teachers College Press.

B-17 Metacognitive Inquiry: Talking Through the Text

M. RUTH DAVENPORT

Introduction   This activity helps learners bring their own reading process to the conscious level. For most students, it is the first time they closely observe themselves as readers or articulate their beliefs about reading. Developing a deeper understanding of the active nature of reading helps my college students become more perceptive of their elementary students as readers. They become better able to consider the thought involved during reading, the strategies readers use, the language cueing systems, the influences on comprehension, and the potential for and nature of a variety of miscues.

Procedures   Begin by introducing the concept of metacognition, or thinking about your own thinking. I demonstrate this procedure by thinking out loud as I read from an overhead. I usually select brief articles from a magazine such as *Science News* because they are about topics for which most of us have no schema, some of the vocabulary is usually unfamiliar, and there are usually other types of orthographic features (e.g., words in all capitals, numbers, abbreviations, and hyphens) that would be common to content-area texts and possibly problematic.

Read a brief passage, stopping after every few sentences to tell the students what you are thinking. I find it best to read something new each time I use this strategy to ensure an authentic response on my own part.

After reading and discussing several paragraphs, pass out another science article, like the example on the following page, and ask the students to tell what they were thinking after they had read the title. Ask for predictions; then ask them to read another few sentences. With the recurring invitation to "tell me what you're thinking," students continue to observe their transactions with this difficult text.

When several paragraphs are finished, students are asked to talk with each other about their experiences during the strategy. Brainstorm a list, which can be put on the board, of the types of things they notice about their thinking during reading, such as calling on background, connecting to another text, or making a graphic analysis of a word.

Close with a reflective writing about how this new awareness of themselves as readers would influence their teaching.

Life Blooms on Floor of Deep Siberian Lake, by R. Monastersky

A joint U.S.-Soviet research team has discovered an oasis of life around springs of heated water along the floor of Siberia's Lake Baikal, the oldest and deepest lake on Earth. Many similar "hydrothermal vent communities" thrive in the oceans, but until now scientists had never seen an example in fresh water.

Expedition members discovered the field of vents at a depth of 1,350 feet in the northern section of the 395-mile-long, crescent-shaped lake, which sits just north of Mongolia. Using a submersible to explore the field, researchers photographed a rich community of sponges, bacterial mats, snails, fish and transparent shrimp, some apparently representing unknown species, says chief scientist Kathleen Crane from Columbia University's Lamont-Doherty Geological Observatory in Palisades, N.Y. Fluids spewed from the vents measured at least 24°F warmer than the normally frigid bottom water.

The discovery surprised some researchers because measurements made during an expedition two years ago showed no signs that the lake harbored vents, says geochemist Ray F. Weiss of the Scripps Institution of Oceanography in La Jolla, Calif. "I was skeptical that they could find any vents at all," he told *Science News*. The recent vent search, conducted during six weeks in June and July, concentrated on a virtually unexplored section of the lake.

Organisms living near hydrothermal vents in the ocean have attracted considerable attention over the last 13 years. While almost all biological communities on Earth derive their primary energy from sunlight through photosynthesis, oceanic vent communities rely on a process called chemosynthesis, drawing their basic energy from chemical nutrients in the warm fluids.

Biologists now seek to determine whether chemosynthesis supports the Baikal communities, says Barbara Hecker of Lamont-Doherty, who has studied photographs from the recent expedition. Researchers will also examine the Baikal organisms to see what characteristics they share with those from ocean vents. Such comparisons could offer insight into the evolution of vent communities.

Whereas most large lakes date back only 10,000 to 20,000 years, Lake Baikal formed about 25 million years ago. Due to its great depth, it holds about 20 percent of the world's supply of liquid fresh water.

The vents found at the bottom of the lake indicate that previous studies have significantly underestimated the amount of heat flowing out of the Earth's crust in the Baikal region, says geoscientist Marcia K. McNutt of the Massachusetts Institute of Technology in Cambridge. Future studies of the vents and local heat flow, she says, will yield more accurate estimates and should help geoscientists resolve a debate about why the Asian continent is splitting along the giant rift that created the deep lake. Many researchers view the rifting as a passive process driven by tectonic stress from the distant collision between India and Asia. But some think the Baikal rift results from a more active process, in which hot material rising from Earth's mantle forces the Asian place to crack apart. (*Science News*, 138, 7: 103.)

Copyright © 1996 M. Ruth Davenport. Stenhouse Publishers. York, Maine

B-18 Children's Multiethnic Literature

HELEN SLAUGHTER

Introduction   The goals of this engagement are to help teachers understand and explore the need for an in-depth "insider" as well as "outsider" view of minority cultures when teaching children's literature; to help teachers begin to review critically the extant children's literature as it relates to specific ethnic groups; to provide a format for sharing among students' own cultural perspectives in multi-cultural teacher education contexts; to expand the perspectives of majority culture teachers and preservice teacher education students regarding minority perspectives on multicultural literature; to establish a framework for broader and more critical reading of multicultural children's literature; and to help set a direction and rationale for encouraging ethnic writers of children's literature.

Procedures   Discuss the issues involved in whether an author writes from "insider" knowledge and perspectives of a specific ethnic-cultural group in contrast to an "outsider's" perspective and how this relates to the positioning and perspectives of the characters and themes in the story itself. An example in children's literature is Jane Yolen's book *Encounter* (1992), an account of Columbus from the viewpoint of a Taino child. In contrast, Peter Sis's picture book about Columbus, which was written from a European perspective, does not touch on the plight of indigenous peoples. Yolen's book is discussed in the *New Advocate, 5*, no. 4 (fall 1992). A serious limitation of Yolen's work is that she is not an ethnic writer, and although she presents the perspective of the indigenous people in a very strong way, because she chose to write about a group that did not survive the European encounter, little is resolved at the end of the book regarding the identity of contemporary indigenous children of mixed ethnic heritage.

In contrast, *The People Shall Continue* (1988), a nonfiction book by Simon Ortiz that attempts to encompass all Native American history, gives children a more hopeful perspective. The children's novel *Morning Girl* (1994), by Native American writer Michael Dorris, is also about a Taino child. Although it is similarly unresolved at its conclusion, it provides a richer account of the possible lives of the original people. All of these books together provide a way to open the discussion about authors' perspectives as well as book characters' perspectives portrayed in multicultural children's literature.

Next, help the group define their own ethnic-cultural identification by asking students to do a free write about their own ethnicity and family history, and share the results with their peers. At the same time, the instructor writes about his or her own ethnic identity and the complexity of describing family origins. Before asking for volunteers to share what they have written, the instructor talks about his or her own background. After a few class members have shared what they have written, break up into small groups to explore the topic.

As a first step, ask the groups to explore issues that they think are important about their own identity, the ethnic-cultural identity of students in the schools in which they are or will be teaching, and whether they believe that their and their students' backgrounds are adequately represented in current children's and adult literature. Ask students to give examples if possible from either their current reading or past school experience. Include the quality of illustrations in the discussion. You may find that students discover they are inadequately knowledgeable about the availability and variety of multicultural children's literature. If the instructor has prior knowledge of the ethnic makeup of the students, text sets of samples of multi-ethnic children's storybook literature can assist students in exploring this topic.

As a second step, ask students to select one of the particular ethnic-cultural groups discussed in their small group and, working together, describe the following:

1. The diversity and complexity within this group of people.
2. Some of the important insider and outsider perspectives regarding the group of people and their role in history.
3. The kinds of themes that authentic children's literature about this group does or should address.

Students may also want to identify stereotypes that they would like to see exploded. Groups can add to the list of questions and issues: a likely possibility is gender issues within an ethnic group. Encourage students to discuss these questions from more than one perspective. This discussion is facilitated if the person whose ethnicity is being described takes the initiative in discussing some of the complexities and controversies regarding his or her own group. Small group findings are shared later in the larger group.

At the end of the session, groups summarize what they know and do not know about the cultural experience and available children's (and adult) literature of the ethnic group that they have expressed an interest in. Future plans for researching the topic more fully, including a search for ethnic writers of that ethnic group, and the interdisciplinary nature of their question (e.g., historical, sociological, literary, contemporary politics) are discussed. A list of criteria for judging the quality of literature in a particular ethnic group is started.

References

Dorris, M. 1994. *Morning Girl.* New York: Trumpet Club.
Ortiz, S. 1988. *The People Shall Continue.* San Francisco: Children's Book Press.
Yolen, J. 1992. *Encounter.* New York: Harcourt Brace Jovanovich.

B-19 *Come Sing, Jimmy Joe,* by Katherine Paterson: A Read-Aloud Selection Used to Stimulate Discussion and Initiate Writing

LAURA A. SMITH

Introduction   The use of read-aloud selections enables participants to hear well-written literature, learn about new authors and titles, and understand the values and pleasures of being read to.

As they enter kindergarten or change schools during their academic careers, many children encounter values and expectations different from those of their families and home communities. The responses of school personnel can greatly influence the actions of the children, sometimes forcing the children to behave in ways even the children feel are unacceptable.

This selection is a good discussion opener for such topics as the attitudes of school personnel toward children of culturally different backgrounds and how children of culturally different backgrounds deal with stressful situations in and out of school. I especially like this selection because it deals with cultural differences. James (Jimmy Joe of the title), who was being raised in the country by his grandmother, has moved with his extended family to the city in order for the family singing group (James performs with the group) to fulfill its professional commitments more easily.

If Katherine Paterson is not a familiar author, you may want to preface the reading with comments on her writing and her understanding of and attitude toward children. (If she is unfamiliar to the reader, scanning *Gates of Excellence: On Reading and Writing for Children* [1981], a collection of her essays, is recommended.)

Procedures In Chapter 6 (pages 55–58 in the hardcover edition) Paterson describes James' experiences as he enrolls in an urban school after having attended only a one-room school in rural West Virginia. The language (school jargon), negative attitude, and lack of understanding of the school secretary are well described as James is forced to lie to protect his family's lifestyle.

Read aloud the description of Jimmy Joe's arrival at General Douglas MacArthur Elementary School, beginning with, "The next morning Jerry Lee drove him the eight blocks to the schoolhouse. The rest of the family was sleeping in late. When his daddy stopped the engine and started to get out, James suddenly didn't want him to come in" (p. 55). Paterson's style lends itself so well to being read aloud that editing of the scene probably won't be needed. A good stopping place would be ". . . pressed a button on the phone and spoke into a box. 'Mr. Dolman, I have a new student for you. Could you send someone down to the office to get him?'" (p. 58). Or, if more of the contrast between James' prior school and his new one is desired, continue through, "At Wesco everybody had been country-white—except one family who called themselves black, but to tell the truth, were lighter than the farm kids who worked in the sun" (p. 59).

My students have easily identified with James' discomfort and universally have condemned the secretary's attitude. Such devil's advocate questions as, "Don't schools have to require adequate records and immunizations when new students enroll?" "How can schools deal with the differences in children's background and the variations between (rural-urban, wealthy-poor, American-foreign, etc.) schools and still attempt to maintain standards?" and "How are children's attitudes toward their homes [toward their schools] formed?" "How do their attitudes affect their school performance?" will usually get the students to share their experiences and attitudes.

Afterword This read aloud and discussion can be followed by writing about uncomfortable experiences students have had, such as moving to a new neighborhood, meeting new people, or starting a new job.

The voluntary reading aloud of the students' writings has been a real eye opener for students who have not had or do not remember such experiences.

References

Paterson, K. 1981. *Gates of Excellence: On Reading and Writing for Children.* New York: Dutton.

———. 1985. *Come Sing, Jimmy Joe.* New York: Dutton.

B-20 *Crow Boy,* by Taro Yashima: A Read-Aloud Selection Used to Stimulate Discussion and Initiate Writing

LAURA A. SMITH

Introduction   (See the introduction to B-19 on the use of read alouds as a way to stimulate discussion and initiate writing.)

This is the story of the school career of a student who was different from all of his peers. Most future teachers have been reasonably successful during their school careers. This gentle story often reminds them of a child they remember from elementary school but did not know very well. The well-written description of the behavior of the child who does not fit in and the impact of the teacher's attitude on the behavior of both the child and the rest of the class is useful in getting students to discuss the child who does not fit in, children's reactions to the child who is different, and the importance of the teacher's attitude toward this child.

Procedures   Read the story aloud, sharing the pictures that are large enough to be seen. The illustrations are very beautiful, but many are too small to be effective if the group is very large. The illustrations can be put on overheads too. Having multiple copies of the book is useful for the groups during the follow-up activities and to give the students a chance to appreciate the illustrations.

After a brief discussion of the story, the students are divided into groups that select writing assignment cards. Each group discusses the assignment, brainstorms relevant information, and decides which parts of the assignment will be done by the group and which will be done individually.

Assignment cards which I have used have included these suggestions:

- Write a script for a discussion of this unusual child in the teachers' lounge. Include Mr. Isobi and other teachers who are familiar with the child.
- Write a letter from the classroom teacher to the principal requesting help for Crow Boy.
- Write a letter from Crow Boy to his grandparents inviting them to his graduation from elementary school.
- Write a journal entry by a fifth- or sixth-grade peer of Crow Boy.

These writing assignments have given the students a chance to take varying points of view regarding the story and to write in a variety of genres.

Afterword   The voluntary sharing of the writing usually starts a new round of discussions regarding point of view and different types of group and individual writing assignments.

Reference

Yashima, T. 1985. *Crow Boy.* New York: Viking Press.

B-21 *The Important Book,* by Margaret Wise Brown: A Read-Aloud Selection Used to Stimulate Discussion and Initiate Writing

LAURA A. SMITH

Introduction   (See the introduction to B-19 for the use of read alouds.)

Even with the recent changes in views of writing and in writing instruction, many future and current teachers do not feel comfortable or confident as writers. Therefore they are easy prey for formulaic patterns for teaching the writing of paragraphs and organizing of papers still found in English textbooks (at all levels), curriculum guides, and teachers' magazines. The poems in *The Important Book* (1949) allow the participants to discuss and experiment with the processes of finding the relative importance of various aspects of any topic, the process of brainstorming as a way of pooling all of a group's knowledge about a particular topic, the use of a poem as a format for organizing knowledge about a topic, and the characteristics of nonrhyming poetry.

Procedures   *The Important Book* is a collection of poems about familiar items in which the most important aspect is highlighted in the first and last lines of the poem. Other characteristics of the item are listed in the middle of the poem. The fact that the poems do not have a rhyming pattern is a bonus in getting less experienced writers to experiment with writing poetry. Subjects of the poems include a spoon, the sky, rain, an apple, grass, wind, snow, and a shoe. Depending on the area of the country, the students' experiences, and the teacher's preference, any of the poems can be used. My personal favorites are an apple, rain, and a spoon.

The poems themselves need little introduction, and, as this "listen, discuss, and write experience" often comes well into the semester, when my students are familiar with the procedure, I usually begin by reading a few of the poems aloud, allowing the students to picture the item being described. If the whole process is new to your students, you will need an introduction. What you use will vary, depending on your specific purpose for the writing experience.

The selected poem is read aloud more than once and discussed by the class (or in small groups) focusing on:

- The content.
- Whether the students would have selected the characteristics that Brown did.
- Whether they feel that she highlighted the most important characteristic.
- How the characteristics are alike and different.
- Whether they are descriptions, actions, comparisons, or something else.
- How Brown phrased her description of each characteristic (Was it simply listed? Was it expanded or illustrated? etc.)

I have found it useful to use a transparency of one of the poems during the discussion.

Small groups of students select a topic for their own important poems. The topics can be totally open or may be limited to those related to the content of the course. In reading methods courses, such topics as reading, phonics, basal readers, children, reading aloud, and reading teachers have been used. In content-area courses, students select topics related to the content field in which they expect to teach. For example, future math teachers have selected such topics as geometry, algebra, the math text, numbers, homework, and calculators.

Each group is then asked to brainstorm a list of characteristics of their topic. This step is particularly important because it creates a list from which to select characteristics that may be used in the poems and that can be ranked in terms of relative importance. In some groups, the process of selecting and ranking can become very heated as members try to support their pet ideas.

The writing of the poems may be a group process, or individual students may wish to write their own poems after the brainstorming and discussions.

In some classes, the topic selection, brainstorming, discussion, and even writing have been done as a whole class, with students or small groups being allowed to split off either before or after the class poem has been written. Classes with not much experience with the process of brainstorming or with a number of individuals who are still reluctant to write often benefit from the extra demonstration of the process.

After the writing, the poems are shared on a voluntary basis. I often have followed the writing of the poem with the writing of a paragraph on the same topic. Discussion of the usefulness of brainstorming and discussion and of the writing of the poems and paragraphs follows. Students often share views of the relative value and the relative difficulty of writing a poem or writing a paragraph.

Afterword   After you have done this for a few semesters, you will have a collection of student poems that are as good as those in *The Important Book*. These can be enjoyed by later classes.

Reference

Brown, M. W. 1949. *The Important Book*. New York: Harper & Row.

B-22   *Mrs. Frisby and the Rats of N.I.M.H.,* by Robert O'Brien: A Read-Aloud Selection Used to Stimulate Discussion and Initiate Writing

LAURA A. SMITH

Introduction   (See the introduction to B-19 on the use of read alouds.)

In this read-aloud selection, the rats' and the researchers' views of reading are well described and provide a good lead into discussions of definitions and aspects of reading, as well as the need for readers to understand what reading is. The fictional setting makes this a nonconfrontational introduction to the subject of basic definitions of reading for current teachers who may feel strongly about a particular teaching method.

Procedures   In the chapter "A Lesson in Reading," Nicodemus' description of how he and the other rats were being taught and actually learned to read is classic. It includes how the rats were taught shape recognition, letter recognition, and phonics; how Jenner discovered what reading was and told the other rats; how the researchers, not recognizing that the rats could read, continued to teach them individual words; and how the rats used their ability to read to open their cages and escape.

A brief introduction to the rats and the story up to this point may be useful, but it may be enough just to explain that Nicodemus, one of the rat leaders, is telling Mrs. Frisby, a mouse who has come to him for help, how he and the other rats learned to read.

The writing reads well aloud, but you need to preview the selection and decide how to handle the intonation of the researcher, Julie, as she is heard on the tape giving the lessons and how you will pronounce the *knob* (I usually pronounce the *k* as the rats at this point do not know what the word means).

Discussion of the actions and comments of the rats and the researchers are used to define their views of reading before the students individually write their own initial definitions or descriptions of reading. We then pool these and try to come to some group consensus. Even when agreement cannot be reached (this doesn't really create a problem since the experience is usually done early in the semester), the discussion does broaden student and teacher awareness of the need to develop a working definition for themselves.

Afterword   Irene Hunt's *Across Five Aprils* (1964), the story of a family in one of the border states during the Civil War, has a short scene in which Jethro agrees to bring a newspaper to an old man who says that he can't read but can recognize his name in print. The old man tells of a neighbor girl who sometimes reads to him but, "She's got a quick sassy way o' readin'; I much doubt that she calls all the words right" (p. 84). This short scene (pp. 84-85) can be used in the same way as the selection from *Mrs. Frisby and the Rats of N.I.M.H.* (1971). It can also be used to look at reading and its role in people's lives now and in the past.

References

Hunt, I. 1964. *Across Five Aprils*. Chicago: Follett.
O'Brien, R. C. 1971. *Mrs. Frisby and the Rats of N.I.M.H.* New York: Atheneum.

B-23 *Pilgrim at Tinker Creek,* by Annie Dillard: A Read-Aloud Selection Used to Stimulate Discussion and Initiate Writing

Laura A. Smith

Introduction   (See the introduction to B-19 on the use of read alouds.)

It is often difficult for adults to remember the time when they learned to do something totally new to them. Some remember learning to drive a standard shift car, but since they have seen others do this before, they bring some prior concepts and experiences to the task. These learning experiences are most often described in terms of unsuccessful attempts to navigate a sloped driveway or negative comments from unsympathetic instructors. The learner's experiences are not usually described in terms of what they didn't know and suddenly realized. The typical "aha!" experience is not a frequent one for most of us.

All of us have read in child development texts that young babies *learn,* to see but we have no recollection of this process and find it difficult really to picture having to learn anything so basic.

Annie Dillard's description of the perceptions and experiences of adults who had cataracts from birth and after cataract surgery "learned to see" has given my students a new understanding of what seeing really means. This selection allows the class to discuss how human beings devise experiments to figure out how new information fits into what is already known, how human beings react to learning, and how experiences influence everyone's understanding of the world and the words that we use to describe it.

All of these help future teachers recognize student behaviors that are signs of new learning and understanding. I highly recommend all of Dillard's book, especially for students preparing to teach science. It is a rare look at the natural world and one woman's attempt to experience it.

Procedures   This read-aloud selection from *Pilgrim at Tinker Creek* (1974) needs little introduction unless you wish to introduce Annie Dillard or her books. She opens the book with, "I chanced upon a wonderful book by Marius von Senden, called *Space and Sight*" (p. 25), and then explains that the book contains case histories of patients who had never seen and then had cataracts removed and learned to make sense of visual information.

After describing von Senden's book, Dillard tells of her experiences trying to see her world as someone who did not know how to process visual information. Her experiences are a good reminder for future and current teachers of how difficult it is to ignore what we already know.

I particularly like the end of the selection as Dillard uses a line from Martin Buber from a story of a young rabbi and his teacher. "Yes," said Rabbi Elimelekh, "in my youth I saw that too. Later you don't see these things any more," (p. 30). After hearing the selection read aloud, students comment on things that they have taken for granted about being able to see. Occasionally students who started wearing glasses at five to eight years of age have recalled the first time that they saw what the teacher was writing on the board or seeing numbers and letters as something other than a blur.

After time for general comments and experiences, use questions to help students explore those ideas you feel are appropriate. My questions usually focus on the need of human beings to learn to do such basic things as see and the wonder of learning a new skill.

Afterword   I leave the writing assignments after this read aloud very open. At times I send students out to look at familiar scenes to try to consider how they would view them if they didn't already know what the scene was. They are then asked to try to describe the scene from a different point of view. Pictures of moonscapes or extreme close-ups of familiar objects can also be used.

Reference

Dillard, A. 1974. *Pilgrim at Tinker Creek*. New York: Harper's Magazine.

B-24 A Polar Map: Experiencing the Impact of Prior Knowledge on Understanding

LAURA A. SMITH

Introduction   All teachers need to be aware of the impact that prior knowledge has on any reader's or listener's ability to make sense of what is being read or heard. Even after struggling to follow income tax directions, identify an unfamiliar piece of equipment from a catalog description, or understand the impact of a business trend predicted in the *Wall Street Journal,* many student teachers (especially those who will be secondary teachers) are often still convinced that the solution to their students' problems is to "find the meaning of the unfamiliar words in the glossary" or "memorize the new terms from the vocabulary list provided by the teacher."

Procedures   Pool the participants' knowledge of maps. This will usually include terms found on a map, the location of various directions on the map (north at the top, etc.), and how maps can be used to find information (how to get to a particular place, what the geography or weather will be, etc.). You may want to facilitate this pooling process by using a map or transparency of a familiar map.

Provide each participant with a copy of a map of the North Polar region. A good source of small maps of this region is *Maps on File,* map 0.012 (published by Martin Greenwald Associates), found in most libraries in the reference section. A transparency or wall map can be used, but I have found more personal involvement in the experience if individual maps are used and the participants are allowed to work in pairs or trios. As the participants try to answer the following questions, remind them to focus on the prior knowledge they are using or assumptions that may be causing confusion.

1. Where is north on this map? (At the center.)
2. Where is south on this map? (All directions away from the center.)
3. How would you draw an east-west route? (A counterclockwise circle with the pole at the center.) West-east?
4. How would you show the directions southwest, southeast, and so forth?
5. Find the places on this map where you would be traveling north but your compass would be indicating that you are traveling south. (Locate the pole and geomagnetic pole.)

Depending on time, your interest in and knowledge of maps, and the amount of frustration your students are experiencing, add questions related to scale, time projection, and location of more familiar places off the edge of the map.

Even students who find the questions fairly easy to answer are often frustrated when they try to communicate their answers and usually resort to pointing.

Return to the list of the participants' prior knowledge about maps and discuss:

1. Assumptions that caused frustration in using the polar map.
2. New understandings they have developed about maps.
3. How the new understandings developed and who or which comments were most helpful in developing these understandings.
4. New understandings about the process of developing new concepts and vocabulary.

Afterword   The personal involvement in this process, each person's ability or inability to answer the questions or even understand the answers given by others, and the degrees of frustration felt by each person make this experience memorable. This also applies to the person directing the experience.

B-25   What Is the Main Idea?

DAVID L. TUCKER

Introduction   I use this engagement to demonstrate to an audience that questions about books and stories don't have one right answer, which sets the stage for exploring the reading process. Children, like adults, have varying opinions and views about the books and stories they read. This engagement helps participants be open to the idea of many interpretations as well as beginning to view the conversation and sharing of stories and books as an interactive, meaning-construction process.

Any story or small book can be used. Using a seemingly easy book makes the point that even what is considered a simple story can create varying interpretations and much discussion. The book that I use is *Harry, the Dirty Dog* (1976) by Gene Zion, with pictures by Margaret Bloy Graham. I chose it because I had an experience in a school with two first-grade teachers who wanted to use literature to determine that a child understood the main idea of a story. This story was common to both their classrooms. These two first-grade teacher themselves couldn't agree upon the main idea of this story.

Procedures   The audience needs a piece of paper and pencil. Read the story out loud; then ask the audience to write down the main idea of the story.

Depending on the size of the audience, have various people share their interpretations or have groups of three or four first discuss their interpretations and then share with the large group. Every time that I have conducted this engagement, someone asks, "Does the story even have a main idea?" Such thinking has to be encouraged and valued.

Reference

Zion, G. 1976. *Harry, the Dirty Dog*. Illus. M. B. Graham. New York: HarperCollins.

B-26   Teaching Teachers About Teaching Writing

MARGARET YATSEVITCH PHINNEY

Introduction   I teach a ten-week graduate course in teaching elementary writing. Most of my students are inservice teachers. One of my objectives for the course is to help these teachers see and *feel* themselves as writers. It isn't enough for them to do a term paper and some responses to the readings in order to say they "can write"; they need to believe they are authors, capable of engaging an audience of their peers. Ten weeks isn't much time to help someone come to this belief, but it can be done.

Procedures A major activity in the course is that the students become a part of a small writing group that produces a published book of writings to distribute to the rest of the class. I explain the project during the first class session but wait until the third session to get underway. I think it is important that they have a couple of weeks to get to know each other, to start building a sense of community and the accompanying trust. I do several trust-building activities during those first two classes (see protocols/engagements earlier in this section).

At the third session, I read a personal piece I have written and ask them to give me feedback in specific areas that are a struggle for me. Recently, it was a first draft of an attempt at a memoir, based on a childhood memory related to a dog we had. I chose this piece as a model because it was a situation that clearly had an emotional impact on me as a young child, and the emotion was starting to develop in the writing, but it is not an adult-world high-risk topic such as divorce, abuse, or major trauma. My experience has told me that adult resistant writers are very much like young resistant writers: they are afraid of the power of writing because it is a window on their fragility. They need to see that there are topics in their lives with which they can take risks without fear of shaming themselves or feeling inadequate or exposed. I open myself up as much as I can to their feedback, inviting them to come in closer to what Calkins and Harwayne (1990) call the "important passions in our lives" (p. 111). I learn so much from them about what is going on with my own writing. They, in turn, see what it can be like for someone to expose herself through her writing in a supportive yet inquisitive and analytical environment. Their feedback turns to questioning of feelings, motives, and deeper emotional undercurrents. It's scary for me, but I push myself. Sometimes I have to turn away a line of comments or questions, but throughout the process I alternate between the writer role and the teacher role. I discuss how my responses and reactions, as well as their comments and questions, connect to the writing process and how these processes might transfer to their own classroom situations. They carry this model with them as they become engaged in the project.

I follow this demonstration with a recap of the intent of the project and hold up samples of past publications that will be available for them to browse through for the remainder of the quarter. I also clearly acknowledge that some people may not want to try very personal writing at all in this situation. On the overhead, I offer a list of genres they might like to consider, depending on the amount of risk they feel comfortable taking.

For those not comfortable with personal topics the following sources are useful:

- Articles aimed at professional publication in newsletters or teachers' magazines.
- Classroom vignettes.
- Descriptions of events.
- Creatively or humorously written recipes or directions.
- Opinions or editorials.
- Creative writing.
- Fiction stories.
- Stories for children.

- Poetry.
- Personal experiences.
- Memoirs (see Chapter 12 of Calkins and Harwayne 1990).

The next step is to have them try out a bit of relatively safe sharing of themselves. I ask them to take a few minutes to write down something about their names: how they feel about their names, why they were named as they were, and so forth. Names are generally important to us or elicit feelings of one kind or another. After five minutes, I ask them to turn to the person next to them and read or tell about what they have written. They are simply directed to practice active, responsive listening for this exercise. I conclude by making up the publication groups. I put the students randomly into groups of three or four. (I have found that three is the best number to allow enough time for giving adequate feedback to each other during the forty-five minutes I allot each week for their publication work.) During this first group session, I ask them to converse, get to know each other, and start talking about writing possibilities that may have come to mind. Mainly, I want the students to start feeling comfortable with each other.

Between the third and fourth sessions, they draft their first piece of writing. During the fourth session, before they get in their publication groups to share those first pieces, I do another activity involving them in a somewhat riskier level of conferencing, this one more engagement than demonstration. The purpose is to warm them up for the real thing and to give them experience with how the writing process works. The steps of the exercise are as follows:

1. Take five minutes to think about and list some events in your life that evoked strong feelings in you (e.g., fear, anger, joy, humiliation, confusion, ambiguity, astonishment/surprise, love, comfort, relief, anxiety, awe). [I have these on an overhead, and give examples of a couple.]
2. Turn to someone next to you and talk about one of those times.
3. Take fifteen minutes to start writing about that event.
4. Turn to your neighbor and share what you've written. The listener tells what he or she heard, what stood out as strong or potentially strong, and what he or she is looking forward to hearing more about.
5. Reverse positions.
6. Each write about possible directions for the piece given the feedback.

We follow this exercise with a discussion of how it went, how they felt, and how it connects with the readings they have done so far on the writing and conferring processes in general. There are comments on the scariness of doing this, but typically they are more comfortable than they realized they would be because of the preliminary exercises and the emphasis on the need for trust. They then start the real process in their comfortable, small groups.

After this third class, I budget time in each class for them to work on their publications. I make myself as scarce as possible during this time, while still being available if they have technical questions. They don't need an outsider leaning over their shoulders making them feel judged or kept track of. Like older children who have been trained throughout schooling to follow directions carefully, many of these teacher students can't quite trust that whatever they decide to do will be an acceptable fulfillment of the assignment. They ask me, "How long should the publication be?" My answer is, "As long as you want it, have time to make it, and can afford to make it, considering you need to supply thirty copies." "Can we write an article together?" "Do we all have to write about the same topic or on the same theme?" "Do we need a table of contents? a title?" "Do we put our names on each piece or only on the cover?"

My answer to all such questions is, "It's your publication. You may present it any way you wish." Their questions may seem trivial, but they are representations of their fear of failure in a system that is structured to threaten failure when details aren't observed. When the inevitable question about grades comes up, I say, "If you participate in the feedback process in your group and you make a contribution to the publication, you will get full credit for this project." My objective is to show them that writing can be an enjoyable, safe, and fulfilling activity providing the environment is supportive, there is plenty of choice to allow for self-regulation of risk, and evaluation is based only on engagement—on trying out the activity. I want the students to experience what I am asking them to have their students experience: writing in a social setting involving sharing and feedback, particularly in the safety of small groups, and, ultimately, for a larger purpose—in this case, publishing for the whole group.

At the eighth session, each group brings enough copies of their publication to distribute to everyone, including me. Their homework assignment for week 9 is to read all the publications and make notes on what stood out for them in each. I tell them, "Think of what kinds of comments *you* would like to hear on a piece of yours that was finished and published." Between weeks 8 and 9 I write responses to each publication and give them out at the ninth session. During group time each group consolidates its comments on each publication, and members of the group divide up the work of writing a letter to each of the other publication groups: one letter from each group to each group. They have my letters as a model if they want to attend to them. At the tenth session, the letters are distributed to the groups, and we have an end-of-quarter celebration.

A small final assignment is that the students are asked to write a reflection on the project, discussing what the experience was like for them and how they see their experience translating into their understanding of classroom learning and classroom practice. Their comments speak for themselves:

"This was a threatening prospect to me when I read the syllabus and listened to you discuss it with the class. However, because of the people I was with for this class project I found it to be a fun and rewarding growth experience for me!"
"It is still extremely difficult to do much personal writing. If it were not for the moral support and guidance of my publication group, I would have been unable to produce what I did. They each gave me confidence to continue and to dwell on my strengths instead of my weaknesses."
"I can see how the process works even better when the group has more time to build that base of trust. I felt that my stories improved, as well as my self-concept as a writer, through the process."
"I have to admit that at the beginning of the quarter, I failed to see the importance of us writing. After all, weren't we here to learn how to help the children become better writers? Well, throughout the quarter, I realized that I learned

more about children's writing through my own experiences with it than anything. Sometimes it's easier to say this is what you need to do rather than showing them strategies or ideas that worked for me. I had never given a thought to what it must be like for them. I was more product oriented. . . . Working with a group of people on this was a great experience. As well as getting to know them and making new friends, I learned we are all writers, we all have it in us to write. We all just need the encouragement to do it, and feel safe doing so!"

Afterword   To be teachers of writing, we must be writers ourselves. By showing my teacher-students first that I am willing to write more than impersonal academic text, then providing them with an opportunity to do the same, I am trying to help them take a small step toward believing they can be models for their own students.

Reference

Calkins, L. M., and S. Harwayne. 1990. *Living Between the Lines*. Portsmouth, NH: Heinemann.

TRANSFORMING CURRICULUM
WITH LEARNERS

Carol Gilles and Shirley B. Ernst, editors

Whole language curriculum doesn't come from a guide or from a publisher's text; it's a reflection of educators' beliefs. Not only is the curriculum the vehicle for the content and process of the course, but it also becomes an entity in its own right, providing opportunities for learning by its very format. Learners understand more fully what integrated curriculum means when they have experienced a course that combines language arts with, say, science or social studies. A course in which learning communities are a major component of the format suggests to participants that learning takes place in a social environment. When students experience the celebration of cultural diversity in their classes and are given opportunities to reflect on what that might mean to them as teachers, they have opportunities to consider language diversity issues.

Curriculum is dynamic. As we grow and change, the curriculum must reflect what we have learned and what we now believe. Our belief systems and those of many of our students are often separated by gulfs of age, experiences, and values. Therefore we must negotiate the curriculum with our students. By engaging them in authentic curriculum experiences, we encourage students to reconsider some of their beliefs about children and learning. The chapters in this part reflect the processes these authors use to design curricular engagements that cause students to reflect. We consider curriculum through descriptions of teacher education courses designed to offer integrated experiences, then move to a focus on particular whole language classes, and finally to a view of an entire program of study. Although the chapters are diverse, there are common curricular themes.

Wayne Serebrin and Joan Irvine offer in Chapter 13 a detailed and powerful explanation of how they collaboratively organized a course concerned with language arts and early-years social studies. The voices of the students who engaged in the new experiences show us the course from the students' perspectives as well as how the course impacted the authors' teaching lives. David Heine and Stephen Hornstein also deviated from the traditional curriculum as they created a collaborative course in which students first experience a whole language curriculum for themselves and then create a whole language curriculum for their classrooms. Heine and Horstein's model demonstrates, with examples, how multidisciplined classes are conceptualized.

The subsequent chapters deal with particular course content taught from a whole language perspective. Yvonne Freeman examines an innovative graduate bilingual education course. Since many of her graduate students teach in classrooms where children speak more than one language, she teaches the class in Spanish and English. She demonstrates that teachers can effectively teach English and content in a bilingual setting.

David Freeman describes a most unusual linguistic course: one that engages teachers in linguistic inquiry so that they can explore language questions with their own students. The course format is explained through three projects about syntax, morphology, and phonology. As teachers see the practical side of linguistics, they are likely to engage in language study with their own students.

Finally, we think of teacher education in broader terms. David and Patricia Heine help us to understand a cohort model of graduate education. They offer five inquiry themes that hold the cohort together and strategies they use for building communities.

Each of these chapters profiles innovative change at work, the reactions of students, and the enthusiasm of the instructors. As we reflect on these chapters and our own teaching situations, we find specific examples to answer our questions and facilitate our own curriculum transformation.

13

Empowering Ourselves to Inquire: Teacher Education as a Collaborative Enterprise

Wayne Serebrin and Joan Irvine

As teacher educators, most of us have heard ourselves or our colleagues complain that "undergraduates don't want theory; they just want recipes and teaching tips." This sentiment grows out of the difficulty education students sometimes have when we expect them to examine their beliefs and values in relation to the practices they are reading about, observing in classrooms, and defining themselves as student teachers. We often feel frustrated by their reluctance to engage in critical, reflexive thinking.

In fairness to our students, though, this may be the first time they have been asked to theorize, and to articulate or question their own beliefs and values. We can empathize with Cindy, one of our students, who wrote: "My first attitude was will someone please tell me where I can find a book with all the answers on teaching. My second feeling was okay there is no book, but Joan and Wayne you know everything about teaching, so p-l-e-a-s-e tell me." At the time, Cindy believed there was one best way to teach, experts knew what it was, and her job was to learn what they told her.

Ironically, because we feel this pressure to provide preservice teachers with answers, we find ourselves engaged in the very model of teaching-as-telling we had intended to challenge through our course of experiences. And this is not the only source of pressure. We also hear our colleagues in universities and in schools talking about the need to cover predetermined curricula to ensure that students will be properly prepared to teach.

The problem is not that we are unaware of the dissonance between the nature of the ideas we are teaching students, but that we have managed to convince ourselves that under the circumstances we have little choice. The large number of students we face, the limited amount of time scheduled to work with them, and the substantial commitment of energy and time it takes to teach in a more collaborative manner all become part of a stock of reasons for not examining and altering our practices as educators. We settle for pointing out to our students that

"of course, we would never teach this way if we were working with children."
Then we encounter a comment like the one we read in Christine's journal:

> The professors in the Faculty of Education often preach about inquiry, methods,
> hands-on experiences, and collaborative learning, but how do they do this? By lec-
> turing, of course. We have seen almost no examples or participated in activities
> that require us to inquire, to do some hands-on work, or to learn collaboratively.
> We have learned to give the professors what they want in terms of answers and
> written work. We have learned to play their game, and to forget what we think
> and feel is acceptable and important.

The sting we felt from Christine's words instantly persuaded us of their significance. Her comments laid bare the inconsistencies in our own curricula and
practices. The two of us were so moved by what we read in our students' journals (a common assignment shared across our courses) that we had no choice but
to bring our own teacher education curriculum and practices in line with what
we knew and cared about as teachers. Together we decided that we would plan
and teach our language arts, social studies, and early-years curriculum and
instructional courses collaboratively—with each other and with our students. By
choosing to work in this way, we felt we had a far better chance of altering our
own roles, relationships, and practices as learners and teachers and of inviting
our students to do the same.

OUR PERCEPTIONS OF RISK

We did not make this commitment to a new model of teacher education without
trepidation. We were well aware of the significant risks within the institutional
context. We knew there would be no support for teaming and sharing course
work and assignments in terms of work load formulas. We understood that
tenure and promotion documents would not recognize time necessary to make
this a genuinely collaborative enterprise; we also knew curriculum negotiation
with students across what would normally have been separate course boundaries
would be difficult. Indeed, the University of Manitoba requires professors to provide, within the first two weeks of classes, separate course syllabi that list topics
to be covered; text selections and assigned readings; a schedule and description
of all course assignments; and specific grading procedures. We were astounded
by how difficult it was even to modify the faculty timetable so that our three
courses, for each of two sections (each with thirty-five students), could be scheduled together at the same time and in the same room.

Of more worry, though, was risking preconceptions of students, who in their
final year of a four-year program would be coming to us with a number of expectations about what and how our courses should be *taught* to them. We predicted
that our students would be uncomfortable with the idea of sharing power with
the two of us. We knew that habitual patterns of interaction—professors talking,
assigning readings and papers; students listening and taking notes, and completing assigned readings and papers—would have to change if we were to engage in
real conversations with one another.

ASSUMPTIONS ABOUT OUR STUDENTS

Our starting point had to be our students. We created a list of assumptions about where our students would most likely be coming from philosophically. Putting these assumptions down on paper made our fears about how our students might respond to our curriculum invitations more tangible, less surprising, and not quite so terrifying.

OUR COLLABORATION

In many ways our collaboration was odd. Joan was nearing the end of a long career in teacher education. Wayne was fresh from graduate work and beginning his. There were differences in age, educational background, experience, and gender. More important than these differences, though, were our shared worldviews, our visions of learning and knowledge, and our excitement for the potential of those visions to transform our students and ourselves. Each of us knew that we would be changed by the experiences we were undertaking. We were aware of how vulnerable we would be with each other and with our students. This awareness charged our partnership with excitement and a sense of adventure, but it also increased anxiety. Strangely, our insecurity and vulnerability (which we decided to share with our students) helped us to understand in a very real way what students had to risk as learners in this program and made us an integral part of a community of learners.

We pooled the time for three courses and agreed to team teach in order to amass six contact hours with each of two sections each week. Each term included ten weeks of classes, followed by a five-week practicum. (These students had a variety of other curriculum courses that were not part of this collaboration and one day of practice each week in the schools.)

PLANNING PRIOR TO THE YEAR

We decided we would not provide a list of the topics to be covered or readings to be completed. But without a prearranged course outline, we knew our students would need some way of maintaining a focus throughout the year. As part of our preplanning we devised sets of questions to provide this focus by setting out the parameters of the three courses:

1. How do young children learn? What kinds of contexts support and extend young children's learning?
2. What is language arts? What is the role of language arts in the learning of young children?
3. What is social studies? What is the role of social studies in the learning of young children?

We shared common assignments for all three courses, and each assignment was stated broadly to allow individual students as much freedom as possible to pursue their own inquiries. We also determined the grade for each student for all three courses. We never imagined how much time this aspect of our collaboration would take.

To start off the year, we felt we needed an initial course experience that would reawaken our students' awareness of, and interest in, their own learning. The primary intent of this experience was to create an inquiry context in which the students were fully engaged in a collaborative, interdisciplinary curriculum. A community exploration provided our students with an opportunity to become involved in firsthand social studies inquiry as adult learners, to feel the wonder of learning something that they chose, and to reflect on themselves as learners.

PLANNING DURING THE YEAR

Once the program began, our collaboration focused on the conversations we had with our students in a variety of settings. These conversations, along with our students' questions, provided us with new directions and potentials for creating curriculum with them. We met regularly to share our perceptions about where our students were and to prepare the supports for continuing curricular engagements. Together, we clarified our beliefs about our roles as teachers in this new way of working with our students; in particular, we questioned the role of our own expertise and the expertise of others in the making of the curriculum. We struggled to develop new language that would be consistent with what we believed. We shared readings and other visions of teacher education with each other, and we raised new questions for ourselves and set new directions for our own learning.

NEGOTIATING CURRICULUM WITH OUR STUDENTS

Central to our vision of teacher education was the belief that our primary responsibility was to work with our students to establish an inquiry community. This meant that all members of our inquiry community needed to feel empowered to assume responsibility for their own learning, and that over time they would also come to care for each other and support each other's learning. The authority we had traditionally held as teacher educators had to be diffused, shared, negotiated, and critically considered in light of whatever knowledge we were pursuing (Bleich 1988).

We engaged our students immediately by asking them to answer the three focusing questions identified earlier in this chapter to accomplish two goals. First, this exercise allowed students to think about their own experiences and what they already knew. Second, responding to questions allowed students to raise their own questions. Next, students worked in groups to share their ideas about what they needed to know. This second experience started the process of learning about each other and established a base for working together throughout the year. The groups put their questions on large sheets of paper, which became public artifacts. Common concerns were identified by the total group, and we started the process of investigating these issues. At the beginning of the course, we took a great deal of responsibility for providing supports for the learning experiences. As the year progressed, the students took more initiative and shared their resources and insights in an ongoing manner.

We established some rituals (Peterson 1992) that continued throughout the year. For instance, at the start of each class, we read aloud to the students, often from a children's story or perhaps a piece that could illustrate or extend an idea we had been working with or might introduce a new idea. The selected pieces were excellent examples of writing and frequently evoked an emotional response.

We established one block of time each week as a period for writing. The students conducted professional interviews with one another in pairs. The purpose of our initial writing experiences was to introduce the authoring cycle (Short, Harste, and Burke 1996; Short and Burke 1991) to our students through experiencing it and to help each student become acquainted with one other person in the class in more depth, in order to continue to develop a sense of community. We made sure the students understood that this was the purpose for these experiences. As well, by working with a student partner ourselves, the two of us were able to share this writing experience and our own thoughts and feelings about it with our students.

In the first week we started a community exploration experience that asked the students to select a site in the community they wished to explore. The sites ranged from historical venues to natural environments to hospitals, restaurants, and farms. Our students gathered their own questions, visited their sites, recorded their findings with cameras, VCRs, and audiotape recorders, took notes, and dragged back various artifacts to class. These trips seemed to bring our students to life. They returned filled with enthusiasm for their inquiries and more relaxed with one another. Each group was given an opportunity to compile its findings and make a presentation to the rest of us. This activity gave us the chance to share adventures with the whole group about ambulance rides, confronting large cows on farm lanes, and meeting backhoe operators eating their lunches in the middle of garbage-strewn landfill sites. We now had a stock of shared stories, which contributed greatly to an emerging sense of our own community.

Our intention was to enable our students to experience the process and the methods of inquiry that we hoped they would pursue with children in classrooms; we believed that our students had to live this kind of experience themselves if we were to expect them to create similar kinds of experiences with children.

These community experiences aroused many questions in our students' minds about the inquiry process, learning in general, and the learning of young children specifically. These questions became the source of new activities in our classes and provided a focus for professional readings. Soon they started to bring books and articles of their own to share with the others.

Next, we asked each small group to develop what we called a playscape: a learning environment that would allow children (who had first engaged in a similar kind of experience to what our students had done) to continue to explore the potential for ongoing inquiry into key aspects of their community study. For example, one group of students had visited a local pizza parlor. When they examined their own questions, they realized that they had focused on the economics of operating a restaurant. This led them to the domain of economics as a focus for creating a playscape environment that would allow children to explore pizza making, advertising, prices, and the day-to-day management of a restaurant. In their playscape, they included a variety of learning materials, such as the ingredients for making pizzas, the recipes, and all of the measuring tools they would need. They included ads and commercials, menus, bills, and boxes from the restaurant they had visited. They also provided materials for the children to develop their own ads, commercials, bills, and menus. The area was supplemented with a wide variety of reading materials about cooking and restaurants. Because these playscapes also included an opportunity for children to play, this group set up both a model kitchen and an eating area, where children could pretend to make pizzas and play at being chefs, servers, and customers.

We asked students to create these environments so they could see the potentials of their community studies for inventing a variety of learning opportunities with children in classrooms. Once the playscapes were developed, we provided time for each group to make a presentation to their colleagues about the potentials of their study.

Regular group meetings gave groups an opportunity to discuss their experiences with each other and with us—to share their perceptions of their own learning and to gather their new questions. These conversations added to our collective thinking about curriculum, learning, and teaching.

While all of this was going on, we continued with writing sessions, immersed ourselves in professional readings, discussions, and demonstrations that arose from our readings and other experiences, and asked and recorded new questions. In addition, our students spent one day a week in a classroom, returning each time with more questions of practice. As the year progressed, the students not only had more questions, but their questions became both more complex and more focused.

The first term culminated in an assignment asking the students to explore in writing their understandings of the three questions we had introduced in the first class of the term. We asked the students to illustrate their work with examples from their own experiences as learners and teachers and to support their positions from their readings.

Our students left us at this point to spend a five-week block in the schools in early-years classrooms. While they were away, we read their papers and spent hours providing each student with written feedback, a joint comment, and a grade. We did this separately first and then met to share our perceptions. We spent a great deal of time sharing our thoughts on what the students had accomplished in the first term and how we could use what we had learned to inform our curriculum in the second term.

When the students returned for the second term, they had many new questions that had arisen from their observations of teacher practice and their own attempts at teaching young children. Many of these questions were challenges to current early-years practices, which we had been studying in the first term, while others were "how-to" questions. When we added our written feedback to their new questions, we had a full agenda for the second term.

Since most of the students seemed ready to take charge of their own learning in the second term, the focus of the curriculum shifted to support a more personal pursuit of inquiry, within the context of an increasingly connected social community. Indeed, many students had developed support groups within the larger class and ways of supporting each other's inquiries.

It also became evident that the students were realizing that they would soon be applying for teaching positions of their own and taking the full responsibilities of early-years classrooms. They appreciated how important it was to be able to articulate *their* beliefs and to be able to support them. They also knew that they needed to be able to envision how they would carry out a program with a group of young children. Our focusing question for this second term became: "If your own classroom is to reflect a collaborative inquiry model of curriculum, what will it be like?"

Again we returned to the challenge of creating an inquiry-driven, interdisciplinary curriculum. This time we spent several weeks engaged in curriculum experiences that explored one of the social studies domains in depth. We selected history as the domain and involved ourselves in personal histories, which made it possible for us to think and act as historians through a series of workshops in which we learned to use artifacts, historical photos, and documents. Then the students brought evidence of their own personal histories in the form of pictures and artifacts. They shared these items as well as stories of their personal lives. While all of this was happening, we read Patricia MacLachlan's *Journey* (1991) and then *Sarah, Plain and Tall* (1985). We involved ourselves in literature circles that enabled us to feel personal and social history themes in a very different way from our history workshops. Through this interdisciplinary curriculum, our students understood more clearly the role of the domains in inquiry-based learning.

Our assignment for this second term was the development of a portfolio, framed by the inquirer's own early-years curriculum questions (within the broader framework of the focusing questions with which we had begun the year's work). This portfolio included evidence of how and why each inquirer had pursued the questions he or she had chosen. In these portfolios were recollections and reflections on the full range of each inquirer's experiences throughout the year, the development of a personal philosophical position on early-years education, an action plan for future learning, and a piece of tentative curriculum planning for our students' final block of student teaching.

This was a heavy agenda for both our students and ourselves. And yet, before we knew it, classes were over, our students were ready to return to student teaching, and we were once again providing written feedback to each student on their portfolios. Each of us was completely exhausted, but also exhilarated and somewhat triumphant. We knew we had accomplished something worthwhile.

THE IMPACT OF THE YEAR'S EXPERIENCES

What an exciting and, at times, frustrating year this had been for our students and for us. Not only had we felt the confidence of our students building throughout the year, but we had shared in their emotional swings from joy to despair as all of us had struggled to take ownership of our own learning.

As we read students' portfolios, we were especially interested in locating evidence of their having found their own voices as learners and teachers, of their having come to value collaboration, and of their having grown to appreciate the importance of their own questions and the changes in those questions over the year. Essentially we were interested in evidence of our students' having become more reflexive learners.

A number of samples from the writings of two of our students, Clare and Denise, serve as an illustration of some of this evidence.

As expected, we found that at the beginning of the year, students had been anxious about the value of their own ideas and were nervous about sharing them. After the first week of classes Clare wrote in her journal:

> I find myself encouraged by the others, although I am a bit hesitant to share all my ideas. I don't want them to think I'm bossy or stupid.

For Clare, this feeling was only gradually replaced by a growing confidence in her own ideas. In February she wrote:

> It seems to me that being a parent has given me a lot of skills in dealing with children and that this is a valid source of educational experience.

In some instances our students went beyond gaining confidence in their own voices to recognizing how their voices had been subordinated by others, perceived by them to have more power. Denise shared her thoughts on this in January:

> All my experiences in school from Grade One to Graduate courses . . . stressed comprehension and analysis of texts for the literary/narrative elements and to determine the author's meaning (singularly). I subconsciously thought that what I did—try to make sense of the meaning of the text in terms of my life—was wrong, unscholarly, and a bit crazy. It has been our experience with *Journey* which has led me to really know what "transactional reading" means. This all seems to be tied to my lack of voice. I have not been encouraged to trust my voice, to trust myself as a reader or a writer.

Throughout our students' writings there was a growing sense of their having become members of a community of learners. Many students had been uncomfortable with this idea when we began. Clare put it this way in a journal entry early in the school year:

> I find I am not so keen on group work. The fear is always that only a few will do the work or that one or two will dominate.

At least initially, Denise was equally uneasy working with her colleagues:

> I seem to have a greater need for order and organizing information than my group members do. I still find group work generally to be difficult.

However, these feelings shifted over the year for most of the students in our class, as we can see in this comment from Denise at the end of the year:

> Within this community of learners each learner was treated as a whole unique human being who had something valuable to contribute to the community and whose questions were vitally important.

From the first day of our courses, we had tried to encourage our students to value their own questions and to keep a record of them. Their questions provided us with many insights into the processes of thinking and reflecting in which they had been engaged. The following collection of some of Clare's questions demonstrates part of her inquiry over the year and reflects her inquiry into more complex and focused issues of learning and teaching:

> I want to consider the issue of play some more. What exactly do we mean by play? I can see all of this for my Kindergarten class but are parents going to buy all of this? [September 20]

> I really wonder if the kids will get so interested in everything. I always have this feeling they'll be missing something from the "real" curriculum. [October 4]

> So is spelling acquired? Is it developmental? Are there some kids who are just more gifted than others? [October 11]

> How do you start teaching reading to very young students? [October 17]

> Why make some kids stop playing and come to circle time? [November 19]

> If my cooperating teacher had prepared for the [dragon dance assembly] the day before and had read a few books, it would have been so much more meaningful. What is the problem here? There is no long-range planning that I can see. [February 3]

> What is the purpose of Kindergarten? What is the role of books and literature in Kindergarten? [February 21]

We believe that records like this helped our students monitor their own growth and shifting perspectives.

Finally, we include a powerful piece from Denise's journal. Rather lengthy, it captures how at least one student thought through an incident that was most upsetting to her. It reveals how powerful old ways of thinking are, how fragile we are when we are attempting to move away from these old patterns, and how promising different practices of teacher education could be.

> Why am I so upset? I think Wayne is right, it has something, no everything, to do with how we understand knowledge.

> I had written to Professor B., a real bona fide historian, to come to my class the first week of our study of pioneers to talk with the kids about what it is like to be an historian and to answer their questions about the methods of an historian and maybe say something about pioneer lifestyles in Manitoba.

> I phoned him this morning and talked to him. He said he wondered if I really knew what I was doing because an historian working at his level doesn't have much to offer a young child. So I told him what I saw him possibly coming to do. He asked me if I had studied and understood Piaget's stages and what I knew about the conceptualizing ability of a seven-year-old. (This immediately made me feel like a fool: I mustn't understand about children, because if I did I certainly would not have presupposed anything so outrageous, he implied, or am I overreacting?)

> I said, "Yes, I understand what you mean—they wouldn't be able to understand at a university level—but I thought you could just answer their questions about what you do, and why, and how, etc." His interests, he told me, were in social

classes (and some other technical terms I've forgotten). He was "not an expert in what foods they ate . . . " I mentioned some questions they might have, like: what were the bathrooms like long ago (recalling Kathleen's first question in our own community exploration brainstorming session). "Well," he said, "I could do something on an historical look at bathrooms long ago. Although," he laughed, "it might upset some of the parents to have their children discussing excrement." No! that's not what I mean, I thought to myself. I don't want an historical diatribe on bathrooms, just answers to children's questions in a simple, meaningful way.

Professor B. said he would come: "it would be mildly amusing for both sides to see how useless it would be to have an historian talk to seven-year-olds." He could see the value in his coming for me, because it would be a failure and that would be an interesting (I presume he meant intellectually interesting) project for me to write up for the Faculty. We were "allowed to have projects that failed, weren't we?" he asked. "Oh, yes," I said. "Anyway, yes," again he said he would come. "Well," I said, "I would feel badly taking you away from your busy schedule when you don't feel it would be of benefit to anyone." "Well, no," once again he said, "it could be of benefit for [me] to see how much of a failure it would be."

I said, "thank you" and that I needed to think about it. He said to talk with an education professor about what children can conceptualize at that level. I said I would get back to him next week.

I got off the phone and I was shaking. I didn't quite know why. My first instinct was to go and see Joan. She would help me sort it out. I found Wayne and then Joan. Wayne and Joan, they listened to me. They heard me right away. Okay. I'm okay. My views do count. I am not a fool! Wayne said, "This is all about how you understand knowledge." Yes, it always is how we see it and how we see young children. Joan was so empathetic. Yes, my idea was great. Oh! Thank God! I'm not an idiot for having had that idea. Wayne said, "Write about it." Here I am. I left Joan's office and came and wrote. Now I understand some of the things that bothered me . . . that triggered this feeling of upset, anger, disappointment, sadness.

11:30 Class is beginning. [February 20]

At dinner tonight I asked my son Timothy (eight-year-old, in Grade 3) what is an historian?

TIMOTHY: I don't know.

ME: Well, what do you think an *historian* [*stressing the first syllable*] might be?

TIMOTHY: A person who studies history.

ME: Yes! What is history?

TIMOTHY: Stuff that happened in the past.

ME: What questions would you ask an historian if he came to your class?

TIMOTHY: What things did they study about the past? What is it like to be an historian? What things were like in the past . . . things like schools and machines and how they ran. How much money does he get? Why he became an historian. [February 21]

So here was a three-minute exchange with very little lead in or input and Timothy came up with good, solid questions.

Why couldn't Professor B. have come and responded to such questions simply and meaningfully? How can children's questions lead to an experience of failure? Now I see why Wayne was so concerned that I was caught up in Piaget's stage theory, or at least caught up enough to write about it in my first Insights Paper. We do owe a great deal to Piaget. But his stage theory is very limiting when you consider children's abilities to understand and learn socially. Timothy may be only eight years old, but he is capable of understanding all kinds of abstraction. Professor B.'s comments about my understandings of Piaget and about children define his stance, his understandings of how children learn and the experiences he sees as relevant to their stage of development. I don't want him to come to my classroom because I respect the children too much and value their questions and their understandings. [February 22]

THE IMPACT OF THE YEAR'S EXPERIENCES ON US

We gained confidence in ourselves and in each other as learners and teachers. With each other's support, we had been able to take the same kinds of risks as learners and teachers that we had invited our students to take.

As teachers we felt vulnerable working with the kind of messy curriculum in which all participants ask their own questions and take more and more ownership of their own learning. It was hard for us to trust that our students' questions would lead them into such focused and in-depth questions of both theory and practice. This was an important lesson.

We learned to listen well to our students as co-learners. This kind of responsive teaching demanded that we become far more systematic in keeping track of their questions and concerns. We came to appreciate our ongoing responsibility to gather and share resources in support of their inquiries.

Most often our students' concerns were tied to the relationship between theory and practice in the real world of young children. While we had tried to live an inquiry-driven, interdisciplinary curriculum with our students as adult learners, many of them had remained uneasy about the practical moves necessary to transform these experiences into curriculum with young children. Our awareness of this discomfort pushed us to keep trying out what we were doing in our university classroom, with groups of young children. We then wove this action research back into our teaching demonstrations and conversations in class. It was not long before our students picked up on these demonstrations and engaged in and shared what they too had tried out with children.

By the end of the year, we knew how incredibly powerful this experience had been for us and for most of our students. New voices had been heard, new conversations started, and we had created a community of learners who wished to continue these conversations (Harste 1989). In the spring our students organized a meeting with the Dean of the Faculty to help him understand why their experiences had been so unique and so valuable.

Our roles, relationships, and practices with our students were not the only ones to change. The two of us had come to know, in an intimate and profound way, what it meant to think together as members of a "thought collective" (Fleck 1935/1979). Collaborative, interdisciplinary curriculum had taken on a whole new meaning. Each of us now had a double perspective. For one of us, this opened up a world of inquiry beyond literature to oral histories, artifacts, photographs, and buildings as sources. For the other, this meant developing a new sense of the critical role of language, and specifically metaphor, in the ways in which we interpret our experiences to ourselves and others. As well, we both came to appreciate that collaborative, interdisciplinary inquiry enables and values the connections that learners make for themselves and that such curriculum invites learners to know and act in new ways, from more than one perspective.

While we have never wondered, for even a moment, whether this experience was worthwhile, it would be misleading not to acknowledge the demands our collaborative planning, team teaching, and joint responding to our students' work placed on our time and energy. Yet neither of us ever wants to work alone again. We feel a renewed need to work more closely with students, teacher education colleagues, and classroom teachers to better understand the constraints of inclusive, collaborative practice. Those of us who are engaged in teacher education "have to get gutsier" (Edelsky 1992, p. 328), and to do this we will surely have to rely much more on one another.

REFERENCES

Bleich, D. 1988. *The Double Perspective: Language, Literacy, and Social Relations.* New York: Oxford University Press.

Edelsky, C. 1992, September. "A Talk with Carole Edelsky About Politics and Literacy." Interview with William H. Teale, ed. In *Language Arts,* 69, 5: 324–329.

Fleck, L. (1935) 1979. *Genesis and Development of a Scientific Fact.* T. J. Trenn and R. K. Merton, eds. F. Bradley and T. J. Trenn, trans. Chicago: University of Chicago Press.

Harste, J. C. 1989. "The Future of Whole Language." In *The Elementary School Journal,* 90, 2: 243–249.

MacLachlan, P. 1985. *Sarah, Plain and Tall.* New York: HarperCollins.

———. 1991. *Journey.* New York: Delacorte Press.

Peterson, R. 1992. *Life in a Crowded Place: Making a Learning Community.* Portsmouth, NH: Heinemann.

Short, K. G., and C. Burke. 1991. *Creating Curriculum: Teachers and Students as a Community of Learners.* Portsmouth, NH: Heinemann.

Short, K. G., J. C. Harste, and C. Burke. 1996. *Creating Classrooms for Authors and Inquirers.* Portsmouth, NH: Heinemann.

LIVING AND LEARNING WHOLE LANGUAGE WITH PRESERVICE TEACHERS

David Heine and Stephen E. Hornstein

As teacher educators, we have been working to put whole language theory into practice in our language arts and social studies methods classes. Our goal has been to create authentic learning experiences for teaching that addressed the needs and questions asked of and by preservice teachers and to demonstrate our whole language philosophy.

We use the following list of premises as a lens to examine and change or accommodate to the constraints imposed by the university (real or imagined) and our own evolving understanding of pedagogy:

- Learning happens best in wholes rather than in disjointed, decontextualized parts.
- Learning happens best when learners perceive and participate in authentic uses of what is being learned.
- Learning happens best when we value and take advantage of the social nature of learning.
- Learning happens best when learners have control over what, when, and how they learn.
- Learning happens best when learners have the opportunity to reflect on their learning.

University faculty who work to change their curriculum to reflect a whole language philosophy find that many of the structures within schools serve beliefs contrary to whole language. Grading, the partitioning of time and subjects, the use of space, and the traditionally defined roles of student and teacher are all inherited from a belief system that assumes that learning is the accumulation of facts that can be sequentially ordered, delivered, and measured. We combine language arts and social studies methods into a single unified course to achieve twice the room and contact hours with each group of students. Adjacent rooms with tables provide flexibility to work in small or large groups. A portfolio assessment and evaluation system help students explore issues concerning assessment and evaluation as they analyze their own and each other's work (see Chapter 18 for details).

A MODEL OF TEACHER EDUCATION

We use the model shown in Figure 14 to conceptualize what we do in our integrated language arts and social studies classes. A reading methods course, a classroom management course, and a seminar on inclusive education are part of our program core. The model has two intertwined strands: Living a Whole Language Curriculum and Creating a Whole Language Curriculum. The work that students complete occurs within the context of a lived whole language curriculum. The activities in which they participate help them to build the understandings from which whole language curricula can be created.

LIVING A WHOLE LANGUAGE CURRICULUM

Our classes revolve around six major themes: Engaging in Invitations, Reflecting on Our Learning, Examining Theory and Personal Belief, Reflecting on Younger Learners, Exploring and Critiquing Pedagogy, and Creating Whole Language Environments (see Figure 14).

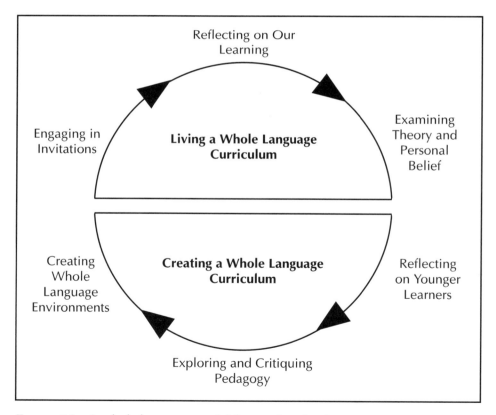

FIGURE 14   A whole language model for teacher development

Engaging in Invitations

Our classes allow students to choose tasks that are personally important and interesting and encourage them to help one another, collaborate on a variety of tasks, and stretch their thinking. Embedded within each of the engagements are opportunities for students to draw from their life experiences; to work, write, read, and think together; to bounce their ideas and thoughts off one another; to refine their thinking, writing, or work; and to share newly created knowledge.

Our intent is to provide firsthand authentic learning encounters within a school context. Because whole language theory speaks to all learners irrespective of age, it is not expected that our preservice teachers "take on the role of children" in these engagements. By living the curriculum, students come to know it from the inside out.

Reflecting on Our Learning

Journals, discussion, self-evaluations, and peer evaluations are tools to help students reflect on their learning. It is through this reflection that they come to understand their learning processes better and how others learn as well.

Because the students are still required to pass through a fairly traditional student teaching program, we include lesson planning as part of our courses. Students work together in pairs and take their work to a modified authors' circle for discussion. Our work with evaluation starts here as students assess their own work and comment on the work of their peers. As the quarter progresses and their planning becomes more and more integrated, students find plans for the typical forty-five-minute lessons less and less appropriate.

Students identify the larger purposes to which their work is directed and suggest how to document student learning as it pertains to their planning. Thus the lesson plans manifest students' emerging beliefs about learning and schools. The lesson planning activities serve as a forum for engaging in all aspects of our model, from living in a social learning community and learning with others, to planning assessment and evaluation.

Examining Theory and Personal Belief

Our students' insights into their own learning are catalysts for examining and extending their personal theory of learning. Typically their assumptions about learning are woefully inadequate in accounting for the generative learning engagements they have been living. Through theoretical readings and discussions, students tease out and create their own personal theory of learning.

Reflecting on Younger Learners

As the preservice teachers develop a guiding theory of learning, it is examined in light of younger learners. Although the context is changed and the personal experiences may be different, the process of learning is fundamentally the same for all learners.

Exploring and Critiquing Pedagogy

In our model, students critique, modify, and create educational practice as they develop a theory of learning. Our class engagements are recast in various forms to become appropriate learning experiences for younger children, and conventional elementary education pedagogy is adapted to support authentic learning.

Creating Whole Language Environments

When our students enter the field, they know how to plan engaging learning experiences for children, but they are not doing activities solely because they are fun. They know that enjoyment is not the goal but rather the result of successful learning. Underlying theory behind authentic engagements distinguishes sound whole language from "spiced-up" skills instruction.

Trina wrote the following as a part of her final evaluation:

> It is very clear that I need to provide an environment and supportive community within the classroom where every individual feels safety, trust, respect and the freedom to make choices. As a prospective teacher I want to act as a guide, I want my students to discover and create their own knowledge. These things that I want were things I saw students [in my field experience] needing. Many of the above beliefs were rooted in the discussions and readings experienced during this course.

WHOLE LANGUAGE ENGAGEMENTS IN THE UNIVERSITY SETTING

We use five major engagements within the context of this model in our integrated language arts social studies methods classes: walking journals, literature circles, inquiry projects, publishing a children's book, and community engagements. Whole language is a theoretical construct, so it cannot be matched directly to activities. When these engagements are added to a top-down teacher-directed model, they cease to be whole language. We must look to evidence of our underlying premises within our class structure and engagements to gain a sense of our success at implementing whole language.

Walking Journals

A *walking journal* is a written dialogue among a group of people (Heine 1988) (see Protocol/Engagement C-8). Each group member has the opportunity to read other people's entries and to add an entry each time the rotating journal is received—generally once a week. In our class, journals typically "walk" among four students and a faculty member. (In the following journal excerpt, the faculty person is our colleague Chris Gordon.)

To get the journals started, we explain what a walking journal is, pass out the notebooks, and ask students to sign up for a day of the week on which they can expect to receive the journal. We ask students to sign up with people other than their close friends as this seems to provide for a greater diversity of opinion. Students may write about anything they wish as long as it pertains to education or to the classes they are taking. The following is fairly typical:

Stanley, October 4

The issue I'm becoming aware of lately is the one concerning mainstreaming. I'm glad we received the assignment in this area because it made me do more research about it. I'm not quite sure I agree with the arguments put up to defend these issues but it does offer a lot of food for thought. I do think it is good for some of these kids to enter our school systems. I do have some questions about maybe putting a deaf person in a classroom where a teacher has to spend a lot of time with that individual and lack of time with the other students. Believe it or not I've seen this case happen in a small school. This is a big thing and I'm not sure all the questions have been answered.

Anyone else have anything to add to this subject matter? I would be interested to hear more about it. I have a friend who had to pick up sign language to deal with this within her classroom. I hope this doesn't become a deterrent to learning for other students who need that extra time with the teacher.

Renae, October 5

I personally have little knowledge (or views) on mainstreaming. If I had any time I would definitely take one of the special education classes just to have some background. However, it doesn't look like I'll have time.

I can easily see myself spending so much time with that one student and leaving the others behind. Yet I think each student wants to be independent.

Sue, October 6

It is interesting that Stan brought up the topic of mainstreaming and integrating deaf children into a "hearing" classroom because the article I am reacting to this week attends to both of these issues. I have not read it thoroughly yet but the message I get is that both the hearing and deaf children can benefit from the integration, especially when the hearing children are guided in the understanding of the existence of the sub-culture of the deaf population. Thus, the experience is one of social studies experience! I should note that the photos in the magazine showed the deaf children wearing the "transistor radio" type thing that aids in their hearing. If any of you want to read the article let me know.

Ginny, October 9

I am aware of the mainstreaming issue. I enjoy children, especially the primary level, but I'm not sure if I can handle the special kids. I don't think I would have the patience and would give extra attention they need. This issue tests my ability to be a good teacher, but I don't know if I will pass the test. It will be my responsibility to work with some special kids this summer, so I can understand and relate to them. I am looking forward to this experience so I can find out for myself if I can teach them.

Chris, October 10

Mainstreaming is an important issue—one that you will face in the classroom. If you feel "lacking" in background on this topic, I'd suggest you do some reading this summer. One of the best situations I've seen in the schools is at Madison

Elementary (in St. Cloud) where the classrooms have the district's hearing impaired. Some wear "amplifiers" and so does the teacher. Some have signers who accompany them to the classes. These students are very accepted by the others because of the way the situation is handled by the classroom teachers. Attitude is *so* important.

The journals provide an opportunity for students to share thoughts, concerns, and resources that might not otherwise arise in the context of the course. In this way students control their own learning and create a community of learners. We use the same journals from quarter to quarter so students also gain insight into what peers taking the course during earlier quarters may have been thinking about. Students see their own concerns as neither foolish nor unique, and thus they feel part of a larger community creating meaning and shared knowledge.

The content of the journals ranges from mundane responses to serious dialogue and reflection. Sometimes topics change as students come to important issues or philosophical crossroads (democracy versus school structure; fairness in schools, etc.). In these cases it seems that the discussions are threatening to students' worldview, someone may suggest a new topic for discussion, and the dialogue starts down a new path.

Text Sets and Literature Circles

A *literature circle* is created when a group of people come together to read, discuss, and respond to a text or group of texts. A *text set* is a related set of books about the same topic or based on a common theme (Short, Harste, and Burke 1996). An overall question or some beginning themes may be suggested by the teacher. From this beginning, the group develops its own reading schedule, discussion topics, and ways of sharing with others.

> In one class, a group of four students worked to answer the question, "How should we facilitate writing in the elementary classroom?" Scott read *Writing with Power* by Peter Elbow (1981), a book that focuses on helping adults to write. Lori read Lanham's *Revising Prose* (1979), concerned with helping writers clean up their prose through the use of active voice, the removal of extraneous verbiage, and so forth. Kirk read Lucy Calkins' *Lessons from a Child* (1983), which details one classroom's move into a process approach to writing, and particularly details one child's development as a writer throughout the school year. Cynthia read *What's There to Write About?* (Dakos 1989) and the section on the authoring cycle from *Creating Classrooms for Authors and Inquirers* (Short, Harste, and Burke 1996).
>
> When they met, each came to the group with a slightly different perspective. Scott was concerned with eliminating distractions and "clearing the decks for writing" and Lori was focused on skills and style and Kirk on how the classroom would actually function. Cynthia wanted to help children find topics and help them help one another. Drawing perspectives together isn't an easy task, but after several extended discussions, they came to some guidelines of what they thought should happen in classrooms. They decided to present their decisions to the class in the form of a booklet that describes an ideal writing curriculum. Each student

wrote a set of vignettes addressing the specific concerns. They planned a how-to book on process writing using their vignettes.

Students bring a variety of perspectives and personal experiences to literature circles and create understandings far greater than any one of them could create alone. We use the literature circle procedures in our classes when students read children's literature as well. Groups of students sign up to read children's and adolescent novels or picture books. They read individually or with a partner and respond to their reading in their literature logs. The students then meet in their groups and share their written responses and other insights from the part of the book they read for that day. When the class has completed the reading and literature discussion, we reflect on these processes and consider how the learning was affected by both the content of the readings and the literature circle process itself.

Inquiry Projects

Helping students discover the power of their own questions, developing tools to pursue their inquiry goals, and coming to value their own learning process are the purpose of the *inquiry project*. In this project, students identify areas of interest that they wish to explore, such as school-related issues raised in a university class, in field observation, from a personal experience, or from a current event in the news media. Topic ideas are shared, and students with similar interests are encouraged to work together. Inquiry projects are developed out of a need to know. Students determine guiding questions and then brainstorm resources for exploring their issue, which might include library research, interviews, polls and surveys, experimentation, and examination of archival documents and artifacts.

Periodically, the students meet in response groups to share their investigations and to help one another. As members of our learning community, students have an obligation to share their insights with others although they choose what to share. Sharing might take the form of formal presentations, displays, debates, creative productions, written documents, or other methods appropriate for their project.

On a visit to a local elementary school, Carrie and Pete were amazed to discover that given the chance, third graders enthusiastically read and discussed literature. This was in contrast to their own elementary experience of assigned basal stories, workbook pages, and comprehension checks. Knowing they could not be satisfied teaching reading the way they had been taught, Carrie and Pete set out to develop a literature-based reading program they could propose to their supervising teacher during their upcoming student teaching experience.

Carrie borrowed several professional books that described literature-based reading programs, and Pete found a network of local teachers who use literature as the core of their reading programs. They also visited a teachers' supply store to look for prepared material for teaching reading through literature. After several weeks of reading, observing, and shopping, they realized that developing a complete reading program was valuable but could not be completed within the time constraints of the course. Sharing their concern with their response group, they decided to develop one of two interesting issues to share with the class: (1) that some literature-based reading programs are no more than warmed-over basal programs and (2) that the best programs involve children in many choices and take advantage of their interests. Although the first issue was important, and they had dreadful examples of basalized literature, they selected the second issue because the response group was very excited about the literature programs they had observed and Carrie and Pete wanted their classmates to see how excited children can be about literature.

Carrie and Pete interviewed children in two fourth-grade classrooms and captured their literature study in slides. For their presentation Carrie, Pete, and three children from the school explained the slides and their literature study time. They shared the students' literature response logs and the self-evaluation folders kept by each child.

Through these inquiry projects, the students take control of their learning. As learners and future teachers, our students need to value and develop the ability to ask and answer their own questions, and they need the skill to assist young learners in exploring their worlds. Inquiry projects provide students the opportunity to live reflective inquiry within a supportive community and in the process to explore the potential of using inquiry as a teaching strategy with children.

Publishing a Children's Book

As part of the integrated class, each of our students publishes a *children's book*. We ask students to write, illustrate, bind, and share a children's book with each other and elementary students. The following vignette captures the supportive interactions that result from peer critique in an authors' circle as our teacher education students worked on early drafts of their children's books.

Ralph had heard about the children's book assignment and had been worrying about his book topic since the previous quarter. He toyed with the idea of a chapter book and even wrote a first chapter. At that point, he realized the task he had set for himself was too large to fit within the time available. He decided to write about a raindrop to coincide with his science unit on the water cycle.

Cindy started from the assumption that she would make this a joint project with her ten-year-old son, Jarran, who would be the illustrator. She and Jarran talked about what he might be able to draw, and Jarran made a few sample drawings. Because he felt he could do well with a boy and a rat, they built their story around these two characters.

Anne wrote a moving story about her memories of her grandfather, who had recently passed away. She talked to other family members about their memories of their grandfather as well.

Amy wrote a story about a bird outside her window. She wasn't particularly satisfied with the results.

On the day reserved for authors' circles (Short, Harste, and Burke 1996) each group member followed a different purpose. Ralph talked the group through a proposed outline for his book and asked for response. Some focusing ideas were discussed, along with different aspects of the water cycle. Anne thought that some of the sections were overly technical and should be eliminated. Ralph argued that the science concepts were central to his message in his book. This led to a discussion on how to make the relatively technical information presented in the book more accessible to young readers. Ralph left the circle with clearer ideas about writing his text.

Cindy was stuck. She had developed some story lines to go with her characters but was unable to go much further. She showed the group some of Jarran's pictures and talked them through the partial story line she and Jarran had developed. The group worked with her on the story line and, in her own vernacular, "got her mind rolling again."

Anne had felt a lot of pressure about her story from family members who now felt ownership of the work too. The group was responsive to the power and emotion of the story. In discussion, they also had some suggested minor changes to ease the flow of the story but encouraged her to keep the content as she wanted. Anne decided to leave the story just as it was, given the outside pressure about ownership.

Amy had a finished draft, but she didn't like it very much and felt it was too bland. She read the work to the group, who were (of course) very supportive. They discussed some problem areas and provided some suggestions. Amy left the group with some new ideas and approaches for revision.

In an authors' circle each student in turn reads or describes his or her working draft. The content of the work is the focus of discussion at this time, setting aside issues of mechanics and style for later consideration. Listeners provide support for the work, ask questions about areas that may be unclear, and provide suggestions about areas of concern to the author or the listener. Each student responds to each other's texts, and the authors are free to accept or disregard suggestions as they choose.

Each of the participants used the authors' circle for a different purpose. For Ralph and Cindy the circle was generative, that is, they used the group as a springboard for their own ideas for writing. For Amy, the authors' circle was responsive, she used the group to get responses in order to revise. For Anne, the authors' circle was simply supportive. She needed the reassurance from the group that she be the final decision maker about what went into her book. She got that support. These uses of authors' circles overlap; authors may be using the circle for more than one purpose at any time.

There is a strong social strand in this assignment. Like any real-world literacy transaction, this project reaches far beyond a class assignment, connecting student to family, community, and a personal sense of history.

We have found that students' previous school experiences with writing often contribute to a fear of writing. Our students need considerable support as they write and share their writing. We describe the authoring cycle in detail to help them see that they will be supported throughout the project.

A variety of strategies help students give one another helpful feedback: brainstorming the kinds of questions that might be helpful to an author, providing students with examples of questions that others have used in authors' circles, asking the authors to come with concerns about their own work, or, at its simplest, asking listeners to respond with "two pluses and a wish" (Mills 1986)— that is, two positive statements about the work and one "I wish . . ." statement that gets at constructive criticism.

As trust is built among a group of writers, students open themselves to greater risks and therefore greater potential for learning as well. The "everything-is-fine" comments give way to constructive critique. The authors' circle becomes a collaborative venture as each participant enters into and contributes to each of the manuscripts.

From the conception of an idea to the binding of an illustrated text, the students grapple with the challenges that authors, illustrators, editors, and publishers must address. This is a powerful experience as they feel the accomplishment of becoming published authors. The books and the process used to create them are later shared with children in a visit to classrooms. Typically, children respond by sharing their own writing experiences as the university students talk about how they created their books. This activity provides an opportunity for authentic dialogue with children about writing and allows prospective teachers to interact with elementary students as co-learners engaged in similar experiences.

Community Engagement

In the following vignette the students are involved with what we call a *community engagement,* a project designed to help students use the community as a resource for creating knowledge and meaning. This particular project involved historical research but such projects lend themselves to other content areas equally well.

> Brigette, Carol, Barb, and Brenda are studying Lake George, a small lake in the center of St. Cloud, where we teach. Carol started by asking her father what he remembered about Lake George as he had lived here his entire life. One memory was of a large ice sculpture of a Native American chief that had been there for several winters. When he couldn't remember anything else about it, Brenda went to the local historical society to see if she could find out more. She was directed to an elderly man who revealed the sculpture was known as Chief Sli-Ski-Ska and was part of a 1930s winter festival known as Sli-Ski-Ska (for Slide, Ski, and Skate). This information enabled the study group to find newspaper clippings about the festival. Brenda and Carol looked at the newspaper clippings, while Brigette and Barb attempted to pursue a Native American perspective on the festival.
>
> In addition to the information on the festival itself, the group uncovered the nicknames adopted by the members of the chamber of commerce who sponsored the festival. The treasurer was "Wampum Hanger On," the secretary was "Chiseler on the Rocks," while the president was "Chief Blizzard in the Beard." They also found out that St. Cloud had once been served by three trains a day from Minneapolis, that the festival was sponsored to bring in outsiders to raise money

for the community coffers, and that the festival had ended shortly before the onset of World War II.

They were outraged by the blatant mockery of Native Americans and even more sobered by their interviews with several Native Americans. One man revealed that his people could not have been concerned with the festival as they were in what he described as a "survival mode" at the time working to preserve their lives and their cultures.

In addition to presenting their information, the group made a scale model of the ice sculpture, and Carol wrote a ballad about the festival. Even the minority studies program on campus was unaware of this bit of history and requested a copy of their work.

The creation of knowledge and insight associated with this activity was powerful to students, and in their own excitement about learning, they could see the responses children would have to such an activity. Simultaneously, they learned about themselves, the topic, and teaching and learning. Students also find the community engagements particularly enjoyable because they necessitate dealing with people in their research. Students develop questions they wish to answer, brainstorm sources of information, make visitations and conduct interviews as appropriate, and use libraries, museums, newspapers, and public records to gather information. We encourage students to explore their topics until they find an angle—a story that needs to be told. Students correlate, prepare, and present their findings. They keep a log of their meetings, discussions, activities, leads, dead-ends, and questions, and develop artifacts that represent their work and their topic of study.

The community engagement is used to investigate any aspect of the community and can expand to include issues in science, health, or math. Bus routes, placements of elementary schools, stop signs or traffic signals, local electricity generation, water purification, and local environmental problems (to name but a few) lend themselves well to this type of investigation. The implicit integration of content and uses of literacy become plainly obvious as students pursue their questions. We conclude the activity with presentations and by discussing what we learned, how we learned, and possible applications in schools.

SUMMARY

The classroom environment and the five engagements we have described are good demonstrations of the processes we would like to see in elementary classrooms. They engage students in authentic activities, facilitate the building of shared knowledge, and involve significant student control of learning.

These lived-through experiences provide the demonstrations necessary for students to create whole language environments for their own future students. The joy and power of learning is too important to talk about or to learn about; it has to be experienced.

REFERENCES

Calkins, L. M. 1983. *Lessons from a Child*. Portsmouth, NH: Heinemann.

Dakos, K. 1989. *What's There to Write About?* New York: Scholastic.

Elbow, P. 1981. *Writing with Power*. New York: Oxford University Press.

Heine, D. 1988. *Teaching as Inquiry: A Sociosemiotic Perspective of Learning*. Unpublished doctoral dissertation, Indiana University, Bloomington, IN.

Lanham, R. 1979. *Revising Prose*. New York: Charles Scribner.

Mills, H. 1986. *Evaluating Literacy: A Transactional Process*. Unpublished doctoral dissertation, Indiana University, Bloomington, IN.

Peterson, R., and M. Eeds. 1990. *Grand Conversations*. New York: Scholastic.

Short, K. G., J. C. Harste, and C. Burke. 1996. *Creating Classrooms for Authors and Inquirers*. Portsmouth, NH: Heinemann.

15

TEACHERS LEARN WHAT IT'S LIKE TO BE A SECOND LANGUAGE LEARNER

Yvonne S. Freeman

"I have learned what it feels like to be in a classroom where the teacher speaks in a language other than mine."

"Having a class that was conducted in part in a language that I didn't know was refreshing, but I got more than that out of it because I resensitized myself to the needs of my students."

"This course helped me to see the benefits of a bilingual program."

"I've been able to see a very controversial, very political subject through another perspective. My eyes have been opened to not only pedagogical advantages of primary language support but also the social and psychological pluses."

These statements came from the self-assessments written by the teachers in my graduate class, Current Theories, Methods and Materials for Bilingual Education. I teach this class in both English and Spanish, although only a small portion of the students who take the course are bilingual themselves. I got the idea for teaching bilingually from a presentation by Robert Milk at the 1989 TESOL (Teachers of English to Speakers of Other Languages) Conference (1989). The presentation described an experimental methodology class taught entirely in Spanish for English as a second language (ESL) and bilingual specialist teachers. The course was designed to meet the language needs as well as the common pedagogical needs of the teachers involved.

Dr. Milk's presentation both excited and frightened me. As a teacher educator in the fields of bilingual and second language education, I had taught courses in language acquisition and cross-cultural communication, theories, methods and materials for teaching a second language, and theories, methods, and materials for bilingual education. In all of these courses, I sought to blend whole language learning theory and research by providing readings that described whole language principles and practices for second-language students (Freeman and Freeman 1992, 1993; Freeman and Nofziger 1991; Hudelson 1984, 1986, 1987, 1989; Rigg and Hudelson 1986), by encouraging teachers to share their holistic teaching practices in class, by doing demonstration lessons and providing whole language checklists, by creating risk-free environments for discussion and shar-ing, and by providing the teachers with the kinds of choices I hoped they would give their students. However, these experiences were not completely authentic (Edelsky, Altwerger, and Flores 1991) because they were done in the context of the college classroom. If, I reasoned, I were to try to demonstrate to the teachers how to teach content in a second language by actually teaching a college course bilingually using a method consistent with whole language principles, I would, perhaps, really be able to practice what I preach (Freeman and Freeman 1991).

In an article published after the conference, Milk (1990) explained that seven-teen teachers in two summer courses were given immersion in Spanish where they could "widen their lexical range in Spanish for the content areas as well as increase their academic proficiency in academic Spanish." In addition, the ESL and bilingual specialist teachers "were provided with intensive simulated class-room experiences in small-group content-based instruction following a coopera-tive learning approach" (p. 413). Like Milk, I could see the value of giving teachers the experience their second-language learners have in schools all the time where they are "learning a new language and having to deal with academic demands in a second language" (p. 412).

The idea of trying to do this with my students was challenging. Unlike Milk's students, my students were not all preparing themselves to be bilingual or ESL teachers. In fact, many students in my graduate classes are classroom teachers in mainstream elementary or high school classrooms who are interested in how best to help the second-language students who are beginning to fill their classrooms. These teachers have often had little or no exposure to learning a second language themselves. In a recent class of forty-three teachers, only one was a native Span-ish speaker. Six were fairly fluent in Spanish, two-thirds had at some point in their lives studied a little Spanish, and one-third of the class had no previous experience at all with the Spanish language.

My own college classroom, then, was like many of these teachers' classrooms: some students who spoke a lot of English, some who spoke a little English, and some who spoke almost no English; some who spoke a lot of Spanish, some who spoke a little Spanish, and some who spoke no Spanish beyond Spanish words that have become part of our English vocabulary such as *patio*, *taco*, and *gracías*. If I could teach the course content and some Spanish to even non-Spanish speak-ers by drawing on whole language and second-language theory and research, I would be demonstrating how teachers could effectively teach English and con-tent in a bilingual setting.

I have taught the ten-week course bilingually now five times. The students have not all responded, at least initially, with enthusiasm. Teachers who enter the bilingual methodology class with little or no Spanish come into the course with anxieties. However, they leave the class feeling that they are better equipped to work with second-language learners in their classrooms even when they do not speak their students' first language. Comments like "I was afraid to take it [the class] because of the Spanish, but I'm glad I did" and "Now I have a real feeling for what works and what doesn't work" have helped to convince me that teachers learn best about theory when they are both studying it and experiencing it.

THEORETICAL AND RESEARCH BASE
FOR BILINGUAL EDUCATION

Teachers working with second-language students recognize the importance of helping their students develop competence in English. It seems logical that the best way to develop English is to immerse students in an environment in which they hear, speak, read, and write English each day. The idea that "more English leads to more English" is logical but not consistent with the research, which shows that the fastest way for bilingual students to develop both academic concepts and English is through their first language. In fact, use of students' primary language helps learners develop English more rapidly than exclusive use of English (Collier 1992; Collier and Thomas 1995; Ramírez 1991; Hudelson 1987).

The rationale for bilingual education has been clearly explained by Cummins (1989) and Krashen (1985). The basic premise of these two researchers and theorists is that bilingual students who are given instruction in their first language easily transfer the concepts of the instruction into English; in contrast, instruction all in English leaves second-language students frustrated and lost. They may not understand enough English to acquire English or learn any of the content. For example, it is nearly impossible to learn Portuguese simply by listening to the Portuguese radio station when the listener does not understand anything that is being said!

When second-language students in English-speaking countries are put into English-only classrooms with no support in their first language, they find themselves in the situation of trying to learn what does not make sense. Smith (1985) explains that although learning is natural and happens all the time, we cannot learn what we do not understand. Learning involves demonstrations (we see people doing things), engagement (we decide we want to do those things), and sensitivity (nothing is done or said that convinces us we can't do those things). When the demonstration is given in English to nonnative speakers, they may not understand what they are seeing or hearing. If they don't understand the demonstration, they probably won't choose to engage in the activity. And if they don't understand what the teacher says, they may become convinced that they can't learn. At all three stages, instruction in English may not be comprehensible enough for learning to take place. These students quickly lose interest and are either directly or indirectly isolated from the classroom community. Just as Smith (1985) discussed the idea that students who do not learn to read and write fluently do not feel they are members of the "literacy club," second-language learners can be in schools in which they never see themselves becoming members of "successful English speaking-students club."

Skutnabb-Kangas (1983) explains how listening to a second or foreign language is more tiring than listening to a first language. Second-language learners may appear to have shorter attention spans than native speakers, but in reality, the second-language students may simply be tired and give up trying to make sense out of their new language.

Use of the first language, then, can help make all instruction, including the instruction in English, more comprehensible. One effective way of providing "comprehensible input" (Krashen 1985) is through a preview, view, and review method. In this format, bilingual students are given a preview of lesson content in their first language before teachers and students work with the content in English. Then when the content is explored in English, bilingual students have a better chance of understanding the lesson and acquiring English at the same time. If the students are also given opportunities to discuss what is going on with their classmates in their first language, they can resolve questions and more fully engage in the activity. Near the end of a unit of study, a review of the content in the students' first language helps them clarify concepts and promotes the acquisition of English.

The research shows, then, that bilingual students who receive instruction in their first language from qualified bilingual teachers are most likely to succeed. However, only a small percentage of bilingual students are in classrooms with bilingual teachers. In my bilingual methodology course, I show teachers, bilingual or not, how they can support their students' first language (Freeman and Freeman 1993).

WHOLE LANGUAGE IN THE BILINGUAL CLASSROOM

Besides having graduate students understand how important it is for them to encourage the use of their students' first languages, I also want them to experience how a whole language approach to instruction supports second-language acquisition. As I plan the course, I keep the following principles in mind:

- Learning in any language moves from whole to part.
- Lessons should be learner centered.
- Lessons should have meaning and purpose for students now.
- Lessons should involve students in social interaction.
- Oral and written language are acquired simultaneously.
- Faith in learners is critical to student success (Goodman 1986; Freeman and Freeman 1992).

For bilingual students to reach their full potential, they need classrooms where teachers apply these principles. Unfortunately, even when there is some understanding of the importance of primary language support in schools, there is little understanding about whole language and how language and literacy are best developed. Bilingual students may receive whole language instruction in English but read and write with a fragmented curriculum in Spanish. In these classrooms, language arts instruction in English might include the reading of quality children's literature and journal and process writing in a curriculum that integrates content study around thematic cycles (Edelsky, Altwerger, and Flores 1991) while the instruction in the students' first language consists of repetitious drills, copying practice, and meaningless worksheets (Freeman and Freeman 1992).

THE BILINGUAL METHODS COURSE

As I organized my graduate bilingual methods course for teachers, I wanted to demonstrate practices consistent with the theories of both bilingual education and whole language. I wanted the teachers to experience how their first language (English) could help them as they study content in a second language (Spanish). I hoped that by the end of the course, they would feel part of the "Spanish speakers club" even if they were not fluent. I hoped that their own struggles in a second language would make them more sympathetic to the second-language learners in their classrooms.

Smith's (1983) three basic aspects of learning—demonstrations, engagement, and sensitivity—would have to be present. I wanted to demonstrate effective strategies and create a community of learners in which the students would become engaged and demonstrate for each other that learning can take place in Spanish as well as English. In this atmosphere, students would feel that learning could take place and that it would not be difficult.

Demonstrating How First Language (English) Supports Second Language (Spanish)

I provided a variety of demonstrations of the importance of first-language support. All of the required reading for the course was in English. There were two texts: a book on the empowerment of minority students (Cummins 1989) and one on the history, politics, theory, and practice of bilingual education (Crawford 1989). Students read in English before the class, and then I discussed the concepts in Spanish using overheads, visuals, role play, and interactive activities. In addition, I had overheads I used in Spanish translated into English. Students would refer to those during group discussion to clarify what I was talking about and doing. For students who were already fluent in Spanish, there were also some optional readings in Spanish (Arellano-Osuna 1992; Dubois 1984; Freeman 1988). The Spanish speakers then led the subsequent discussions of those articles.

The fluent Spanish speakers helped non- or limited-Spanish speakers understand the content in Spanish. The first night of class, students classified their own ability to speak and understand Spanish. They signed a sheet that indicated, "*Sí, hablo español*" (Yes, I speak Spanish), "*Hablo un poco*" (I speak a little bit of Spanish), or "*No, no hablo español*" (No, I do not speak Spanish). I put students in heterogeneous groups of four or five, which became a kind of "family" with at least one fairly proficient Spanish speaker and one or two non-Spanish speakers in each group. During class I asked students to discuss what I had presented in Spanish in their families. I suggested that proficient Spanish speakers not translate but instead encourage those who felt less confident with Spanish to summarize what they did understand and ask questions. These groups sat together for most of each class period and developed a fairly strong bond by the end of the course.

To help reinforce that their first language, English, was a valuable resource, I had students write class responses and papers in English unless they chose to write in Spanish. For their group presentations, students became experts on different topics of interest related to bilingual education. Most of that reading was in English so students could rely on their first language, learn in their first language, and share what they learned in their first language. Because their knowledge and learning in their first language was supported, the students felt less anxiety about also learning content in a second language.

Engagement with Natural Language and Sensitivity

As I planned for classroom interactions, I tried to keep in mind two of Krashen's ideas of second-language acquisition: (1) second-language acquisition occurs when language is used in a natural, comprehensible way, and (2) language will be acquired only when the "affective filter" is unclogged. Students do not engage with language unless it is real language used for some authentic purpose. The open affective filter that allows language learning to take place can be clogged up by fear, lack of confidence, or lack of interest (Krashen 1982). This idea is similar to Smith's idea of sensitivity.

I introduced topics, provided demonstrations, and suggested interactive activities in Spanish in a natural and authentic way. I believed that even complex Spanish could be understood without simplification, vocabulary lists, or grammar exercises if I made the content comprehensible by finding relevant and current reading materials in Spanish. Just after the 1992 presidential elections, when classes began, one of the first readings I used was from *Scholastic News* in Spanish, entitled "*¡Nuestro nuevo presidente!*" (Our New President) (Scholastic 1993). To introduce the reading, I first showed a large poster of *la casa blanca* (the White House). I also showed large photos of both Bill Clinton and ex-president Bush and talked briefly about the election. As I talked, I not only pointed to the pictures and poster but also gestured and dramatized.

Next I gave the students the newsletters and asked them to read to themselves and make as much sense as they could from the text. Then the students talked to each other about what they had understood and asked each other questions. We then discussed what did or did not help them understand the Spanish. They listed previous knowledge, having the poster and pictures first to help them predict what the passage would be about, having pictures with the reading, and recognizing *cognates* (words similar to English) such as *presidente* (president), *líder* (leader), *gobierno* (government), and *eligido* (elected or chosen). The students began to see that they did not need to translate every word to understand the Spanish. They also realized how being able to discuss the lesson with their family members in their first language made the Spanish more understandable.

The family buddy system helped to alleviate the anxiety that many non-Spanish speakers felt in class. However, unclogging the affective filter was still often my greatest task. To make the class atmosphere relaxed and nonthreatening, I constantly assured students that they were doing well and that their grade was not going to be determined in any way by their Spanish proficiency.

Drama also helped students to see that language is best understood in a natural setting and learned best when the affective filter is not clogged. On one occasion, different families made up short classroom skits to depict some of the many different ways of organizing a bilingual classroom, including concurrent translation (everything said in one language is immediately translated into the second), pull-out (non-English speakers get first language instruction in a pull-out situation), and preview-view-review. Not only did the class discuss the pros and cons of the approaches but also how they felt about being involved in the role plays.

Choice

To give students choice as they learned in a second language, I provided expert topics for study: History of Bilingual Education in the United States, Bilingual Education Models and Instructional Modes, Paulo Freire and Critical Pedagogy, Bilingualism and Intelligence, Politics of Bilingual Education, Successful and Effective Programs, Two-Way Immersion Programs, Bilingualism, Mother Tongue, or related topics of their own choosing. Students formed their own groups and worked together to decide how they wanted to share what they learned. The only limitation for the sharing was that the other students in the class had to be involved and that some part of the sharing be in a language other than English. Students have come up with many creative ways to share, including drama, art, poetry, live murals, songs, time lines, jigsaw activities, brainstorming, reading, and response activities. One group enacted a court scene with bilingual education being on trial. The judge and attorneys asked questions about the rationale and politics of bilingual education in English, and the defendent (bilingual education) answered in Spanish.

Students had choices in videos or television programs to view outside class. They were asked to watch for at least a half-hour something in a language they did not already speak or understand. There were videos in Spanish and Hmong on reserve in the library, or students could choose a TV program in one of several other languages. The teachers then wrote about the experience, commenting on their ability to make sense of the video, their own attention spans, what helped make the input comprehensible, and their own emotional responses.

Demonstrations

To highlight the importance of both context and background knowledge, I did several demonstrations in Spanish. On the first night I read *¡Puedo leer dondequiera!* (I Can Read Everywhere) (Avalos 1991), a book about reading environmental print, and then asked the students to watch for environmental print in languages other than English during the following weeks. On the third night of class, family groups listed on butcher paper the kinds of print they saw (billboards, ads, newspapers and magazines, warning signs, want ads), where they saw the environmental print (in stores, in newspapers, in elevators, at construction sites, at auto repair shops, different parts of town), and what some of the words or phrases were that they had seen. Each group shared what they had found and many noticed how more environmental print in Hmong, Laotian, and Spanish was found in poorer sections of town.

The following week, I gave students different advertisements for familiar products in Spanish, such as Colgate toothpaste and Tide detergent, and asked them to individually decide what the ads said. Afterward, we discussed how students who had never studied or spoken Spanish could use context and background knowledge to figure out what the words must mean. Each family was then given more ads in Spanish to talk about together in English. After looking at the ads in both their own environment and the ones I had provided, we talked about the importance of environmental print for developing reading and self-esteem. Each family then wrote an announcement or sign in Spanish that could be put up in their own classrooms using the slogans from the ads I had brought into class (Figure 15).

A similar activity was done with greeting cards in Spanish. We first brainstormed a list of occasions for sending cards and then listed some common English phrases found on different cards. Family groups were given a collection of eight to ten greeting cards in Spanish. They predicted the occasion for the cards and the messages, using the art work and their knowledge of the language. The teachers then worked together to write their own greeting card in Spanish using the language from the cards they already had. Afterward the class discussed how they were able to comprehend the language and construct their own messages because of their background knowledge and the supportive context of the cards.

To demonstrate how teachers could make content comprehensible, I demonstrated a health lesson. Though I spoke only Spanish, I was able to draw on their background knowledge and use enough visuals to make the input comprehensible. I first asked students to brainstorm the names of fast food restaurants and make a list of the food people buy there. I accepted answers in Spanish and English, writing down the responses in Spanish. Students then discussed in their family groups what they liked and did not like about fast food restaurants, and their group experts helped them express those ideas in Spanish. Three students volunteered to tell us their favorite fast food restaurant meal, which I wrote on the overhead. With the help of commercial pamphlets in Spanish listing the nutritional value of foods at different fast food restaurants, students discussed what made the different meals healthy or unhealthy. I then showed an overhead of the food pyramid in Spanish. Students were given pictures of different foods and physically put themselves into the proper place on the pyramid. At the end of this activity, many non-Spanish speakers talked about how surprised they were at how much they could understand.

The students themselves provided another type of demonstration. In pairs they presented a book or other materials such as newspapers or ads in a language other than English to the rest of the class. Materials were presented in French, German, Chinese, Korean, and Hmong as well as Spanish. Some teachers read a book, others acted something out, and still others explained how they would use the materials with students. For example, one pair of monolingual English-speaking teachers used a cookbook in Spanish and prepared the recipe and had us try the results. Another pair dramatized *The Giving Tree* (Silverstein 1964) in Spanish, French, and German, complete with props.

Student Response

One of the main goals of the course was to show teachers that in a class where all students' languages are valued, students relax and participate. In my class students gave presentations in many languages, and they realized the benefits of a multilingual setting. Lian, a student from the People's Republic of China, read a children's story to the class in Chinese. After she finished, she told the class with an obvious show of emotion, "I just want to tell you all that it must be very important for children to have their first language spoken in school. I am a

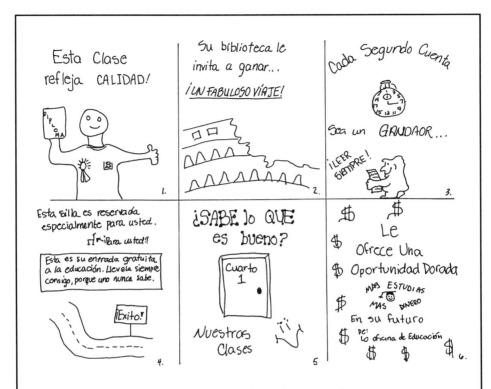

1. Esta Clase refleja Calidad!: This Class Shows Quality!
2. Su biblioteca le invita a ganar … ¡UN FABULOSO VIAJE!: Your library invites you to win … A FABULOUS TRIP!
3. Cada Segundo Cuenta … Sea un GANADOR … ¡LEER SIEMPRE!: Each Second Counts … Be a WINNER … READ ALL THE TIME!
4. Esta silla es reservada especialmente para usted. (On ticket) Esta es su entrada gratuita a la educación. Llevela siempre consigo, porque uno nunca sabe. (On sign) ¡Exito!: This chair is reserved especially for you. (On ticket) This is your free entry to education. Keep it always with you because one never knows. (On sign) Success!
5. ¿SABE lo QUE es bueno? (on door) Cuarto 1. Nuestras Clases: Do you know what is good? (on door) Room 1. Our Classes.
6. Le Ofrece Una Oportunidad Dorada. MAS ESTUDIAS MAS DINERO En su futuro De: La oficina de Educación: You are offered a golden opportunity. MORE STUDY AND MORE MONEY In your future From: The Office of Education.

FIGURE 15   Teacher signs and translation

graduate student and you don't know how much it means to me to be able to read this book to you in Chinese!"

Just as Lian's experience helped her understand how important first-language support is, this bilingual methods course helps English-speaking teachers understand how it feels to be taught in a language other than English. Comments such as "Now I really know what it's like for my students to sit all day and try to learn in a different language" and "I am already using more techniques to 'make the input comprehensible;' I see how much using visuals, gestures, and overheads helps *me* in this graduate class" are indicators that theory and practice come together when teachers experience the same kind of instruction that they can use with their own students.

Teachers who were not bilingual felt the course gave them ideas about working with their second-language students even if they could not speak their students' first language. Annette wrote in one week's response, "I seem to pick up something new with each class. I've noticed more improvement overall with this year's non-English students than any of the other years I've taught."

Teachers came to understand how support in the first language helps learning and understanding a second language. Julie wrote how this concept became real for her:

> What really hit home for me was how helpful it was to be able to talk in English to my classmates to figure out what was going on or just to confirm that I was on the right track. When I had already learned something in English, it was much easier for me to listen to it in Spanish, but if it was a new concept to me in English, there was too much anxiety after a while I found myself doing what the kids do—getting frustrated and tuning out.

CONCLUSION

When I decided to teach this course bilingually, I had the fears that all whole language teachers face when they put something they believe about learning into practice. Like other teachers attempting to implement whole language, I know I still have a long way to go. This is proven to me each time I teach the class and each time I interact with a new group of students. I try new things, they respond in different ways, and we learn together. However, one thing I do realize: I can never return to teaching about bilingual education without also demonstrating how to put the theory into practice.

REFERENCES

Arrellano-Osuna, A. 1992. *El lenguaje integral: Una alternativa para la educación.* Mérida, Venezuela: Editorial Venesolana.

Avalos, C. 1991. *¡Puedo leer dondequiera!* Cleveland, OH: Modern Curriculum Press.

Collier, V. 1992. "A Synthesis of Studies Examining Long-Term Language-Minority Student Data on Academic Achievement." In *Bilingual Research Journal,* 16, 1 and 2: 187–212.

Collier, V., and W. P. Thomas. 1995. Language Minority Student Achievement and Program Effectiveness. Research Summary of Study in Progress. Washington, DC: National Clearinghouse for Bilingual Education.

Crawford, J. 1989. *Bilingual Education: History, Politics, Theory and Practice*. Trenton, NJ: Crane.

Cummins, J. 1989. *Empowering Minority Students*. Sacramento, CA: CABE.

Dubois, M. E. 1984. "Algunos interrogantes sobre comprensión de la lectura." In *Lectura y Vida*, 4: 14–19.

Edelsky, C., B. Altwerger, and B. Flores. 1991. *Whole Language: What's the Difference?* Portsmouth, NH: Heinemann.

Freeman, D. E., and Y. S. Freeman. 1991. "Practicing What We Preach: Whole Language with Teachers of Bilingual Learners." In *Organizing for Whole Language*. K. S. Goodman, Y. M. Goodman, and W. J. Hood, eds. Portsmouth, NH: Heinemann.

———. 1993. "Strategies for Promoting the Primary Languages of All Students." In *Reading Teacher*, 46, 7: 552–558.

Freeman, Y. S. 1988. "Métodos de lectura en español: ¿Reflejan nuestro conocimiento actual del proceso de lectura?" In *Lectura y Vida*, 9: 20–28.

Freeman, Y. S., and D. E. Freeman. 1992. *Whole Language for Second-Language Learners*. Portsmouth, NH: Heinemann.

Freeman, Y. S., and S. Nofziger. 1991. "WalkuM to RnM 33: Vien Vinidos al cualTo 33." In *Organizing for Whole Language*. K. S. Goodman, Y. M. Goodman, and W. J. Hood, eds. Portsmouth, NH: Heinemann.

Goodman, K. S. 1986. *What's Whole in Whole Language?* Portsmouth, NH: Heinemann.

Hudelson, S. 1984. "Kan You Ret an Rayt en Ingles: Children Become Literate in English as a Second Language." In *TESOL Quarterly*, 18, 2: 221–237.

———. 1986. "ESL Children's Writing: What We've Learned, What We're Learning." In *Children and ESL: Integrating Perspectives*. P. Rigg and D. S. Enright, eds. Washington, DC: Teachers of English to Speakers of Other Languages.

———. 1987. "The Role of Native Language Literacy in the Education of Language Minority Children." In *Language Arts*, 64, 8: 827–840.

———. 1989. "'Teaching' English Through Content Area Activities." In *When They Don't All Speak English: Integrating the ESL Student into the Regular Classroom*. P. Rigg and V. Allen, eds. Urbana, IL: National Council of Teachers of English.

Krashen, S. 1982. *Principles and Practice in Second-Language Acquisition*. New York: Pergamon Press.

———. 1985. *Inquiries and Insights*. Haywood, CA: Prentice Hall.

Milk, R. 1989, March. "Immersion for Teachers: Preparing Personnel for Effective Instructional Practice." Paper presented at the TESOL (Teachers of English to Speakers of Other Languages) Conference, San Antonio, TX.

———. 1990. "Preparing ESL and Bilingual Teachers for Changing Roles: Immersion for Teachers of LEP Children." In *TESOL Quarterly*, 24, 3: 407–426.

Ramírez, J. D. 1991. *Final Report: Longitudinal Study of Structured English Immersion Strategy, Early-exit and Late-exit Bilingual Education Programs*. 300-87-0156. Washington, DC: U.S. Department of Education.

Rigg, P., and S. Hudelson. 1986. "One Child Doesn't Speak English." In *Australian Journal of Reading,* 9, 3: 116–125.

Scholastic. 1993. "¡Nuestro nuevo presidente!" In *Scholastic News,* 49, 4: 1–4.

Silverstein, S. 1964. *The Giving Tree.* New York: HarperCollins.

Skutnabb-Kangas, T. 1983. *Bilingualism or Not: The Education of Minorities.* Clevedon, UK: Multilingual Matters.

Smith, F. 1983. *Essays into Literacy: Selected Papers and Some Afterthoughts.* Portsmouth, NH: Heinemann.

———. 1985. *Reading Without Nonsense.* 2d ed. New York: Teachers College Press.

Urzúa, C. 1987. "You Stopped too Soon: Second-Language Children Composing and Revising." In *TESOL Quarterly,* 21, 2: 279–297.

16

Putting Language
Back into Language Arts:
A Linguistics Course for Teachers

David E. Freeman

Each year more teachers attempt whole language. In classrooms all over the world, teachers are reading to their students and with their students. These teachers are using literature, not basal reading programs, and teachers and students are engaging in literature studies (Short and Pierce 1990). In these classrooms both students and teachers are also engaged in authentic writing. They write for a variety of purposes and a variety of audiences (Calkins 1991; Graves 1983). Curriculum in these whole language classes is often arranged around theme cycles (Edelsky, Altwerger, and Flores 1991). Students and teachers explore questions together, and in this process, they draw on information from various content areas (Watson, Burke, and Harste 1989).

Teachers and students in whole language classes use language to mean. They learn language, they learn through language, but, ironically, in a number of whole language classes, students and teachers don't learn *about* language (Halliday 1975). The reason for this is simple enough. Many whole language teachers hesitate to lead their students into linguistic inquiry because of the kind of experiences the teachers themselves have had with language study.

Generally, students in teacher education programs take one class in grammar—either a traditional grammar class or an introduction to linguistics. In a traditional class, students review the parts of speech and study rules of usage. They learn, for example, that commas go inside quotation marks, and they may do some sentence analysis. When these students become teachers, they teach their students parts of speech, rules of usage, and some sentence analysis.

In other programs, students take an introduction to linguistics, a course that normally covers phonology and phonetics, morphology, and syntax. It may also cover a number of other areas, such as language acquisition, language change, or the history of language. These introductory courses include a number of different areas that are touched on briefly. Students are often nervous about taking linguistics, and their fear is justified if they are asked to solve phonology problems, transcribe sentences, and draw tree diagrams. Linguists who teach these introductory courses are often more interested in linguistic theory. They seldom have had personal experience in teaching at the elementary or secondary level, and they rarely consider possible applications of linguistics for teachers to use in public school teaching. As a result, students leaving an introductory linguistics course are not usually prepared to involve their own students in linguistic inquiry.

Professors who teach traditional grammar courses assume that their students should know and teach traditional grammar in a prescriptive manner. College professors who teach linguistics assume that their students should be exposed to a number of areas of linguistics because they will probably not take any further courses in the area and need some general knowledge about language. Neither of these approaches prepares teachers or future teachers to involve students in the study of language.

If, on the other hand, teachers understand how language works and have some basic tools for analysis, they can engage students in a variety of language study projects. For example, if students in the class speak different languages or different dialects, the teacher can investigate the differences. Are there differences in the way words are formed, pronounced, or put together into sentences? Many students find the study of word histories fascinating, and if teachers have resource books available, students can research their name, the name of their town or city, names of animals, and so on.

implications of linguistics for spelling instruction

Teachers can approach spelling in a whole new way. For instance, students and teachers together can try to list all the different ways we spell the sound of *k* and then try to determine the distribution of these spellings. We generally use the letter *k*, for example, at the beginnings of words if the following vowel is *e* or *i* but *c* if the following vowel is *a*, *o*, or *u*. As students study questions like these they become more aware of spelling patterns. If teachers receive a useful introduction to language, they develop the confidence to explore questions about language with their students.

I have developed a course to introduce teachers to linguistics in a way that empowers them to involve their own students in language study. My course, like any other course taught by someone attempting whole language, keeps changing. Yet although the particular class activities vary in different semesters, the course is organized around certain basic questions that my students and I are trying to answer. In this process of inquiry, both my students and I learn more about language and about how to learn about language. My hope is that after taking this course, teachers will experiment in their own classrooms with ways to put the study of language back into their language arts curricula.

COURSE GOALS

The goal of the course is to engage teachers in linguistic inquiry so that they can explore language questions with their own students. Unlike many other linguistics courses, this course is not designed to help teachers learn grammar in order to teach grammar more efficiently. Research has consistently shown that the study of grammar doesn't make people better readers or writers (Goodman et al. 1987).

Instead I pose a basic question: What are the rules that native speakers of English use to construct, pronounce, and comprehend sentences in English? Native speakers of any language can produce and understand sentences, but they are usually not aware of the rules they use to do this. They lack metalinguistic awareness. Linguistics attempts to make implicit rules explicit. Students begin to see that by "rule," a linguist means a generalization that describes what native speakers do.

To answer this question, then, we take a descriptive rather than a prescriptive approach. The prescriptive position was articulated clearly more than three hundred years ago by Robert Lowth:

> The Principal design of a Grammar of any Language is to teach us to express ourselves with propriety in that Language; and to enable us to judge of every phrase and form of construction whether it is right or not. The plain way of doing this is to lay down rules, and to illustrate them by examples. But, besides showing what is right, the matter may be further explained by pointing out what is wrong. (Gleason 1965, p. 69)

Many students dislike grammar study because teachers have defined their roles in Lowth's terms as one whose job is to "judge of every phrase and form of construction whether it is right or not." Rules, for teachers following this approach, are prescribed by experts.

In a descriptive approach, on the other hand, rules are discovered by testing hypotheses. Rules describe patterns of natural language use. The descriptive approach was well stated by the scientist Joseph Priestly, who was a contemporary of Lowth but took a very different approach:

> It must be allowed that the custom of speaking is the original and only just standard of any language. We see, in all grammars, that this is sufficient to establish a rule, even contrary to the strongest analogies of the language with itself. Must not this custom, therefore, be allowed to have some weight in favor of those forms of speech, to which our best writers and speakers seem evidently prone? (Gleason 1965, p. 70)

Priestly advocates a scientific approach toward language study: observe the best writers and speakers, and take their standard as what is right. My hope is that my students can adopt a similar attitude toward language study, forming and testing hypotheses about language by observing the way people actually use language.

COURSE FORMAT

The linguistics course meets for three hours one night a week for a semester. During that time, as we attempt to answer the general question, How do people construct, pronounce, and comprehend English sentences? we focus on the subfields of syntax, morphology, and phonology. For each area, students carry out a project in an attempt to answer more specific questions that relate directly to their teaching. As they complete each project, they put into use the concepts and methods linguists use.

In the sections that follow, I describe the course by explaining each of the three projects and related class activities. Although students do one project at a time, we devote part of every class to each of the three areas of syntax, morphology, and phonology. In that way, we can focus on the area of the project but continually think about how that area relates to the other two. Students work in teams of three or four for each project.

Syntax

Linguistics, like most other sciences, breaks language down into small parts for study. Whole language teachers, on the other hand, attempt to begin with the whole and look at the parts in the context of the whole. I begin this course with syntax, because syntax deals with larger units than morphology or phonology. Syntax looks at sentences rather than words or sounds. Sentences, though, aren't the whole; texts are. As we look at sentences, we look at how they function in discourse.

Focusing each project around certain questions also helps to keep the part we are studying in the context of a meaningful whole. A basic question for syntax is: What are the basic structural patterns of English phrases and clauses? Related questions include: What are some rules for transforming the basic patterns? How does the syntax of student writing contrast with the syntax found in textbooks? and How does English syntax compare with the syntax of other languages?

I begin by asking students to make up their own rules to describe English sentence structure. Their answers give me valuable insights into their background knowledge of English grammar. Generally, students realize that to describe English syntax they need to refer to the order of words in a sentence, word categories, such as noun or verb, and sentence constituents, such as subject and object.

Since many of the students are a bit rusty on terms like *noun* and *verb,* we talk about the differences between intuitive ideas for these terms (a noun names a person, place, or thing) and grammatical tests for parts of speech (many nouns add *s* to form plurals). They begin to see that in linguistics, as in any other science, it is important to define certain terms and set up basic categories. Rather than learning that a word is a noun for the sake of being able to identify it, they understand that if they want to describe sentence structure, they need to classify the words in the sentence into different categories. It may help students to understand some linguistic tests, such as the plural *s* test for nouns, to identify different parts of speech, but I suggest that they approach this topic with their students by reading to them the beautifully illustrated series of books written by Ruth Heller. Each book focuses on one part of speech. For example, *Kites Fly High* (1988) is about verbs. I have listed Heller's other books related to language at the end of this chapter.

I then ask students to think about structurally ambiguous sentences, such as, "He saw the girl with a telescope." None of the words here is ambiguous, but the sentence has two possible meanings. Either the boy or the girl could have the telescope. This leads to the idea of a two-level analysis. On the surface we have one sentence, but underlying that sentence are two different structures.

Students begin to see that a grammar contains two kinds of rules, one set generating basic sentence structures and the other transforming those basic structures into different surface forms. For example, if we say that statements are basic, we can write a rule for changing a statement into yes-no questions. Throughout our discussion, I emphasize that what we are trying to do is to make explicit the rules they already have in their heads. They all agree that a statement such as, "He can sing," would be transformed into the yes-no question, "Can he sing?" The problem, then, is to write a rule that produces the correct result.

Some students enjoy working on rules because they enjoy this kind of exercise. My students, however, are teachers, and they see more of a purpose in studying syntax if they can apply what they learn. For that reason, they start by taking some sentences from a linguistics textbook, putting those sentences into basic form, and analyzing the ways they have been transformed. The linguistics text contains typical scientific writing similar to what their students would read in content-area textbooks. Then they bring in samples of their own students' writing and carry out the same procedure.

In analyzing student writing, teachers are not concerned with correcting the syntax. They are looking at the patterns students are using and at the complexity of the sentences. Many of the teachers have students who speak English as another language, and they consider how the students' first language influences their English syntax. Often teachers have students do creative writing, and they begin to become aware of the syntactic differences between the fiction students write and the nonfiction that students may be reading in their social studies or science textbooks.

As students work in teams to analyze the textbook and student sentences, they raise questions and solve problems. They really do the kinds of things linguists do. For example, students with a background in traditional grammar aren't sure what to do with verb particles like *up* in a sentence such as, "We wrote up the results." Many of them want to call *up* a preposition. This leads to a discussion of the difference between prepositions and particles. I ask students to write in their logs all the verbs they can think of that can be combined with *up*. Often the teachers involve their own students in this project. They become aware of the great number of particles used in English. They also realize that second-language students have difficulty using the particles because verb particles are generally quite idiomatic.

Although the project focuses on English syntax, we also look at how English compares with other languages. For example, we compare English reflexives with reflexives in other languages such as Russian, Japanese and Spanish, using exercises from *A Linguistics Workbook* (Demers and Farmer 1990). The teachers see that different languages carry out the same functions in different ways and that one way is not better than the others. My students can then ask their second-language students to carry out similar comparisons between their own first and second languages.

We certainly don't solve all the mysteries of English syntax in a semester, but students come away with a practical knowledge of basic structures and the concepts linguists use to study syntax. More than that, they develop ways of looking at the syntax of writing that their own students are doing. They often come to see that students' syntax may reflect students' first language and may also reflect the kinds of reading students are doing. This knowledge helps teachers plan experiences with students to improve their writing.

Morphology

The basic question I pose for the study of morphology is: How do words come into our language? In answering this question, students look at the structure of words, the rules for creating words, and the way individuals develop their own vocabularies.

As a background for the main project, the class looks at different ways new words come into a language, through such means as borrowings or coinings. As part of their study of etymology, they investigate their own names. Where did their name come from, and what does it mean? We also study eponyms, such as *sideburn* or *diesel*. My students (and their students) find it interesting to think about becoming famous and having their own names go down in history.

We also look at abbreviations and acronyms. Students are often surprised to find that in words like *laser* and *sonar* each letter stands for something. Again, my students often ask their own students to try to find acronyms, or they bring examples from our class into their own classes to discuss.

Since many teachers of both first- and second-language students spend a good deal of time in language arts teaching vocabulary, the main morphology project centers around the question: Should we teach vocabulary directly? Related questions are: What do we know when we know a word? Can we learn vocabulary through the study of prefixes, bases, and affixes?

Students begin the morphology project with a sample of words taken from our linguistics textbook. During the project, they classify the words in a number of ways. First, they divide them into function words and content words. Then they subdivide the content words into simple, compound, and complex. For the complex words, they decide whether they are inflectional (adding *s* to *tree* to make *trees*) or derivational (adding *al* to *nation* to make *national*).

One result of the study is that the students realize that only a small percentage of the words in any sample, even a sample from a science text, are made by combining roots and affixes. This raises the question of how effective it is to teach vocabulary through teaching roots and affixes. We also look at words such as *cognate* to discuss the difficulty of identifying the parts and combining the meaning of the parts to find the meaning of the whole. I suggest that we seem to understand word meaning first and then, if we know the meaning of the parts, we can see the connections. Working from part to whole for word meaning doesn't usually work (Freeman 1991).

As a result of carrying out the morphology project, most of my students conclude that vocabulary is acquired during conversation and reading rather than learned as the result of direct teaching. At the same time, they understand that knowing a word involves much more than simply knowing a synonym for the word. Through our study of morphology, students begin to see that playing with words, word histories, and word meanings can be fun and that if students begin to enjoy thinking and talking about words, their vocabularies will increase without the need for the direct teaching of vocabulary.

Phonology

Linguists raise certain questions about how to represent and describe sounds and systems of sounds. Phonology may seem quite abstract, so to make these questions more relevant for my students, the question I ask is: Should we teach spelling? Related questions that we investigate include: What is the nature of the relationship between sounds and spellings in English? What is the normal developmental pattern of spelling acquisition? What are some ways spelling has been taught?

The phonology project is based on a study reported by Smith (1971), who found that it would take a great number of rules and exceptions to describe the spelling-to-sound correspondences of a sample of words taken from basal readers. Smith concluded that the number of rules is too great to be learned through direct teaching.

My students take one hundred different words from a book they use. They transcribe each word and then connect the phonemes with the spellings. For example, for the word *little,* students would transcribe it and then connect the sounds and spellings as shown below:

After transcribing the words and matching the sounds with the spellings, students make a list of possible spellings for each phoneme. Each team does one hundred words, and then we combine the class totals. Using this data, students write their conclusions about teaching spelling by teaching phonics rules.

At the same time that they carry out their project, we read about children's spelling development (Wilde 1992; Chomsky 1970; Read 1971). We look at how school texts approach teaching spelling, and we analyze the invented spellings teachers bring to the class. Once students have taken a scientific approach to phonics, they are in a better position to explain to parents and administrators why they don't teach spelling (or reading) by teaching phonics directly.

Linguistics Logs

In addition to the projects, students keep a linguistics log. They have two notebooks, and each week they turn one in for me to read and respond to. In the log they write questions and observations about the subfield of linguistics we are currently studying. Students can write whatever they wish in the logs, but I also give them questions to think about. In answering these questions, students need to be aware of the language that they and others use every day. For example, in the area of syntax, students might look for sentences that are structurally ambiguous as they read. Another week they try to formulate the rules for turning statements into questions. Or they might list all the verbs they can find that add the particle *up.* In morphology they might write about the meaning of their own name or the meaning of acronyms like *modem*. As we study phonology they might list words that end in *e* and try to formulate different reasons for the final *e* in English spelling. Or they could try to figure out if the spelling of the *k* sound is the same in English as in Spanish or some other language. Although there are always specific questions, the questions are open-ended, and many of my students who are teachers involve their own students in answering the questions.

Evaluation

When I began teaching linguistics, I gave students quizzes and tests to see whether they could transcribe words, diagram sentences, and so on. I found that students were very apprehensive about the quizzes, and even though they felt they were gaining worthwhile ideas during the course, their concern for the exams predominated, bringing back early memories of traditional grammar tests (which many of them had failed).

When I asked students to do things like transcribe words on quizzes, I realized another problem with the testing: I was testing a skill outside the context of its use. This realization led me to change from tests to logs and projects. By having students keep logs and work collaboratively on projects, I am able to engage them in meaningful activities during which they do the kinds of linguistics research that linguists do, and in this process they carry out activities such as transcribing and diagramming. Students clearly demonstrate their understanding of the concepts needed to carry out linguistic investigation, and the project-log format reduces anxiety. As a result, students develop a more positive attitude toward linguistics, an attitude that is more likely to result in their trying some linguistics with their own students.

Recently, I have stopped using the linguistics textbook. I give short lectures, and students learn key concepts as they engage in the projects. I still use a workbook that has problems from a variety of languages so we can do some cross-linguistic comparisons.

CONCLUSION

Most teachers have taken a course in modern English grammar as part of the work for their credential. Unfortunately, most grammar courses are taught by linguists who are not interested in the practical problems teachers face or by professors of education who are passing on a prescriptive approach to grammar that has changed little since Lowth's day. With this kind of background many whole language teachers concentrate on teaching reading and writing but leave language study out of their language arts programs.

One goal for my class is to help students realize how insights from linguistics can inform their teaching in areas such as sentence structure, vocabulary, and spelling. At the same time, by carrying out linguistic investigations in areas of interest to them, the teachers in my class develop the conceptual tools and background knowledge they need to engage their own students in linguistic inquiry. By basing the course grade on their linguistic logs and group projects, I create a situation in which everyone can succeed and build a positive attitude toward language study. Above all, I try to involve students in a number of activities that show them that they and their students can learn language, learn through language, and have a good time learning about language.

REFERENCES

Calkins, L. M. 1991. *Living Between the Lines*. Portsmouth, NH: Heinemann.

Chomsky, C. 1970. "Reading, Writing, and Phonology." In *Harvard Education Review*, 40, 2: 287–309.

Demers, R., and A. Farmer. 1990. *A Linguistics Workbook*. Cambridge, MA: MIT Press.

Edelsky, C., B. Altwerger, and B. Flores. 1991. *Whole Language: What's the Difference?* Portsmouth, NH: Heinemann.

Freeman, D. E. 1991. "Teaching Vocabulary: What's in a Word?" In *The Whole Language Catalog* (pp. 110–111). K. S. Goodman, L. Bird, and Y. M. Goodman, eds. Santa Rosa, CA: American School Publishers.

Gleason, H. A. 1965. *Linguistics and English Grammar*. New York: Holt, Rinehart and Winston.

Goodman, K. S., E. B. Smith, R. Meredith, and Y. M. Goodman. 1987. *Language and Thinking in School: A Whole Language Curriculum*. 3d ed. New York: Richard C. Owen.

Graves, D. H. 1983. *Writing: Teachers and Children at Work*. Portsmouth, NH: Heinemann.

Halliday, M. A. K. 1975. *Learning How to Mean*. London, UK: Edward Arnold.

Read, C. 1971. "Pre-school Children's Knowledge of English Phonology." In *Harvard Education Review*, 41, 1: 1–34.

Short, K. G., and K. M. Pierce. 1990. *Talking About Books: Creating Literate Communities*. Portsmouth, NH: Heinemann.

Smith, F. 1971. *Understanding Reading*. New York: Holt, Rinehart and Winston.

Watson, D. J., C. Burke, and J. C. Harste. 1989. *Whole Language: Inquiring Voices*. New York: Scholastic.

Wilde, S. 1992. *You Kan Red This! Spelling and Punctuation for Whole Language Classrooms, K–6*. Portsmouth, NH: Heinemann.

Ruth Heller's books about parts of speech are published by Grosset and Dunlap and are available in bookstores.

A Cache of Jewels and Other Collective Nouns (1987)
Kites Fly High: A Book About Verbs (1988)
Many Luscious Lollipops: A Book About Adjectives (1989)
Merry-go-Round: A Book About Nouns (1990)
Up, Up, and Away: A Book About Verbs (1991)

A Cohort Model for Whole Language Study in the Graduate School

David Heine and Patricia Heine

They've been doing it alone—reading, kidwatching experimenting, and sharing insights with their colleagues. How can those of us in teacher education programs support whole language teachers as they transform their classrooms and their teaching? I think the short answer is, we can't until we can call ourselves whole language educators too.

There is a revolution going on in schools today. Classroom by classroom and school by school, teachers are discovering that they can no longer bring themselves to spoon-feed children a junk food diet of overprocessed skills and drills stripped of real-world purposes and contexts. Sometimes enduring open hostility by colleagues or administrators, they continue to seek out conferences, journals, and professional texts that help them chart a new course for their teaching. As we became aware of the growing number of teachers in our community who were searching for a new paradigm of education we began to explore how we could support their quest. The result is chronicled in this chapter about the development of the Language and Literacy Institute, a whole language cohort consisting of a sequence of five graduate courses.

Three conditions convinced us that we should develop a language and literacy cohort to support the whole language teachers in our area. First, as teachers took initial steps in whole language, we were inundated with requests for courses that built on their growing expertise in whole language practice and theory. Second, teachers needed a long-term commitment of support. Becoming a whole language educator is a state of being. The cohort combines the shared vision camaraderie and commitment over time of Teachers Applying Whole Language (TAWL) groups and the rigor of university courses. Third, we were alarmed by the proliferation of "whole language materials and programs" hawked by publishers and the whole language "experts" offering make-and-take workshops. To recognize theoretically sound goods and services and to avoid the hype and misrepresentation of whole language opportunists, school districts need in-house educators recognized for their knowledge about whole language theory and teaching. Cohort participants can serve this role.

Perhaps most important, we realized that our whole language model was as much a model for graduate education as it was for elementary education. Our personal challenge was to address our own transformation as whole language teacher educators.

CREATING A WHOLE LANGUAGE PROGRAM

We wondered if there was sufficient flexibility within the university structure to implement a whole language program at the graduate level.

The design of the whole language cohort stands in sharp contrast to the information transfer model of learning and teaching typically practiced in university settings. The Language and Literacy Institute is theoretically grounded in a transactive, multidisciplinary model of learning based on insights from psychology, sociology, semiotics, early childhood education, critical theory, and literary response theory. It is also designed to take advantage of the community that evolves as a group of teachers learn and grow together. It is conceived not as a string of courses but as a continuous curriculum over five quarters of study.

The cohort format of five unified courses fits into the existing university structure for students pursuing graduate degrees, continuing education credits, or nonprogram professional development. We work with our department and the graduate office to ensure that the block of five courses fits within our elementary education, middle school, and reading master's programs. The cohort courses provide about one-third of the total credits required for the master's degree.

Our core group of teachers didn't fit the model of graduate students. They were more interested in learning and doing whole language than in the requirements of the degree programs the university offered. The cohort is intended to serve all interested educators. Although the courses fit the requirements of the master's program, most participants do not take it for that reason. They are interested in experiencing and understanding whole language theory and practice. Their motivation helps us attain our goal of attracting a diverse group of educators. This is important based on our belief that learning is a social process and people learn best when they learn together within a diverse community. The whole language cohort is targeted for twenty to twenty-five teachers, media specialists, and administrators who work with students of different ages. This number provides the diversity needed to hear a variety of voices and yet is small enough so everyone can get to know one another.

Because we feel it essential that cohort members have a basic knowledge of whole language and a commitment to transforming their classrooms, we ask that each candidate for the cohort first take an introductory course in whole language or demonstrate understanding of the theory through professional involvement or readings. To facilitate whole language transformation, we offer cohort courses only during the school year. In this way teachers have the opportunity to apply strategies immediately and research what they are learning within their classrooms.

An early concern of ours was how many courses, and perhaps more important, how long a time is necessary to support real change in teachers. Although whole language content is important (and we do address that in our courses), our first concern is how to facilitate change and how to assist the cohort members in becoming change agents in their schools and districts. We are finding that a sequence of five courses, three quarter-hour credits each, appears to be sufficient to build an in-depth understanding of whole language theory. It allows time to put that theory into practice and provides time for long-lasting relationships and support networks to develop among the participants. The following courses are currently included in the whole language cohort:

Literacy Through Literature for Elementary Teachers.   This course is designed to help teachers explore the concept of literacy—both their own and their students'. We examine the role of literature in literacy development at all levels of education. We broaden our focus to include multiple literacies. Teachers experience the literature cycle (Short, Harste, and Burke 1996) using both professional and children's literature. From this base, they begin or continue to develop their literature-based reading program.

Reading Process and Practice.   In this course participants explore the reading process. What happens when we read? What strategies do proficient readers use? What happens when children struggle with their reading? Reading assessment and evaluation are explored through observation, data collection, and analysis. Participants analyze their reading curricula in light of recent insights into the reading process.

Process Writing.   This course focuses on writing in the classroom. How do we engage students in the purposeful creation of various kinds of texts? Teachers experience writing firsthand for a variety of purposes and begin to see themselves as authors. The course explores the complex nature of writing and highlights journaling, the reading-writing connection, publishing in the classroom and school, and ways of evaluating writing.

The Social and Political Foundations of Whole Language.   Cohort members examine the family tree of whole language. They look at its past, present, and future and develop strategies for informing and collaborating with students, parents, colleagues, and administrators. Current criticisms of whole language theory and practice and political challenges to child-centered education and teacher professionality are examined.

Curriculum Development.   Cohort members examine and create a seamless curriculum. They contrast theme units and theme cycles. They modify and extend their curriculums to focus on inquiry, negotiated curriculum, group projects, and child-focused research.

These five courses are intended to support and extend one another. The lines between the courses are intentionally blurred. Having the same group of learners in all five courses offers a great deal of flexibility within each course. Specific content is highlighted during the course but is not exclusively experienced within that particular time frame.

New learning opportunities have opened up as the lines between courses blurred. Understandings and insights from one course are carried over into the following ones. Because participants are not bound by the university calendar, projects are often begun in one course and completed in another. For example, a group of fourth- and fifth-grade teachers decided to create minilessons to support their literature program in the first course. During the reading process course, they developed minilessons to help their struggling readers, and during the writing course they expanded their project to include minilessons for their writing workshop. A third-grade teacher developed a series of parent letters throughout all five courses.

Cohort participants are encouraged to take on curricular projects that reflect their current needs and interests irrespective of the course title. One teacher decided to do a research project on spelling during the first cohort course (Literacy Through Literature) because several parents had recently expressed concern about her "lack" of spelling instruction. By not tying projects directly to a specific course, the cohort community develops a wide collective base of expertise.

As the course lines blur, course textbooks and readings become part of the participants' professional library and are used as needed through the sequence of courses. For example, a group of first-grade and multiage teachers chose Carol Avery's . . . And with a Light Touch (1993) as their book. They used parts of this book in the reading, the writing, and the curriculum courses. Another benefit to a continuum of courses is that strategies can be introduced, adapted, and extended across courses in varying contexts. For example, literature study is introduced as a strategy in the first course through children's multicultural literature. It is later experienced as a strategy for exploring professional books.

Graffiti boards (chart paper used collectively by a group of participants for writing, doodling, model making, lists, etc.) are used as a tool to explore the concept of literacy in the first course. For example, the students represent literacy in some way using their graffiti board as a record of their ideas. These boards are passed to each of the other groups for additions, questions, and insights and then returned to the original group and discussed. This strategy is used again in the next course to support research projects. Early in the project, each teacher or group creates a graffiti board for her or his inquiry, including the inquiry area, knowledge known about the area, questions to pursue, and possible resources. This circulates among cohort participants for additional information, questions, and resources. Everyone contributes to the board and becomes familiar with all the research projects. The power and utility of each strategy grows as teachers explore its potentials in different contexts.

CREATING A WHOLE LANGUAGE CURRICULUM

Some issues refused to submit to the parameters of a single course. We came to realize they were the warp of the whole language tapestry—strands that held it all together.

It is impossible to carve a field of study as complex as whole language into a sequence of five courses. The power behind whole language theory is realized through the interrelationships of process and practice, research and theory, and content and change. As we structure the curriculum, five strands surface that are critical to any exploration of whole language. These five strands or inquiry themes run through all five courses and tie them together in a web of understanding:

Theory and Research.   These are the foundation for all of the courses. Each course examines current research findings from the growing database of whole language, and participants have the opportunity to conduct their own classroom-based research. Participants examine and develop their personal theoretical base and explore how to use their theory to create a cohesive whole curriculum.

Classroom Practice.   The whole language cohort focuses on practical application of whole language theory and principles. Participants learn about and then create a wide range of whole language engagements for their classrooms based on the authoring cycle, inquiry cycle, literature cycle, and theme cycle.

Assessment.   Ongoing comprehensive assessment by all stakeholders in the classroom is central to a whole language program. This strand presents an array of authentic assessment strategies for documenting and evaluating children's learning, the appropriateness of the curriculum, and our effectiveness as teachers.

Politics of Whole Language.   Education is not only social and academic, it is political. Each course includes issues such as exploring the role of children in the curricular process and society, informing and involving parents and others, hearing a variety of voices, and working effectively with colleagues, administrators, and legislators. Issues of censorship and current criticisms of whole language are examined.

Supporting Teacher Change.   Related to the politics of whole language is the question: How do we put political insights into action? Whether participants are interested in sharing whole language with a single colleague or helping a grade level, school, or district move into whole language, we explore strategies that invite and assist others in examining and transforming their teaching in light of what we know about language and learning.

Although we view the interrelationship of the five courses and the five strands of inquiry as a strength in our program, it also poses a problem for us: we cannot say with certainty what issues, readings, and activities will be addressed in any given course since we believe curriculum is negotiated with the participants and that content changes as the lines blur between courses. We need a structure to help us keep track of this dynamic curriculum across five courses, including up to five instructors. Our answer is a curricular grid (Figure 17) that allows us to plan each course and assists us in keeping a record of the topics, issues, readings, and activities that have been addressed. This information is available to each instructor, and new information is added to the grid throughout the five courses.

Course: *ED 678*	**Term:** *Winter*	**Location:** *Brainerd*	
Topic	**Issues**	**Reading**	**Activities/ Strategies**
Definitions of literacy	Multiple sign systems Role of context	Cecil's *Literacy and the Arts: Alternative Ways of Knowing*; Graves' *Discover Your Own Literacy*; Smith's *Insult to Intelligence*; Cambourne's *The Whole Story*; various dictionaries	Graffiti board

FIGURE 17 Curricular grid example

We needed a class structure that invited a negotiated curriculum. The participants were trusting us to plan the course, and yet we knew and valued that they came with their own agenda. We had to find a way to value their inquiry questions within the framework of exploring whole language.

Course structure can be a roadblock to student ownership and participation in schools. How we arrange time and activities can either invite or discourage student engagement. To facilitate participant involvement, we create a course structure that is predictable, is made public, and is open to change through consensus. Each course is designed to provide time to share insights and experiences, time for an interactive presentation of theory and practice, and time to work together on projects or issues of concern. A typical structure might include these segments:

- *Opening.* Because many participants come early in order to work together, we find it useful to signify the beginning of class with a focusing experience. Someone shares a favorite book or poem.
- *Open discussion.* This may relate to current issues, concerns, or reactions to readings. Participants bring articles from local newspapers, professional journals, programs from workshops they attend, and notices of upcoming events.
- *Presentation.* Instructor-planned activities explore theoretical issues—for example, experiencing literature circles and analyzing the activity using Brian Cambourne's (1988) conditions of learning.
- *Workshop.* Participants engage in group work, work on projects, or explore materials.

- *Closing.* One or more participants sign up to share quotations, articles, books, or personal writings or demonstrate strategies such as choral reading and readers' theater.

CREATING A COMMUNITY OF LEARNERS

We find ourselves using the metaphor of learning community for the whole language cohort. Our learning theory reminds us that the metaphors we choose shape our reality. The message here is to choose metaphors wisely. What does a community of learners look like in a graduate school setting?

Our metaphor of learning community is useful in making curricular decisions in planning the cohort courses. Although we have a few key readings in each course that provide foundational experiences for all the cohort members, self-selected texts, journal articles, and small group literature studies compose the majority of readings. For example, in the writing course we use Ralph Fletcher's *What a Writer Needs* (1993) as the common text. Book talks are given by the instructors and the teachers for choice texts, which groups of teachers then choose and order. Participants are not competing for mastery of the same knowledge but rather pursuing their interests and needs and sharing their insights with others. Collectively we hold far more knowledge than any of us holds individually.

A "getting-to-know-you" strategy that helps build a sense of community is a class-published yearbook. On the first day of class, we take instant pictures of each participant and all cohort instructors. Partners interview each other, and then present their partners to the class. Outside of class they use the interview information and picture of their partner to create a page for the yearbook and make enough copies for everyone in the cohort. Initially we found the yearbook useful in learning the names and faces of our co-learners. Later, we found that the yearbook was useful for keeping notes about each of the participant's unique experiences, special areas of expertise, research projects, and interests.

Inquiry is at the heart of the cohort curriculum. Each course syllabus includes course goals. Participants add personal goals to the course goals and choose several goals to pursue. They also include strategies for meeting their goals, and time is provided weekly for working on them. To foster this inquiry and facilitate ownership in the course, we ask participants to identify and keep a record of their educational interests, needs, questions, and goals. We use reflective journals as part of this self-monitoring process. Through both formal and informal sharing of their journals, cohort participants find colleagues with similar interests to pursue their inquiry goals. A goal update is written in the middle of the quarter with goals being added, changed, and deleted. At the end of the quarter, participants write a reflection on their goals, including any goals they wish to pursue the following quarter.

Communities are inherently active. We learn by participating in the community and then reflecting on the meaning of our actions. In the whole language cohort, participants live the curriculum they are studying. Some of the strategies explored and experienced are literature cycles with professional books, picture books, and young adult novels. Choral readings and readers' theater have been developed. Participants have written and published children's books. A group of cohort members have written letters to parents, legislators, and colleagues along with professional articles and book chapters. Participants have used miscue analysis to understand their own reading processes and the processes of their students better. Areas of personal interest have been studied using the inquiry cycle, and growth has been documented with portfolios. Cohort members create a portfolio that represents their learning through the five courses, beginning it during the first course and adding to and changing it throughout the cohort.

As members of a community we have the collective responsibility to transform it. Beyond helping one another explore and grow, members of the cohort are active in supporting change in their schools, colleagues, and the profession. One quarter we held a conference, with cohort members presenting projects and research to each other. Cohort members have presented to their schools and neighboring schools on literature study, miscue analysis, spelling strategies, invented spelling, and publishing children's work. Members have also presented at our statewide whole language conference, at state reading conferences, and at a national language arts conference. One group of cohort members was asked and provided the fall inservice for their district.

We are learning as we are going. It seems that each class, course, and new cohort group provides challenges to our theory and new possibilities for putting our theory into practice.

The cohort structure and the curricular decisions we have made are intended to create a curriculum responsive to participants' needs, consistent with whole language theory, and reflective of our goals for the cohort. The cohort concept provides a model through which we have been able to meet the needs of teachers and other educators, the requirements of the university, the rigor demanded by whole language theory, and our very personal agenda of empowering ourselves and others through whole language. It is allowing us to share our insights with others, understand ourselves better, learn from valued colleagues, and continue our own whole language journeys. We look forward to the evolution of this model through future cohort groups at St. Cloud State University and through adaptations by others who may find it useful at their institutions.

REFERENCES

Avery, C. 1993. *. . . And with a Light Touch*. Portsmouth, NH: Heinemann.

Cambourne, B. 1988. *The Whole Story: Natural Learning and the Acquisition of Literacy in the Classroom*. Auckland, New Zealand: Ashton Scholastic.

Fletcher, R. 1993. *What a Writer Needs*. Portsmouth, NH: Heinemann.

Short, K. G., J. C. Harste, and C. Burke. 1996. *Creating Classrooms for Authors and Inquirers*. Portsmouth, NH: Heinemann.

PROTOCOLS/ENGAGEMENTS

See the introduction to the Protocols/Engagements in Part A for a full explanation of this material (page 61).

C-1 Thinking Through Curricular Decisions and Influences from Outside the Classroom

ELLEN H. BRINKLEY

Introduction   Few preservice teachers can recall instances when they experienced censorship as students, since censorship seldom is visible to its victims. Sometimes currently practicing classroom teachers similarly are not aware of specific complaints and nationally organized challenges to books, materials, or class experiences that are a part of whole language classrooms. As classroom teachers are expected to make more of the curricular decisions about the texts and experiences used in their classrooms, however, it is important that they consider carefully how their curricular choices might be viewed by diverse groups of parents. My hope is to nudge students to become wise decision makers who can articulate the reasons for their decisions and defend what they believe will best serve literacy learning.

Procedures   Near the end of the semester, I bring to class trade books and textbooks (and accompanying paraphernalia if I have it) that classroom teachers might be asked to consider adopting for their own classroom use. (As classroom teachers, it is likely that they will find themselves in such situations, perhaps serving on district-wide textbook selection committees.) Working in small groups, my students review the materials and generate a list of what they like and can support professionally and what they don't like and can't support. I ask them to keep in mind anything they notice that they think parents or administrators might find objectionable and to weigh the pros and cons carefully.

After working together for a couple of hours (or over a couple of class sessions), we share our findings with the class. It is gratifying to notice the skill with which they can identify texts likely to engage students' interest and to lead to authentic uses of language. I am pleased as well when they realize which texts contain racial or gender bias and which place heavy emphasis on decontextualized, fill-in-the-blank exercises that draw students' attention away from meaning. I encourage them to generate carefully reasoned rationales for each decision.

As they discuss their choices and rationales, I occasionally step into the role of the unconvinced school board member or an angry parent. Unless censorship has come up in our conversations earlier in the semester, undergraduates are often shocked to discover particular texts or class experiences that protestors have sought to have removed. Although they may have some awareness of past textbook controversies, they frequently can't imagine why parents might object to particular books or class experiences that seem so appropriate for whole language classrooms.

At that point they come to understand the frustration that teachers feel when their well-intentioned classroom decisions are called into question. This session(s) can be followed by reading accounts of recent controversies and by discussing censorship and intellectual freedom issues that preservice teachers today must expect to be confronted with (some of the CELT Hotline materials work well for this purpose. The telephone number for the Hotline is (602) 929-0929). We can consider ways to circumvent problems when possible without self-censoring and to respond to the protestors when necessary.

C-2 Computer Journals

SHIRLEY B. ERNST

Introduction   This engagement is appropriate on campuses with e-mail accessibility or when the students have personal access to computers with the capability of connecting with a campus e-mail network.

There are several purposes for this engagement. The first is to involve students in a journal-keeping experience in which they can reflect on their shared experiences and individual learnings. A second purpose is to give them the opportunity to become familiar and comfortable with computers as a classroom tool. A third purpose is to demonstrate the importance of communication and community.

Procedures   At the start of the semester, I provide the paperwork for each student to sign up for computer access so they can utilize the e-mail component of the campus system. I prepare a class list with names, addresses, phone numbers, and e-mail addresses for each member. Directions are given for setting up a distribution list so that one message can be sent to all members of the group. Generally I begin the dialogue by sending a message having to do with a class session or an assigned reading. After that, each student is expected to contribute to the dialogue. The dialogues often are sparked by newspaper articles and political actions that affect education as well as by class discussions and readings. Often the students go exploring with the e-mail function and find interesting Internet opportunities. Most feel much less threatened by technology by the end of the semester.

C-3 Methods Share

DAVID E. FREEMAN AND YVONNE S. FREEMAN

Introduction   Because we are looking at whole language principles and theory and trying to help our graduate students understand how theory translates into practice, we want them to experience different methods of teaching language that are currently being used. Students often discuss on course evaluations how important it is to *experience* the methods in order to understand their effect on students and learning.

Procedures   Students are asked to become experts in a second-language learning method, which they will demonstrate to the whole class. After we briefly review the methods through a jigsaw activity and minilesson, students sign up in groups of their choice for a method. We try to give students their first or second choice of methods. Books and journals are on reserve in the library to assist students in research about their method. In addition, we give each group a folder that contains articles and handouts about their method collected from previous classes.

On the second and third nights, we demonstrate some methods that we feel students need to experience but would prefer they not spend a lot of energy researching, such as the audiolingual method, the direct method, and silent way. We do this in a language other than English. After each lesson, we evaluate the experience as to whether the method is consistent or inconsistent with principles of whole language learning.

Students have approximately twenty minutes to demonstrate the method to the class. We encourage students to use a language other than English. We have had demonstrations in Spanish, French, German, Korean, Japanese, Chinese, Tagalog, and Thai. At the end of the demonstration, they pass out a summary of features of the method plus appropriate resources.

After the method is demonstrated, the whole class evaluates it, looking at how it is consistent and inconsistent with whole language.

C-4 Share a Meal

David E. Freeman and Yvonne S. Freeman

Introduction   In whole language classrooms it is important to create a sense of community. When students share a meal each class evening, they have the opportunity to get to know one another in a personal way. At our college, all the classes in the language, literacy, and culture programs share an evening meal. Many of our students have included the importance of the meals we share as part of their evaluation of the class. They often talk about the community created, going so far as to suggest it is a family-like meal.

Procedures   The first night of each class, the instructors bring a simple meal to demonstrate the share a meal experience. After the dinner break, students sign up in teams to bring the meals for the rest of the class sessions.

We collect 25 cents from each person to buy inexpensive plastic plates and cups, which are reused each week. These are dishwasher proof, and the next week's committee is responsible for taking the tableware home to wash for the following week. After the dinner break each week, we make a point of thanking the night's team and giving them applause.

The last night of class, after the final sharing, the class comes to our home to eat food the students bring.

Afterword   In warmer weather we provide rolls, lunch meats, lettuce, cheese, chips, carrot and celery sticks, fruit, cookies, and beverage. In colder weather we bring chili, carrot and celery sticks, french bread, apples, cookies, and a beverage. After students have taken one course in the program, they begin to volunteer to bring food for the first night of the next class in their course sequence. This often allows the instructor a chance to volunteer to help with meals only when convenient and saves panic on the first night of class.

Over the past year, the system of reusing the tableware has been so successful that we can pass the plates, cups, and plasticware on to the classes the following semester. There always seems to be someone in each class moving on. When students split off into two or three classes, we divide the tableware so that each class has a start.

C-5 Whole Class Response to Student Responses

DAVID E. FREEMAN AND YVONNE S. FREEMAN

Introduction In our classes, we have students write responses to the outside reading and other experiences in which we ask them to engage. For example, they might do a literature study or a case study of a second-language learner. In these written responses, we want them to explore ideas, test out hypotheses, relate what they are learning to the classroom, and ask questions. For many, the kind of response is new and alien compared to their past experiences of "giving teachers what they want." Therefore, sometimes our adult students need demonstrations. Several students make such insightful comments each week that we want the whole class to benefit from reading them. Others need encouragement. We think these responses serve several useful purposes.

Procedures First, we read and respond individually to each student's response. We do this as a kind of "written conversation," writing either in the margins as we want to respond to something they have written or at the end of their responses. As we respond, we always come across several student responses that make excellent points, give exciting classroom examples, or ask insightful questions. In addition, the same misconceptions or questions are often made by a large number of students. As we come to these, we make note of them.

Immediately after we have finished reading and responding to each individual, we write a one- or two-page whole class response, drawing on the examples we have chosen as we read.

In the following class, we hand out our response to their responses, which we ask them to read silently and note comments that strike them. As they are reading, we hand back their individual responses so they can also read our personal comments. They then share in pairs or threes. They can comment on something they wrote or on something from our response. We then have a short general discussion. This process serves not only to answer questions and review major themes but also to bring up new questions.

Here is one of our responses:

All of you have important things to share as you reflect upon the reading. David and I really learn a lot from every one of you. Since it is impossible for all of you to read every other person's response, we like to share parts of student responses with everyone through a written response as well as through small group sharing.

As usual, your responses were varied and represented a vast difference in background experiences.

Laurel shared a prayer from a book entitled *Recess: Prayer Meditations for Teachers* (Murphy 1988).

> Lord, before I met her, I thought, "Oh, great!
> I don't know how I'll deal with this—
> to get a kid who's new to this country,
> who speaks no English,
> whose name I can't even pronounce.
> How will I cope?"
> But then
> with what sweet courage she
> walked into our babble,
> and coped.

The second-language student in the poem/prayer survived. Many do. However, we do not know what the child went through to cope.

Alicia shared how *Crossing the Schoolhouse Border* (Olsen 1988) brought back painful memories:

> The immigrant student goes through tremendous hardships, isolation and discrimination. . . . I ought to know; I have lived the experiences of being ignored because I didn't have the language and therefore I was thought of as dumb. Each chapter reminded me either of my childhood or situations that I have encountered as a teenager or now as a professional.

Sonia also remembers how it was when she first came to this country as a young adult to study:

> The book made memories come back like a flash. How truthful those children's statements were! As I was reading them I found myself saying: "Yes, that's exactly how it is!" And yet, I was saddened by this crude reality.

Laura, Kelly, Debi, Ted, and others spoke about what an eye opener the book was. We are not dealing with "problems." We are dealing with people. In order to do that, there is a lot we must know and be sensitive to. Maria shared honestly about her recent learning:

> I finally woke up! I spent eighteen years teaching, quite content I was doing a good job of teaching our immigrant students. But for the last three years, I have been getting bits and pieces of what "language acquisition" truly means. . . . I can speak Spanish, so I and my administrators believed I was truly qualified to teach in a bilingual classroom. Huh!

I suspect Maria is much too hard on herself, but her comments are important. There has been much suspicion about bilingual education and even studies showing it was ineffective. However, what those studies failed to point out was that teachers in "bilingual classrooms" were usually not only not trained but many were not even bilingual! In addition, many times teachers who are bilingual don't understand the rationale for first language support and so they refuse to use the students' first language. They believe they are doing what's best for their students; however, they do not understand enough about language learning. Maryann told of two classic cases at her school: in one, the child's first language was well developed. In the other the child was transitioned to an all-English classroom too soon. The first is succeeding in our system. The second is not.

Many of you talked about funding and other problems, including illegal immigration. Marsha pointed out, "I don't believe that the citizens of California can afford the costs of the solutions that this study recommends. . . . Those things might be ideal, but who is going to pay for them?" It appears that if we are going to begin to meet the needs, we must do it individually. The fact that you are all in this class shows you are doing something—a lot!

In case any of you think you have it hard, read about what Gloria is trying to do:

> I have gotten a teaching and counseling position. . . . It consists of four teaching periods: ESL 3, U.S. History, Guided Skills, and ESL Math. I also have one planning period and one counseling period. Can you imagine ONE counseling period! So many students, so many needs. I also am facing the task of teaching without a developed curriculum, misplaced students, class sizes growing on a daily basis, and the faculty cafeteria as my classroom.

Yet, Gloria maintains her enthusiasm and is convinced that her job is "well worth it and the students are definitely worth it!" She goes on to describe all the ideas she wants to try to make things better for her students. I think Tim's final comment describes Gloria and all teachers like you who are trying to do their best in California: "It [teaching] is a difficult and demanding profession that takes an understanding and devoted person to make it work."

References

Murphy, E. C. 1988. *Recess: Prayer Meditations for Teachers.* New York: Baker.
Olsen, L. 1988. *Crossing the Schoolhouse Border: Immigrant Students in the California Public Schools.* San Francisco: California Tomorrow.

C-6 Watching (Written) Language Grow During Pen Pals

DOROTHY MENOSKY

Introduction   The undergraduates who take my Introduction to Literacy course all dream of becoming teachers but have not yet been in a classroom as professionals. They believe that first graders can copy but not write or create meaning through writing. They believe that first graders just starting their second semester can read only simple words and phrases. This learning engagement allows students to discover just how much language a six year old possesses. They become acquainted with invented spellings and learn how to write their own letters in such a manner that they elicit writing style, spelling, and other changes on the part of their first-grade pen pals.

Procedures   Undergraduates are given the name of a first grader in a local public school. They initiate the letter writing by introducing themselves and asking questions of the child to whom they are writing. I take pictures of my students as they write these first letters, so that they can be included in a future missive. We also receive pictures from the first graders. The letters are hand delivered, early the next morning, to the public school.

For the first-grade writers, time is usually given during the week for them to read and write their letters. When that's not possible, they may write them at home. (Parents are gently instructed not to make any kind of changes, not even spelling.)

The children's letters are delivered the night before my next weekly class meeting.

My students soon learn they can indeed read invented spellings by reading the letters aloud and using the context. What a revelation! Now a new rule is added: My students may not make corrections in regard to spelling or grammar, but they are encouraged to use the same phrases and words the child used, only with a standard spelling. As the letters are collected, my students make notes in their journals and discuss what they are discovering about children's language development with each other.

At the end of the semester, we have two culminating projects. My students submit the letters they have received, along with a detailed, specific accounting of how their pen pals have grown in regard to written language. They also include an explanation of what they know about written language development and the natural development of phonics, using citations from professional books and articles, along with examples from their pen pals' letters.

The second culminating activity is a celebration. We meet our pen pals at their school for an afternoon of school sightseeing, reading, writing, gift exchanges, music, refreshments, lots of talk, and love. Parents participate for the first five minutes so they can take pictures. After that, parents are shooed away, the teacher and I step aside. The afternoon belongs to the kids.

Afterword   My students and I have been doing this engagement for twenty years now. We've been associated with the same school and same teacher during all these years. It's one of the best learning experiences we have. Each semester, some of the circumstances change, but what remains constant is the depth of real authentic lasting learning.

Kay Moss' undergraduates also correspond as pen pals with a local class of first-grade children. At the point in her class that students are ready to complete a miscue analysis, she arranges for her undergraduates to spend the day with their pen pal class. They arrive before lunch and eat with their pen pals in the cafeteria. After lunch, each student reads a story to his or her pen pal; then the pen pal reads a story. These stories are taped, and each student uses this material for miscue analysis work. Throughout the semester, students observe the writing products and the reading process of their pen pals and use this material to analyze the language learning of children.

[handwritten margin note: need to get to Lois to audio tape some first graders]

C-7 Encouraging Mentorship

KAY MOSS

Introduction   This engagement is designed to provide a mentor for each undergraduate student and to encourage graduate students to explore and share experiences as thoughtful practitioners. The engagement also introduces undergraduates in teacher education to learning experiences beyond their degree program. As pre-service undergraduates and graduate students correspond with one another throughout the semester, our community of learners is widened beyond our classroom door.

Procedures   Early in the semester I pair up the students in my undergraduate and graduate reading courses. These students correspond as pen pals approximately once a week, sharing experiences, ideas, questions, and concerns. As an additional experience for the undergraduate students, they attend my graduate class some time during the semester. At this class the graduate student meets the pen pal and introduces him or her to the class as a prospective teacher. The undergraduates then participate in the engagements, discussions, and activities of the graduate class.

C-8   Traveling Journals

KAY MOSS

Introduction   Many students in education have small groups of friends with whom they work and socialize. Traveling journals cross these lines to establish new communities of learners among the students. Students are encouraged to reflect on their learning as they write entries and read the entries of others.

Procedures   I purchase enough spiral notebooks for every four or five students in my undergraduate reading methods course. Within the first week or two of class, I establish what we call traveling journal groups, mixing students of varying experiences and backgrounds. Each group is given one spiral notebook and makes arrangements for writing journal entries and passing the journal to the next member of the group. Throughout the week, each member of the group reads the other members' entries and writes an entry. Students pass the journal when they see one another in other classes. The goal is for each journal group to complete at least one entry per student each week. When the last person in the group finishes writing an entry, the traveling journal is given to me. I read all of the entries for the week and write my own entry. I then return the journal to the first member of the group for the cycle to begin again. In the journal we respond to our class, our text, and one another as learners.

Afterword   This engagement originated with David Heine and Steve Hornstein at St. Cloud State University (see Chapter 14). Also see Chapter 20 by Mary Bixby for a thorough explanation of how journals can be used as part of evaluation.

C-9   Beyond "Topic" in the Thematic Curriculum

STEPHEN B. KUCER

Introduction   An unfortunate dimension of many thematic units is that the materials and activities are linked to the topic but little else. A deeper, more conceptual relationship among and between materials and activities frequently is absent. This demonstration helps students develop meaningful links within thematic curricula.

Procedures   Students are given a bibliography for the theme topic, "Getting to Know About Me, You, and Others." As students can readily see from the titles of the books, all materials address the topic in some manner. I then put students into groups and give each group approximately twenty books taken from the bibliography, such as:

Angel Child, Dragon Child (Michelle Surat, Illus. Vo-Dinh Mai, Raintree, 1983)
Big Al (Andrew Clements, Illus. L. C. Yoshi, Picture Book Studio, 1991)
Crow Boy (Taro Yashima, Puffin, 1976)
Earl's Too Cool for Me (Leah Komaiko, Illus. Laura Cornell, Harper, 1968)
Arnie and the New Kid (Nancy Carlson, Viking, 1990)
Oliver Button Is a Sissy (Tomie de Paola, Harcourt, 1979)
William's Doll (Charlotte Zolotow, Illus. William Pene DuBois, HarperCollins, 1972)
Emily Umily (Corrigan VanKempen, Annick, 1984)
Ira Sleeps Over (Bernard Waber, Houghton Mifflin, 1972)

I tell the students that they are to read each book and then group the books into sets that go together in some manner. I note that all the materials are related to the theme topic but can be grouped by other, more specific similarities. For each text set formed, students are to list the ways in which all of the books are alike.

After each group of students has had the opportunity to share their text sets and the characteristics for each set with the class, I build upon what has been shared and discuss the difference between facts, concepts, and generalizations. I give students the handout in Figure C-9 to facilitate the discussion. During the discussion I point out that generalizations and concepts are not inherent to the material but emerge from a transaction among reader, text, and context. Using the text sets that have been previously shared, I can usually point out instances in which different books were grouped differently by different groups of students and that perceived similarities varied depending on the readers.

I tell students that when they begin to gather materials for their thematic unit, they need to consider how the various materials might be linked conceptually as well as in terms of common generalizations. As the course proceeds and we begin to develop thematic activities, the identified concepts and generalizations serve as a base for the activities.

Afterword   I have found the power of this demonstration to be that it helps students avoid the selection of materials and generation of activities that have no meaningful link to the topic. For example, I recently observed a second-grade classroom where the topic was bears. Students read the book, *Ira Sleeps Over* (Waber 1972) and then practiced their counting using gummy bears because Ira had a bear in the story. The use of the book in this manner missed more significant issues such as the fear of the unknown and how people cope with their fears.

Reference
Waber, B. 1972. *Ira Sleeps Over*. Boston: Houghton Mifflin

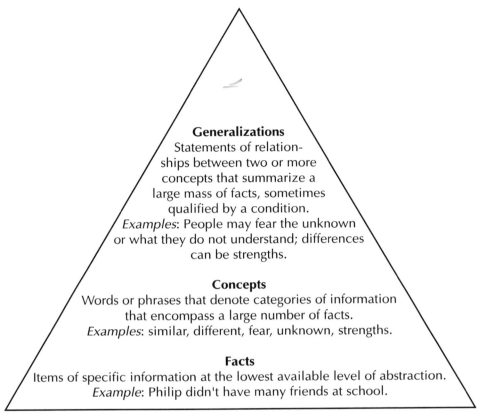

Generalizations
Statements of relation-
ships between two or more
concepts that summarize a
large mass of facts, sometimes
qualified by a condition.
Examples: People may fear the unknown
or what they do not understand; differences
can be strengths.

Concepts
Words or phrases that denote categories of information
that encompass a large number of facts.
Examples: similar, different, fear, unknown, strengths.

Facts
Items of specific information at the lowest available level of abstraction.
Example: Philip didn't have many friends at school.

FIGURE C-9　Generalizations, concepts, and facts handout

Copyright © 1996 Stephen B. Kucer. Stenhouse Publishers, York, Maine.

C-10 Implementation Goals

LYNN RHODES

Introduction   This strategy was developed in an inservice setting; I met with teachers periodically over a semester and wanted them to try out some new (to them) instructional strategies in the interim periods between our meetings. The Implementation Goal sheet (Figure C-10) allows me to individualize instruction that I provide to teachers. In turn, the teachers benefit from making decisions about strategies they use to meet individual needs in their classrooms and from reflection upon what happened during the implementation. In the setting in which this strategy was developed, where teachers were being introduced to writing workshop for the first time, they were not asked to choose a strategy to meet the needs of individual students as the first item on the Implementation Goal sheet indicates. Instead, the first item became, "What specific goal do you have that you hope will result in the improvement of your teaching and learning during writing workshop?" Since then, this strategy has been used in graduate classes dealing with individualizing literacy instruction—hence, the first item on the list.

Procedures   An implementation goal can be generated following the reading of a chapter or article about instructional strategies or following the presentation of instructional strategies in class. In the classes for which I've used this strategy, implementation goals are submitted periodically throughout the semester. For example, during a recent semester, teachers submitted three completed Implementation Goal sheets which were used as a basis for discussion. The Implementation Goal sheets affected the degree to which the teachers applied what they read and heard. As the teachers explored a topic in class or read about literacy instruction, they considered how to address a particular student's literacy needs.

In class or following the reading, teachers complete the first item on the sheet. That is, they generate the implementation goal and the reason for that goal, using any assessment information they have about the student. Teachers note that the completion of this section helps them understand that they deal more effectively with instructional needs by carefully articulating the student's behaviors and naming or creating a strategy to address needs. The goal sheet is then set aside, and the goal itself is implemented by the teacher in his or her classroom. Completing this first item and sharing the goal with colleagues encourages many teachers to try instructional strategies that are new to them.

Following the implementation of the goal, teachers complete the remainder of the goal sheet. In the second item, they record what they have read that supports implementation. Whether teachers read a variety of materials or read a common textbook, we see what specifics they use to generate their goals.

For the third item, teachers write about how the implementation actually goes in their classrooms and how they feel about it. Teachers often make adaptations to the original strategy, and the sharing of these adaptations in class adds to their learning, especially when more than one teacher attempts the same strategy.

In the last portion of the goal sheet, teachers ask questions that reveal issues not covered in their readings or in class up to that time. Their questions also reveal any confusions. Further, teachers raise new questions about the students

Your name _____ Date _____

Student's name _____ Grade _____

1. What specific goal do you have that you think will result in more
    effective literacy learning for the student named above? What
    assessment information led you to decide this goal was appropriate? If
    possible, name or describe particular instructional strategies you will
    use.

    _____

    _____

    _____

    _____

    _____

    _____

    _____

2. What did you read to help yourself think about this goal?

    _____

    _____

    _____

    _____

    _____

    _____

    _____

3. How did you do with regard to the goal you set?

    _____

    _____

    _____

    _____

    _____

    _____

    _____

4. What do you wonder about as a result of implementing this goal?
    What new assessment questions do you have about the student?

    _____

    _____

    _____

    _____

    _____

    _____

FIGURE C-10   Implementation goal sheet

Copyright © 1996 Lynn Rhodes. Stenhouse Publishers, York, Maine.

on whom they had been focused during the implementation process. Thus, the instruction assessment cycle begins again.

Afterword   As I read the completed Implementation Goal sheets, I make notes about what will be shared with the entire class, what questions should be raised, and what problems might be discussed. I suggest that they also select items they want to share, along with questions and problems they think should be raised. I write individual notes to the teachers about their specific students and lessons.

Debriefing of the Implementation Goal sheets is not always done with the entire class; sometimes we form smaller groups. For example, those teachers who had implemented the same or similar strategies, or those with the same grade-level considerations, are grouped together.

C-11 Literacy Progress Report

DAVID L. TUCKER

Introduction   More traditional programs in colleges and universities for the training of reading specialists were built on the idea of a clinic, and "problem" readers were brought to the clinic for help in reading. As part of the experience, clinical reading tests were administered to determine the strengths and weaknesses of these readers, instruction at the "appropriate" level was given, and then a clinic report was written. The clinic notion may be disappearing from the preparation of reading teachers, but the idea of a practicum has remained. If this practicum is approached from a meaning-based, language-based philosophy, what type of report should be written that can be shared with schools and parents? This literacy progress report replaces the traditional clinical reading report.

Procedures   Present an introduction that briefly explains that tutoring follows language principles. Therefore, no standardized testing, no test scores, and no grade-level designations are reported. Tutors conduct interviews to elicit students' perceptions of their own reading strategies, and miscue analysis serves as the basis for instruction.

The report has three main sections:

Part I: Assessment

- Strengths from the initial assessment, giving examples.
- Strengths from the ongoing assessment (instructional assessment).
- Areas that need improvement.

Part II: Instruction

- Areas in which learners were tutored, including time devoted to reading aloud to the learners and the strategies taught.
- Areas in which progress in strategy use was seen with examples.

Part III: Recommendations

- Recommendations for home.
- Recommendations for school.

C-12 Eavesdropping

JAYNE DeLAWTER

Introduction I use eavesdropping in a semester-long graduate course that meets once a week and in which a publishable paper is one of the course requirements. I schedule it after the first draft is written—about one and one-half months into the class. Before eavesdropping, students have worked with each other in small groups to select and clarify the topics and questions their paper will address. They have also engaged in discussion groups about current educational issues. This activity provides authors with response and feedback on their work in progress. It is a variation of "Save the Last Word for Me" (Short, Harste, and Burke 1996).

Procedures In the first of two class sessions students bring four copies of an early draft of their paper to class. As a whole class, we discuss the kinds of response and feedback authors find useful when they are in the early stages of writing. We examine sample formats for student peer response to writing from a variety of grade levels and settings.

Trios of students then discuss ways to adapt, refine, or invent a response format that will provide them with the information they want and need to proceed with their own writing. Consensus within the trio is usually reached but is not necessary. Students then exchange drafts with their two partners; their homework for the week is to respond in writing to each paper following the response format they have generated.

The trios reconvene at the next session. Two students sit facing each other and talk about the writing of the third, who sits with her or his back to the pair. The eavesdropping student author takes notes on the conversation about his or her draft, without entering the dialogue. The pair may talk generally about their reactions to and understanding of the content of the piece or refer specifically to strengths and concerns from their written responses. When time is called (about six to ten minutes usually works well), the eavesdropper turns around to join the conversation. The author poses questions that arose from listening to the conversation, and the pair locate points in the draft to which they referred. The eavesdropper does not try to convince peer readers or provide long explanations to answer their questions; rather, he or she seeks information that will help improve the next draft.

The conversation after the eavesdrop helps to clarify strengths in the piece as well as areas that need attention. It also invites the author to ask general questions about content and form that may not have been addressed in the eavesdropping time.

Drafts and written responses are returned to each author in the trio after all have eavesdropped to avoid focus on written comments before full attention is given to each conversation. Students with whom I have used eavesdropping say it is "delightful to have uninterrupted talk about your writing and then to join in to clarify things you want to work on next."

Reference

Short, K. G., J. C. Harste, and C. Burke. 1996. *Creating Classrooms for Authors and Inquirers*. Portsmouth, NH: Heinemann.

✳

C-13 Transparency Talk

JANE WHITE

Introduction   This strategy can be used with large or small classes of education students, but I have found that it builds a sense of community almost immediately in large classes of thirty-five to forty students. The strategy allows small groups of students to center their talk on a task, the creation of a transparency to share, but in fact, they talk about many peripheral aspects pertaining to the topic. At the beginning of the semester when students are uneasy or unfamiliar with group work and beginning new acquaintanceships, this strategy works wonders. The students must talk about important ideas that they understood from their readings or clarify difficulties, gradually reaching a consensus about what information should be included on the transparency. The clarification, embellishment, and shared understandings as classmates talk are remarkable. The students also are engaged in collaborative learning; they begin to understand its power and to enjoy the learning that occurs.

Procedures   Students have often read the same texts—chapters in books, journal articles, position pieces; other times they've read different texts centered on the same topic. As they read the assignments at home, they follow their normal procedure for school reading, and I ask them to mark anything they find confusing or unclear.

When we meet as a class, students form groups of their own choosing (usually four to six members) to talk, seek clarification, and discuss ideas they consider most important, most controversial, or most meaningful. The group's goal is to create an overhead transparency to share. My instructions are simple: "Represent the ideas that you agree were most important to you in any way you'd like." They're often disconcerted initially with the lack of direction on what the transparency should look like. Groups often discuss and create the transparency in twenty to thirty minutes, but some topics extend the discussion dramatically and in such groups it takes forty-five to sixty minutes to generate the transparency.

The talk is active, generative, and wide ranging as they begin to plan. First, they must come to consensus on what was important. Not all agree but as they talk, they see different points of view, defend their own, and generate new understandings. The first time the groups create the transparencies, many list important ideas, as if in outline form. But the second or third time some groups try mapping, small pictures to illustrate a point, or a chart to air arguments or agreements with the author. As the groups share their transparencies, everyone considers innovative possibilities. By the third or fourth time we share transparencies and discuss them, groups generate creative, personalized pictures of their comprehension; i.e., drawings, or word plays, or cartoons.

As the groups finish the transparencies, we meet as a whole class, and each group explains the information they've represented. No one goes to the front of the room or presents a formal talk. Instead, they sit and share the group's thinking. As the transparencies become more diverse, I often ask others in the class to describe what they see in the representation, what it means to them, and why they think the group organized the information in such a way. As the outsiders talk about the transparencies, the originating group gets a new perspective on what they have created.

Everyone realizes that while the transparencies look different and often contain unique information, there are threads that are represented in them all. That validation underscores the value of collaboration and sharing in any classroom.

C-14 Using Children's Writing Collections in Whole Language Teacher Education

Elizabeth A. Franklin

Introduction   Recent work in literacy evaluation has stressed the important idea that knowledge of the individual child must inform teacher curricular decision making. Kidwatching, a now-popular term coined by Yetta Goodman, captures the essence of this idea. In order to know what to teach, teachers must first be deeply informed about and connected to the children with whom they are interacting.

Many whole language teachers make portfolios, or collections, of children's written classroom works (Harp 1991; Tierney, Carter, and Desai 1991; Valencia 1990). These works are then studied in a variety of ways to document children's interests as well as their development in reading and writing. With descriptions of writing collections, teachers learn to document development in a way that respects the choices and meaning of individual children, framed by the writing traditions of cultures and communities.

At the University of North Dakota, we have an archive of the works of thirty-six children who attended Prospect School in North Bennington, Vermont, from the time they were five until they were thirteen. In addition, my collection of the written and visual works of seven first-grade Dakota children living on the Devils Lake Sioux Indian Reservation has 300 to 700 pieces per child. A similar collection, gathered over two years from six preschool children with special needs, has 200 to 300 pieces of work per child. Teachers in our graduate program often make and study collections of works of children in their own classrooms as part of course and/or master's thesis requirements. These teacher collections also inform our ongoing discussions of children and their works.

The use of writing collections serves several purposes:

- Many samples of work within one genre written over time are available for descriptive study.
- It is possible to study literacy development in a way that respects the complex relationships that exist between meaning, choice of genre, and use of writing conventions.
- The study of children's collected work provides a window on the person learning within varied social and cultural contexts, including gender.
- The study of writing collections helps teachers connect to children as thinking people. By reading their work seriously, as literature, teachers better understand children's meaning-making efforts.

Procedures   These procedures have been adapted from the reflective and descriptive processes for child study developed by Carini (1983).

My students and I first view the child's entire writing collection. Selected works (usually ten), taken from various times in each child's life, are then reread more carefully. These selected works are read aloud, paraphrased (to ensure a focus on meaning and not conventions), and then described and responded to in great detail. When studying a particular area, such as fiction writing, all examples reflective of the particular genre are viewed first as a group, followed by more detailed description of individual pieces.

After collectively reading the fictional works of a child, teachers are asked to write a descriptive response about the child as a writer of fictional literature. In their responses, the teachers are asked to refer to specific stories and address patterns of both change and continuity in the child's fiction writing life.

At no time is the child "psychologized." Instead, teachers read children's works from a reader-response perspective, drawing on their own life and text experiences in order to understand a child's meaning (Peterson and Eeds 1990; Rosenblatt 1978). Readers usually discuss genre characterization, setting, plot, and other literary features. Similarities between the text being studied and other texts are often noted. Because we are a group talking about our reading of the same child text, our individual interpretations are enriched and deepened by the various responses we share.

An example of how I use collections of children's works to help teachers better understand children as fiction writers will illustrate these points. In a graduate course, teachers read and study the collected fictional works of Oscar and Carly, children whose works are housed in the Prospect Archives at the University of North Dakota. Excerpts from the written responses of two teachers are shared below.

Cindy Blue, a second-grade teacher, wrote the following:

When reading Carly's selections, storytelling came to my mind. I found myself reflecting back to stories I have read in the same genre. Her writings were like a window into literature.

. . . From the selected stories I read, Carly wrote five fairy tales, five fantasies, three fantasy/horror, one story that is realistic fiction, a mystery, and a mystery/horror. As Carly gets older, she writes fewer fairy tales and fantasies and ventures into other genres. She appears to write about experiences she has acquired through literature and life. . . .

Carly interwove a variety of themes together in her stories. When she was young, the idea that good things can happen to you if you wait long enough was very apparent. She often interwove this theme with the theme of rags to riches. As she got older, the concept of struggle was added. Magic was also included in many of her stories. As she got older she began to add special twists and tricks that her characters had to endure. When she wrote about the supernatural, she effectively let the reader feel the unknown and the uncertainty in life. . . .

Carly usually had two or more characters in her story. Her characters were developed through description, gender, and a variety of roles. [When she was younger], the stories started out with a male being the main character, as in the story about "Mack and Mrs. White." Her main character changed over to female as Carly grew older. In "The Story" and "The Will," the female characters were very strong protagonists. Some of the characters seemed to be the age of Carly when she wrote the stories. . . .

In many of the stories, Carly's characters worked cooperatively. They solved problems together. In many of her stories, there was a happy couple who helped each other through many adventures. This happened, for example, in a "Moon Adventure."

Sixth-grade teacher Laurie Robinson studied and described the fiction writing of Oscar:

I was very impressed with the stylistic expression that was uniquely Oscar's throughout all of his work. From the very beginning he used humor—"and it knocked the hell out of him"—which fit the sentiment of his story . . . He used parentheses in several places to clarify a point—"While Frank was having a sword fight (well, you might call it a knife to sword fight)." These little "bonuses" made his writing full of color, description, and personality! I laughed out loud when I read a story constructed as an eleven-year-old regarding his experiences down at the railroad tracks and he came upon two characters who wore t-shirts that read "Waterbury Institution for the Criminally Insane." . . . I had many strong feelings about Oscar's writings. I would love to meet him.

The reading and study of children's collected written works helped these teachers better understand the richness of the writing life of individual children.

Afterword   The use of extensive collections of children's works also allows for the study of the gendered child/person learning within a specific writing context. My experience is that teachers are often unaware of how culture influences definitions of gender, how gender shapes the meanings that people construct, and how gendered worlds are created by children in the fiction that they read and write (Christian-Smith 1987; Gilbert and Taylor 1991; Holland and Eisenhart 1990; Radway 1984; Willinsky and Hunniford 1986). I always provide a series of research-based readings that address gender in children's writing. The study of gender helps students realize that the child's choice of genre is related to gender considerations in complex ways.

References

Carini, P. 1983. *The School Lives of Seven Children: A Five Year Study.* Grand Forks, ND: North Dakota Study Group on Evaluation.

Christian-Smith, L. 1987. "Gender, Popular Culture, and Curriculum." In *Curriculum Inquiry,* 17, 4: 365–406.

Gilbert, P., and S. Taylor. 1991. *Fashioning the Feminine: Girls, Popular Culture, and Schooling.* North Sydney, Australia: Allen and Unwin.

Harp, B., ed. 1991. *Assessment and Evaluation in Whole Language Programs.* Norwood, MA: Christopher-Gordon.

Holland, D., and M. Eisenhart. 1990. *Education in Romance.* Chicago: University of Chicago Press.

Peterson, R., and M. Eeds. 1990. *Grand Conversations: Literature Groups in Action.* Richmond Hill, ONT: Scholastic.

Radway, J. 1984. *Reading and Romance*. Chapel Hill, NC: University of North Carolina Press.

Rosenblatt, L. 1978. *The Reader, the Text, the Poem*. Carbondale, IL: Southern Illinois University Press.

Tierney, R., M. Carter, and L. Desai. 1991. *Portfolio Assessment in the Reading-Writing Classroom*. Norwood, MA: Christopher-Gordon.

Valencia, S. 1990. "A Portfolio Approach to Classroom Reading Assessment: The Whys, and Whats, and Hows." In *Reading Teacher*, 43, 4: 338–340.

Willinsky, J., and K. M. Hunniford. 1986. "Reading the Romance Younger: The Mirrors and Fears of a Preparatory Literature." In *Reading-Canada-Lecture*, 4, 1: 16–31.

D

DOCUMENTING PERSONAL
AND SOCIAL LEARNING

David Heine and Patricia Heine, editors

The whole language transformation of teacher education is not complete without addressing evaluation, assessment, and grading. We have learned from our elementary and secondary colleagues that these issues cannot wait until our curricular ducks are in order. Evaluation, assessment, and grading shape and are shaped by the curriculum. Therefore, as we reconsider teaching and learning, we also have to reconsider how we go about documenting that learning.

Generally teacher educators are given wide latitude in how they teach. The notion of academic freedom works in the favor of innovation. Assessment procedures, however, are less likely to be given the same degree of latitude. Most colleges still require instructors to assign letter grades or other markers that reflect their evaluation of their students' academic performance. Because of these political constraints, less exploration and experimentation is undertaken in the areas of evaluation and assessment.

The mismatch between whole language teaching and traditional evaluation is no less important in the college classroom than it is in any other classroom. Before we can expect authentic assessment to be recognized as a legitimate alternative in the college classroom, we need a clearer understanding of the potential that whole language theory offers for documenting learning.

We know that what we teach and how we teach reflects what we value. And what we value determines how and what data is collected, what purpose data serves, and how data is reported. As whole language teacher educators turn their theories inward on their own teaching, they are inventing new curricular structures that support inquiry-centered learning communities. Through this process the very nature of evaluation, assessment, and grading is also being transformed. A number of chapters earlier in the book include discussions of evaluation. In this part, whole language teacher educators focus their efforts more specifically on how they document the essence of learning they see in their students.

Several themes emerge from the following chapters that create a frame of reference for the potential that whole language offers to our emerging understandings of evaluation, assessment, and grading:

- A shift from instructor as holder of knowledge and students as recipients of knowledge to instructor and students as co-learners, supporting one another's inquiry.
- A shift from viewing students as independent agents to students as members of a learning community embedded within even larger extended communities.
- A shift from evaluation as a tool for ranking students by the instructor to evaluation as personal reflection for both student and instructor.
- A shift from grading of performance to thick description of learning.
- A shift from the transmission of knowledge to the personal construction of knowledge.

Unless students experience firsthand and have opportunities to explore assessment, evaluation, and grading from a whole language perspective they will carry their traditional views of evaluation with them into their teaching. In "Assessment, Grading, and Whole Language in University Classrooms," Stephen Hornstein shares the development of an assessment model within a block of integrated methods courses built on student goal setting, self and peer assessment, and a reflective stance on learning to inform teaching. Hornstein argues that grades work at cross purposes to the learner-centered democratic classroom, and although for political reasons he has not eliminated grades, he has upstaged them with students' documentation of their own growth.

As we move from content-centered curriculum to process-centered curriculum, it is important to develop authentic contexts for exploring, learning, and evaluating. "Continuous Evaluation in a Whole Language Preservice Program," by Richard Meyer, Yetta Goodman, and Kenneth Goodman, presents a collaborative site-based project between method block instructors at the University of Arizona and teachers at Borton Primary Magnet School in Tucson, Arizona, for preservice elementary education students. This chapter describes how assessment and evaluation are not afterthoughts to instruction but rather integral to and grounded in a set of expectations created by university instructors, classroom teachers, and students.

Collaborative journal writing has become a valued component in many whole language college classrooms. We know that shared written discourse is an important tool in learning, and yet we have only begun to explore its use in understanding and documenting student growth. Mary Bixby begins this exploration in "Journal Keeping as a Window on Change." Bixby highlights six modes of discussion that support her students' professional growth. We can adapt the process Bixby used to explore her students' journals for understanding our own students' growth.

Evaluation and assessment in the whole language college classroom hold promise for university instructors as well as students. If we view ourselves as learners, then we need to look at how we go about evaluating and assessing our own learning. "Transforming Practice Together: Teacher Education and Collaborative Inquiry," by Leslie Patterson and her colleagues, documents the power of collaborative inquiry among faculty in assessing and evaluating their own teaching. These teacher educators utilize a traveling dialogue journal to record their teaching decisions, write reflexive narratives on theory and practice, and analyze their journal entries for patterns of response and support.

If we believe that knowledge is theoretically grounded and personally constructed, then we have to develop structures within the curriculum that invite students to explore and document their emerging realities. In "The Struggle for Voice in Learning to Teach: Lessons from One Preservice Teacher's Portfolio," Dana Fox shares the power of personal reflection and theory building through an in-depth look at one secondary teacher education student's portfolio.

Finally, evaluation—coming to know and value ourselves as learners—requires self-exploration and reflection. Roxanne Henkin reminds us in "Something Just Clicked: Reflection Through Portfolios" that we develop our literacy as we explore ourselves through writing. Henkin tracks feminist themes embedded in the personal narratives found in the portfolios of her female graduate students.

We are at a critical point in teacher education. We are transforming our courses to be more consistent with whole language theory and now must explore ways to transform evaluation, assessment, and grading as well. The authors in this part share their insights and strategies as they attempt to transform their teaching.

ASSESSMENT, GRADING, AND WHOLE LANGUAGE IN UNIVERSITY CLASSROOMS

Stephen E. Hornstein

For the past five years, I have been working with my colleague Dave Heine to create a whole language approach to our university teaching methods courses and to develop an environment and a set of engagements that support language and content learning in genuine contexts. That work is reported in Chapter 14. The further we got into this work, the less comfortable we became with assigning grades to the work students were doing. We were uncomfortable with the way grade points are used in the marketplace (it is nearly impossible to get a teaching job in Minnesota without a grade point average of 3.5 or above). In addition, a comparison between our students and students who had experienced other kinds of settings would mean nothing.

Finally, we felt the process of grading contributed little, if anything, to learning and more often than not had a negative effect on what students learned and how they perceived their own learning. We had concerns about hidden curricula and the meaning students would create from their experiences in our classes. When someone other than the learner has the power of approval or disapproval over a student (typically indicated by a grade) honest intellectual pursuits become secondary to pleasing those with power. The questions and answers of those in power take precedence over students' questions and their own creation of answers. In addition, when we grade, we are in essence positing that the student with an A is better than the student with a B and therefore deserves some sort of greater reward. As Holt (1964) noted,

> We destroy the . . . love of learning in children . . . by encouraging them to work for petty and contemptible rewards, gold stars or papers marked 100 and tacked on the wall, or A's on report cards, or honor rolls or dean's lists, or Phi Beta Kappa Keys, in short for the ignoble satisfaction of telling that they are better than someone else." (p. 160)

When we grade our university students, we tell them that it is okay to make this differentiation. But if we believe in acceptance of diversity, pluralism, and multiculturalism we can't give students the message that some can be judged as better than others. We need to stop doing this ourselves and to find ways to help students navigate this quandary.

Despite what we say, our students see our classroom experiences as demonstrations and then emulate them in their own classrooms. If we continue to assign grades, it is likely that this structure will flow into our students' classes as well. Our task must become helping our students live other ways of assessing their own and their students' work, so that these engagements become the demonstrations for what can be done in place of grading.

BEGINNINGS

We presented our work on bringing whole language to university settings at the Whole Language Umbrella Conference in Phoenix in 1991. The many concerns our colleagues raised and the spirited discussion of grading in such settings demonstrated to us the necessity of doing something different. [Previous to this time we were simply giving students credit for work completed, and although they weren't threatened by such an approach, little was learned about assessment.] Our colleagues around the country indicated similar approaches, including contracting for grades, simply giving everyone A's, averaging an instructor-assigned grade with a student-assigned grade, and a variety of other strategies. Most of us didn't like what we were doing but had yet to develop much of an alternative.

With these concerns in mind, and with the intention of helping students to live a whole language approach to documenting learning, reflect on how this approach works for them as students, and learn how to document learning in their own classrooms, we decided to try a new approach beginning with the fall quarter. We were still required to submit grades at the end of each quarter. However, instead of being graded, students were asked to write a self-assessment for each of the five major projects they completed during the quarter. Students also wrote assessments of at least two projects their peers completed. Finally, we asked them to keep an "evaluation, assessment, and grading journal," which was passed to others once a week for response.

Before students wrote their first assessments, we brainstormed the kinds of information that might go into them. As instructors we agreed to read a minimum of two projects (of their choice) per student and to provide in-depth, substantive response both in person and in writing.

At the end of the quarter, students were asked to submit a portfolio containing all of their work and all assessments written by or for them, to write a self-assessment, and assign themselves a grade. We accepted the grade requested in almost all cases. In two cases (out of more than 100 students) we felt that students had not really engaged in the class. These students either retook the course or redid major portions of the work.

Over the course of the quarter, we saw interesting changes in our students' understanding and beliefs about grading, assessment, and evaluation. Based on their experiences, many students moved from seeing grading as legitimate and necessary (if imperfect), to viewing it as harmful, finally to seeing it as

I'm not sure I agree?

inconsequential and unrelated to learning. Similarly, their views of assessment changed from seeing it as discrete and decontextualized, to seeing the need for assessment to be ongoing within a specific context. Initially evaluation was seen as an evaluation of the learner by the teacher, measured against a prescribed standard. By the end of the quarter, many students saw evaluation in a larger context: the evaluation of the learner and the curriculum, by all involved stakeholders, with the purpose of documenting change and growth.

Knowledge was initially seen as linear (echoing the hierarchical skills approaches with which students are familiar). Later it was seen as volume as students recognized how much they learned. Finally, some students saw knowledge as ever changing and connected to other areas.

The self and peer assessments students wrote echoed their changing views of schooling and knowledge. Some simply celebrated the completed work and said little else, noting how much they liked the project, how creative it was, or how hard they had worked. Other more thoughtful assessments, although starting with a celebration, also cataloged what had been learned and suggested further questions, approaches, or avenues for investigation.

The most powerful student assessments revealed changes in the learner beyond the scope of learning about teaching and schools. Brigette's experience with her Living Social Studies project is a good example:

> I think one of the most profound things I got out of this project sounds so simple at first and yet has a very deep meaning for me. During my interview with Art, he talked about how the Native American peoples at this time in history were experiencing genocide of their culture and were basically in a survival mode. Even though I've been exposed to this over and over before it was never real. He didn't expand on the issue at all; the impact came from sitting two feet away from someone who this had directly happened to and hearing the word survival in his own voice.
>
> . . . And then to think that things like the Sli-Ski-Ska festival, as degrading and mocking as it was, wasn't that big of an outward issue for the Native American population because they were literally trying to keep their culture and their people alive on the reservations. And the fact that there are people alive today who are still deeply affected by what had happened. . . . I have a better understanding of how their problems of today go deeper than we can imagine because generation after generation of their people were submitted to so many incidents—some large events and some small; but all of them had lasting effects.

Brigette may never have pursued this project in this depth, may never have been cognizant of her internal change, and in all probability would not have told us about it were it not for the self-assessment process and the fact that the project and class were not graded. Students tell us they have never worked as hard or learned as much as they do in our classes, because of the fact that we don't grade them. They now decide for themselves when something is completed rather than assuming that something will merit a specific grade. In addition, they note that the people they share their work with will be their peers for their entire careers, and thus peer opinions are important. They do their best because they are professionals, not because a grade is riding on it.

LOOKING BACK

The first major lesson we learned from engaging in the self-assessment process was that we didn't know very much about assessment either. As we began to write assessments, we found that we didn't have much more to say than the students. Many students were content to write or receive assessments that simply said, "I liked it," or, "You worked hard." These same kinds of assessments showed up in their suggestions for kidwatching (Y. Goodman 1978), as they planned their projects with children and in their assessments of children. Like most other teachers and students, we simply had no experience with describing learning rather than judging. I began to use a model that included celebrating completion and effort, describing, cataloging, and commenting on things I could see students had learned, and making some suggestions for students to consider in the future.

We shared this model with students, but it seemed to have little effect. We got the same tired comments. Something was still missing. It took much discussion about the nature of assessment and several months for me to realize that the missing ingredient was context. Dave and I had a context for writing our assessments because we had internalized goals for what we wished students to consider and had set up classes and engagements with a universe of outcomes in mind. Our students had no such context. Our task now became helping to build contexts for assessment.

MOVING FORWARD

As we built a context for assessments we had to think about what we were trying to achieve and rethink our goals for students. Following are goals for the Living Social Studies Project and the Children's Book assignment:

Living Social Studies Project Goals

- To understand the nature and teaching of history in a new way and to see new potentials for teaching social studies in elementary classrooms.
- To apply these experiences, along with information from the readings and discussions, to develop a classroom social studies program.

Children's Book Goals

- To experience what it feels like to be an author, including struggling with topic, voice, response, revision, writer's block, fear, and success as an author, and to see new potentials for writing in elementary classrooms.
- To apply these experiences, along with information from the readings and discussions, to develop a classroom writing program.

In essence, we are informing students of what we intend they will gain from these experiences. We also ask students (at the time we make the assignment) to set their own goals for the project. I suggest at least two sorts of goals: (1) what they are going to do and (2) what they hope to learn. A third important goal in some cases might be, "How do you want to use this information?"

By the end of the school year, I was convinced that although we were on the right track, something was still missing. Again we got some insightful self-evaluations and some in-depth consideration of personal goals and growth. On the other hand, some students still told us, "I'm not very reflective," or in describing their process in writing indicated that they had done the project, then reconvened with their group to decide what their goals had been.

It became clear at this point that we still had missed an important aspect of the context of our students' lives. Their history is about doing tasks assigned from the outside, for other people's purposes, and jumping through teachers' hoops. They have little experience with looking at their own learning or with setting goals for themselves. We needed to develop a process that recognized these realities.

A MODEL FOR PROMOTING SELF-ASSESSMENT

Based on our experiences and in consideration of our students' past school experiences and the need to provide a context and structure for assessment, we developed a classroom model using the following components.

Public Files

To communicate the importance and centrality of assessment to all teaching, we now keep a hanging file system, with a file for each student, in the classroom. The files contain an initial philosophy statement written by the student, our list of class goals, the student's initial class goals and any changes throughout the quarter, and goal statements and assessments for each engagement. These files need to be public so that students who are writing peer assessments of projects can gain access to individual students' previous work and goal statements.

Goal Setting

In order to ensure early goal setting students are given a week to develop their own goals for each engagement. We respond to their goals and ask the peer reviewers to respond. The goal sets and responses are placed in students' files.

Writing Philosophy/Belief Statements

A philosophy and belief statement is required as part of the materials students complete for their placement files, which makes this an authentic activity with a genuine purpose. We ask students to write a draft of their statement at the beginning of the quarter and to share it with one other person. At the end of the quarter, students rewrite this statement in preparation for opening their placement files. These two documents provide the students with artifacts with which to see themselves at different times and assess growth and change.

Self-Assessments

We set a context for writing and a set of expectations regarding what a self-assessment might include:

1. How have you met your goals and the goals we set for this engagement? What have you learned and how did you learn it? How does the evidence you have collected document your learning?
2. How would you modify this activity so children can share a similar experience? Or . . . How would you change this activity? Why make these changes? (Kids can answer this second question too!).
3. What questions or concerns do you still have about this topic or activity? How will you pursue them?
4. What have you learned that is outside the parameters of your stated goals? Will you be pursuing these ideas further? How?
5. How have you been changed by this experience? What effect will these changes have on you and/or on your work with children?

The response using this model has been promising, as excerpts from Kristi's Children's Book self-assessment show:

> I think I successfully met my goals in writing this book. I wanted it to be something to be used in a classroom as a discussion starter. I also wanted it to have an effect on readers/listeners that would once more drive home the dangers of drinking and driving. After having several classmates read it, and reading it myself to a few 6th graders and a class of fourth-fifth graders at Centerpoint School, I think I can safely say these goals have been met.
>
> The initial reaction of readers and listeners alike is always silence. Then they ask a few tentative questions. I think if time and the situation permitted, a discussion about drinking and driving and/or death would develop. This happened in my author's circle. Someone suggested it as a discussion starter especially when someone (or the class) has experienced the death of someone close as a way to help in dealing with the grief and loss.
>
> I think I may also have had a hidden agenda in choosing this topic. Now that I look back at the process, I can see that it helped me to deal with my own grief and loss, even though this happened over eight years ago. When this assignment was first given, I had no idea what to write about. I guess one could say I had a bad case of writer's block. I also wonder if my subconscious planned that. When the idea came for this book, I ran with it and I knew it was the topic I needed to write on. It was what I was waiting for. I don't think I would have been as satisfied or as successful writing about something else.
>
> Now that I am done with "I Remember When," I am always looking for another topic for another book to jump out at me. I want to try some of the illustrating ideas I have seen others use. I have the writing bug!
>
> All in all, I am glad we had this assignment. Not only did I learn a lot about the authoring process, I now have a family keepsake that I hope will last a long time. My parents will also receive a copy. They also found the book both touching and healing.

Peer Review

As we moved into this goal-setting and response model, we expanded the role of the peer reviewer. Peer reviewers serve as mentors and consultants. Each student has the opportunity to serve as a peer reviewer. They meet with small groups or individuals to comment on, extend, or help students revise goals. If necessary, they help students collect evidence to document their learning. As work is progressing, the peer reviewer encourages, provides response, refocuses questions, and plans for further exploration. At the conclusion of a project, the peer reviewer prepares a typed written summary of the process used and evidence of growth.

The quality of the peer assessments is exemplified by Tracy's response to a group who had just completed a project using the inquiry cycle to investigate the topic, "Setting Up a Whole Language Classroom."

> I very much enjoyed watching your presentation as well as examining the documents that show how and what you learned. I'm glad that I got this opportunity because I learned many things from your description, published work, and assessments.
>
> It was neat to see that every member of the group came away learning something different. Your group not only described the primary things you learned, you told where and how you learned them. I believe you accomplished your main group goal by finding out some of the essential components of setting up a whole language classroom and experiencing setting them up for your presentation.
>
> I also see that you accomplished much more. You all now have names of books that can be valuable resources in your future teaching. You have seen the importance of immersion, demonstration, etc. . . . . the seven conditions of a child centered environment [Cambourne 1988]. You found out how the inquiry cycle can be implemented into an elementary classroom by experiencing it yourselves. Finally you found that as a beginning teacher it is best to take it slow and gradually incorporate the components of a WL classroom.
>
> So, because you learned many things in this process, are you interested in finding out more about WL classrooms? I want to know more just from reading your project. If so, how will you go about finding new information? Did you find talking to WL teachers was more beneficial than reading books? What new questions do you have about WL classrooms? Would you use the inquiry cycle again in pursuing these questions? Thanks for giving me the opportunity to assess your project.

Instructor Assessment and Accountability Checklists

Included with the packet of materials we give to students is a document entitled "Accountability Checklist," listing the specific components of each assignment and providing a space for Dave or me to sign off as each piece is finished. This ensures that students complete all of the assignments and eliminates the need for us to receive all of the materials at the end of the quarter. The checklist for our "Choices" project has these components:

- Goals
- Project description
- Meeting log
- Artifacts
- Publication
- Presentation
- Self-assessment
- Peer assessment
- Instructor
- Date

The project description and the self and peer assessments must be typed or handed in on computer disk.

The checklist informs the students that we intend for them to complete all of the required projects despite the fact that we are not grading and informs the instructors that everybody completed all assignments. Before I sign off on a project, I make sure that the self-assessments and peer assessments are thoughtfully completed.

The fact that we don't respond to all student work in depth but do insist on completion sends two important messages to students: expectations are important and the quality of one's learning is not necessarily predicated on a teacher's validation of it. A student's own reflections and reporting of learning and the responses of their peers are given more attention than are the responses of the instructors. In short, we believe our students are learners, we trust them to be reflective, and we believe they will use their reflections as tools for further learning.

We do respond in much greater depth to two projects for each student. As our students become more reflective in their self-assessments, recognize their own progress toward their goals, and how their project may apply to a classroom, we respond to different issues. Following is my response to a group of students (Lauralee, Becca, and Judi) investigating a local sculpture:

> Wow! In addition to meeting your goals I can see that you are learning many different lessons from your work on this project. You've all done an excellent job in recounting your achievement of your goals so I won't address that here. I guess I'm more interested in the more global effect this project may have on your teaching.
>
> I think Judi's question "Why are we working so hard if we are not being graded?" is important. The answer you found is what I believe to be the key to a meaningful education . . . it has to be interesting and of importance to the learner. As you can see it isn't necessary for there to be *total* freedom in this. Dave and I made a specific assignment for which we had specific goals. Within that assignment we left room for individuals and groups. How can you work from this assumption throughout your school day?
>
> I'm also impressed with your sense of responsibility to your group. Coming out of your classroom experiences do you have suggestions for helping kids gain this sense of responsibility? I think it's also extremely important that children choose their own groups (as you did) because trust is so important! Group members need

to trust one another and I *always* let kids choose their own groups unless there is some compelling reason why they shouldn't. I encourage kids to seek diversity and work with new people but forcing it has never worked and never will. We can't force friendship or trust and a grade hanging over our heads or the potential for a petty reward doesn't make us like each other any better.

I do have several questions for you . . .

1. Are all the possible perspectives really here? Are there people who were against the sculpture? If so, why? Are there people who don't like it? I didn't hear anything about these issues. What would you have to do to find them?
2. I also felt your presentation was a bit lengthy. I understand that you had a great deal of information about which you were very excited. But the fact that someone thought it was important has been the reason for *everything* that has ever been placed in a formal curriculum. So the question is, how do we take our interests, and make them "engaging" for others, so others are "invited in" to participate and extend what we are doing rather than just having our findings transmitted. I think you'll find this to be an important issue with your students too.

In conclusion, I can see that you really have accomplished our goals as well as your own. I can tell you've also had a lot of fun here! Congratulations on a job well done!

Final Assessment and Portfolios

At the end of the quarter students are asked to prepare a portfolio documenting their learning for the quarter. They are encouraged to include anything that documents their learning in the context of their own goals, the goals Dave and I established for the block of classes, and the questions included in the "Final Assessment" (Figure 18).

Our results in using this model have been promising. Because students are able to focus on both our goals and their own, they are a lot more cognizant of what it is they wish to gain from our class and from the specific projects. As expected, this model is finding its way into their practicum classrooms as well.

We are happiest with the depth of reflection in our students and in ourselves. Students now have a better ability to apply what they have learned in our class to their own classroom settings. Using the Final Assessment questions as a guide, Bryan wrote in his portfolio:

> My understanding of Assessment has completely changed. . . .
>
> Previously assessment meant taking tests, writing closed book essays, memorization, etc., Now it seems assessment furthers learning, synthesizes process, teaches others, etc. As you can see these are two totally different results. It seems clear to me which one is more beneficial. . . .
>
> I now realize there are a variety of ways to assess students that do not include stress, rote rehearsal, senseless knowledge, and numerous other tasks that have no real world context. Grading seems for me to be obsolete. Unfortunately I do not think my opinion will reflect that of most school districts and parents. When

Please think about how your understanding of the following issues has changed during this course. In each area, consider what experiences, discussions, readings, etc. have prompted these changes, what evidence of this growth you have included in your portfolio, and how this evidence documents your growth.

1. Children, learning, and schools.
2. Assessment, evaluation, and grading.
3. The nature and teaching of reading.
4. The nature and teaching of language arts.
5. The nature and teaching of social studies.
6. Your views of classroom organization, discipline, management, and curriculum.
7. Multicultural and inclusive education.
8. Curriculum and the politics of education.
9. Would you be any different if your own school experiences had fit more closely with the vision for schooling expressed in this class? If so, how and why would you be different?
10. What have you learned about yourself as a learner as a result of this class? What impact will this understanding have on your work with children?
11. What have you learned that is outside the parameters of these questions and the topic of schooling in general? What do you perceive to be the implications for such "incidental" learning in schools?
12. Has the reflective process implicit in this assessment changed your perceptions in any way? If so, please describe.

FIGURE 18   Final self-assessment

discussing the matter with classroom teachers the consensus seems to go something like the following. Parents want to know how their children are doing and teachers need to assign some sort of accountability to their students. Without this accountability we will not know if the students are learning anything. This has been embedded in education for centuries. Although I do not believe grades have any worth I probably will need to assign them. . . . While I know of many ways to assess my students, I can not find a fair way to assess students well enough to assign them a grade which I feel has no relevance to their education.

My opinion has changed due to the assessment techniques used in this class. . . . I can not think of one time that a test this quarter would have furthered my learning. If anything it would have stagnated. After a test students generally never see the material again. . . . In our class I have learned that learning needs to be built on a personal level. Students need to be empowered. . . . What I know is personally important, practical, and useful to me, therefore, I have learned it well and I am able to utilize the information in real life situations. I believe assessment techniques that are adapted from our class can be just as valuable to students in the elementary grades.

If we want students to understand whole language they need to be able to live whole language in their own lives. If we want students to be able to assess their own work, and we want teachers and schools to move beyond grades, we need to provide a context within which growth can be documented. Finally, if we want teachers to be reflective and to encourage reflection in their own students, teacher education students need to be immersed in an environment in which reflection is a genuinely valued aspect of daily life in the classroom.

REFERENCES

Cambourne, B. 1988. *The Whole Story: Natural Learning and the Acquisition of Literacy in the Classroom*. Auckland, Australia: Ashton Scholastic.

Goodman, Y. M. 1978. "Kidwatching: An Alternative to Testing." In *National Elementary Principal*, 57, 4: 41–45.

Holt, J. 1964. *How Children Fail*. New York: Pittman.

CONTINUOUS EVALUATION IN A WHOLE LANGUAGE PRESERVICE PROGRAM

Richard J. Meyer, Yetta M. Goodman,
and Kenneth S. Goodman

> Things that have been most wonderful about the block are those that have taken
> place outside of the Wildcat room, but that is far from being a negative reflection
> on the class. What this shows is that the Whole Language block has the room
> within it for such things to happen.
>
> —Cheryl

As whole language teaching has become increasingly visible pedagogy in schools
in Tucson, Arizona, it seems logical that preservice teachers will benefit from
being immersed in whole language teaching. This chapter documents the continuous evaluation of the experiences of apprentice teachers in a field-based whole
language methods block we have developed with the principal and teachers at
Borton Primary Magnet School. Yetta and Ken Goodman have taught in the
block in alternate years. Rick Meyer, now at the University of Nebraska, coordi-
nated and taught in the block during its first two years.

We believe that "evaluation is part of curriculum: it cannot be divorced from
classroom organization, from the relationship between teachers and students,
from continuous learning experiences and activities. . . . There is no way to separate the role of evaluation from the dynamic teaching/learning transaction"
(Y. Goodman 1989, p. 4). Our discussion of evaluation in the block program
follows a framework for the curricular experiences and opportunities planned
for the students. Our evaluation strategies and criteria are integral to our expectations for the whole language apprentices in the block program.

A THEORETICAL FRAMEWORK

The Goodmans' experience with field-based programs began in the 1960s and
1970s at Wayne State University in Detroit. At that time teacher educators were

convinced that preservice teachers received the richest kind of professional development if they worked directly with children at school sites. That experience was invaluable in planning this program. The principal and a representative committee of teachers and parents spent a full year collaboratively developing the block program with us.

We came to the whole language block with two major principles: it should have *a firm theoretical framework* and should provide *authentic experiences* within the reality of a school that supports that framework. In our whole language block we see the students as apprentices, learning through active experiences with children and teachers to develop the flexibility to work in a variety of classrooms. Experienced whole language teachers help the apprentices understand what they do in their classrooms and why. The methods class sessions, held at the school, provide opportunities to read, discuss, and explore academic knowledge and theory as it is played out in the whole language classrooms.

The methods block experience at the University of Arizona is planned for the semester prior to student teaching. It integrates language arts, social studies, and reading with experiences in the school. The students are also together on campus during math and science classes, where the science and math faculty coordinate their teaching with the block program and relate their assignments to Borton classrooms. They join us in meetings with the Borton faculty.

BORTON PRIMARY MAGNET SCHOOL

Borton is a public primary magnet school (K–3) located in the barrio of Tucson. The school has had a long history of commitment to progressive educational concepts. The principal, Bob Wortman, taught as a kindergarten and first-grade teacher for thirteen years, primarily at Borton. He brings his teaching experiences and his philosophy of whole language and early childhood to his work as a principal. Borton teachers are confident and experienced. Most have completed their master's degrees, and some are working on further degrees. The teachers are actively involved in professional experiences; they write for professional publications, give workshops and conference presentations, teach professional education courses, and actively participate in professional organizations. As the principal and the teachers became more knowledgeable about whole language, they began to use the term *whole language* to describe their educational program and philosophy.

An average of twenty undergraduate preservice teachers participate in the block each spring. Bob Wortman, with the support of the district superintendent, accommodates our program in various classrooms on the school site so that the university faculty and the apprentices become part of the school community. The classrooms at Borton all have names such as the Rainbow, Zoo, and Cookie Rooms. The university apprentices chose Wildcat Room as our name and logo, consistent with the name of the university sports teams. That made sense to Borton students. We are *their* Wildcats, a valid part of the school community.

UNIVERSITY FACULTY AND THE BLOCK PROGRAM ORGANIZATION

The block staff includes Ken or Yetta Goodman in alternating semesters, a graduate teaching assistant who supervises the apprentices' practicum work in classrooms and is the liaison, and several graduate interns who receive credit for their experience. The staff shares the responsibilities for teaching, responding to journals, and conferencing with apprentices for evaluation purposes.

The apprentices meet at Borton for three mornings and one full day each week. On two mornings, the apprentices and the university faculty explore theoretical and curricular issues concerning language, literacy, and social studies. The apprentices spend one whole day and one additional morning in the classroom with children. They travel to campus for the math and science methods courses two afternoons each week. Figure 19 illustrates the schedule.

During the mornings in the Wildcat Room, Borton teachers, the principal, and university faculty share their expertise with the apprentices. Over the years teachers have presented on various topics. For example, Teri Melendez presents on her use of sociograms in her kindergarten classroom, unit development, and discipline. Caryl Crowell presents information on her bilingual teaching, her use of miscue analysis in Spanish and English, the ways literature is used in her classroom, and the integration of subject matter. Kathy Lohse presents on ways to develop home-school relations through parent-teacher communication, her person-of-the-week program, and issues of bilingual education. Perry McCauley presents with members of her nongraded primary classroom on mediation as a problem-solving process. Joann Romero Achevederra presents her collection of kindergartners' Spanish and English writing samples and explains how she encourages such writing and what the samples show her about the children's writing development. Kay Stritzel presents on the importance of the role of play and on sex education in an integrated kindergarten curriculum. Kay Rukasin, the fine arts teacher, describes the art and music artifacts the children can take home and shares the big books she has written on art concepts for use with Borton students. Pat Young discusses the importance of children becoming knowledgeable about their bodies through movement and dance. Liv Stevens and Betty Houser, librarians over the years, discuss the ways they are available to integrate the school library with curriculum in the classroom, and how the children use the library in their research projects. The university faculty and the apprentices learn a great deal and appreciate the scholarly expertise of Borton teachers.

Bob Wortman presents often. He loves to read to the apprentices in the same way he reads to the children. He demonstrates teaching reading strategies to young children and discusses the philosophy and mission of the school. He helps apprentices understand that curriculum is organized to accommodate to children's backgrounds and experiences to minimize classroom discipline problems. Bob demonstrates how whole language administrators work positively and collaboratively with teachers, parents, and the university community.

	Monday	**Tuesday**	**Wednesday**	**Thursday**	**Friday**
8:00 A.M. –noon	Class Meetings, Wildcat Room, Borton	Class Meetings, Wildcat Room, Borton	With children in Borton classrooms	With children in Borton classrooms	Individually scheduled time
1:00 P.M. –3:00 P.M.		Math and science methods on campus		Math and science methods on campus	

FIGURE 19   Weekly methods schedule

A PROFESSIONAL SEMESTER

After a few weeks of visits to all Borton classrooms, the apprentices select one room where they spend the rest of the semester. They get to know one teacher and a group of children well. The school is small, so there are usually two apprentices in each room. For students who are interested in upper grades, we arrange for placement at other schools, where there are whole language teachers and an interested, knowledgeable principal.

A whole language classroom, whether at the elementary or university level, is one in which the curriculum is constantly being negotiated to meet the needs and reflect the interests and questions of the students and teachers. Although we plan ahead, we follow the lead of the apprentices. It is not unusual to postpone topics or spend more time on some ideas than planned.

Our flexibility and learner centeredness is directly related to the evaluation procedures. Although university grading is required, it is only one aspect of evaluation. We evaluate student growth through journals or logs, written and oral presentations, and small group and individual conferences held a number of times during the semester. Written reflections and oral conferences involve self-evaluation and are the most powerful and meaningful assessments. We believe that the faculty and program should also be continuously evaluated, so apprentices critique the block program at midterm and at the end of semester. These sources of data constantly influence our planning.

The apprentices experience whole language learning as they plan and evaluate with the university faculty. We explore the processes of how children use reading, listening, writing, and speaking while solving problems and building concepts in social studies, maximizing integration of content in our curriculum. We examine these processes in relation to the whole language pillars of teaching, learning, language, curriculum, and the social community as discussed by Ken Goodman in *What's Whole in Whole Language?* (1986). Evaluation is part of all planning. The Borton staff works with us to develop the curriculum, including the objectives, the focus of the program, and the expectations.

EXPECTATIONS FOR THE WHOLE LANGUAGE APPRENTICES

As each year begins, apprentices receive copies of the objectives of the program and the expectations. We discuss the expectations for clarification and negotiation any time during the semester when we sense there is anxiety building or when apprentices ask questions or suggest alternatives. Following is one year's set of expectations. Each begins with a self-reflection from an apprentice's journal.

At midsemester and during the last week of classes, the students formally reflect in writing their progress toward each of these expectations. A faculty member holds a conference with each student and responds in writing. At the end of the semester, final grades are negotiated during individual conferences. (The collaborative evaluation form we use to structure these reflections is Protocol/Engagement D-5.)

Expectation 1: Assuming a Role in the Profession

> There are those times when I've felt like a professional instead of a student: When Howard [a graduate student intern] asked me to consider including some of my ideas about music in a book he is working on and when Kay [the fine arts teacher] asked me if I would mind if she used some of my ideas about music in her program. To me this says that my ideas are being read as a colleague's, not as a student's. (Teresa)

Our major expectation is for the apprentices to believe that they are part of a school faculty and part of an active and dynamic profession. We discuss this expectation with the apprentices throughout the semester, as they share specific classroom experiences. We explore their role, the teacher's role, and the ways different children respond. We frequently talk about the apprentices' anxiety with their personal learning. Differences in philosophies about teaching, learning, testing, and grading are explored in relation to their goals as future teachers.

As professionals, the students assume responsibility for the organization and running of the class and for establishing a positive relationship with the Borton faculty. We organize committees to discover the professional resources available to teachers, to maintain the environment of the Wildcat Room, including refreshments and to share information (articles from professional journals, pieces of children's literature, announcements of related conferences and community events, etc.). The apprentices participate in local and state conferences, become active Teachers Applying Whole Language (TAWL) group members, and join national organizations.

We could never have assigned the activities that students themselves have assumed responsibility for over the years. One semester, a student sewed name tags for each of us so that we were instantly recognized as members of the Wildcat Room. Another year a committee maintained a bulletin board to inform us of current national and local issues concerning education. Another semester, apprentices contributed to a biweekly newsletter that included all the reports from committees, short vignettes from apprentices about their teaching, lists of resources, and favorite quotes.

The seriousness with which the apprentices take their responsibilities gives us ample opportunity to evaluate how their experiences contribute to professional development. Indicators of professionalism are found during discussions, class time with children, and off campus and are noted by the faculty and recorded for formal assessment conference summaries. We document how apprentices assume initiative, participate collaboratively, are creative, and develop a sense of ethics.

Expectation 2: Classroom Introductions

My first day in Teri's [kindergarten] class I saw my educational psychology class in action. Piaget talked about the stages of development and in one stage (supposedly ages seven to eleven) students develop the concept of conservation of number. Well, Teri asked the students to make three separate lines depending on which type of fruit they wanted for a snack. After the lines were formed side by side, Teri asked the class which line had the most. The students answered "the apple line" which had nine students in it. Teri then took the pear line (with five students in it) and spread them out so the pear line was longer than the apple line. Then she asked which group has more now? Some students understood that the apple line still had more and explained to the class that Teri had just put more space between the people. Other students were sure the pear group now had more. Teri tried to get those students to count the children in the lines to see which had more but this had no impact on those students who did not have conservation of numbers. This experience was like my textbook page had come alive and was presented to me with a real-life example. It made my learning more meaningful and that is certainly exciting! (Nancy)

We call this expectation an introduction because it requires apprentices to learn about the organization of their classroom, the children, and the teacher and at the same time to leave something tangible for each classroom. The Borton staff receive no financial remuneration from the university for their participation in the whole language block. The introduction each apprentice develops is a product useful to the teacher.

Each apprentice works collaboratively with the children and the teacher to develop an introduction that is interesting not only to the members of the classroom and school learning community but also to the many visitors who come to Borton. The introductions typically include the teacher's philosophy. Apprentices create pamphlets, large posters, mobiles, albums or notebooks of photos and artifacts, or videotapes that show highlights of their classrooms.

The classroom introductions celebrate the activities of students at Borton. The apprentices interview the teacher and students and gain insights into how the teacher's understanding of whole language translates into daily practice. They establish a relationship with the classroom teacher and the students that grows throughout the semester. Through this project, the apprentices reveal their observation abilities, their knowledge of individual differences in children, and their understanding of classroom activities and teacher decision making. These indicators of their learning are recorded by the faculty as the apprentices present their introductions. Responses from the children and the classroom teacher are also part of the evaluation.

Expectation 3: Theme Cycles

> The most significant comment of the entire discussion was when Howard asked why those of us in the majority (with the power) would have any interest in changing the status quo, why would we want everyone to be equal and treated fairly? . . . What did we, the majority, have to gain from that? I fight for the equality of people and will try to instill that fight in my students because I do not want to live in a society that does not place equal value on every person regardless of race, sex, color, religion, handicap. . . . Because a society that does not hold every person as equal to every other person is a society in which resentment develops and turns into hatred and hatred leads to violence. . . . These are my "pie in the sky" dreams, but if we push our dreams aside and let reality take over then we will always find a justification for not hiring a Black applicant, or overlooking the beating of a Mexican undocumented worker. . . . It is not easy to undo all the stereotypes that have passed on from generation to generation, but we must work to open our minds as well as our students' minds and strive to appreciate differences instead of fighting them. (Nancy's response to class discussion about her unit of study)

The apprentices develop a theme cycle or some aspect of a theme already in effect in the classrooms with the support of their cooperating teachers. We talk about different ways to plan and highlight the importance of themes being significant studies based on the interest and research questions of the children. Borton teachers often share how they generate ideas for theme cycles with their children, how this impacts children's learning, especially in social studies, and what they see as the teacher's role in the process.

 Through these explorations apprentices learn that there are unique ways for each teacher to work, even though the teachers follow similar beliefs. They come to understand how a theoretical framework forms the base of classroom practices, expressed in varied classroom activities and teaching strategies. Opportunities to plan and teach theme cycles provide insights into the apprentices' ability for integrative planning, their innovative abilities, and their knowledge of various subject matter areas.

Opportunity for evaluating the theme cycles occurs when the apprentices put their plans into action. When the students see the results of their curriculum ideas, see the response of children, and discuss how the learning experiences went with other professionals, they reflect and self-evaluate. Along with each moment of self-evaluation comes more sophisticated planning ability.

Expectation 4: Interactive Logs

> I have always been very private about my writing. I keep many personal diaries in which I try to write every day. When the idea of interactive journal groups came up, I just cringed! I was even angry about it. Writing is so personal to me and in a way, I felt a bit selfish to think that I had to share my writing with others. I mean, my deepest thoughts come out in my writing. However, the responses I've gotten have only been supportive and positive. I've gotten to know others well by reading their journals (which I also didn't like because I found it an invasion of others'

privacy). But, we find that there are things we feel that are the same, we find support and help from one another, and I can look back and say . . . it's not so bad. So, I confess that at first I despised the ideas of interactive journal groups, but now I like them and hope to get the most from my participation in them. (Jamie)

The apprentices maintain a journal reflecting their understandings of whole language, responses to activities in the Wildcat Room, reactions to life in their classrooms, evaluation of their readings, concerns regarding their successes or problems in the program, and any other issues. Apprentices exchange journals regularly, sometimes with each other but especially with the faculty. We respond as soon as possible.

The journals serve as a link between the Wildcat Room and life in the apprentices' cooperating classrooms. The apprentices also regularly share their journal with their cooperating teachers. The teachers respond in writing or have oral conferences with the apprentices.

The journals are more than a vehicle of communication. They serve as an ongoing form of evaluation. We witness apprentices' growth, ask them questions, suggest readings, and offer advice. Apprentices reread their journals regularly to get a sense of their growing understanding of life in a whole language classroom and school. The journal provides essential data for the apprentices to self-evaluate their learning in narrative form at the middle and end of the semester. One indicator of learning in journals is the demonstration of critical response, when students have confidence and knowledge to disagree with a presentation or reading, to provide evidence to support their arguments, and to verbalize their growing personal philosophy.

Expectation 5: The Portfolio

The day when Yetta and the class were discussing racism and prejudice, was a day that brought back some painful experiences I had in elementary school. I had shared my excitement of discovering that my Great-grandmother was a Sioux Indian with my class. Instead of openness they teased and ridiculed me. They called me names and said hurtful things about my heritage and I quickly stopped sharing. I now realize that our discussion about prejudice has increased my awareness and sensitivity. (Pat)

Apprentices collect their professional experiences in a portfolio. We believe that preservice teachers will use portfolios for evaluation purposes in their own classrooms if they experience them firsthand. When the idea of portfolios is introduced, it brings into the open the typical schooling experienced by the apprentices. They ask faculty: "What do you want?" and "What goes into one of these things?" We suggest that the apprentices organize and collect information about their experiences as students throughout their schooling history. We discuss their histories as readers and writers both in and out of school and relate these to their growth in thinking about literacy and social studies, classroom procedure processes, and being part of the teaching profession. They struggle with this expectation, but the struggle is enlightening and productive.

Some apprentices have sections in their portfolios with samples of their own writing and reading from preschool through their early college years. Others include their journals and lists of influential books and other readings. They have sections for ideas about theme cycles, educational issues, and favorite magazine articles and quotations.[Each section includes a narrative about the influence of the section for the student's professional development.]We spend a number of class periods at the end of the semester examining each other's portfolios. The variety of portfolios is rich and informative for us as university staff and for the apprentices as future teachers. Right up until the final minutes of class, they are busy writing down ideas from each other as much as from the faculty. "Make me a copy of that" often seems to be the theme of the day.

Portfolios are a good beginning for the apprentices to define themselves as professionals. We suggest that the apprentices continue the portfolios during their student teaching. Then, upon completion of student teaching, they can present the portfolio, or parts of it, to prospective employers. A number of the apprentices report that their portfolios have been instrumental in securing their first teaching job. The interviewing teams at the schools where they apply are impressed with the quality of work they accomplished during the block program and their student teaching.

Expectation 6: Professional Readings and Staying Informed as a Professional

> I have never enjoyed a college class so much. The only problem for me has been not enough time to read all I want. My summer reading list is becoming extensive with children's and professional books. (Wren)

The apprentices are expected to read widely, to respond to their readings in their journal, and to present their readings in class for discussion with others. *The Whole Language Catalog* (Goodman, Bird, and Goodman 1991) is required reading. We do not expect them to read the entire catalog but provide them with a "A Hitchhiker's Guide to the Whole Language Catalog" (1991), developed by Ken Goodman to share with the apprentices ways to explore the catalog. As we discuss whole language theory and practice, the apprentices follow up on classroom discussion by reading on specific topics throughout the catalog, or they can follow a particular interest, a series of topics, or an author of their own choosing.

We want the apprentices to experience the excitement and responsibility involved in being part of a professional literature group. They choose a book from a large collection available at the local TAWL group and form groups. One year, for example, groups read *In the Middle* (Atwell 1987); *Creating Classrooms for Authors* (Harste, Short, and Burke 1988); and a related set of books: *Grand Conversations* (Peterson and Eeds 1990), *What's Whole in Whole Language?* (K. Goodman 1986), and *Whole Language: Inquiring Voices* (Watson, Burke, and Harste 1989). Each group presents the impact of the book on their learning to the rest of the class.

These presentations are more than book talks. The apprentices involve their colleagues in a variety of activities gleaned from their readings, such as interactive discussions, or some innovative experience suggested in the book. Some groups produce handouts, elaborate mobiles, or posters. Our belief that professionals learn from one another as experts is demonstrated through the book groups.

The apprentices are also expected to read additional professional books and articles, which they select and share in class at appropriate times. They also read and present a children's book as an opening to the day's experiences. This becomes a time of community sharing since apprentices often choose books that represent important celebrations and issues (Year of the Woman, Martin Luther King, Jr. Day, ecology, etc.).

The professional readings provide the apprentices with a sense of the collaborative effort inherent in whole language. They become immersed in the language of education and join the professional educational community. We also make available professional journals concerning language arts, early childhood, reading, and social studies. The students maintain collections of their readings, sharing bibliographies and copies of their favorite articles with each other. They keep records of their readings, which become part of their portfolio. Final reflections show that students recognize how well read they are before they move into their student teaching experience.

Expectation 7: A Case Study

> I conducted a reading and writing interview with Aaron. His response to what his dad does when he is reading and doesn't know a word was classic. He said that his dad probably did the same thing he did: figured the word out by context, because they had the same genes. I looked back at the same interview done at the beginning of the year. His response to that question was that his dad probably used a magnifying glass when he came to a word he did not know. Aaron was so enthusiastic about sharing his writing and books about geckos with me. He was thrilled when I asked him to share the books he and his friends had collaborated on. It is neat that kids get so involved in their writing and are proud of their accomplishments. It makes me realize the rewards of being a teacher and the support and encouragement we can offer in a child's learning process. (Wren)

Each apprentice prepares a case study of one child in their classroom. For some of the apprentices, this turns out to be the most powerful experience. They typically choose a student who touches them in some way.

The apprentices interview their cooperating teachers, the principal, and sometimes even the parents about their case study child. They observe and work with the child in the classroom. They gain insights into the child's literacy activities. Some examine the quality of the miscues the child makes while reading, others discuss the child's reading preferences or collect and analyze samples of the child's writing. They interact with the child in an individual conference setting and observe the child in small groups and whole class settings.

The apprentices often take time to interact with the faculty and each other about the data they are collecting for their case studies. We present and discuss critical issues of evaluation and assessment and offer ways for them to sort and interpret their data. They rely on each other, the Borton staff, their readings, and the university faculty to organize the information into a useful format. The greatest impact of the case study is the empathy it instills. The apprentices become sensitive to issues of language, culture, sexism, and racism inherent in testing and how deeply an experienced teacher can impact the success a child has in school. Through careful observations of children, they become thoughtful kidwatchers (Y. Goodman 1978). When we discuss individual children, we also consider the power structure of a classroom. Many of the apprentices are reminded of their own learning experiences. We uncover the importance of knowing who you are in order to know how you teach.

EVALUATION OF THE WHOLE LANGUAGE BLOCK

In the same way that we use the expectations for the evaluation of apprentices, we use the expectations for continuous evaluation of the block program. When apprentices report that their expectations are significant to their learning, we know that insight is important. When expectations cause undue anxiety, we have to rethink and make appropriate adaptations. We rely on the apprentices' journals and the classroom teachers' responses to provide insight into the impact of the program and the expectations.

For some of the apprentices, the whole language block is the first time in their educational history that they have experienced self-directed learning. The portfolios help us understand what aspects of preservice teachers' lives influence their professional development. When apprentices hand in just a collection of books or articles without much narrative, we consider that the experience was not significant in the development of the student. We respond by providing additional frameworks and other kinds of invitations. Although most of the apprentices find the portfolios important to their professional development, some are not completely satisfied. This reaction causes us to reconsider our use of portfolios.

In addition to the apprentices' evaluations of the expectations, we meet regularly with the Borton faculty committee to make sure the program is running smoothly. Suggestions for changes and improvements made by apprentices over the years include the following:

- More regularly planned time for work in small groups.
- More structure and guidelines for portfolios, units, and case studies.
- Earlier due dates for expectations.
- Expectations spread out more evenly throughout the semester.
- More response in journals from faculty and teachers.
- A checklist to record readings.
- Assigned readings for all to discuss together in class.
- Regular conferences with faculty throughout the semester.

We consider all suggestions and involve the apprentices in understanding our perspective when we disagree. Comments of cooperating teachers and university supervisors when the apprentices move to student teaching the semester following the block, also help us to assess the success of the block and of individual apprentices.

Our students feel prepared and confident for student teaching and their first year of teaching. Virtually all graduates are teaching in the Tucson area and entering master's degree programs. Many are actively participating in the local TAWL group. They often return to the block as speakers, to answer questions and tell stories about their own experiences with the teacher education program and their early careers.

A CULMINATING EVALUATION EXPERIENCE

One year in a graduate whole language class the students decided to evaluate the semester by putting on a Whole Language Fair, now a traditional culminating event for that course. The graduate students invited the whole language block undergraduates to the fair. Since the first invitation, the undergraduates have become integral to organizing for the fair. The apprentices select from their collections of experiences to present at the fair.

The Whole Language Fair takes place at Borton the last week of the semester. The occasion is announced in the local TAWL newsletter, and flyers are posted throughout the college of education and in the schools. One year, a student arranged for a group of Tohono O'odham dancers to perform and lead some dances. Local storytellers, book authors, and book stores are invited to set up informal presentations. This rich evening gives the apprentices a sense of being part of a community of educators.

Our experiences and the experiences of the apprentices at Borton have supported and strengthened our commitment to whole language teacher education. Like whole language itself, each year is not quite like any other as we learn from our holistic experiences.

REFERENCES

Atwell, N. 1987. *In the Middle: Writing, Reading, and Learning with Adolescents.* Portsmouth, NH: Heinemann.

Goodman, K. S. 1986. *What's Whole in Whole Language?* Portsmouth, NH: Heinemann.

———. 1991. *A Hitchhiker's Guide to the Whole Language Catalog.* Unpublished manuscript. Tucson, AZ: University of Arizona.

Goodman, K. S., L. B. Bird, and Y. M. Goodman, eds. 1991. *The Whole Language Catalog.* Santa Rosa, CA: American School Publishers.

Goodman, Y. M. 1978. "Kidwatching: An Alternative to Testing." In *National Elementary Principal,* 57, 4: 41–45.

———. 1989. "Evaluation of Students: srehcaeT fo noitaulavE." In *The Whole Language Evaluation Book.* K. S. Goodman, Y. M. Goodman, and W. J. Hood, eds. Portsmouth, NH: Heinemann.

Harste, J. C., K. G. Short, and C. Burke. 1988. *Creating Classrooms for Authors: The Reading-Writing Connection.* Portsmouth, NH: Heinemann.

Peterson, R., and M. Eeds. 1990. *Grand Conversations: Literature Groups in Action.* Portsmouth, NH: Heinemann.

Watson, D. J, C. Burke, and J. C. Harste. 1989. *Whole Language: Inquiring Voices.* New York: Scholastic.

20

JOURNAL KEEPING AS A
WINDOW ON CHANGE

Mary Bixby

Ken Goodman (1982) says that miscues serve as windows on the reading process. In a similar way, journals are artifacts that may serve as windows on change in teachers-to-be. As an investigator of journal keeping, I studied the students' and teachers' writing and their perspectives on journal-keeping experiences in Dorothy Watson's preservice course, Methods of Teaching Reading at the University of Missouri, Columbia (Bixby 1989). I wanted to portray what the members of the classroom community did with their journals and how they described those experiences. In doing so, I made some discoveries about the ways students and teachers support one another's learning. In this chapter, I suggest modes of communication that teacher educators can look for as they evaluate students' learning through journal writing events.

Students in Dorothy's class kept personal-response journals and were members of roving or group journals that were passed among four to five members, including Dorothy and a graduate student intern (see Protocol/Engagement C-8). Students wrote in their individual journals approximately three times a week for sixteen weeks, and the group journals circulated through the groups about every ten days. Dorothy and the intern collected and wrote in individual journals every three weeks.

This methods class consisted of three graduate and twenty-six undergraduate education majors and two health-related-profession majors who took the course as an elective. All students were women. Many of the students had no journal-keeping experience; a few had kept journals in language arts classes in high school or in college composition classes, but most of their prior journal keeping had been teacher directed rather than student directed. Although Dorothy suggested that they write in their individual journals at least three times a week, students chose what and when to write. The journals played an integral part in the curriculum; they became the students' records of class activities, responses to assigned or selected texts, questions to teachers or to themselves, or connections with past or future experiences. The group journals became contexts for sharing ideas and experiences or learning about other teachers-to-be.

In order to understand the functions and power of the journals, I analyzed the entire texts of the individual and group journals of fourteen students who were in five-member roving journal groups. (Two groups had five student members; one group had four student members, with Dorothy as the fifth member.) In addition, I interviewed with nine students, the graduate teaching assistant, the graduate intern, and Dorothy.

Six distinctive modes of discussion appeared in the students' journals. These modes were ways in which the students preserved and discussed ideas and issues presented in the course and in course-related activities, such as conferences, meetings, and aiding experiences. The modes of discussion were categorized in the following manner:

1. *Recording.* A summary or chronicling of events for the self or another; may or may not include a personal connection or response by the writer.
2. *Conversing.* Questions, answers, or thanks to another; dialogue between writers.
3. *Reflecting through "playing with time."* Using past or future time references to explain or understand experiences; adopting a stance as a child, prior learner, or future teacher.
4. *Reflecting.* Considering or reconsidering experience through means other than adopting a past or future point of view; may involve reconsideration of prior journal entries.
5. *Working through dysjunctions.* Testing or developing beliefs through encountering and resolving conflicting points of view; working toward decision making.
6. *Deciding.* Stated decisions that may or may not have resulted or emerged from the other five modes of discussion; development of informed points of view for future action.

Teacher educators who use journals might use these categories to assess the writing and thinking processes their students utilize. The categories show the richness of students' responses and reflect their individual growth over time.

DEMONSTRATIONS FROM STUDENT JOURNALS

What was it like for these future teachers to be introduced to the world of children as they are initiated into literacy? How did the students manipulate and experiment with information in order to inquire about reading instruction and the future classrooms in which they would become responsible for learners?

The following section includes unedited illustrative quotations that show the students' uses of the six modes of discussion to answer the previous questions that show how students change over time as they consider ideas and issues about the teaching of reading. Here the students' voices (students' names have been changed) emerge to tell their stories and create their texts about the world of teachers-to-be. Their words show the subtle influences of whole language teaching in their reading methods classroom on their attitudes about the possibility of their whole language teaching in the future. Their words provide the teacher with opportunities for continuous evaluation.

Recording

The students associated recording class experiences with remembering information. Students remarked that they preferred to write about a class as soon as possible after it, because recording information helped them "remember what happened" in the class. Most recording occurred in the individual journals, where the entries were the recording or rehearsing for the self.

Amy was the most regular, consistent recorder of the class. Her journal was the only one that contained an entry for every class session, with highlights from each day from the beginning to the end of the semester. Amy's entry from the first day of class illustrates her style of recording and commenting on class activities:

> The first day of class we were introduced to Teaching of Reading. . . . Although we didn't cover any material the first day there were many things Mrs. Watson did that I thought would be very helpful for me when I teach. One of the things she did was write morning messages on the board everyday. For example, one message read "Happy Sunshine, Merry First Day." At first I thought gosh, this is different, because most college teachers don't write sweet messages on the board, but now I understand why. Morning messages would be great for children in a classroom. It makes the day brighter and puts the class in a cheery mood. It lets the children know that you're friendly.
>
> The second thing we did in class was read. Mrs. Watson read us the story, "A Dragon Takes a Wife." It was the neatest story. I love children's books. I had never read "A Dragon Takes a Wife," but it would be a great book for children of all ages. It's funny, sweet, unique, and suspenseful.

Dorothy has always encouraged students to attend professional conferences as options for or in lieu of class projects. As it turned out, the Teachers Applying Whole Language (TAWL) Fall Renewal Conference, held locally during the sixth weekend of the semester, became one of the most educative experiences that the students had. They felt that it helped them to understand about teaching and learning and what it was like to be a member of the profession. Jackie mentioned that the conference had enabled her to understand whole language. Her journal entry shows how she recorded that highly relevant preprofessional experience:

> Today I went to the TAWL conference. It was FANTASTIC! I loved it. I learned so much. I also think the information I took in will help me with [this class].
>
> Yetta Goodman is very impressive. She really knows her "stuff." She talked about how in order to evaluate your students you must get to know them. You must also be a part of the classroom. If they read (SSR) [Sustained Silent Reading] then you must read also . . . [Here Jackie continued to record at some length Yetta Goodman's comments.]

Conversing

In the individual journals, students initiated and participated in purposeful conversations with the teacher, the graduate teaching assistant, and the intern. The teachers, in turn, initiated conversations with the students. Since Dorothy and the teaching assistants collected and responded in the journals every three weeks, there were five opportunities for exchanges between teachers and students.

Interviews showed that students were influenced highly by the opportunities for written conversations with their teachers. Sue's entry from September 20 told the graduate intern of the class exactly how she felt about the teacher responses:

> I guess I would like to address this journal entry to you, Marcia, if I could. I would like to tell you that you are *very* appreciated. I love your encouraging and thoughtful comments! . . .
>
> I have not had that encouragement in two years. It was often very difficult for me to be excited about writing anything. I would receive my papers back with harsh comments and red marks. . . (I was not used to that at all!) I must add that I think I write better when dealing with personal experience . . .
>
> Anyway, I want to thank you Marcia just for who you are and how you represent yourself. You have made my day! Please know that encouragement and constructive criticism is greatly appreciated!

Marcia, the graduate intern, replied:

> They say we're just supposed to say "Thank you" for compliments. I really do appreciate your comments, Sue—and especially that you took the time to do so. I guess it makes us think about how actions and words affect others.
>
> I shared your note with my husband, who said, "I guess that made your day!" He was right!!! I told him I tied my 21 and 24 year old daughters to a chair and made them read it too!

This exchange also reveals how the comments in the journals influenced the motivation and perception of journal-keeping experiences of the teachers as well as the students.

Reflecting Through Playing with Time

Students did a great deal of personal responding to experience in their journals; they frequently wrote entries that involved a unique reflection on experience through references to the past or future. The writers adopted past stances as children or students in the school, or they took the stances of future teachers. The notion of playing with time in writing has been discussed variously by several language and learning theorists. Freire and Macedo (1987) showed that "critical literacy" involves storying about past, present, and future. Smith (1982) and Vygotsky (1978) discussed the use of language to move a writer in and out of experiences, while Progoff (1975) described writers' movements in time in intensive journals that helped them to understand their lives better.

Karen wrote more entries that contained references to past and future than any other student. Excerpts from her journal from September 7 through December 6 illustrate how she made sense of experiences by playing with time during these three months. These entries are presented together to illustrate the cumulative nature of her discussion and so her thinking over time can be examined.

> I just want to let you know how much I enjoyed writing my paper on "How I Learned to Read and Write." When the assignment was first given my initial reaction was like so many others. I can't remember. However, once I really got started, I really took off with memories. [September 7]

> When I was young, before I went to school, I preferred story books. I didn't want to read "See Jane. See Jane run." It wasn't a story, it was just a repetition of sounds. When I was in school I liked worksheets, but I always did well on them. This was my way of showing off. [September 12]

> My mom . . . was asking me one day how one learns not to read every word. I told her I was not sure, It was just something I picked up. I think I did this even when I was younger because I used to read a lot of books where you did not have to read every word to get the plot of the story. [September 29]

> In high school and even some of my other college courses we have done journals. . . . I think the journals are going to prove to be very useful in the classroom setting. [October 11]

> When I get a teaching job, I hope to get into a school where the teachers are mainly whole language. [October 25]

> I got to thinking back to the day in class when [the graduate teaching assistant] did the basal reading lesson. . . . I can't imagine sitting in front of a group of children asking all those minimal questions. It would also be hard for me to convey to children how important reading is. If I feel (as the teacher) that something is boring it is going to be tough to make the kids feel it is not boring. [November 19]

> [An] article made me think back to my own writing experience. It also has helped me realize that just because textbooks don't make writing an important part of a school's curriculum, that doesn't mean I can't. *I am the teacher and I can have them do writing that goes along with what I am teaching.* [emphasis added] [November 17]

> From looking at [my pen pal's] journal, I decided that I would really like to use journals in my class. [December 1]

In her interview, Dorothy commented on students' shifting their thoughts to the past and future. This excerpt shows her acknowledgment of the richness of entries that utilized this mode of discussion:

> Some of the best entries, I think, are those that have caused the students to think about something that's happened to them in their past . . . they've gone back and they've retold that. . . . Or when they're criss-crossing back and forth and you can see ideas coming up there; there's a network of ideas. . . . If you ask them a question [about what is unique in the journal-keeping experience] I suppose they'd say it gives them a chance to rethink what's going on in the class, in their heads, about their futures. [December 4]

Reflecting

When students wrote using this mode of discussion, they exhibited reflection that referred not to specific past or hypothetical future experiences but to reconsidering responses to course information or rethinking their own or another's literacy and learning.

Mary experienced a change of heart about reading instruction. At the beginning of the semester, students received lesson plans for a basal reader lesson. Mary reflected on her earlier reaction to the lesson plan:

> I read it once and highlighted it thinking how neat it was to already have a lesson plan pertaining to reading, After I read it a second time (today) I couldn't believe I felt that way! The lesson was so simplistic it was entertaining to read. . . . I found myself a little embarrassed for high-lighting the lesson. [October 22]

Jean used her journal to express her discovery upon reflection on her journal-keeping experiences. In an entry written on October 17, she had been discussing the presidential election and her feeling that more people should vote, when she suddenly shifted gears in her thinking and reflected on her own journal keeping:

> My journal is getting really wild. I jump from issue to issue. I've never kept a journal like this before—it's kind of fun. At first, I didn't know what to write and I had to force myself to do it. Now, I do something exciting or just think of something interesting and start writing. Sometimes I am surprised at what I write because it turns out to be different than what I started out thinking. . . . It's becoming apparent how useful journals will be in my classroom. I'm sure my students will go through many of these same experiences or stages that I have.

Working Through Dysjunctions

This mode of discussion in the journals used the concept of a dysjunction as an occasion of divergence or disagreement and acknowledged Barnes' (1976) assertion that learning occurs when one is faced with a "dysjunction between his implicit beliefs and those of the persons he is interacting with" (p. 106). I discovered this mode of discussion only after reading the students' journals from beginning to end, for this mode developed recursively over time.

Throughout the course, students were faced with pedagogical, curricular, and instructional issues against which they tested their existing beliefs. For example, they were challenged to investigate the contents and accompanying teaching materials of basal readers; they looked at phonics instruction materials and at whole language teaching methods. Each student had a pen pal at a local elementary school. When they read their pen pals' letters, students were encouraged to investigate the children's literacy practices. Here is Amy's response to her first pen pal letter:

> Yesterday in class we got our first pen pal letters. The letters were so cute. My first grader . . . drew a colorful picture with flowers, sun, and clouds. She didn't write very much, and she didn't answer my questions. She wrote "Dear Amy Love you from pen pal . . ." [She] did very well at writing her letters, though, and the words

were written correctly. Her letter format was very well also. She included a greeting and an ending. She also included the date. I'm not sure if she followed the letter format from my letter, or if her teacher taught the class. She did very well, and I am excited to write back to her and tell her how much I enjoyed the letter and the picture. I'm anxious to see how well her writing and words improve throughout the semester. I'm going to get her to tell me something about herself.

Mary revealed within her journal her joys and confusions about entering the world of teaching and in doing so disclosed to her teachers the vulnerability that she and her peers were experiencing. She had gone to a presentation given by the language arts coordinator of the local school district and began to feel nervous about getting into the profession. The semester was drawing to a close, and she knew she had gained a lot of useful knowledge about reading instruction and learners, yet she felt unsure. Her November 10 entry illustrated her sorting through dysjunctions stemming from an awareness that her beliefs and those dominant in the "real world" might not be totally compatible:

> I know she was explaining her job and how she and others decide what types of books they will order for the teachers, but she also talked about first-year teachers. It kind of made me nervous to think about interviews and then what the heck do I do to teach these kids. I know I'm learning a great amount of information about education and types of methods to use when teaching, but what about when it comes time when I actually have to do it? I know it is easy for me to say, well, of course I'll use [literature] groups and try not to rely on the basal, but that school may really believe in the basal & the skills model. As my first year of teaching I just feel that it will be a very nerve-racking year for me! I've talked to girls who are teaching and they say they're at school from 6:30 A.M. to 6:00 P.M.!

Deciding

Deciding was an extension, but not necessarily a result, of the five other modes of discussion within the journals. As students retold experiences and personalized them, they moved toward decisions for their futures as professionals. This mode included stated opinions and decisions about preferences in classroom materials and practices. Students stated decisions about future teaching when they truly understood the issues.

After attending the TAWL conference, Amy stated an opinion she had formed about her future model of teaching reading:

> I learned so much Saturday, probably more than I learned in a whole semester in some of the classes I've taken. I learned so many ideas and ways in which teachers use the whole language method in the class. I feel very confident that I want to teach the whole language model in my classroom.

The students responded to in- and out-of-class experiences as readers respond to written texts, by recording to understand and remember, but with much more versatility. They wrote also to converse, reflect, work through dysjunctions, and make decisions about their future teaching. To borrow the words of Rosenblatt (1983), writing in their journals about episodes in their lives helped those episodes become "lived-through" experiences and extended the meanings of the original events. The classroom, then, was itself a response-centered environment from which the students extended their educative experiences, and their thinking about those experiences, into their journals.

JOURNALS AND INQUIRY

All inquiry begins with a problem—a need for a good answer to a good question. The students no doubt were not consciously aware that they were performing their own private inquiries as they proceeded through the semester, yet every one of them was in pursuit of a satisfactory answer to an important question that was both unspoken and sometimes reflected within their writing: "How am I going to teach kids to read?" or, "What do I believe about how the reading process works?"

Inquirers need to be versatile in seeking answers to their questions. The modes of discussion, or modes of inquiry, enabled the journal keepers to be versatile discussants and versatile inquirers. The students' inquiries would not have been as thorough or rewarding if the entries had been recordings with little or no personalization. Because the journals were not directed and topics were not dictated by the teachers, students wrote to discover what they were thinking, to find or ask for answers to smaller, more focal questions, such as, "What is a basal reader?" in order to move themselves forward to answers to larger questions, such as, "Do I really want to use a basal reader series?"

The students often wrote on the edges of what they knew, for an answer to one question moved to the asking of another. Therefore, the inquiry was generative (Watson, Burke, and Harste 1989, p. 12), propelling students' thinking forward. Watson, Burke, and Harste observed that, in an inquiry, "questions produce more questions" (p. 22).

At the beginning of the semester, most students had never heard of whole language, and many did not know what a basal reader was. Therefore, they wrote at first to clarify and experiment with the terminology associated with reading instruction. Once the students felt comfortable with the terminology, they could begin to converse with others, to reflect, or to work through dysjunctions that they encountered during their investigations into methods of teaching. The journals, then, were inquiry oriented, just as the course was.

A glimpse into Sara's journal reveals the power of preservice students' writing and thinking about teaching that is possible when they are given room and support to wrestle with the issues and to evaluate new ideas in light of their own and others' belief systems. Sara considered carefully the ideas from her courses, and she tested them against her prior schooling experiences, situations she had observed in aiding experiences, ideas she had heard at conferences and professional meetings, and the point of view of her mother, who was certified as a teacher but had never taught.

Sara clearly agonized over conflicting beliefs about basal readers. Excerpts from her journal illustrate how she used the different modes of discussion in her journal. Several entries are presented together to illustrate Sara's thinking over

[handwritten margin note: writing on the edges of what you know]

time and to show the power of the journal to promote and sustain inquiry. She takes ownership through her journaling of a model of teaching and learning. Sara was very aware of the importance of her journal-keeping experience to her growth and movement toward the profession, and it is she who will finish the story about the coming of fledgling whole language teachers.

Now that I've read this article [on basal readers] and I've had a chance to compare how I felt about basals when I was young to my neutral feeling about them recently, I can form a new conclusion. Basal readers should not be used as sole means of teaching reading. [September 6]

It finally dawned on me today what it was that made me love second grade. First you have to understand how my second grade classroom was run. [She described in detail the teacher and the daily schedule.] . . .

Obviously, although I didn't know what it was called, I have been a student in a whole language classroom. . . . Thinking about this today has also inspired me to write to my second grade teacher to let her know what a great influence she has been. I'm also anxious to ask her advice and listen to any suggestions she may have. [September 22]

My second grade teacher wrote me back! . . . She has offered to have me over some afternoon so we can talk. She wants to show me some of her ideas and said I'm welcome to use any of them. [October 1]

I thought I had a definite opinion against the basal readers. I spoke with my mom however and she shed new light on the subject. . . . She said basal readers were very important to her as a child. . . . All of my mother's positive experiences with basals made me really think about my views. I do think they have a place in the classroom, but not in the large extent that they are being used. [October 4]

It seems as if basals mechanize reading lessons. The teacher becomes the "robot" and the students are know-nothing learners. [October 12]

What a great article [about standardized tests] this was! . . . Tests are becoming much more important, scores are the all important bible, directing teachers as to which course to start next.

Let's stop this all encompassing cycle! All of this could begin with getting rid of the overabundance of standardized tests. Let teachers relax, motivate students, be creative, and do their jobs! Next as part of this eliminating testing process, let's throw away the basals! [November 20]

[This semester] I've learned a lot about specific methods of teaching that I especially like, and I've also seen a lot of examples of methods that I don't like at all. . . . Beyond all I've learned about education, I think I've also learned a lot about my instructors. . . . I also think that for the first time my instructors know me. . . . If I can voice my views, refine them, and change some of them from hearing other people's experiences, I think I will become a better professional and even a better individual. I'm glad I've been exposed to such an abundance of hours all at once.

I'm especially glad I've had this journal to write down how I feel. [December 11]

REFERENCES

Barnes, D. 1976. *From Communication to Curriculum.* New York: Penguin.

Bixby, M. K. 1989. *Descriptive Inquiry into Preservice Journal Keeping for Teacher Educators.* Unpublished doctoral dissertation, University of Missouri, Columbia, MO.

Freire, P., and D. Macedo. 1987. *Literacy: Reading the Word and the World.* Amherst, MA: Bergin & Garvey.

Gilles, C., M. K. Bixby, P. Crowley, S. R. Crenshaw, M. Henrichs, F. Reynolds, and D. Pyle, eds. 1988. *Whole Language Strategies for Secondary Students.* New York: Richard C. Owen.

Goodman, K. S. 1982. "Miscues: Windows on the Reading Process. In *Language and Literacy: The Selected Writings of Kenneth S. Goodman, Volume 1. Process, Theory, Research.* G. Gollasch, ed. Boston: Routledge & Kegan Paul.

Progoff, I. 1975. *At a Journal Workshop.* New York: Dialogue House.

Rosenblatt, L. M. 1983. *Literature as Exploration.* 4th ed. New York: The Modern Language Association of America.

Smith, F. 1982. *Writing and the Writer.* Portsmouth, NH: Heinemann.

Vygotsky, L. S. 1978. *Mind and Society.* Cambridge, MA: Harvard University Press.

Watson, D., C. Burke, and J. C. Harste. 1989. *Whole Language: Inquiring Voices.* New York: Scholastic.

21

TRANSFORMING PRACTICE TOGETHER: TEACHER EDUCATORS AND COLLABORATIVE INQUIRY

Leslie Patterson, Mary Robbins, Phil Swicegood, Genevieve Brown, Joan Livingston Prouty, and Bess Osburn

As teacher educators, we ask students to reflect on their instructional decisions, to document their students' learning, and to explain their instructional rationales. We also invite them to join a supportive community of colleagues. When our students go home, we close the doors of our university classrooms, return to our offices, and write about how others can improve their teaching. Occasionally we confess to a trusted colleague that we should probably take our own advice and study our classroom practices, but there is simply never enough time.

As colleagues at a midsized state university, we were interested in portfolio assessment as a way to encourage students to take more control over their learning. Genevieve teaches educational leadership courses, Phil teaches special education, and Bess, Mary, Joan, and Leslie teach courses in literacy. All of us had been planning to try portfolio assessment and thought that if we worked together, we could learn from one another. We didn't have time for meetings, so we decided to collaborate on paper.

To do that, we used a traveling dialogue journal, a "polylog," which made the rounds approximately once every two weeks. In this spiral notebook we recorded our instructional decisions, concerns, and students' responses and reflected on them. We also responded to each other's entries in the margins beside the reflections. Often we found ourselves returning to previously read entries, adding even more comments in the margins. The effect was that we always began reading the polylog from the beginning, creating, in effect, layered relived experiences. Truly we were immersed in our shared journey.

This journey of collaborative inquiry has so far had three paths, each making its unique contribution to our collective and individual growth. The first was the actual polylog. In it we recorded teaching decisions, observations, and reflections. We responded to one another and responded on second and third readings. That experience by itself changed the way we saw one another and our students. Another path of this journey happened when we individually wrote reflexive narratives of the changes we had made in our theory and our practice. Approximately eight months after we began the polylog, as we were preparing to present what we learned at a conference, we each told the story of our changes. Those stories corroborated what we had experienced when we first wrote in the polylog and what we had seen in our analysis. Working together, we learned from one another; working individually, we changed in ways that we hadn't expected. Yet the third path was our analysis of the polylog. When we sat together, we read and reread the polylog, together identifying categories that described our entries and our responses to one another. Those categories demonstrated to us that we had participated in the kind of reflective teaching that is described again and again in the literature. We were surprised to see how that reflective inquiry process was so clearly represented in the polylog.

The following discussion explores each of these paths of our collaborative inquiry. As we reflect, we see these three paths as options that might be helpful to others who are working together to make changes: collaborative reflection and inquiry, reflexive narratives, and collaborative research.

THE POLYLOG: COLLABORATIVE REFLECTION AND INQUIRY

The initial concerns we recorded were primarily technical, like questions about procedures for assigning and grading portfolios. We also recorded our reports about what we did and how our students responded. We confessed our nervousness about trying something new in our classrooms and about sharing our attempts and mistakes with colleagues. The polylog was a contract among us: a promise to one another that we would try new things and keep one another informed. It also captured our thinking so that we could revisit our plans and reflections. The polylog made it possible for us to reflect collaboratively, to learn from one another, and to offer encouragement as we changed our assessment practices. Together we made discoveries and took risks that none of us would have experienced independently.

REFLEXIVE NARRATIVES: RELIVING AND EXTENDING THE EXPERIENCE

Soon our focus moved from portfolios to conceptual and theoretical issues about student ownership, reflection, and self-assessment. Our initial questions about the use of portfolios as an assessment tool in teacher education classes no longer seemed critical. We each wrote a reflexive narrative to learn how our theory bases and courses were changing as a result of this inquiry. Those reflexive narratives suggest that we all made significant changes in our instructional practices and understandings about student ownership and reflection. Most important, those narratives showed that the polylog enabled us to take risks, making changes in our courses that we might not have tried individually. Each moved through this process in unique ways, but a spiral of increasing risk taking and innovation was the theme of all of our narratives. Here are excerpts from Phil's and Joan's narratives that demonstrate this increased risk taking:

> How have I changed? . . . I am becoming more outspoken about the lack of critical theory and belief systems which should be guiding the classroom practices of teachers. . . . My professional development has turned down a road toward exploring topics of qualitative change, critical theory, and reflective teaching. (I am continually taken aback by the vast wealth of information and resources with which I am unfamiliar.) . . . I am beginning to keep my own logs, journals, and personal reference points. The importance of conducting personal dialogues with myself about whether or not I am achieving personal and professional goals, uniting theory and practice, etc. has become evident for me. (Phil)

> After several attempts, I felt frustrated and confused that I could not seem to manipulate the course content to better fit what I believed a portfolio should reflect. Why was this so difficult? As the semester progressed, I shared these concerns through the polylog and continued to wrestle with these many issues. (To my surprise, the students seemed to find it not nearly as complex as I did!) Then as time passed, I began to confront more realistically my preconceived notions about my teaching. Even though I espoused collaborative experiences, reflection and empowerment for the learner, I still kept control in a way I had not realized. All of my struggles over the implementation of portfolios were over this issue. I simply did not know how to give up this control! (Joan)

Confronting the discrepancies between theory and practice is never easy. The polylog prompted our reflections, and the reflexive narratives gave us an opportunity to voice what we were learning.

COLLABORATIVE TEACHER RESEARCH: DATA ANALYSIS AND THEORY BUILDING

When our proposal to document this whole process was accepted for a conference presentation, we had a deadline and an audience. The polylog seemed to be an appropriate way to document our collaborative inquiry. What happens when a group of teachers works together to transform their teaching, use a response journal as a tool for that collaboration, and analyze the data together?

To answer those questions, we sat down with copies of the polylog and slowly read through the first fifteen pages, categorizing the entries and responses we saw. We suggested labels for categories, discussed the implied meanings, and elaborated on the contexts of the entries. When we decided on categories, we independently analyzed the rest of the polylog and met again to compare our analyses. Through this process we identified categories of responses throughout the polylog. These discussions during the data analysis sessions generated at least as much excitement and as many discoveries as the original polylog experience. From these categories we developed a model of collaborative reflective teaching, including four phases of instructional decision making. These phases of reflective teaching follow, with excerpts from the polylog (representing entries from all of us).

Inquiring: Asking Questions, Reading, Kidwatching, Experimenting

These are my first impressions. 1) All the students seemed to make thoughtful choices and thorough . . . reflections. 2) Their selections varied widely, including these things: Excerpts from their journals . . .

I'm going to try portfolios in a different way from Leslie.

Futuring: Planning, Hoping, Dreading, Wishing

I need to study this more before I decide how to handle that aspect.

I am looking forward to the portfolio party on the 25th. It will be a first opportunity to see where one 568 class is on pfs [portfolios] vs. this term's group.

I wonder if, when we are more convinced of the value of portfolios, we will be able to let something else go to make time for conferences.

Acting: Working with Students

I basically told them that we would be accumulating portfolio type information and that I wanted them to begin to locate a student.

I gave them full credit. Well, except for two or three students for whom it was clear they had "reflected" in the car on the way to class.

Remembering: Looking Back and Interpreting Actions

Of course, this kind of decision-making by me is really not the best for what I envision as a pf [portfolio], but I'm stuck with it this semester.

They have taken the assignment in stride, even though it's open-ended.

One thing that I have done this semester that I feel good about is talking with the 370 students about fundamental differences—synthetic vs. analytic, deductive vs. inductive.

Our understandings of portfolio assessment grew as our colleagues made discoveries. Because others were making substantial changes in their instruction, we were able to take more courageous steps. Together, we were able to articulate what we were doing, confront the inconsistencies between theory and practice, and make the changes we saw as necessary. Our analysis of the polylog enabled us to see that we were the reflective teachers we read about in the literature.

Many educators have pointed out the importance of reflective teaching, but our data analysis emphasized that the power of the polylog is its collaborative nature. We worked together on a common problem. We made ourselves vulnerable to questions and critique from colleagues and celebrated together, congratulating one another on our successes. As we analyzed the polylog, we began seeing patterns in the ways we responded to each other, patterns we call *collaborative links*. Following are examples of the kinds of responses we believe are critical to our collaborative growth.

Connecting

But Genevieve has given me some good ideas—stopping the class, asking them to turn to their neighbor.

Since we are at the stage of identifying patterns, I'm attempting to construct continuums and dichotomies. Here are some of the patterns that seem to run through the project . . . process vs. product . . .

Disclosing

I am definitely uneasy about implementing this plan, particularly the evaluation of the portfolios.

I know I still have much to learn about this.

Inviting

What do you think? And how should the portfolios be evaluated then?

After what you saw in the portfolios, I think that it would be a good idea to have another faculty review them.

Valuing

I liked Mary's focus on "reader friendly" portfolios.

I liked this idea.

Sanctioning

Why grade them? What message are we sending them if we feel it necessary to grade these?

Bad-Bad-Bad.

Reminding

I can't find the question.

But there you go again, focusing on outcomes and products.

Assisting

Can we do self-assessment with the students on a 4/29 meeting?

Requesting

Please share when it comes in.

Leslie, could I get copies of your 485 handout?

Extending

And how can we get that information?

The depth and spread of the Pfs [portfolios] may be related to the long-term exposure to school kids and classroom learning—their growth as a teacher who comes to feel at peace and confident as a professional.

Clarifying

This is a process—of decision-making and evaluation as they have to write and analyze their products.

These collaborative links are the linguistic evidence that we supported one another as learners, were committed to a common goal, and respected one another as professionals. Through this process we came to know and trust one another more than before, and we began to see significant connections across our three fields. We have subsequently participated in other collaborative projects, writing grant proposals and articles and making presentations together. We have formed informal coalitions, and we participate on committees within our college and among our departments.

CONCLUSION: WORKING AND LEARNING TOGETHER

Our collaborative risk taking and instructional innovation represents a significant shift from the way we had always taught. For most teachers in universities and in public schools, instructional decision making is a lonely process. Glickman (1992) says that the halls of our schools are lined with one-room schoolhouses, each classroom an isolated place where teachers learn how to teach. This polylog project set in motion a collaborative professional growth process that drove us to examine practice in light of theory and to transform both. The following excerpts from the reflexive narratives illustrate the power of colleagues working together, building the courage to examine professional decision making and to open the doors of our classrooms:

> When they began to talk about a polylog project, I immediately volunteered myself to participate. That experience opened up so many new doors for me! I changed as a professional "person" as well as a teacher. I was, suddenly, free to ask others how they would teach or "do" something! I was free to express in the polylog concerns, frustrations, fears, etc. And there was someone to respond, to validate me. In addition, the ideas they shared helped me clarify my thinking, improve my teaching, etc. . . . Having this support group to validate my ideas and encourage me gave me the courage to do something different! I have felt so much better about my teaching recently. I feel very "revived"! . . . There was also a terrific sense of bonding. My polylog partners became my very special professional friends and co-mentors. I got to know them so well and to respect them so much more than I ever would have any other way. (Genevieve)

> As I think about what has happened for me personally, the recurring major thought is how the polylog and subsequent interactions forced me to look more critically at what I was doing in my classes. I use the word "force" intentionally—I felt inwardly compelled to look much deeper than the usual "refinements" I did with each semester's syllabi. I think it was a combination of colleague support and higher risk taking that our group engendered. (Joan)

> It was that time last fall when we began to analyze the polylog in an attempt to understand how we had implemented portfolios in our classrooms that we began to explore what we had become and were becoming to each other. Soon we were less interested in the implementation of portfolios and fascinated by the level of trust and camaraderie which had developed among a group of people whose lives sometimes touched, but not frequently. It was this time that we spent together

sorting out how we had helped each other learn how to use portfolios that we understood that the study was not about how we implemented portfolios in our classrooms, but how the polylog helped us develop a community of learners. (Mary)

As teacher educators, we made the time for collaborative, reflective inquiry, and together we transformed our practice.

REFERENCE

Glickman, C. 1992. League of Professional Schools Workshop. Unicoi, GA.

22

The Struggle for Voice in Learning to Teach: Lessons from One Preservice Teacher's Portfolio

Dana L. Fox

Be patient toward all that is unsolved in your heart and try to love the questions themselves. Do not seek the answers, which cannot be given to you because you would not be able to live them. And the point is to live everything. Live the questions now. Perhaps you will . . . gradually, without noticing it, live along some distant day into the answer.

—Rainer Maria Rilke

Critics of teacher education programs point to the gap between the situated complexity of life in classrooms and the decontextualized, formal principles that are often transmitted through university curricula. In the past, teacher knowledge has regularly been described in terms of specific skills or predictable routines, and teacher educators believed that such static knowledge could be delivered to novices in preservice course work and applied later in classrooms. Recently, however, researchers have attended to the complexities of teacher knowledge (Carter 1990) and have suggested that effective teachers are those who move beyond simple routines by learning to reflect—by learning to examine their own practice critically and to search continually for ways to improve it (Grossman 1991, 1992). In such professional education experiences, teacher candidates have opportunities to become knowledge producers rather than knowledge receivers, moving from what Kutz (1992) calls "unconfident answer-knowers to confident question-askers" (p. 69). Fosnot (1989) represents the teacher educator's voice in rethinking such course work:

> In looking at my own practice, I realized that I had always given an exam as a way to evaluate whether my students had learned or not, yet I was coming to see this procedure . . . as being in direct contradiction to the principles I had been advocating. I wanted instead to capitalize on the *process* of learning, rather than evaluation of a *product;* I wanted to maximize the opportunity to probe my students' understanding in a way that would cause them to continue questioning,

rather than to accept rote answers. In particular, I wanted students to leave my class with a desire and thirst for continued inquiry. (p. 40)

This chapter describes the reconceptualization of a composition methods course in secondary English education, narrating the development of one preservice teacher who was enrolled in the course. Inquiry, reflection, collaboration, and theory building were themes of this preservice education course in the teaching of composition. Readings for the course included Atwell (1987), Kirby and Liner (1988), Miller Cleary (1991), Tierney et al. (1991), Welty (1983), and an array of professional articles by classroom teachers. Much of the course content centered on exploring, extending, and even transforming future secondary English teachers' beliefs about writing instruction and assessment. This chapter chronicles the events that led to the initiation and development of preservice teacher portfolios, as the preservice teachers began to take the first steps toward the construction of their own "personally-situated theories" of teaching, learning, and assessment (Kutz 1992). This "theory making" enabled one teacher candidate (Anne, a pseudonym) to find her voice as an emerging secondary English teacher—a voice that will help her to live the processes of inquiry and reflection and ultimately to sustain creative teaching practice in her own classroom.

PORTFOLIOS AS A VEHICLE FOR THE DEVELOPMENT OF VOICE

Enabling individuals to find their voices as teachers has become a central concern of teacher educators (Carter 1993; Elbaz 1991; Schubert and Ayers 1992; Witherell and Noddings 1991). I define voice as the actual speaking or writing of personal thoughts, feelings, beliefs, questions, and experience. Richert (1992) suggests that "voice is a vehicle for reflective practice which results in ongoing learning in teaching" and that "being heard and hearing others . . . must be central to the curriculum in teacher education" (p. 192).

In order to foster the emergence of individual voice the beginning teachers used narrative modes as they wrote personal histories and autobiographies, collaboratively discussed teaching cases or stories of teachers and teaching, wrote teaching cases, and conducted and reported ethnographic research. The culminating experience in the course was the development of a portfolio that contained representative writing samples and demonstrated reflection and growth.

Advocates of the use of portfolios in literacy education underscore the importance of teacher autonomy, student ownership, self-expression, developmental process, and diversity (Tierney et al. 1991; Wolf 1989; Graves and Sunstein 1992). "There is no right way to implement portfolios," Tierney and his colleagues write. "Each classroom will reflect a unique approach to authentic assessment, and . . . each child's collection of documents will be different" (p. vii). Advocates of teacher portfolios echo these beliefs, maintaining that portfolios should reflect "schoolteaching as a form of expression, a humane project, an evolving state of affairs, and a situated accomplishment over time" (Bird 1990, p. 249). As portfolio keepers, prospective teachers begin to see teaching as an expressive, constructivist process.

Because I wanted the preservice teachers to understand—and actually live through—Tierney's notion that "there is no right way to implement portfolios," I consciously refrained from providing them with a set of rigid guidelines or requirements. Throughout the course, we continually negotiated what might appear in the portfolios. This process of negotiation was unsettling and troubling for many of the teacher candidates, and although they continually pushed me to provide guidelines ("What do *you* want us to put in these portfolios?"), I refused to give them a recipe. Each of the completed portfolios was a unique reflection of individual growth; however, my retrospective analysis revealed that certain artifacts were apparent in many of the preservice teachers' portfolios in the composition course:

- *Introductory and/or concluding statements.* Statements that demonstrated an ability to reflect on one's own work, revealed growth and risk taking, discussed the potential value the portfolio might hold for readers, and assumed an active role for the future by asking, "What's next?"
- *Individual goals.* Individual lists of writing goals that incorporated references to negotiated class goals.
- *Personal histories/autobiographical writings.* Pieces that explored memories of learning to read and write, of continued literacy development. Took the stance of an informed critic or autobiographer.
- *"Think" pieces.* Personal essays that considered important questions on the teaching of writing. Intentionally speculative in tone. Topics varied widely.
- *Biography of one "think" piece.* Drafts of one personal essay and reflective statements of the individual writer's process in composing the piece. Highlighted readers' responses to drafts as well as self-evaluation.
- *Group case study project.* A written summary and self-evaluation of a small group project. Each group completed a close examination of a student writer profile or case study (Miller Cleary 1991) and then engaged the class in a discussion of the case.

Anne's portfolio was organized into six parts: personal history, personal writing goals, "think" pieces, biography of a "think" piece, student ethnographic project, and final retrospective piece. In addition, self-evaluative writings were interjected throughout her portfolio, as were written responses from peers and the instructor.

The following qualitative analysis of Anne's portfolio conveys a sense of the whole through my discussion of the predominant themes that emerged from Anne's record of her growth. Because her use of introductory quotations in the portfolio highlights many of these themes, I include some of them here. Anne's portfolio invites the reader to accompany her on the first steps of her intellectual journey in learning to teach writing, an eventful journey fraught with both discomfort and joy. The straight path was lost indeed. Searching for the answers, Anne discovered the importance of living the questions.

ANNE'S PERSONAL HISTORY:
THE STRUGGLE FOR VOICE

Anne's reflections on her memories of schooling reveal her struggle to find a voice, to feel confident in her own abilities. In her early elementary years, she recalled "trouble with reading" and being assigned to the lowest reading groups. After repeating the second grade, she moved to a new school, was assigned to a higher reading group, and "felt much more successful." Seventh grade brought her "boring" experiences with sentence diagramming; in eleventh grade, Anne listened to Mrs. Miller's lectures on different writers' lives and their works. But she didn't view herself as a writer. "I have been a lover of books all my life, and I am still amazed that the thoughts of others can move me to tears or anger or fear or laughter," Anne wrote. "That's the beauty of writing for those who can do it well, and the frustration for those who can't."

Struggle, frustration, doubt. Learning to trust her own voice wasn't easy for Anne. Ironically, her portfolio revealed the strength of her writing, of her individual voice:

> I think I see things as a writer would, but I have never felt I was able to put the beauty of my thoughts into words. It's frustrating sometimes to be able to see a moment in your mind, capture all its qualities, hold it like a snapshot, only to find yourself losing it when you try to write it down. That's the worst, I think. To know there's a voice inside wanting to speak, but not quite knowing how to say it in words.
>
> As a child, I spent a lot of time making up stories in my head. I have always been a writer of the mind and not of the paper. I have often admired those people who could somehow write the things I had been thinking, but that I couldn't quite put into words. Perhaps I am too self conscious of my writing to ever be courageous enough to write from the heart. I think that's what really good writers are able to do.

Looking inward, Anne realized that her search for "correct answers" had permeated her life as a reader and writer. "Writing is not like working an algebra problem," she reflected. "With writing, there is no correct answer. That's the hard thing about writing for me; it's individual. And I always questioned, 'Did I do it right?'" Constantly comparing herself to others, Anne believed that she lost much of her creativity and confidence: "I have spent my life looking over my shoulder wondering if I was doing it wrong."

Most of her positive literacy experiences stemmed from private moments reading with her father at bedtime or from watching her mother read: "I knew she was in a special place that I wanted to visit." Powerful reading experiences with her peers took place outside classroom walls: "During lunch, I sat with a group of girls and listened as Judy Blume's *Forever* (1975) was read aloud. We were mesmerized by it, yet conscious of its importance to us." In school, teachers affected Anne's sense of self and her literacy development in mostly negative ways. She remembered teachers who "bled on my papers" in red ink, who "forced grammar upon me in large doses." As she began to articulate her vision of herself as an English teacher, Anne was clear:

> As a teacher, I want to learn with my students. I don't want to be the kind of teacher who stands in front of the class lecturing, and claiming to know all the answers. I feel students have much to teach us if we are only open enough to listen and learn from them. I want to teach kids to think for themselves, question their

beliefs, explore life, dream impossibilities, and refuse to accept defeat as final. I want to be the kind of teacher who listens, understands, challenges, and motivates students.

Moving toward a realization of this vision proved to be difficult for Anne. She had to move beyond familiar territory, be willing to live with ambiguity, and embrace questions with no easy answers: "That's my dilemma, to learn to listen to my own voice, and trust it to find its way, . . . and to know that it is important because it is mine."

Setting Individual and Collective Goals

The teacher candidates set their own goals so that they might monitor their progress more authentically, demonstrating an approach I hoped would surface later in their own classrooms. From initial individual lists, we negotiated a class list and prioritized goals, which became course objectives. Anne's personal goals fell into four categories: (1) completion of specific pieces of writing (such as a writer's notebook or a children's story), (2) specific goals as a writer (including "to write something every day" or "to develop a timeline to guide my writing"), (3) goals for overcoming anxiety about writing, and (4) goals for thinking through her beliefs about the teaching of writing.

Specific pieces of writing became part of Anne's course portfolio, but she viewed her portfolio as a fluid document. The collection of works would change over time, for she wanted to keep a student teacher's portfolio during upcoming months and later a teacher's portfolio. She longed to have a piece of writing published, to write more and regularly, and to put more of herself into her writing. Again, she recorded the importance of the search for voice and feelings of self-confidence, "to overcome anxieties about allowing others to read my work."

Think Pieces: Of Questions, Metaphors, and Change

My course syllabus invited individuals to use "think" pieces (speculative writings) to connect theory to practice, to consider the course readings and discussions in light of their own experiences as learners. Think pieces focused on key issues in the teaching of writing that emerged during class discussions: adapting the writing workshop, managing response to student writing, teaching skills in a process classroom, and so on. These personal essays extended teacher candidates' own questions and purposefully remained exploratory in nature.

As the quarter progressed, we negotiated eight working criteria for effective pieces that helped us focus our responses to one another: genuine questions raised, sense of voice, sense of movement/flow, evoking reader's response, evidence that thinking was influenced by texts or current theories in teaching writing, conclusions or further questions raised, realistic alternatives for teaching explored, and evidence of technical skill in writing. We participated regularly in writing groups in order to share drafts and "finished" products. I published anonymous excerpts from all think pieces at various points during the quarter, and community building occurred as individual voices resonated during read-alouds. These think pieces allowed teacher candidates to "think aloud" together, to engage in the processes of articulating their own ideas, of listening to the ideas of their peers, and of comparing those ideas with their own.

Think Piece 1: Tearing Down Walls of Self-Doubt

Anne often used metaphors to explore her questions and concerns in think pieces. In her first piece, she blended her own experiences and her emerging ideas about teaching writing and tried to envision herself in the role of teacher. Her words echoed the themes of voice and self-confidence:

> Writers who lack self-confidence are often the hardest to reach because they have barricaded themselves behind a wall of self-doubt. It can be a long and tedious process to tear down these walls, . . . but as teachers it is our responsibility to try.

Anne believed that teachers should move toward creating an atmosphere of trust in their classrooms. As a teacher, she envisioned herself eliminating student competition and creating community. She saw herself fighting fear, stress, and anxiety by providing multiple opportunities and choices for student writers. "Teaching students to trust their own voices and their own creativity is the basis for building confident writers," Anne announced. She vowed to "tear down the walls of self-doubt, one brick at a time."

Think Piece 2: Tearing Down Old Beliefs

Letting go of the past is never easy, especially when moving into unknown territory. "I find myself challenged with the dilemma of tearing down old beliefs to make way for something new, but I am still searching for answers as to what that something new will be," Anne worried. Images in her second piece revealed her inner struggle to match her evolving ideas about teaching and learning with notions of evaluation and assessment:

> I find myself still trying to grab hold to the sides of the ship as it slowly sinks into the deep dark nothingness where educational ideas that were destined to fail go to rest. I struggle and I fight my urge to cling to that which is familiar and safe. What is this loyalty I feel to a grading system that has been my enemy for so many years? I am caught in the dilemma of wanting to build confident student writers while at the same time knowing I must assign a grade. . . . I am watching my ship sink as the red ink trails behind it.

Anne believed that young writers need encouragement as well as constructive criticism that nudges them to improve. She felt "caught somewhere in the middle, . . . wanting to incorporate the best of both worlds in the writing classroom." Elbow (1983) describes Anne's feelings when he writes that "good teaching seems a struggle because it calls on skills and mentalities that are actually contrary to each other and thus tend to interfere with each other" (p. 327). He portrays the painful process of transformation that Anne was undergoing in this course:

[L]earning involves both assimilation and accommodation. Part of the job is to get the subject matter to bend and deform so that it fits inside the learner. . . . Just as important is the necessity for the learner to bend and deform himself so that he can fit himself around the subject without doing violence to it. Good learning is not a matter of finding a happy medium where both parties are transformed as little as possible. Rather both parties must be maximally transformed—in a sense deformed. There is violence in learning. We cannot learn something without eating it, yet we cannot really learn it either without letting it eat us. (p. 223)

Learning to embrace contraries in the teaching of writing was very difficult for Anne, something she described as the "tightrope teachers must walk." She recognized the difficulty of "critiquing writing without destroying creativity and confidence" but tried to seek a balance:

I don't know all the answers. I'm convinced no one does. I find myself continually walking this tightrope in my own thinking, knowing all the while my students are the ones at risk of falling if I lean too far to the left or too far to the right. I always seem to return to find a balancing point somewhere in the middle where there are no definitive answers, only instincts and glimmers of hope.

Think Piece 3: Living the Life of a Writer

"Teachers can't possibly expect to understand how to teach writing if they don't write themselves." Anne's own experiences again surfaced as she wrote about herself as a "teaching writer" in her third piece. She clearly defined her belief in the importance of writing with students: if we want students to value writing, we must value it ourselves; if we are not writers, we will never be able to empathize with our students' struggles; and if we share our drafts with students, they will learn to view writing as a continual process of thinking and rethinking.

By the time Anne had written this piece, she had moved toward insights and a clearer vision of herself as a teacher: "What students really need is for teachers to come down off their pedestals and join them in their writing." Finally, Anne equated the process of writing with the process of teaching: "For me, writing is a continual challenge. That's what I like best and sometimes what I fear most. I think that's probably the way I'll feel about teaching writing."

Think Piece 4: Living the Questions in Learning to Teach

All twenty-seven teacher candidates arrived in my course wanting to learn a set of recipes that would make them good teachers of writing. "It is not surprising that my students want answers," Wilson (1992) writes:

School has taught them that knowledge about teaching or history or mathematics or biology is conclusive, final, concrete. They have never been exposed to the exciting aspects of knowing: refutation, argument, construction, interpretation. No wonder learning is boring to them—even distasteful at times. On the way to the classroom, the very characteristics that make knowledge worth knowing got lost. (p. 140)

Throughout Anne's portfolio she dealt with her continual longing for answers. Her fourth think piece focused solely on this issue and thus became a rallying cry for all the future teachers in the class. One peer responded that Anne had touched on the most important theme in the course: "Obviously, you addressed everything we've been wondering about, everything we've been bitching about. I like your conclusion that we should quit bitching and be glad to build our own theories."

In her fourth and final think piece, Anne began,

> As a child, I would go to my father with my homework and say, "Dad, what's the answer to this problem?" And he would excitedly begin to go through a long, drawn out explanation of how you go about getting the answer. After a few minutes, I would stop him and say, "Dad, I don't need to know all this, just give me the answer." With frustration in his voice, he would always refuse, making me sit for what seemed like hours listening to his lengthy explanations. Afterwards, my father would say, "Anne, you can't always expect someone else to give you the answer; what I'm trying to show you is how to find answers on your own."

"It's not surprising," Anne reflected, "that I would sit in this class and mumble to myself, 'Just give me the answer!' But like my father, you never would." How did Anne and the others reconcile their fears of coming up with their own answers, of building their own theories of teaching and learning? Encountering "no clear and easy answers," Anne formulated her "salad bar theory of education":

> In sorting out my feelings about this class, I began to search for an analogy that described how I felt. As funny as it sounds, I see this class as a big salad bar. In the past, when I ordered a salad in a restaurant, they brought it to me. I never asked questions about the salad; I just ate it. Recently, I tried a new restaurant called education. "I'll have a house salad," I announced. To my surprise, the people there looked at me kind of funny and replied, "I'm sorry, but you'll have to make your own salad."
>
> I angrily thought, "What kind of restaurant is this, making me fix my own salad?" But I decided to stroll over to the salad bar to check it out. Peering down the line, I was overwhelmed by all the different items. How would I ever be able to decide? What if I made wrong choices? Many experienced eaters gave me conflicting advice. Standing in the middle of a salad bar war, I decided (since I was new at this) to try a little bit of everything. I began to pile my salad as high as it would go while the other more experienced salad-makers heckled me, saying I was doing it all wrong.
>
> I ignored them and continued building my salad. I haven't gotten to taste my salad. I'll probably find things that I don't like about it, but that's okay. Every day I'm seeing new things to put on my salad. I still have a lot to learn about salad making.
>
> The most important thing that I've learned during the ten weeks that I've been eating at this restaurant is this: every person's salad is going to be different. There are no right or wrong salads, and no one can tell me how to make my salad. I have to learn that myself. I'll admit that ordering a house salad is much more simple, but now that I've been at the salad bar, I like it better. I get to discover my own answers and choose, for myself, what goes on my salad.

AN ETHNOGRAPHIC PROJECT: THE POWER OF INQUIRY

> I tell you one thing, if you learn it by yourself, if you have to get down and dig for it, it never leaves you. It stays there as long as you live because you had to dig it out of the mud before you learned what it was.
>
> —Aunt Addie Norton, in *Sometimes a Shining Moment* (1986)

Kutz and Roskelly (1991) and Cochran-Smith and Lytle (1993) maintain the importance of formal inquiries, which enable teachers and teacher candidates to create their own pedagogical theories. "What is missing from the knowledge base of teaching," Cochran-Smith and Lytle (1990) write, "*are the voices of the teachers themselves* [italics added], the questions teachers ask, the ways teachers use writing and intentional talk in their work lives, and the interpretive frames teachers use to understand and improve their own classroom practices" (p. 2). Lytle and Cochran-Smith (1990) have expanded our definitions of teacher research to include teachers' journals and personal essays, as well as more formal classroom ethnographies or case studies of individual students. Teacher research, they argue, may be defined as "systematic, intentional inquiry by teachers about their own school and classroom work" (1993, pp. 23–24).

Throughout this preservice course, I asked the teacher candidates to become engaged in such research, and I continually reminded them that such work would become a regular part of their teaching lives. This course immersed Anne in all sorts of systematic inquiry: autobiographical writing, written explorations about critical issues in the teaching of composition, an individual case study project, and continual written reflection concerning these and other activities. Anne began building her own theory of writing instruction.

For Anne, the case study project proved to be most meaningful. She observed two eighth graders in a local language arts class and conducted interviews with them about their writing. The research project took place at a time when Anne admitted feeling "cynical":

> I was questioning not only my talent to be an effective teacher, but also the practicality of all that we've learned this quarter. Sure it worked for Atwell [1987], but would it work for me? Did I even want to teach? I found the answers to both during this project.

Observing the class, Anne began to connect the theories she was reading about to actual practice. "Everything we've learned suddenly began to take shape," she reflected. She was amazed by the students' enthusiasm for writing in this classroom:

> The students could have easily been quoting from Atwell as they talked with me about writing groups, revising, peer editing, time to write and share their writing in class. I can never put into words the enthusiasm these students had about this English class. For the first time in their lives, these students were learning to write. And they were excited about it.

Digging deep in order to find answers on her own, Anne continued to move forward. She referred to this case study project as the most powerful learning experience during the quarter. "I had no idea two eighth graders could teach me so much," Anne concluded. "If Nancie Atwell were here right now, she would say, 'I told you so.' But it has never been enough for someone to tell me it will work; I have to be shown. I see now that these approaches can work—and work well."

ENDING THOUGHTS, BEGINNING THOUGHTS

> I leaped headlong into the sea, and thereby have become better acquainted with the soundings, the quicksands, and the rocks, than if I had stayed upon the green shore, and piped a silly pipe, and took tea and comfortable advice.
>
> —John Keats

> "Come to the edge," he said.
> They said, "We are afraid."
> "Come to the edge," he said.
> They came.
> He pushed them. . .
> And they flew.
>
> —Guillaume Apollinaire

"I have struggled for answers in this class—answers about teaching and about myself," Anne wrote in her portfolio's concluding statement. Participating in the course proved to be a transformative experience for her: "This class brought me both agony and exhilaration, moments when I painfully had to look at myself and the way I wanted to teach." She continued:

> As a class, we questioned everything. We continually demanded that you give us answers. I realize now that a really good teacher doesn't give answers but leads students toward the discovery of finding answers on their own. I was so busy asking for answers that often I didn't take the time to listen or to see that you were pointing me toward the answers without my even knowing it.

Anne's experiences in the teaching of writing course helped her formulate new definitions of teaching and learning. "Learning is not merely finding one simple answer for a problem or situation," she discovered, "but rather a continual journey in which we discover and rediscover many different answers and solutions to our questions."

Fosnot (1989) suggests, "If change is to occur in teacher education, the new models advanced must be based on what we know about teaching and learning, and they must aim at producing teachers who are decision makers, researchers, and articulate change agents" (p. xiii). This course's emphasis on inquiry, reflection, collaboration, and theory building enabled teacher candidates to begin to view "learning as construction and teaching as a facilitating process to enhance and enrich development" (Fosnot 1989, p. xi). As the teacher educator, I pushed these preservice teachers to reflect on their own experiences in school and to voice their own beliefs about teaching and learning. As Richert (1992) explains,

> Learning to teach is just like learning anything else that is difficult, uncertain, complex, and infinitely challenging. . . . One place where "giving voice" is essential in

teacher education, therefore, is in the articulation of ideas and beliefs about teaching as one enters the field. (pp. 188, 191)

All of the structured course experiences invited these teacher candidates to write in their own voices and to engage in a reflective dialogue with others. In particular, the portfolio-keeping process helped Anne find joy in her learning and in her investigation of the teaching-learning process. Documenting her own growth as a teacher candidate, she moved toward becoming a thoughtful, reflective, autonomous decision maker. In addition, in constantly working with others, she learned the importance of collaborative inquiry. Perhaps some would say that Anne's "theory" remained largely underdeveloped as she completed this course. I argue, however, that she took the first important steps toward the articulation of a personal theory of teaching, learning, and assessment in writing classrooms. Because she completed her *own* portfolio, Anne began to name a theory of assessment that emphasized student responsibility, process, and personal empowerment. In her own way, she began to redefine or reinvent herself as a learner and a teacher. As Anne's journey reveals, the struggle to develop a portfolio—and in doing so, to develop a voice as an emerging teacher—can in itself be one of the most important experiences a future writing teacher can have:

> At the beginning of this quarter, I was first and foremost a STUDENT. I lived from assignment to assignment, quarter to quarter. I have been steadily transformed over the past ten weeks, however, into a more self-actualized person with a vision of my future. . . . My perceptions of English and what it means to be a teacher have evolved into a personal philosophy that is exciting, but not yet completely comfortable. That is as it should be, I think. I have grown so much this quarter, but I want to keep going. *I feel like this is the beginning rather than the end. . . .* And I have finally come to terms with the possible advantages of portfolio assessment for my own future students. I must admit that even the Tierney [1991] book did not completely erase my doubts about such an approach. But working on my own portfolio *did.*

REFERENCES

Atwell, N. 1987. *In the Middle: Writing, Reading, and Learning with Adolescents.* Portsmouth, NH: Heinemann.

Bird, T. 1990. "The Schoolteacher's Portfolio: An Essay on Possibilities." In *The New Handbook of Teacher Evaluation: Assessing Elementary and Secondary School Teachers.* J. Millman and L. Darling-Hammond, eds. Newbury Park, CA: Sage.

Blume, J. 1975. *Forever.* New York: Macmillan.

Carter, K. 1990. "Teachers' Knowledge and Learning to Teach." In *Handbook of Research on Teacher Education.* W. R. Houston, ed. New York: Macmillan.

———. 1993. "The Place of Story in the Study of Teaching and Teacher Education." In *Educational Researcher,* 22, 1: 5–12.

Cochran-Smith, M., and S. Lytle. 1990. "Research on Teaching and Teacher Research: The Issues That Divide." In *Educational Researcher,* 19, 2: 2–11.

———. 1993. *Inside Outside: Teacher Research and Knowledge.* New York: Teachers College Press.

Elbaz, F. 1991. "Research on Teachers' Knowledge: The Evolution of a Discourse." In *Journal of Curriculum Studies,* 23: 1–19.

Elbow, P. 1983. "Embracing Contraries in the Teaching Process." In *College English,* 45, 4: 327–339.

Fosnot, C. T. 1989. *Enquiring Teachers, Enquiring Learners: A Constructivist Approach for Teaching.* New York: Teachers College Press.

Graves, D. H., and B. S. Sunstein, eds. 1992. *Portfolio Portraits.* Portsmouth, NH: Heinemann.

Grossman, P. L. 1991. "Overcoming the Apprenticeship of Observation in Teacher Education Coursework." In *Teaching and Teacher Education,* 7, 4: 345–357.

———. 1992. "Why Models Matter: An Alternate View on Professional Growth." In *Review of Educational Research,* 62, 2: 171–179.

Kirby, D., and T. Liner. 1988. *Inside Out: Developmental Strategies for Teaching Writing.* 2d ed. Portsmouth, NH: Heinemann Boynton/Cook.

Kutz, E. 1992. "Preservice Teachers as Researchers: Developing Practice and Creating Theory in the English Classroom." In *English Education,* 24, 2: 67–75.

Kutz, E., and H. Roskelly. 1991. *An Unquiet Pedagogy: Transforming Practice in the English Classroom.* Portsmouth, NH: Heinemann Boynton/Cook.

Lytle, S., and M. Cochran-Smith. 1990. "Learning from Teacher Research: A Working Typology." In *Teachers College Record,* 72, 1: 83–103.

Miller Cleary, L. 1991. *From the Other Side of the Desk: Students Speak Out About Writing.* Portsmouth, NH: Heinemann Boynton/Cook.

Richert, A. E. 1992. "Voice and Power in Teaching and Learning to Teach." In *Reflective Teacher Education: Cases and Critiques.* L. Valli, ed. (pp. 187–197). Albany, NY: SUNY Press.

Rilke, R. M. 1934. *Letters to a Young Poet. Letter No. 4.* Trans. M. D. Herter. New York: Norton.

Schubert, W., and W. Ayers. 1992. *Teacher Lore: Learning from Our Own Experience.* New York: Longman.

Tierney, R. J., et al. 1991. *Portfolio Assessment in the Reading-Writing Classroom.* Norwood, MA: Christopher-Gordon.

Wigginton, E. 1986. *Sometimes a Shining Moment: The Foxfire Experience.* Garden City, NY: Doubleday.

Wilson, S. M. 1992. "Thinking About Teaching, Teaching About Teaching." In *Exploring Teaching: Reinventing an Introductory Course.* S. Feiman-Nemser and H. Featherstone, eds. New York: Teachers College Press.

Witherell, C., and N. Noddings. 1991. *Stories Lives Tell: Narrative and Dialogue in Education.* New York: Teachers College Press.

Welty, E. 1983. *One Writer's Beginnings.* New York: Warner Books.

Wolf, D. P. 1989. "Portfolio Assessment: Sampling Student Work." In *Educational Leadership,* 46, 4: 35–39.

SOMETHING JUST CLICKED:
REFLECTION THROUGH PORTFOLIOS

Roxanne Henkin

Portfolios are part of the inquiry-based evaluation I promote in my graduate education classes. Because I believe in the importance of students' self-evaluation in the learning process, I explore options that portfolios might offer. I use portfolios to document and assess my students' progress toward understanding a feminist liberatory perspective on educational issues and to further my own understanding of the feminist themes of searching for an authentic voice, posing questions, and taking risks.

FEMINISM IN UNIVERSITY CLASSES

It's so funny how the students in our class think I'm an expert at the Writer's Workshop. It's only my second year teaching. I wish I was an expert, so I wouldn't have to struggle with everything. I've enjoyed hearing people say that Writer's Workshop would not work in first grade, because my class is living proof that it can. I love teaching the writing process, even though I don't consider myself a good writer. Maybe I should practice what I preach.

This excerpt was written by Amy, a student in my graduate class and a second-year teacher. Her portfolio was organized around the title "Great Expectations" and documented her questions and doubts as she tried to integrate new ideas and searched for her own personal and professional voice.

For another student, Holly, the integrative quality of the portfolio bridged theory with practice through reflection on her work in Bolivian schools:

As I look at my portfolio and remember the thoughts that were going through my head before I started this class, I am impressed by a curious circling back. I started out wondering how to train Bolivian teachers to help children think and have ended up with . . . thinking! Yet although I have started and ended with thinking, my beginning concept was vague, and I felt lost in a myriad of unconnected thoughts and questions. Now, however, I can recognize some of the trees in the forest, and I have some notion of where the paths could possibly lead.

The integrative quality of portfolios helps students bridge the gap between theoretical knowledge and classroom practice (Garman and Piantanida 1990). The portfolio is a place where life stories are told, examined, and reflected upon, where students can live "wide awake" lives. Greene (1978) challenges us that "curriculum ought to provide a series of occasions for individuals to articulate themes of their existence and to reflect on those themes until they know themselves to be in the world and can name what has been up to then obscure" (p. 19). The portfolio provides a place for this to become explicit. Greene reminds us, "The point is that learning must be a process of discovery and recovery in response to worthwhile questions rising out of conscious life in concrete situations."

> It's been 21 years since I graduated from Northeastern Illinois University. During those 21 years, I've stayed home and raised my four children. Having children was very important to my husband and myself. Seven years ago, when my youngest child started kindergarten, I decided to work as a substitute teacher and as an instructional aide. I applied for three full time teaching positions, but was rejected. One principal suggested that I should go back to school and take a reading course. So here I am, excited and scared to take my first graduate course and compete with so many intelligent people.

Grace's life story was interwoven in her life as a student, teacher, and learner. The role of autobiographical narratives in portfolios provides a place for the questions to be asked and an opportunity for them to be explored given that storytelling is a way of coming to know (Howard 1991).

Finding an Authentic Voice

For women, the possibilities that portfolios provide for examining life stories may offer safe havens for tentatively finding and asserting one's authentic voice. Tannen (1990) says that women and men often talk at cross-purposes. Women trade stories in a show of empathy and see gossip as a positive way to share life stories honestly. The empathetic experiencing that women share in conversation may be, according to Tannen, our "greatest aid in escaping our inevitable limitations in understanding people from different cultures, races, belief systems, sexes, places and time" (p. 196). One of the strengths of portfolios is the opportunity offered to students to reflect critically on the meaning of their lives and educational experiences and to challenge their existing stereotypes and prejudices. Ellsworth (1989) challenges dominant members of society to educate ourselves about oppression, sexism, bigotry, homophobia, racism, and anti-Semitism so that the minority members in society don't assume that responsibility.

Posing Questions

Portfolios provide extended invitations for women especially. "Women's question posing when faced with moral conflict indicates a sensitivity to situation and context" (Belenky et al. 1986, p. 149). Belenky et al. report the difficulty many women have in finding their authentic voices and for some women to find the courage to speak at all. As women find their voices, they "resist premature generalizations" and pose questions they assert are "central to the constructivist way of knowing" (p. 149).

Taking Risks

Portfolios offer a safe place for question posing and searching for authentic voices. For women in particular, the male model in academia—of challenging students and putting them on the defensive—can have serious consequences. Rather than responding to the professor's challenge women doubt their ability to contribute and retreat into silence. Doubting is debilitating rather than energizing for women (Belenky et al. 1986). Schweickart (1990) discusses the need for women to encourage and facilitate each other's speech. She states, "truth, to the extent that it depends on speech, is likewise fragile, elusive and must be coaxed out and cultivated and is likely to emerge distorted in uncaring argumentation" (p. 91).

Because the student controls the portfolio process and interprets its meanings, this is a more powerful and supportive model for women students. The role of the teacher is one of caring and response. The supportive teacher acknowledges the "complication of the situation" and encourages students to "integrate an ideal of personal and moral integrity with an ethic of responsibility and care" (Gilligan 1982, p. 140).

Bateson (1989) points out that women's lives are often asymmetrical and interrupted; women's "energies are not narrowly focused or permanently pointed to a single ambition" (p. 9) and "fluidity and discontinuity are central to the reality in which we [women] live" (p. 13). The portfolio offers opportunities to reflect on, in Bateson's words, the "composition of our lives" (p. 1) and the way that "living life as an improvisatory art can/has . . . evoked creativity" (p. 3).

The journal is central to the portfolio, perhaps the core where reflection begins. The review process is particularly significant for women, because, as Bateson notes, "we are engaged in a day-by-day process of self-invention—not discovery, for what we search for does not exist until we find it, both past and the future are raw material, shaped and reshaped by each individual" (p. 28).

Most of my students are women, and so I'm interested in the opportunities that portfolios can offer them in the process of coming to know. Portfolios are no less valuable for men, however, because of the occasions provided to reflect on life stories and to integrate content. All students are asked to reflect on curricular issues in portfolios. Portfolios add to liberatory classrooms another venue to support the work we do together. They become vehicles through which we "focus on how we construct the very examination of our teaching and research processes" (Miller 1990, p. 13).

THE PORTFOLIO PROCESS

As I read students' portfolios, I wondered how feminist themes might emerge. I asked students to follow Hansen's (1990) recommendations: to collect, select, and reflect in their portfolios. Students were asked to collect all evidence of themselves as thinkers, learners, readers, and writers. Everything in class represented potential inclusion—class projects, class discussions, readings, dialectic journals—as did artifacts collected from their lives that reflected their experiences as literate human beings. They were encouraged to include alternative forms of documentation, such as audiotape or videotape.

Students then chose selections for their portfolios that best represented their growth. They wrote "Dear Roxanne" letters that explained why work was included and what it represented. The resulting portfolios were diverse. Some students included large sections of their dialectic journals and few other artifacts. Others used alternative forms to express their literacy growth.

Joan included a picture of the roses her husband had given her on their twenty-fifth wedding anniversary. She said that, like the rosebuds, she was in the process of opening and growing in her literacy knowledge. Janice was a student in my children's literature class who was mentioned in other students' journals for her ability to articulate ideas beautifully. Her journal began with a "Dear Roxanne" letter that said I probably wouldn't want to read the next part of her portfolio but it was important that she included this section. She said that creating the portfolio along with her work over the past year was about finding her voice, for she had long been silenced, having been molested as a child.

STUDENT PORTFOLIOS

The portfolios I received from my graduate students represented various parts of the educative process and the different options available, and they highlighted the integration that happened.

Many of the following selections reflect the safe atmosphere that portfolios provide for students to *find authentic voices*, to *pose questions*, and to *take risks*.

For Grace, the homemaker for twenty-one years, finding her voice was difficult. She shared her anxiety:

> It is now around 11:00 P.M.—Wednesday night. This is my first reflection. How am I after the first class? SCARED and NERVOUS. I feel so insecure. Talk about the competition. I'm the lowest on the educational totem pole. I'm in deep, deep trouble. I want to thank you for telling me tonight that I'll do fine in this class. A teacher never, never said that to me. Thank you. Thank you. That really meant a lot to me. I hope I can keep up. I'll do my best, but a lot of times, that's not enough. I'm still *scared!*
>
> Who cares how or what I think about the class? I should acclimate myself to the class and to you. Right! And to think that of all people, you my teacher want to know what I think of the class. WOW! A new experience for me. You are such a caring person. My mother never cared that much.

The fears of returning to school after a long hiatus while raising children were evident in Gail's portfolio too:

> I was a bit curious about what the difference would be in this reading class and how "whole language" would change my mind. This must be a common "fight" because our handouts had the description of my feelings in the first set, the "encapsulation" of the teacher's mind as she reenters formal education. I've read

and reread this handout numerous times, the fact that the dialectic journal was foreign to me made me uncomfortable the first two months.

A number of my students return to the teaching profession after raising families. Many of these portfolios included life stories about their asymmetric and interrupted lives. But even the young students talked of being uprooted, of moving because of husband's job changes. Brenda wrote this in her opening letter:

On completing this class, I began to reflect on how the methods of teaching beginning reading fit into my teaching and my life. The last two years have been filled with transitions, decisions, and a need to redefine myself and I think a brief explanation of this will help explain why I chose the theme of freedom for my portfolio.

My husband and I moved to Chicago from the West a year ago for [him] to attend law school at the University of Chicago. I was excited by the move, but didn't know what the move would bring for me, since I was leaving a good job and didn't have an Illinois Certificate and we were moving far away from family and friends.

While Brenda reflected on the composition of her life, Holly focused on curricular questions. Holly had taught in Bolivia and hoped to return. She titled her portfolio, "Emerging Thinking About Literacy and Bolivia," and divided it into four sections: emerging questions, emerging skills, emerging issues, and emerging path. She documented her journey in this way:

I think more than anything else, my experience in Bolivia has made me see how important a "whole-to-part approach" is. A child living in a highly literate home is more likely to understand what he reads in spite of inadequate instructional strategies. But a student who never sees books either at home or at school will have a difficult time building the conceptual base needed for effective reading.

And so I come up with a lot of questions. How can I use what they already know about reading and build on that? Is it necessary, especially on the rural level with teachers who have limited educational background, to change an entire paradigm? What about taking small, concrete steps first to create a more literate environment? Where do you start?

For Holly, the portfolio became a place to ask and examine questions about teaching and learning. She moved away from previously formed generalizations and began to think in new ways. The portfolio became a safe place for question posing and contemplation:

I was on the El train on the way home from class last night, thinking about some educational issue in Bolivia. Suddenly I started listening to myself. Before taking the class, my thoughts would not have sounded the same. I was using vocabulary that I wouldn't have previously used, but now those very words and the concepts they represented could not be separated from my thinking. I can almost feel the shape of my mind changing.

Holly documented her growth and related it to literacy praxis. As she examined the curriculum of the course, synthesis became possible:

I stopped two paragraphs into another paper, stuck, when suddenly something just clicked! I've just abandoned the paper because I want to explore this and somehow pull all of those floating puzzle pieces together. I wish right now words came easily and my mind could transmit clear messages instead of muddled ones. But maybe it will take form as I write.

Reflection. That's the word that shouts at me. That's what I'm looking for! How could I have missed it? It started the very first day in class—I remember, we were to be a "thought collective". The purpose of the portfolios was to reflect on our growth as learners. Reflection was stamped over every discussion. I even remembered thinking about reflection and told everyone how my head was buzzing with thinking about thinking. I saw that was what we needed our kids to do—reflect. And in class we were learning ways to make that happen.

In my mind I have been thinking, "How do we get teachers to help children think?" I've been processing what seems to me so far to be all the essentials—deeper discussions, authentic purpose, keeping things whole and meaningful, kid-watching, creating a secure climate. I have been wondering how to help teachers in Bolivia do this. All of this time I have been focusing on philosophy and methodology and have overlooked the obvious: just as we want our kids to reflect, we as teachers need to reflect. And that is the first step.

The portfolio provided a safe haven for exploration, integration, and synthesis, both professionally and personally. Amy's portfolio centered around her title, "Great Expectations." She explained:

I've chosen the theme of "Great Expectations" because of my desire to always do the best because of the expectations that were placed on me. When someone has expectations for me to do well, I usually do. I used to want to be the best daughter, friend, girlfriend, aunt, teacher, mother (not yet), wife, etc. However, now I'm learning to do more things for myself.

My life started out with high expectations from my family. Now I have them for myself. Expectations are important as long as you don't go too far and are never satisfied. As a first-grade teacher, I want to be on top. I want to be the most innovative, creative, energetic, knowledgeable teacher possible. I want to be proud of myself and have others proud of me, too.

Now I feel like I'm trying very hard, but I need more information. I think teaching is a very frustrating profession if you're always trying to do your best. There needs to be a point where you reach satisfaction with yourself as a person.

While Amy was aware of her high expectations, she hadn't anticipated the difficulties she would face as a whole language teacher. She described some of these difficulties in the segment "Frustrations":

I've included this section because of all my feelings as a new teacher. It is overwhelming and frustrating to teach in an innovative, creative, individualized whole language way using inquiry-based instruction. That's why I keep wishing that I had a few years' experience.

I was at a sharing meeting, hearing ideas I didn't agree with. It bothered me that I was so negative. Everything I have learned in this class conflicts with their ideas. I know how I want to teach, but why should I critique others?

> I wish there were more teachers like me that I could share ideas with. It would make me feel more part of a group. Right now I feel isolated and unusual, almost as if I was a rebel.

Amy struggled as an emerging whole language teacher. The portfolio was a place to identify and describe her struggle.

Grace alternately shared and asserted her voice in her portfolio. She tentatively offered part of her life story to class members:

> Tonight was our last formal class. It is so sad to think we have only one more class together. Tonight seemed very special. I never thought that talking about our family and multicultural issues could get so complicated. Our discussions became so deep and personal, I suddenly became bonded to everyone.
>
> My views toward group discussions have dramatically changed. I really honor what other people have to say. Everyone has something special to contribute. When you stopped our class discussion and asked us to reflect, you could feel everyone's emotional vibrations. What I shared about my mother is something I never said in public before. A bunch of ladies came up to thank me for sharing and even gave me hugs!!!

For Grace, this multicultural discussion about under-represented groups was a significant breakthrough highlighted in her portfolio. The multicultural discussions in class were important for other students, too. Portfolios capture an integration of class curriculum with individual insight. Jane shared:

> When I think of multicultural, I get a peculiar, puzzled look on my face. I attended a predominately white, all girl, Catholic School in Chicago. I can honestly say that I never learned anything concerning my Black heritage. I felt the pain you expressed when you stated you never learned about the Holocaust nor Jewish history throughout your schooling. I have a painful memory of my Freshman year of history that I can remember so vividly.
>
> We were learning about different ethnic backgrounds and what countries many of our ancestors came from. Being the only Black in the classroom, naturally it was assumed that my ancestors were from Africa. During this time, my only vision of Africa was jungles, apes, and Tarzan movies. I remember feeling ashamed to be Black and wondered why God would let the torture and disparity that slavery brought last such a long time.

Jane confronted painful educational memories acknowledging the injustice that stereotypical ideas and prejudice inflicted on her life. Portfolios were venues for reflection on class discussion, promoting empathetic understanding and moving praxis toward action for a fairer world. The contributions of both Jane and Grace to our discussions inspired and moved other class members. Karen summarized:

> This session turned out to be the very best and most interesting session. Our class discussion on multiculturalism paved the way for everyone to participate in the discussion and express their views. We proved we were a group that evening. We demonstrated to each other the fact that our diverse viewpoints could be expressed and we could maintain a level of respect for one another, too.

We didn't solve any earth shattering problems, nor did we solve the dilemma of how to address sensitive issues in our classrooms, however, we did become more cognizant of our differences and vowed to make a conscious effort to be inclusive in our teaching and not assume that difference[s] don't exist or [difference] doesn't matter. We realize we have to make conscious efforts to not exclude any of our students or make assumptions based on stereotypical remarks, but to treat each student as an individual and accept him/her for who he/she is, not where he/she is. We also realized that we will make mistakes, but will not perpetuate those mistakes by compounding them. Most importantly, we learned what community in our class had been established by Roxanne previously and how this sense of community helped us reach that point.

The significant moments that occur in classrooms may be reflected in our students' portfolios. If we establish caring, safe spaces where controversial issues are examined and action is promoted, student contemplation and integration of these themes and ideas emerge. I've presented representative samples to illustrate some of the themes and issues that my students explored in portfolios. My analysis of these portfolios suggests they help support the liberatory, feminist classrooms we seek to create by offering personal and alternative opportunities for reflection. The portfolio is a place where curriculum is explored in conjunction with life stories.

Portfolios extend the work in our classrooms and continue the dialogue that takes place in journals. Whether portfolios continue to be used is less important than the effort they represent to honor student growth. It is the essence of the portfolio that interests me, that reflective quality that I will continue to affirm and support in my students' work. Selections from Grace's portfolio serve as a testament to the process that I am both committed to and continually revising:

> My theme of my portfolio is a balloon being blown up. Why a balloon? I feel as if I'm a balloon, and all that extra reading I do is being pumped into me. My portfolio also reflects on how I've grown in my reading and writing literacy.

Grace included a section about her family. They encouraged and supported her work in class. Each week she shared what she had learned with them.

My Family's Comments:

> Mom has been putting a lot of effort into this class. I'm very proud of her because she shows her effort by staying up sooo late and spending time during the day finishing her projects. I'm happy for her because she seemed like she was happy that she took the class. It showed that she liked the class because she was very satisfied. (Carolyn)

> Mom has worked almost every night this past week to finish her report! I try to tell her to get some sleep because she's always so tired, but she stays up to 1:00 or 3:00 working. It's amazing that she's still happy. I don't understand but I guess she likes learning. I think that I have heard and seen about every report and good book that she wrote or read. (Kenny)

> My mom has spent a lot of time for this class. Countless times I've seen her reading in our den or in her room, with books upon books. I would have much better grades if I worked as diligently as her! It's really good to see her enjoying herself

in her first class back in school. The excitement in her voice and look in her eyes tell it all. Thank-you for making her time enjoyable and a wonderful experience. I'm sure she'll cherish it. (David)

REFERENCES

Bateson, M. C. 1989. *Composing a Life*. New York: Penguin.

Belenky, M. F., B. M. Clinchy, N. R. Goldberger, and J. M. Tarule. 1986. *Women's Ways of Knowing*. New York: Basic Books.

Ellsworth, E. 1989. "Why Doesn't This Feel Empowering? Working Through the Repressive Myths of Critical Pedagogy." In *Harvard Education Review, 59*: 297–324.

Garman, N. B., and M. Piantanida. 1990. *The Academic/Professional Portfolio*. Unpublished manuscript.

Gilligan, C. 1982. *In a Different Voice*. Cambridge, MA: Harvard University Press.

Greene, M. 1978. *Landscapes of Learning*. New York: Teachers College Press.

Hansen, J. 1990. "Literacy Portfolios: Keep a Good Idea Alive." Paper presented at the National Council of Teachers of English Annual Convention, Baltimore, MD.

Howard, G. 1991. "Culture Tales. A Narrative Approach to Thinking, Cross-Cultural Psychology, and Psychotherapy." In *American Psychologist, 46*: 187–197.

Miller, J. 1990. *Creating Spaces and Finding Voices*. Albany, NY: SUNY Press.

Schweickart, P. 1990. "Reading, Teaching, and the Ethic of Care." In *Gender in the Classroom*. S. Gabriel and I. Smithson, eds. Urbana, IL: University of Illinois Press.

Tannen, D. 1990. *You Just Don't Understand*. New York: Ballantine.

D

PROTOCOLS/ENGAGEMENTS

See the introduction to the Protocols/Engagements in Part A for a full explanation of this material (page 61).

D-1 The Developing Teacher Interview

MARK W. F. CONDON AND JEAN ANNE CLYDE

Introduction   The assessment instrument in Figure D-1 is used repeatedly throughout our teacher preparation program to assess how effective we are in developing in our students the concepts of student-centered and holistic education we hope to instill. It was designed to document the evolution of our students' conceptualization of teaching and their own professional growth over time. Single items or groups of the questions in the instrument might be adapted to shape teacher education discussions. Or individual students can respond to the questions (perhaps in a narrative form) in journals or in preparation for midterm or final self-evaluation.

Afterword   A fuller treatment of this instrument and the research based on its use is found in: J. A. Clyde, M. W. F. Condon, Kyle, and Hovda. 1993. "A Constructivist Basis for Teaching and Teacher Education: A Framework for Program Development and Research on Graduates." In *Journal of Teacher Education*, 44, 4: 273–278.

1. Do you see yourself as a good teacher of K–4 children? (If "no") Can you name someone who is a good K–4 teacher?
2. What do you (she/he) do that makes you (him/her) a good K–4 teacher?
3. If K–4 pupils were having trouble learning to do something on their own, what might you do to help them learn how to do it?
4. What kinds of help can you offer a K–4 learner now that you haven't felt confident about offering in the past?
5. Give a single example of the very best teaching you have seen or experienced. Explain what made that teaching good.
6. Describe specifically an example of the best teaching you personally have done. Explain what made that teaching good.
7. What would be the most important indication to you that someone was having trouble with teaching?
8. If someone you knew were having this kind of trouble teaching, how would you help?
9. What is the most important thing that you would like to work on next in your teaching?
10. What experiences would you like to have in the near future that you believe would help you become a better teacher?
11. Think about what you can do well in addition to being a teacher (e.g., in a hobby, job or profession, as a spouse or parent, as a friend or sibling). How are those strengths reflected in the teacher that you are?
12. What issues were important to you at one time in your teaching career that are less important now? What has happened to effect this change?
13. What issues are important to you now that were not part of your thinking before? What happened to effect this change?
14. What is your idea of an ideal teaching situation?
15. What is your idea of the ideal pupil?

FIGURE D-1   Assessment instrument

Copyright © 1996 Mark W. F. Condon and Jean Anne Clyde. Stenhouse Publishers, York, Maine.

D-2 Big-Kidwatching

RICHARD J. MEYER

Introduction   We begin our understanding of evaluation by reading about kid-watching (Goodman 1978). We start by watching each other because we can have many levels of conversation going on at once. We explore how it is we learn, what we choose to learn, and the conditions that most support and facilitate our learning. This engagement demonstrates that evaluation is quite complex and extends far beyond traditional notions of tests.

Procedures   Three or four class members volunteer to come to the center of a circle. On the table at the center are a wok, an electric hot plate, and the ingredients and recipe for egg foo yung. The volunteers make egg foo yung for the class.

This is a unique experience for the preservice teachers because many have not previously cooked with a wok. The rest of the class is responsible for taking copious notes about the language and learning that they see as the cooks prepare the recipe.

The cooks are encouraged to talk and think out loud as the rest of the class is watching. The cooks are intent on following the recipe and having an edible result in the end. Their discussion is rich in the stuff of classrooms in which language is cultivated and explored. I watch and work with the kidwatchers, peeking into their notebooks as they record observations.

Once the cooks' jobs are divided and decisions are made, they become efficient, confident, and sometimes even silly. Their reactions add to the kidwatching experience as we discuss what takes place and changes over time. I present Halliday's (1975) concepts of field, tenor, and mode to help us interpret what we are seeing. We discuss the relationships between the cooks, and the cooks join in the discussion as they share what they were thinking and feeling. Discussion also provides insights into language use as a window into understanding and an indicator of the authenticity of a learning activity.

When the clean-up is complete and we're all in the circle again, I focus the discussion on text, context, and community as issues of evaluation. We have changed, having eaten together. We share inside jokes about eggshells, Michele and her distaste for mushrooms, and other community knowledge we have developed. These are important texts for us to understand because of how they impact the literacy of our classroom. We end the day by reflecting about critical issues of evaluation in our journals.

References

Goodman, Y. M. 1978. "Kidwatching: An Alternative to Testing." In *National Elementary School Principal,* 57, 4: 41–45.

Halliday, M. A. K. 1975. *Learning How to Mean: Explorations in the Development of Language.* London, UK: Edward Arnold.

D-3 Dialogue Folders

KAY MOSS

Introduction   The purposes of this engagement are to demonstrate a portfolio-style assessment tool, to establish an instructor-student dialogue throughout the semester, and to facilitate student self-reflection and self-assessment. Many students will share thoughts in a dialogue folder that might not be shared in class.

Procedures   At the beginning of the semester, I have each student bring in one manila folder. Each time an assignment is turned in, the students place it in their manila folder. On the inside cover of their folders, students write the date, their reactions to the assignment, or their reflections as learners in our class. Each time these are turned in with a new assignment and a new dialogue folder entry, I respond to the assignment and write my own comment below theirs inside the covers of their folders. Throughout the semester we might write about reactions to class, a practicum experience in the schools, or events in their lives that have influenced their thinking and learning.

Afterword   This engagement was adapted from one used by Bonnie Chambers at Bowling Green State University.

D-4 Journal Portfolios

JEAN ANNE CLYDE AND MARK W. F. CONDON

Introduction   Personal journals offer learners one of the most effective tools for clarifying and extending their thinking. Representing one's ideas enables the learner to shape and reshape them, rethink and revise, and outgrow current beliefs. However, the time required for teachers to keep up with responding personally to fifty or more student journals that include several entries each week often seems overwhelming and unmanageable. Inviting students to create journal portfolios offers them the opportunity to select a few entries from their journals to share with their teacher (or peers) for the purposes of receiving response. More important, the process of identifying the most significant entries requires the learner to adopt an evaluative stance. Finally, personal journals offer students a firsthand experience from which they can project the value of such journals to the children in their classrooms.

Procedures   Students are invited to record their thoughts, feelings, personal responses to class experiences, readings, and discussions. They are encouraged to write informally, jotting down ideas as they occur, and searching for connections across course topics. (The teacher keeps a journal as well, providing a demonstration that writing is a valuable tool for all learners.) Students are also informed that their journals will be shared. To avoid creating a journal that is too public to hold deepest feelings, pages that they feel too personal for others to read may be stapled closed.

Students are informed that the teacher will collect the journals during the third or fourth class in order to respond to their ideas.

The teacher collects the journals and responds to each one, providing response about ideas, asking questions to prompt in-depth thinking, and encouraging students to pose and explore answers to questions of personal importance to them. This initial response provides several important demonstrations: (1) all ideas are valued and respected; (2) the teacher sees her or his role as a supportive one; and (3) the teacher identifies the kinds of responses that are appropriate (e.g., reflective responses rather than simply summaries of readings, experiences, or events).

Students are invited to submit their journals for teacher response at any time, but because the teacher may not see a particular student's journal until the semester's end, she or he may also wish to arrange peer readings so that students are receiving periodic response on their ideas. Peer sharing enables students to identify with others who have similar concerns and confusions and provides a safe place in which students can begin to have professional "conversations" with one another. Those conversations often lead students to clarify their thinking.

At the end of the semester students review their entire collection of entries to identify five entries that:

1. are, in some way, especially significant to the student;
2. provide evidence of searching for and making connections across readings, class discussions, field experiences, and disciplines (i.e., reading/language arts and art); and
3. demonstrate progress as a learner.

Students are to insert paper clips or bookmarks or easy-to-find dates to help locate each entry. In addition, each entry might be clearly marked, with a circle or star, for example.

Having identified their five entries, students compose one additional entry in which they justify why they have chosen the particular set of journal entries.

D-5 Collaborative Evaluation

YETTA M. GOODMAN, KATHRYN F. WHITMORE, AND RUTH SÁEZ-VEGA

Introduction   The form in Figure D-5 provides students with an opportunity to summarize their reflections and self-evaluations at least twice during the semester in response to the stated expectations of the program. It is particularly appropriate when students have already developed personal goals and objectives for the learning at the beginning of a course. The expectations for the whole language block at Borton Primary Magnet School (described in detail in Chapter 19) are provided here as an example. The goals of this engagement are to invite students to initiate the evaluation process, to provide a structure for mutual assessments by the student and the teacher, and to encourage students to prepare thoughtfully for the conference that follows completion of the written form.

Procedures   At the beginning of the course, students write their own objectives for their learning, as well as explore the preliminary objectives of the professor(s). The form in Figure D-5 is completed at midterm and again at the end of the course. Each time, the students write several reflective sentences in each section of their column.

Copyright © 1996 Yetta M. Goodman, Kathryn F. Whitmore, and Ruth Sáez-Vega. Stenhouse Publishers, York, Maine.

Student's evaluation	Faculty response
Professionalism	
Introduction to the Classroom	
Child Case Study	
Theme Cycle	
Interactive Journal	
Portfolio	
Class Readings and Additional Professional Readings	

Look back at your personal objectives for the semester and assess your progress thus far. Would you like to change them? Have you already met your goals? Write a narrative response that reflects on your objectives and summarizes your self-evaluation of the expectations.

Faculty comments:

Signatures:
Student _____   Faculty _____
Date _____

FIGURE D-5   End-of-semester student-faculty evaluation

The student and the professor meet to discuss each section. Students bring samples of their work to the conference, their journal, or other forms of documentation they want to share. As the pair discusses each expectation, the professor writes parallel comments in the faculty column. If a grade needs to be assigned, the student and the faculty member negotiate it during the conference.

At the conclusion of the conference, each participant signs the form, and a copy is made so that the student and faculty member each has a record of the discussion and decisions.

D-6 Negotiated Evaluation: Living the Process to Truly Learn About It

HEIDI MILLS

Introduction   The powerful demonstrations and engagements that have become central to our teaching have pushed us to rethink our evaluation strategies. The ways in which we have traditionally assessed preservice and inservice teachers are theoretically inconsistent with what we believe about curriculum and evaluation. Therefore, I devised an evaluation strategy that would involve students in creating a class-developed instrument to evaluate their own growth and determine a grade for the course. The student-generated devices help me better understand what the students value while providing a functional opportunity to discuss the tensions, struggles, strengths, and weaknesses of various forms of evaluation. I find that although the instruments vary from class to class, we consistently learn to think seriously about the possibilities and limitations as well as the content and form of evaluation devices.

Procedures   I begin by writing explicit descriptions of class projects in the syllabus. I embed belief statements to make clear connections between my beliefs about teaching and learning and the way the course is organized. I take a great deal of time reviewing the syllabus and share sample projects from former students so that the class will realize that the course is very organized and that the projects are intentionally open-ended so that each student will be provided opportunities to personalize the theory. I also spend time explaining that at the end of the course the group will devise the evaluation instrument. I tell them that they will need to experience the strategies firsthand to appreciate their learning potential and to create appropriate categories for each engagement. The course begins.

Usually the second-to-the-last day of the course is devoted primarily to the development of the evaluation device. I ask the class to divide into groups equaling the number of course projects or issues that were listed on the syllabus. Each group selects one engagement and discusses what they learned from the experience. I ask them to take the important lessons they generated and to identify features of the experience that were most important to them as learners. They then create a list that represents their thinking and promotes thoughtful reflection from their colleagues working in other groups. They frequently frame the essence of their discussion in question form—for example, What connections did I make between the readings and my own story? Did I demonstrate that I developed a professional voice?

Class Participation (5 points)

Did I come to class on time and well prepared?
Did I participate consistently?
Did I contribute to the growth of the whole group?
If my opinions were not always supportive, did I generate differences appropriately with justification?

Student _____
Instructor _____

Class Newspaper (Biography, Different Topics, Text Sets) (7.5 points)

Were my articles on time and well prepared?
Did I respond to my colleagues in supportive, constructive ways (3 +'s and wish)?
Were my pieces well thought out, helpful, and informative to my colleagues?
Did I follow the format generated in class?

Student _____
Instructor _____

Literature Study Group (5 points)

Did I hold my own in the group and make important contributions to the project?
Did I make the assignment meaningful?
Was I a risk taker?
Was the medium chosen for presentation appropriate for the book?
Did our presentation portray the book well?

Student _____
Instructor _____

Professional Essay (10 points)

Did I ground my paper in the literature/research?
Did my paper reflect personal growth?
Was my final draft edited for grammar and other elements that affect the presentation?
Did I include a bibliography?

Student _____
Instructor _____

Journal (7.5 points)

Did I make connections and raise legitimate questions?
Did I discuss the research?
Did I keep up consistently?
Was I well prepared so that I could exchange my journal and turn it in on time?
Did I give my colleagues good feedback?
Did I make connections and solid comments in my letter to my colleagues when we exchanged journals?

Student _____
Instructor _____

Case Study (15 points)

Was my work with the child and my analysis based on research?
Did I use strategies discussed in class or create my own?
Does my case study reflect personal growth on my part?
Did I work with my child consistently?
Do I believe that the child has grown?
Was I supportive?

Student _____
Instructor _____

FIGURE D-6   Negotiated evaluation

Copyright © 1996 Heinemann. Stenhouse Publishers, York, Maine.

Finally, each group determines the number of points that each project should be worth, given that all of the projects together should equal 100 points (50 points decided by the student and 50 points decided by me). After a great deal of discussion within groups, they share their thinking with the class. I find that the class usually frames reflection questions that represent critical incidents in their growth. They are usually very complimentary of the ideas presented. A debate often emerges when we discuss point totals with the whole group. At times we come to consensus and other times agree to disagree and create a format that allows individuals to determine point totals within agreed-upon limits.

I pose questions throughout the discussion that will promote reflexivity. This strategy encourages students to get in touch with their own learning, to reflect carefully on their own growth, and to understand better that evaluation is a stance or perspective we take. Ultimately, how we evaluate determines what we evaluate. Figure D-6 documents the decisions made by one class.

D-7   Student-Developed Tests

YVONNE SIU-RUNYAN

Introduction   As an elementary classroom teacher for grades 3–6, I frequently involved my students in the development of tests to evaluate what they have learned. Because my students were the ones who provided the topics about which they felt they should be tested, as well the questions themselves, several things happened: they studied, they didn't complain about the test being unfair, and, most important, they took more responsibility for their own learning.

Five years ago, I made the move to teach in higher education. Because I had positive experiences with my elementary students in the development of their own evaluation, I knew that this would be a valuable process for teacher certification students. Besides, I wanted to demonstrate this process for them so that they would experience the benefits of student-developed tests. In addition, I discussed with my university students how important it is for them to involve their future students in the evaluation process.

Despite my interest in involving my teacher certification students in their own evaluation, I was afraid that they would develop weak test items, take advantage of me, and wouldn't study because they already knew what would be on the test. Mostly I was afraid student-developed tests wouldn't work in a university setting.

How wrong I was.

Procedures   For the midterm examination, I announced to my students I wanted to "walk my talk." The students were astonished. Some of their comments: "Really?" "How do we do this?" "Do you think we can?" "We'll all get A's. Aren't you concerned about this?"

After discussing the reasons for their involvement in the evaluative process, I asked: "Now what topics do you think you should be tested on? Please discuss this in your cooperative learning groups."

The topics for possible inclusion on the midterm were listed on the chalkboard. To my surprise, the same topics I already had on a prepared midterm were the ones the students identified as important. "This is good news," I thought to myself. "Perhaps this will work after all." I was encouraged.

They thought the following topics were important:

- Alternatives to standardized tests: portfolios, anecdotal records, observations and conversations, interest and attitude inventories, reading and writing interviews, writing samples, think-alouds, learning logs, self-reflections.
- A model of proficient silent reading and how language cue systems are used when reading continuous text.
- The interpretation of the results of a norm-referenced, standardized test.
- Reasons for assessment and evaluation.
- Instructional strategies.
- Conditions of language learning.
- Testing issues: validity, reliability, error measurement, norm-referenced tests, criterion-referenced tests, norming population, stanines, grade-level equivalent score, percentile scores.

After the topics were discussed, students developed test items, by themselves or in collaboration with others, and turned them in at the end of class so that I could compile, rewrite for clarity, and develop their midterm. I felt developing a graphic organizer or web was an important strategy to use for studying, so for the midterm, they were to develop a web, which they used during the exam. Their web counted as one of the questions.

On the day of the midterm, I brought in their tests. The questions were done. Now we had to decide cooperatively the points each question should be allotted. I shared my initial thinking about how I thought the 200 points should be distributed. For the most part, the students agreed. However, they felt that the web should be worth forty points instead of the thirty I had offered and that the first question, which asked them to discuss at least five alternatives to standardized tests, should be dropped from forty points to only thirty. I agreed and the students proceeded to take the midterm exam.

Following the administering of the midterm exam, I gave the students a questionnaire to complete. I wanted to find out what they thought about developing their own midterm and whether they thought it was a valuable experience.

All twenty-three students said that the exam was fair. Some of their comments were:

"It was fair because we discussed, in small groups and as a total class, topics, information, and issues we felt were important and should be covered on the exam. Together the class and the teacher selected specific topics that would be on the exam. The class also had input about the number of points each question would be worth."

"There were no trick questions, no punches pulled. It gave us the opportunity to think about what we felt was important."

"Everyone in the class contributed what they thought was important. I knew what to expect and I knew what to pay special attention to when preparing my concept map. There were no surprises."

Only one student did not think developing a web was worthwhile. The other twenty-two students thought it was an excellent strategy to use, as the following comments explain:

"In creating the web I was able to visualize all my thoughts and also I was able to connect the ideas together better. By connecting ideas, the concepts became more clear and relevant to me and therefore I understood better the information."
"My web took a long time to complete. I really had to look at which ideas were connected and how. I had to find relationships among all the topics. With the relationships I found that I could remember the information easier. It wasn't simply a matter of memorizing information. I really understood it."
"Creating a web really helped me pull everything together."

Afterword   Because of my experience with this student-developed test, I have decided that I need to involve my students much more in the process of evaluation. If we want future teachers to involve their students in the evaluative process, then we need to demonstrate its values and how this process supports learning in the university classroom.

EPILOGUE AND PROLOGUE

We consider this last chapter both an epilogue and a prologue. As an epilogue we summarize and revisit many of the issues explored in the previous chapters by embedding the issues within the political context of the university. As a prologue we consider the connections to the political arena in order to push open the doors of academia to liberate our teaching. The act of writing and reflecting about these issues helps us be consciously aware of our teaching and sophisticated about its political nature.

Heightening Political Awareness and Action: Liberating our Teaching

Yetta M. Goodman and Kathy G. Short

Because of our concerns for the empowerment of learners in elementary and secondary schools, Center for Expansion of Language and Thinking (CELT) members are actively involved in many capacities to develop powerful teaching and learning environments. As we turn this concern to our teaching and scholarly pursuits in university[1] settings, the significance of the political issues that affect us and the students with whom we work has become a major focus of our attention. We especially want to support nontraditional students and faculty: men and women from underrepresented ethnic and racial groups and those who are the first generation in their families to complete university degrees.

For more than a decade, CELT members have been raising and discussing serious questions about the political nature of teacher education through the lens of our beliefs about whole language. In this chapter, we pose these questions through our focus on three major concerns: (1) creating opportunities to become politically sophisticated about the culture of academe, (2) organizing the university setting to create democratic communities of learners, and (3) developing collaborative networks and creative environments to promote dynamic and innovative teaching and research.

LEARNING THE CULTURE OF ACADEME

- How do we support graduate students and colleagues new to academe in becoming sophisticated about university procedures and policies to enable them to survive in the system?
- How do we support adaptation to the hegemonic aspects of academe and remain in a position to critique and change the autocratic nature of the system?

If we borrow and extend Frank Smith's metaphor about joining the literacy club (Smith 1988) and carefully consider what we do to become successful in joining the academic club, perhaps we can help students and colleagues new to the academic scene to do the same. We survive most easily by becoming part of, and knowledgeable about, the culture of the university without losing our own ideological identity and by working with colleagues to become equally sophisticated in dealing with university structures.

Knowing the Academy

We need to know the university system and our colleagues. Various groups of faculty members representing females, differing research and philosophical paradigms, and racial and ethnic groups meet regularly at universities. It is helpful to participate in such groups to develop support networks and discover colleagues across the academic spectrum with similar political and pedagogical views. Although the physical and social science faculties have different agendas from the professional schools, there are physicists, mathematicians, anthropologists, and others concerned with exploring issues about teaching and learning similar to ours. When we find opportunities to work with these colleagues, they become more sensitive to issues of teaching and learning and more respectful of the faculty in education and teachers in elementary and secondary schools. We can work with these groups in a variety of ways, such as having them speak in our classes, serve as outside evaluators on research projects and dissertations, and set up formal and informal opportunities for interaction.

When faculty members understand the power networks and their players in the university, it becomes apparent which policies are absolute, such as grading practices and promotion and tenure procedures, and which can be questioned or waived, such as the ways in which syllabi are organized. Such knowledge helps us decide on which issues we want to expend our energy.

Since all members of the academic workplace are significant to the learning community and necessary to its success, it is essential that secretaries, custodians, and other staff members are included in decision making and treated with respect. Departmental staff, for example, should be included in regular department meetings, departmental committees, and social events.

Committee Responsibilities

Accepting responsibilities for major university committees allows us to be in positions to raise questions and challenge regressive cultural practices. We need to challenge practices that violate our belief in a democratic and politically safe workplace:

- The privilege of one kind of research over others.
- The privilege of single authorship over collaborative writing.
- The hierarchical nature of ranks from instructor to full professor.
- The meaning of "peer" in peer review.
- The relationship and status of teaching, service, and research.
- The status of those who work with undergraduates as opposed to those who work with graduate students.
- The issue of recruitment and retention of women and people of color.
- Grading and scheduling practices.

If we expend our academic committee energies on such issues, we may affect the elitist nature of the academic institution as a major barrier to more equitable status for all. It is imperative, however, to be highly selective of the university committees on which we serve and to agree to participate only in those that have significant impact. Service is not highly prized in promotion and tenure considerations, and it is vital to guard valuable time for scholarly work.

Department committees should include graduate students as members. Graduate students, especially in the field of education, are often professionals with years of experience in the teaching establishment. They have innovative and relevant contributions to make to the organization of university programs and procedures. It is not necessary to set up artificial mentoring systems if faculty view graduate students as colleagues and collaborators.

Some faculty take the position that it is not ethical to treat students as insiders because it makes them responsible for procedures over which they have little or no control. Although students should not be placed in politically untenable situations by sharing information with them that would make them vulnerable or by giving them responsibilities that might keep them from their work, it is empowering for graduate students to know that their knowledge and abilities are respected and appreciated. Committee membership also provides them with a safe environment from which to view the culture of the academy.

Responsibility for Others

Each of us is responsible to graduate students and beginning faculty who have not yet taken academic positions or achieved the status of tenure. These colleagues benefit from advice about questions to ask administrators to ensure the best benefits in relation to work load and initial salary, to protect their whole language orientation regarding teaching beliefs and research agendas, and to understand other aspects of academic positions so the road toward promotion and tenure is as smooth as possible.

Opportunities for discussion among faculty reduces professional isolation. One of the reasons for the organization of CELT was the need for a support group for those of us exploring new paradigm questions and understandings often at odds with those of other faculty. CELT is a strong model to use to organize support groups at local sites. This kind of support is helpful not only in terms of workplace negotiations but in research and consulting opportunities. An established e-mail network facilitates long-distance mentoring.

Another essential part of a nurturing climate is support for graduate students and beginning faculty to participate in professional local, state, and national conferences, write publishable papers, and research with more experienced faculty. In keeping with the principle that assignments are authentic in nature, many faculty are encouraging students to write papers for courses that are of publishable quality. Colloquies can be planned regularly so students can present research in sheltered situations before presenting at national conferences.

Faculty must support such endeavors by their presence and participation. Student presentations are often well received by the audience, but unfortunately few people typically attend. A note to colleagues in our own universities as well as those in other places asking them to attend students' sessions is a good idea. At the same time, it is important to prepare students for the possibility of a limited audience. Walter Loban, a language development researcher at the University of

California, Berkeley, loved to tell about his first national conference presentation that he gave to three people. Although he was disappointed as he surveyed the audience, he decided to be as powerful as he had planned to be to a cast of thousands. Later he discovered that one of the people was a major scholar in the field who eventually promoted Loban's work. The other two sought him out years later to tell him how important that presentation was to the development of their own teaching and research.

Politics plays a big role in whose voices get heard in journals and at conferences and who gets referenced by whom in writing. Our bibliographies should recognize our whole language colleagues, graduate students, and other avant-garde scholars with related ideas to our own. A range of voices needs to be raised at journal and conference review board meetings and with editors of books and journals.

Such recognition allows us to be aware of teaching and teacher education in its broad historical, political, and universal contexts. We need to show more conscious awareness of academics outside our own field, such as philosophers, artists, and historians, as well as linguists, anthropologists, and psychologists. We need to know the international scholars, including those from developing nations, who are doing related research. We also need to recognize the power of historical references.

Teacher education faculty are likely to be the first members of their family to attend a university. Teaching has been the road toward upward mobility for a long time in North America. *Strangers in Paradise: Academics from the Working Class* (Ryan and Sackney 1984) includes profiles of a number of first-generation faculty. Exploring such stories is helpful to students or faculty who have not experienced the culture of the university life. Those of us who have been successful in the academy should write about and tell our stories. Through narratives like those told in this book, we help colleagues to know the frustrations and hard work involved in establishing a secure although sometimes uncomfortable place in academia. Patty Anders, a professor at the University of Arizona, Tucson, tells about growing up as a farmer's daughter who was yelled at for reading in the silo instead of pitching down the ensilage and for reading on the tractor while racking the hay field and turning it into a mess. She had to fight cultural tendencies to believe that reading is worthwhile and significant. We need to share episodes that show how we resist the status quo and still remain part of the academic club. In this way we enlarge the boundaries of the academic culture to include greater numbers of scholars concerned with the transformation of educational institutions. We also help those from cultures not comfortable with academe believe that there are ways to become part of the university community without losing one's personal and cultural identity.

CREATING DEMOCRATIC LEARNING AND TEACHING ENVIRONMENTS

- In what ways do we demonstrate commitment to empowerment for undergraduate and graduate students?

- How do critical pedagogy and the nature of democracy and education relate to the classes we teach, our teacher education programs and curricula, and our relationships with students?

CELT members discuss ways to create democratic communities of learners within our university settings. We've documented some of those experiences in the previous chapters. Our questions focus on self-reflection, collaborative teacher and student planning and evaluation, and the importance of valuing diversity as they relate to building a powerful democratic learning community.

Self-Reflection on Our Teaching

Through reflection we make changes that break down the hierarchical structures and transmission models of learning that characterize higher education. This reflection involves self-evaluation of our own teaching and learning and our students' self-evaluations and responses to our teaching and to the learning experiences and structures we create within a particular course.

The most common form of evaluation for teacher educators has been university-mandated student evaluation forms. The items on these forms and the way they are used often reflect a transmission model of teaching, not the kind of transactional teaching described throughout this book. Regardless of required university forms, whole language teacher educators gain insights into their courses when they ask students: In this class, what was most important to your professional development? What aspects of this class should be changed or eliminated? What are your specific recommendations that will help me plan a better class the next time I teach this course?

We need to participate in university committees to work toward alternative forms of faculty evaluation. Teaching portfolios, for example, might include a faculty member's philosophy of teaching, course descriptions, photographs of learning engagements, videos of teaching, and student responses to open-ended evaluation questions. Faculty could organize a showing or presentation of their teaching as already occurs in art and music faculties.

Whole language teacher educators involve students in considering why they teach in a particular way. Yetta Goodman uses the term *metapedagogy* for those critical teaching moments when something has worked well—or has really bombed—and we stop to ask students to consider what has occurred and why. When we share our reasons for what we are doing, it helps students consider the hegemonic aspects of academe and at the same time critique and shape the system. Students see us put our beliefs into action and see and hear how we form our arguments. It is instructive for students to see us make mistakes, hear our frustrations, help us figure out what went wrong (or right), and help us formulate new and better responses and engagements. These moments of conscious oral reflection on teaching are opportunities to examine the role democracy plays in university classrooms and to critique the instruments that perpetuate the status quo.

Collaborative Planning with Students

In addition to evaluation, students participate in planning class goals and projects, choosing their own inquiry paths, and making classes relevant to their own purposes and experiences. We make efforts to provide direction and a clear structure for courses in our syllabi and still allow room for student collaboration and negotiation. The previous narratives and protocol/engagements in this book are teeming with ideas to accomplish collaboration goals. These include: open-ended discussions, self-selected and unique assignments, critical debates, dialogue journals, and regularly scheduled individual conferences. Through conferences and logs, students' personal voices emerge as they consider multiple ways to answer their individual questions and discover varied ways to present their ideas to others. Portfolios have been thoroughly discussed in Part D, but they are also considered formats for negotiated and student-determined planning.

These whole language teacher education experiences are even more powerful when the teacher educator participates in them with the students. It is easy to allow committee work and administrative responsibilities to interfere with such participation, but we must value our roles as learners in our classrooms by engaging in similar learning experiences as those of our students.

Valuing Diversity Within Teacher Education Classrooms

Diversity is central to creating a strong democratic community in university classrooms. Our presentations and invitations reflect conscious awareness of the range of people and ideas represented in the world. Every syllabus and curriculum plan is critiqued to ensure inclusion of females, authors of color, new scholars, historical references, and whole language advocates. Time is spent in class highlighting and understanding the reasons for these inclusions.

A strong sense of community and a value of diversity are encouraged when we spend time at the beginning of each course to discover the literacy and learning histories of our students. Many times, students' previous experiences in school contexts have been so negative that this exploration provides the time necessary to deconstruct those experiences and discover the joy of learning. This time creates an environment within which students feel safe in exploring their ideas with others and in pursuing their own inquiries rather than feeling bound to what they think the teacher wants (see protocols/engagements B-4 and B-5).

One way to achieve the centrality of diversity in the curriculum is to establish an extensive collection of writing, art work, audiotapes, and other artifacts by children and adolescents from a range of ages and abilities who have diverse backgrounds: American Indians, African Americans, Latinos, and bilinguals and biliterates, among many others (see Protocol/Engagement C-14). Members of these groups need to be identified in specific, not generic, ways to avoid stereotyping. It is essential that students perceive these children as real human beings with histories and cultures and not just as statistical objects represented by labels and test scores. When university students describe and analyze writing, taped oral readings and retellings, illustrations, diagrams, videotapes and audiotapes of plays, storytelling, and simulations, they are able to connect to the meanings and subjectivity of the children and young adults whose stories are being told. Teachers in elementary and secondary classrooms can participate in building a selection of works from their classrooms that reflect a diverse cultural collection. Textbooks and resource materials are evaluated with similar sensitivity. Such experiences help preserve and inservice teachers build appreciation for diversity, respect their own cultures, and demystify the deficit view of children and young adults.

It is helpful to be aware of programs on campus concerned with and sponsored by Latinos, African Americans, Asian Americans, American Indians, and women's studies. A prominently displayed list of courses concerned with the literature, language, and culture of various peoples suggests how to expand graduate education offerings.

Faculty members need to find ways to attract nontraditional students into graduate classes and programs. It is critical that we include teachers from a range of backgrounds so that discussions are informed and viewed from a range of perspectives. Audiences of teachers are becoming more white and more female. We need to address the feminization of American education as well as its middle-class and Caucasian nature. We need to attend to issues of race and gender that occur in small groups in classrooms to ensure that all members have equal opportunity to express personal opinions that may not be popular ones without being ridiculed or ostracized.

CREATING A TRANSACTIVE ENVIRONMENT FOR TEACHING AND RESEARCH

- How can we demonstrate our beliefs about learning and teaching within a university structure that imposes many constraints?
- In what ways do critical pedagogy and beliefs in democracy influence the nature of the kinds of research that we do?
- How does the collaborative nature of our research with teachers and graduate students demonstrate political awareness?
- How do we support the concept of teacher as researcher in relation to political awareness?

In order to create new environments that have an impact on whole language teaching and research in university settings, we need to think creatively and critically about dealing with university constraints on teaching and redefining research and scholarship within the academic world.

Constraints on Classroom Teaching

While the field of education is moving away from transmission to interactive and transactive models of literacy learning, many university classrooms remain based in transmission models. In many different contexts, including this book, CELT members explore how to teach transactionally within a system that primarily consists of isolated and fragmented courses where knowledge about teaching is passed on to passive students sitting at desks. We cannot expect either preservice or inservice teachers to teach on the basis of new models of learning and literacy if our classrooms continue to operate from old models.

While the new perspectives on language and learning that pervade current educational research and theory have affected what is taught in teacher education programs, they are only beginning to influence how innovative educational content is taught and learned. We face the task of considering our beliefs about language and learning within a university context that includes many obstacles to change. To create more powerful learning environments, we need to examine critically the constraints within university settings so *how* we teach is consistent with *what* we teach.

While we believe that learning is both active and reflective (Dewey 1938), the university setting rarely encourages active engagement in doing or time for reflection. There is still too much talk about reading, writing, learning, and teaching rather than actually involving learners in those experiences. Time periods for university classes are based on lecture formats, and so the large blocks of time needed for reading, writing, and exploring with others are not available.

We need to push the university to recognize that different class structures require different types of scheduling. Some of the authors in this volume have been able to arrange longer class times by integrating several courses or by adding laboratory time. Others have negotiated alternative class meetings times to which all students agree at the beginning of a course. Time is a serious problem in institutions using quarter systems, where it seems that the class barely begins before it is over. If courses meet over several semesters or quarters the time needed to form a community and process the ideas being discussed is extended.

During summer, we often schedule classes more flexibly for longer chunks of time. It is often prohibitive, however, for us to teach during the summer because of low university salaries and large classes. If teaching a full load in the summer would count as a regular semester, then some faculty could teach in the summer and have either fall or spring semester off. This arrangement would allow faculty to have more time available for work in schools and make more courses available for teachers over the summer. Teaching in the summer often leads to the formation of a strong sense of community that can be continued by reunions in the late fall to share new and continued learning and classroom experiences and artifacts.

Frank Smith (1981) points out that learning is not something an individual comes to be able to do; it is synonymous with life. Learners are continually drawn to the ambiguous, to the "yet to be understood," and their questions, not someone else's, initiate their own learning processes. Most students, however, do not establish their own agenda and learning goals but have an agenda imposed on them by textbooks, syllabi, and tests. Students often come out of teacher education programs without a sense of their own voices or themselves as decision makers. By giving our students a strong voice in pursuing their own inquiry projects and negotiating course goals and experiences, they are able to search out and pursue the questions that matter in their lives as teachers. Students should be encouraged to explore a variety of perspectives through different sign systems such as drama, art, or music in addition to using written language as a way to construct and share meaning.

We are moving away from whole group discussions of a single textbook for a course to small groups where students select their own texts or use text sets of articles on a particular topic. Some teacher educators are required to use textbooks and university bookstores are often unwilling to order multiple copies of different titles for small groups. To overcome this constraint, books can be ordered through local TAWL groups, a local bookstore, or a publisher's representative.

The use of a variety of professional books and children's literature in courses brings up issues of funding. Funding for nontextbook materials is generally not available. Bonus points from paperback book clubs can be used to build a collection of multiple copies of books for literature discussions within the courses. Books can be requested from children's literature publishers to be reviewed by teachers. Book fairs can be held to raise money to buy books. Other options are to argue for money to be allotted in the university budget or to charge a small materials fee as part of children's literature courses. Storage of these materials is often an issue. Faculty often negotiate for an additional room, a large closet, additional shelves, or cabinet space for faculty storage.

The world learners live in is ambiguous; there are few right or wrong answers. Both faculty members and students must be willing to live with ambiguity and the tension of knowing that they must act on their current knowledge, while remaining aware that their understandings are incomplete. We want to create an environment that focuses not on producing right answers but on the value of diversity and critical inquiry; where students are given many opportunities to reflect on their thinking with others; where completed assignments are not considered final drafts but rough drafts or work in progress; and where students are encouraged to become risk takers. Otherwise we realize that our students will feel stress, not tension, and accept a restricted view of their capacity to take risks in their learning.

Learning is a search for connections to make sense of the world. We are attempting to contextualize learning within the complexity of our students' understandings about the past, present, and future. The search for connections is a social search. Our intellectual lives as learners depend on being social. Through interactions with others, students take new perspectives on their own learning as they try to explain their thinking to others and listen to the ideas that classmates offer. While the profession has largely rejected the concept of reading readiness, preservice teachers are still made to feel that they are not yet "ready" for teaching and must be trained. We want our students to feel that they are part of a collaborative community, in terms of both their own classmates and the larger teaching profession.

The physical structures of classrooms and colleges of education often do not encourage social interaction in small groups, nor is the environment inviting and warm to class members and conducive to the building of community. We have struggled with finding rooms with tables that will support small group interaction and reading and writing experiences. Moveable furniture allows for rearranging the room. When we are assigned to rooms without moveable furniture, we ask students to bring cushions and folding chairs or move into a lounge area for class. Since putting posters, murals, and other examples of student work on the walls of classrooms is often not allowed and we rarely teach classes in the same room, we include a moveable message board on the cart used to transport materials to class. We recognize that our teaching environment need not be a university classroom; using schools and the community as sites for learning offers many possibilities for broadening our definition of education. In transforming these environments, we also deal with the perception of faculty members in other disciplines that the increased activity, laughter, and talk in our classrooms means that our courses are somehow less "rigorous" and "academic" than their courses.

These changes in the environment may also be disquieting to students, who come into our courses expecting a lecture format.

When students actively engage in learning within a social context, many possible demonstrations and understandings about learning are available to each individual (Smith 1981). The learning events that we plan must be open enough to allow students to be actively involved in learning, to observe others around them, and to connect to the demonstrations that are most important to them as learners.

In our collaborations with each other in integrating courses and co-teaching, we live more openly as learners and provide other demonstrations of teaching and learning for students. This includes co-teaching with classroom teachers who offer undergraduate and graduate students powerful demonstrations from their own teaching. Learning with other students is encouraged through open-ended explorations rather than class assignments that lead to convergent responses.

Expanding Definitions of Research and Scholarship

Various forms of collaborative, classroom, ethnographic, and interpretive research methodologies are flourishing. These forms of research raise the need to explore new ways for writing dissertations and culminating doctoral programs. Discussion with faculty in other disciplines may show us the way. In the public health school at UCLA, for example, students may choose to write publishable articles instead of writing a dissertation.

We need ways to respond to the language of experimental, positivistic researchers so that forums for a range of research types are available. Although researchers who are actively involved in interpretive research have forums for their work, many doctoral students and new faculty members remain constrained by narrow definitions of what counts as research and what journals are considered prestigious. We need to work toward the legitimatization of a range of research designs that relate to research questions. We need to document book chapters as refereed research publications and coauthored articles as necessary to our work.

Our active involvement in the dialogue taking place in a number of professional organizations concerning teacher and collaborative research can demystify the word *research*, conceptualizing it in terms of its political and historical influences and in relation to how it is used in different fields of study.

Active research in communities, classroom, and schools must be legitimatized rather than lumping it under "service." Fieldwork is part of the scholarly pursuit of professional educationists as well as anthropologists and linguists among others. If we promote the use of the term *scholarship* rather than *research*, we can explore how research is one aspect of scholarship that informs the field of education.

Creativity is often part of the scholarship category in promotion and tenure procedures for fine arts and literature faculties. Perhaps the *scholarship* term can be expanded to mean scholarship and creativity or scholarship including research and creativity. A dialogue with philosophers, historians, and others who do not engage in positivistic research will help us legitimatize a broad conceptualization of scholarship in every field of knowledge.

The political issues of the academic community are significant to the development and survival of whole language teacher education as it has been conceptualized and described throughout this book. To liberate our teaching, we continuously work to walk our talk, to practice what we teach.

Additional contributors to this chapter are: Patty Anders, Margaret A. Atwell, David Bloome, Carole Edelsky, Carol Ewoldt, Karen Feathers, Elizabeth A. Franklin, David E. Freeman, Wendy C. Kasten, Dorothy F. King, Amy McClure, Dorothy Menosky, Richard J. Meyer, Pamela Perkins, Kathryn Mitchell Pierce, Lynn Rhodes, Pat Shannon, Helen Slaughter, Sherry Vaughan, and Kathryn F. Whitmore.

NOTE

[1] The word *university* is used to represent all the institutions in which we work that are post secondary school. Although in the United States the term *college* often relates to teacher education institutions, it refers to different kinds of institutions in other English-speaking countries.

REFERENCES

Dewey, J. 1938. *Experience and Education.* New York: Collier.

Ryan, J., and C. Sackney. 1984. *Strangers in Paradise: Academics from the Working Class.* Boston: South End Press.

Smith, F. 1981. "Demonstrations, Engagements, and Sensitivity." In *Language Arts,* 60, 5: 558–567.

———. 1988. *Joining the Literacy Club.* Portsmouth, NH: Heinemann.

INDEX

Also available from Stenhouse...

INVENTING A CLASSROOM
Life in a Bilingual, Whole Language Learning Community

Kathryn F. Whitmore and Caryl G. Crowell

This ethnographic study is a success story of how, over the span of a school year, students in a bicultural third-grade classroom within a bilingual, working-class neighborhood work and develop together as a community of learners called "The Sunshine Room." You will discover how the Sunshine Room, like many whole language classrooms, invents itself; and how in this process the children themselves are continually inventing oral and written language, culture, and curriculum.

   In two separate collaborative voices, the authors relate critical events in the life of the classroom and follow the developing relationships that are symbolic of the experience fostered in this true whole language environment.

1-57110-002-4   Paperback

CURRICULAR CONVERSATIONS
Themes in Multilingual and Monolingual Classrooms

Steven B. Kucer, Cecilia Silva, and Esther Delgado-Larocco

Curricular Conversations is a concise and helpful book on the "whys" and "hows" of building and implementing a thematically unified curriculum. The authors give you ways of using the communication systems of language, mathematics, art, music, and movement, and the disciplines of literature, science, and social studies to explore concepts and generalizations within a wide range of themes.

Exploration and Discovery, Emotions, Freedom, Survival, the Environment, Continuity and Change are just a few of the topics that are rich for investigation. These themes are not presented as prepackaged activity sets but in a framework with outlines of strategies and techniques.

1-57110-016-4   Paperback

LEARNING TOGETHER THROUGH INQUIRY
From Columbus to Integrated Curriculum

Kathy G. Short, Jean Schroeder, Julie Laird, Gloria Kauffman, Margaret J. Ferguson, and Kathleen Marie Crawford

For teachers who have been exploring process approaches and thematic units in language arts and other areas, the logical next step is inquiry. Based on the authoring cycle, the inquiry cycle provides one possible curricular framework for supporting inquiry within classroom contexts. Through inquiry learners engage in a process of searching for questions that are significant in their lives and finding multiple ways to examine and research those questions.

Learning Together Through Inquiry is an accessible guide to applying the inquiry cycle and negotiating curriculum around a broad concept. It is also a compelling snapshot of how teacher researchers collaborate to enrich their own and their students' learning.

1-57110-033-4   Paperback

For information on all Stenhouse publications,
please write or call for a catalogue.

Stenhouse Publishers
P. O. Box 360
York, Maine 03909
(207) 363-9198